Inequality and Exclusion in Southeast Asia

The **ISEAS – Yusof Ishak Institute** (formerly Institute of Southeast Asian Studies) is an autonomous organization established in 1968. It is a regional centre dedicated to the study of socio-political, security, and economic trends and developments in Southeast Asia and its wider geostrategic and economic environment. The Institute's research programmes are grouped under Regional Economic Studies (RES), Regional Strategic and Political Studies (RSPS), and Regional Social and Cultural Studies (RSCS). The Institute is also home to the ASEAN Studies Centre (ASC), the Singapore APEC Study Centre and the Temasek History Research Centre (THRC).

ISEAS Publishing, an established academic press, has issued more than 2,000 books and journals. It is the largest scholarly publisher of research about Southeast Asia from within the region. ISEAS Publishing works with many other academic and trade publishers and distributors to disseminate important research and analyses from and about Southeast Asia to the rest of the world.

Inequality and Exclusion in Southeast Asia

Old Fractures, New Frontiers

EDITED BY
LEE HWOK AUN • CHRISTOPHER CHOONG

First published in Singapore in 2021 by
ISEAS Publishing
30 Heng Mui Keng Terrace
Singapore 119614
E-mail: publish@iseas.edu.sg
Website: http://bookshop.iseas.edu.sg

All rights reserved. No part of this publication may be reproduced, stored in a retrieval system, or transmitted in any form or by any means, electronic, mechanical, photocopying, recording or otherwise, without the prior permission of the ISEAS – Yusof Ishak Institute.

© 2021 ISEAS – Yusof Ishak Institute, Singapore.

The responsibility for facts and opinions in this publication rests exclusively with the authors and their interpretations do not necessarily reflect the views or the policy of the publisher or its supporters.

This publication is made possible with the support of Konrad-Adenauer-Stiftung.

ISEAS Library Cataloguing-in-Publication Data

Name(s): Lee, Hwok Aun, editor. | Choong, Christopher Weng Wai, editor.

Title: Inequality and exclusion in Southeast Asia : old fractures, new frontiers / edited by Lee Hwok Aun and Christopher Choong.

Description: Singapore : ISEAS – Yusof Ishak Institute, 2021. | Includes bibliographical references and index.

Identifiers: ISBN 9789814951203 (soft cover) | ISBN 9789814951210 (pdf) | ISBN 9789814951227 (epub)

Subjects: LCSH: Equality—Southeast Asia. | Marginality, Social—Southeast Asia. | Southeast Asia—Social policy.

Classification: LCC HM821 I43

Typeset by Superskill Graphics Pte Ltd
Printed in Singapore by Markono Print Media Pte Ltd

CONTENTS

List of Tables	vii
List of Figures	x
Acknowledgements	xv
About the Contributors	xvi

1. Introduction: Inequality and Exclusion in Southeast Asia   1
   Lee Hwok Aun and Christopher Choong

2. Cambodia's Experiences in Addressing Inequality   22
   Piseth Keo and Vannarith Chheang

3. Inequality and Exclusion in Post-Soeharto Indonesia   51
   Mohammad Zulfan Tadjoeddin

4. Inequality and Exclusion in Malaysia: Macro Trends, Labour Market Dynamics and Gender Dimensions   87
   Lee Hwok Aun and Christopher Choong

5. Inequality in Myanmar: Structural Change, Policy Outcomes and Gender Dimensions   133
   Ngu Wah Win, Zaw Oo, Jana Rue Glutting, Aung Htun and S. Kanayde

6. Structural Inequality in the Philippines: Oligarchy, Economic Transformation and Current Challenges to Development   169
   Philip Arnold Tuaño and Jerik Cruz

7. Inequality and the Social Compact in Singapore:
   Macro Trends vs Lived Inequalities 218
   Nathan Peng

8. Inequality in Thailand: Income, Socio-economic and
   Wealth Dimensions 261
   Vimut Vanitcharearnthum

9. Trends and Drivers of Inequality in Vietnam 295
   Trang Huyen Dang, Cuong Viet Nguyen and Tung Duc Phung

10. Conclusion: Old Fractures and New Frontiers 323
    Lee Hwok Aun and Christopher Choong

Index 335

LISTS OF TABLES

1.1	Southeast Asian Countries: Economic and Demographic Profile, 2019	12
2.1	Cambodia Human Development Index	29
2.2	Measured or Estimated Population by Residence	35
2.3	Cambodia: Policies on Poverty Reduction and Inequality	40
5.1	Growth and Structural Change of Myanmar's Economy	135
5.2	Myanmar: Share of GDP Contributions by Economic Sectors	138
5.3	Human Development Index (HDI) in Myanmar and Southeast Asia: Score and Rank, and Gender Inequality Index (GII) Rank, 2017	139
5.4	Myanmar's HDI Trends	140
5.5	Myanmar and Selected Countries: Inequality and Human Development Index	141
5.6	Myanmar and Selected Countries: Gender Gaps in HDI Components	143
5.7	Indicators of Inequality in Myanmar, 2015	146
5.8	Myanmar: Stunting Rates in States and Regions, 2015–16	149
5.9	Myanmar: Electrification Rates Across State and Region	151
5.10	Myanmar: Relative Distribution of Higher Education Institutions (HEIs) per capita	153
5.11	Myanmar: Female Students as Percentage of Total Enrolment, by Level of Education	156
5.12	Myanmar: Women Staff in Basic Education Sector (Number and Percentage of Total)	159
5.13	Myanmar's Position in Global Gender Gap Rankings	162

6.1	Political Dynasties in Selected Philippine Congresses	172
6.2	Philippines: Regional Contribution to Gross Regional Domestic Product, 2002 and 2018	180
6.3	Philippines: Share of Employment and Underemployment by Economic Sector and Class of Worker	182
6.4	Philippines: Proportion of 15–24-year-olds by Education Level and Income Decile, 1998 and 2013	185
6.5	Philippines: Population for Each Type of Government Health Professionals, 2013 vs. 2018, Selected Regions	186
6.6	Philippines: Selected Infant and Child Mortality Rates, per 1,000 Infants/Children, 2003 and 2017	188
6.7	Philippines: Proportion of Children Below Five Years of Age Stunted, Underweight and Wasted, 2013 and 2015, by Wealth Quintile	189
6.8	Philippines: Households by Expenditure Class, 1997–2015 (as Percentage of Total Households)	190
7.1	Singapore: Summary of Inequality Trends	221
7.2	Singapore: Home Ownership Rate by Type of Dwelling	230
7.3	Singapore: Nominal Changes in Property Prices, Q1 2000 to Q4 2019, by Residence Type	231
7.4	Singapore: Correlation of Parents' and Child's Income Rank	233
7.5	Singapore: Average Household Monthly Expenditure on Private Tuition and Other Educational Courses	235
8.1	Thailand: Wealth Distribution of Adult Population	264
8.2	Thailand and International Comparison: Within-Generation Educational Inequality	270
8.3	Intergenerational Mobility in Education: Thailand vs Sample Average	270
8.4	Thailand: Percentage of Total Population with Healthcare Coverage	273
8.5	Human Capital Index: Thailand and International Averages	276
8.6	Thailand: Net Enrolment in the College Level by Expenditure Deciles	276
8.7	Thailand: International Standardized Test Scores by Geographic Area	278

8.8	Thailand: Cumulative Distribution of Household Income by Regions, 2017	280
8.9	Thailand: Distribution of Financial Assets across Regions, 2019	281
8.10	Comparison of Medical Resource Adequacy Between Bangkok and Other Provinces	284
8.11	Thailand: Education Attainment by Regions, 2017	284
8.12	Thailand's Richest Stockholders, 2019	287
8.13	Thailand's Richest Persons/Families, 2008 and 2019	288
9.1	Vietnam Living Standards Indicators: Per Capita Income and Expenditure, and Housing Value, 2002–16	301
9.2	Vietnam: Inequality Measures of Per Capita Expenditure	304
9.3	Vietnam: GMM Regressions of Income Inequality Indexes	316
A9.1	Vietnam: Income Inequality Measures	319
A9.2	Vietnam: Electricity Consumption Inequality Measures	319
A9.3	Vietnam: Housing-Value Inequality Measures	319

LISTS OF FIGURES

1.1	Poverty Rate: Headcount Ratio, Based on National Poverty Line Income	13
1.2	Gini Coefficient of Household Expenditure	14
1.3	Gini Coefficient of Household Income	16
2.1	Cambodia: Minimum Wage in the Apparel and Textile Industries	31
3.1	Long-Term Gini Index, 1976–2019	56
3.2	Wage-Productivity Ratio and Gini Index (33 Provinces, 2001–11)	58
3.3	Provincial Gini Index and Manufacturing Share (%) of RGDP, 2000–15	59
3.4	Resource Boom: Expenditure Gini Index (Indonesia) and Global Commodity Prices (2010 = 100), 1993–2018	60
3.5	Theil T Index of Household Expenditure (Overall, Between and Within Provinces), 2000–18	64
3.6	Theil T Index of Household Expenditure (Overall, Between and Within Sectors), 2000–18	66
3.7	Median Earnings by Income Groups (Top 10% = 1), 2001–18	67
3.8	Median Earnings by Education (Primary, Secondary, Tertiary; Tertiary = 1), 2001–18	69
3.9	Median Earnings by Area (Urban-Rural; Urban = 1), 2001–18	69
3.10	Median Earnings by Type of Employment (Regular Employee = 1), 2001–18	71
3.11	Median Earnings by Gender (Male = 1), 2001–18	72
3.12	Median Earnings of Persons with Disability (No Disability = 1), 2016–18	74

List of Figures

4.1	Malaysia: Gini Coefficient of Gross Household Income, by Area Type, 1984–2019	91
4.2	Gini Coefficient of Gross Household Income, by Ethnicity, 1984–2019	92
4.3	Real Annual Average Growth of Gross Household Income, by Income Bracket, 1989–2019	94
4.4	Interethnic and Urban-Rural Household Income Disparities, 1984–2019	97
4.5A	Top 20 per cent, Middle 40 per cent and Bottom 40 per cent Chinese to Bumiputra Average Household Income Ratios, 1989–2019	99
4.5B	Top 20 per cent, Middle 40 per cent and Bottom 40 per cent Indian to Bumiputra Average Household Income Ratios, 1989–2019	100
4.6	Interethnic Average Wage Ratios, by Gender, 2010–18	102
4.7	Gini Coefficient of EPF Savings Accounts (Proxy for Wage Inequality), 2004–18	106
4.8	Share of EPF Savings, by Segment, 2004–18	107
4.9A	Employees' Salaries: Ratio of Salary Relative to Managers, by Occupation Group, 2010–18	108
4.9B	Employees' Salaries: Ratio of Salary Relative to Managers, by Occupation Group, 2010–18	109
4.10	Female:Male Ratio in University Intake, Enrolment and Graduation, 2010 and 2018	112
4.11	Malaysian Mean Wage by Gender, and Gender Wage Gap, 2012–18	114
4.12	Malaysian Female Employees (Share of Total Female Employees) and Gender Wage Gaps, by Occupation, 2018	116
4.13	Employees: Gender Wage Gap, by Age Group, 2012–18	118
4.14	Wage Share Gap, by Age Group, 2012–18	120
4.15	Labour Force and Participation Gap, by Marital Status, 2018	121
4.16	Share of Employment, by Employment Status, 1998, 2003, 2008, 2013, 2018	122
A4.1	Gini Coefficient of Gross Household Income, by State, Lowest to Highest Average Income (2012 → 2014 → 2016 → 2019)	124
A4.2	Household Income, by State, per National Mean (Peninsular Malaysia West Coast States)	125

A4.3	Household Income, by State, per National Mean (Peninsular Malaysia Northern and East Coast States, East Malaysia)	126
5.1	Myanmar: Poverty Incidence under Two Different Methodologies	144
5.2	Myanmar: Labour Force Participation Rates across State and Regions, 2014	155
5.3	Myanmar: Gender Division of Labour by Economic Sector, 2015	158
5.4	Myanmar: Average Daily Wage Rate by Economic Sector, Per Civil Service, 2015	161
6.1	Philippines: GDP by Sector, 1998–2015	173
6.2	Selected Southeast Asian Countries: Market Capitalization of Family-Owned Conglomerates, by Sector	174
6.3	Philippines: Total Employment, by Economic Sector, 1995–2017	175
6.4	Philippines: Sectoral Labour Productivity, Nominal Pesos per Worker, 1995–2015	176
6.5	Philippines: Poor and Subsistence-Poor Individuals, Millions and Percentage of Population, 1991–2015	177
6.6	Philippines: Gini Index, National, Urban and Rural, 1991–2015	179
6.7	Philippines: Gini Index, by Politico-Administrative Region, 1997 and 2015	180
6.8	Philippines: Gini of Land Ownership, 1960–2012	183
6.9	Philippines: Share of Savings Deposits, 2012, 2016 and 2019	183
6.10	Philippines: Gini of Educational Attainment (Years of Schooling for Population 15 Years or Older), 1993–2013	184
6.11	Selected Southeast Asian Countries and China: Proportion of Poor Households to Total, 1985–2015	192
6.12	Selected Southeast Asian Countries and China: Proportion of Middle-Class Households to Total, 1985–2015	192
7.1	Singapore: Gini Coefficient of Per Capita Household Income	223
7.2	Singapore: Percentage Reduction in Gini Due to Government Taxes and Transfers	224

List of Figures

7.3	Singapore: Average Monthly Household Per Capita Income (Top 10 Per Cent vs Bottom 10 Per Cent)	224
7.4	Singapore: Real Household Per Capita Income Change, by Decile, 2000–18	225
7.5	Singapore: Real Household Per Capita Income Change, by Decile, 2014–18	226
7.6	Singapore: Average Monthly Expenditure Per Capita (S$), by Income Quintile	227
7.7A	Singapore: Ratio of Average Monthly Expenditure Per Capita, Top 20 Per Cent vs Bottom 20 Per Cent	228
7.7B	Singapore: Ratio of Average Monthly Income Per Capita, Top 20 Per Cent vs Bottom 20 Per Cent	228
7.8	Singapore: Wealth Gini Coefficient	229
7.9	Singapore: Share of Luxury Cars	230
7.10	Singapore: Percentage of Children Born to Parents Earning the Lowest 20 Per Cent of Income Who Reached the Top 20 Per Cent of Income	233
7.11	Singapore: Average Household Monthly Expenditure on Private Tuition & Other Educational Courses (Percentage)	236
7.12	Singapore: Probability of Completing Tertiary Education Based on Parents' Education (Low/Medium/High)	237
7.13	Singapore: Income Earners by Geographical Planning Zones	239
7.14	Singapore: Ratio of Resident Households in Condominiums/Apartments and Landed Properties vs HDB 1–3 Room Flats, by Geographical Planning Zones	240
7.15	Singapore: World Values Survey—How Proud of Nationality	241
8.1	Thailand: Gini Coefficient of Household Income, 1988–2017	265
8.2	Thailand's Gini Coefficients Based on Household Income and Consumption Expenditure	266
8.3	Thailand: Income Inequality, by Region	267
8.4	Thailand: Consumption Inequality, by Region	267
8.5	Indicators of Thailand Improved Standard of Living: HDI and GDP per capita	268
8.6	Thailand: Convergence in the Enrolment Rate in the Secondary School Level by Income Quartile	269

8.7	Thailand: Estimated Number of Households (Thousands) Falling into Poverty due to Medical Expenses (Protected from Health Impoverishment)	274
8.8	Bangkok's Gross Provincial Product (GPP) as Percentage of National GDP, 1995–2016	279
8.9	Thailand: Average Household Monthly Income, by Region, 2002–17	280
8.10	Thailand: Deposit Distribution across Regions, 1995 and 2019	282
8.11	Thailand: Credit Distribution across Regions, 1995 and 2019	283
8.12	Thailand: Top Income Brackets (Percentage of National Income), 2016	286
9.1	Vietnam: Gini Coefficient of Income, Expenditure and Housing Value, 2002–16	302
9.2	Gini Coefficient and GDP, Vietnam and the Countries Worldwide, 2012	304
9.3	Vietnam: Per Capita Expenditure of Kinh and Ethnic Minorities	306
9.4	Vietnam: Expenditure Poverty Rates of Kinh and Ethnic Minorities	306
9.5	Vietnam: Poverty Rate of Ethnic Groups, with 90 per cent Confidence Interval, 2016	308
9.6	Vietnam: Education Enrolment Rates, 2016	309
9.7	Vietnam: Decomposition of Expenditure Inequality by Urban/Rural Areas and Provinces, 2006 and 2016 (Theil-L Index)	311
9.8	Vietnam: Decomposition of Expenditure Inequality by Ethnic Groups, 2006 and 2016 (Theil-L Index)	312
9.9	Vietnam: Decomposition of Expenditure Inequality by Head of Household Characteristics, 2016 (Theil-L Index)	313
9.10	Vietnam: Income Inequality and Per Capita Income, by Province, 2002–16	315

ACKNOWLEDGEMENTS

This book is the culmination of a regional research project based at the ISEAS – Yusof Ishak Institute, Singapore and funded by the Konrad Adenauer Stiftung (KAS). We gratefully acknowledge KAS' financial support, and the Institute's facilitation of forums that allowed works in progress to be presented and critiqued. All the country chapters in this book benefited from the proceedings of a March 2019 in-house workshop and July 2019 public conference, both held at ISEAS. We also benefited from feedback received at the SEAsia Biennial Conference of December 2019 in Taipei. Earlier versions of a few chapters have been published in the December 2019 Special Issue of the *Journal of Southeast Asian Economies*. We extend our gratitude to the journal for the review process that helped sharpen the papers, and the coverage given to this subject from political economy perspectives.

We must express our heartfelt appreciation to the authors for their diligence and perseverance in drafting and revising their chapters, amid pandemic-triggered disruptions. This collective endeavour, in which we journeyed together for two years, has been enhanced by their camaraderie and commitment to the research subject. The product is a richer and diverse compilation of Southeast Asian perspectives. We gratefully acknowledge the authors' respective organizations for granting the flexibility and time, as well as supporting with additional resources where applicable, to complete the book chapters. There are also many individuals—peers and colleagues—who have commented on these chapters, above and beyond what is required in the formal peer review process, and we are thankful for these contributions. We heartily thank ISEAS Publishing, especially Rahilah Yusuf, for refining the manuscript into this book. Last and definitely not least, we are immensely indebted to our family members, not only for their moral support but also the unpaid care rendered to make all these possible.

ABOUT THE CONTRIBUTORS
(by Chapter)

Chheang Vannarith is President of the Asian Vision Institute (AVI), an independent think-tank based in Phnom Penh, Cambodia. He is a public policy analyst specializing in geopolitics and political economy of Southeast Asia. **Keo Piseth** is AVI's Vice President, and a researcher, practitioner and consultant in sustainable and inclusive development and environmental management. AVI aims to promote inclusive, adaptive and sustainable societies in Asia through knowledge co-creation and multi-stakeholder partnerships. Major research areas include geopolitics, political economy and sustainable development.

Mohammad Zulfan Tadjoeddin is Associate Professor and Director of Academic Program – Humanitarian and Development Studies at Western Sydney University, Australia. He had visiting research appointments at the Queen Elizabeth House, University of Oxford and the International Institute of Social Studies, Erasmus University Rotterdam. He is an economist by training and his research areas include conflict and development, employment and labour market as well as inequality and human development. He has published two books with Palgrave Macmillan, *Explaining Collective Violence* (2014) and *Employment and Reindustrialisation* (2018). His articles are published in leading academic journals such as *Journal of Development Studies, Oxford Development Studies, Journal of East Asian Studies, Journal of Peace Research and Journal of International Development*. He has consulted for the Asian Development Bank and various United Nations agencies.

About the Contributors

Lee Hwok Aun is Senior Fellow and Co-ordinator of the Malaysia Studies Programme at the ISEAS – Yusof Ishak Institute, Singapore. He holds a PhD in Economics from the University of Massachusetts, Amherst, and an MSc in Political Economy of Development from SOAS, University of London. His main research interests are affirmative action, discrimination, inequality, labour and education. He is the author of *Affirmative Action in Malaysia and South Africa: Preference for Parity* (2021), and of articles in *Journal of Contemporary Asia, Journal of Asian and African Studies, Journal of the Asia Pacific Economy, Journal of Southeast Asian Economies,* as well as ISEAS' *Perspectives* and *Trends in Southeast Asia* series.

Christopher Choong Weng Wai is the Deputy Director of Research at Khazanah Research Institute (KRI) and an Atlantic Fellow for Social and Economic Equity at the International Inequalities Institute, London School of Economics. His main research interests pivot around the everyday reproduction of inequalities and exclusion, and the care economy. He was the lead author of the following reports: *Time to Care: Gender Inequality, Unpaid Care Work and Time Use Survey* (KRI, 2019) and *Welfare in Malaysia Across Three Decades: The State of Households 2020 Part I* (KRI, 2020). Prior to joining the Institute, he was the Economist for the UNDP Country Office of Malaysia, Singapore and Brunei Darussalam.

Zaw Oo is Executive Director of the Centre for Economic and Social Development (CESD), an independent and non-political think-tank. **Ngu Wah Win** is CESD's Senior Policy Coordinator; **Jana-Chin Rué Glutting**, **Aung Htun** and **S. Kanayde** are Research Associates. CESD supports evidence-based policy research, results-orientated knowledge sharing, and people-centred public advocacy to support the peaceful and sustainable transformation of Myanmar. Major research areas include labour market reform, food security and value chain development.

Jerik Cruz is a Lecturer at the Department of Economics of the Ateneo de Manila University, and a PhD student at the Massachusetts Institute of Technology. He completed his Master's degree at the Graduate Institute of International and Development Studies, Geneva in 2016. He is also a fellow of Action for Economic Reforms and the Labor Education and

Research Network, and has co-authored policy studies commissioned by ADB, ILO, Friedrich Ebert Stiftung, and the Philippine Institute for Development Studies.

Philip Arnold Tuaño is an Associate Professor and Chair of the Department of Economics of the Ateneo de Manila University. He is a project coordinator of the Philippine Human Development Network as well as acting manager of the Philippine Chapter of the Sustainable Development Solutions Network. He has also served as Director of Macropolicy of the Philippines' National Anti-Poverty Commission. He completed his PhD from the University of the Philippines in 2015, and has published papers on social and economic mobility, the welfare impacts of trade and tax reform and climate change, and the digital divide.

Nathan Peng is a Lecturer of Political Science in Singapore Management University (SMU) under the Faculty Development Scheme. He is currently pursuing graduate studies at the University of British Columbia as an SMU Overseas PhD Scholar. His research focuses on the political economy of development in Southeast Asia. His larger research agenda has two parts: the first examines the link between patterns of politics and the development potential of a country. The second looks at strategies countries adopt when economic growth does stagnate and their implications; specifically, what kinds of politics and policies better sustain quality of life relative to others in these states of slow growth. Ultimately, he hopes his research will help narrow the development gap between nations as well as the socioeconomic gaps within them.

Vimut Vanitcharearnthum is Associate Professor at the Department of Banking and Finance, Chulalongkorn Business School, Chulalongkorn University. He received a doctoral degree in Economics from the University of Chicago. His areas of expertise are macroeconomics and development economics. His recent publications are on top-income share and inequalities in Thailand and business accounting for the Thai economy.

Tung Duc Phung is the director of Mekong Development Research Institute (MDRI), an independent scientific research agency in Vietnam. **Cuong**

Viet Nguyen is a vice director of MDRI. **Trang Huyen Dang** is a research analyst at MDRI. MDRI aims to contribute to social change and regional development in the Mekong region through development policy research and sectoral studies. Major research areas include poverty reduction, ethnic minority, labour and immigration, and education.

1

INTRODUCTION
Inequality and Exclusion in Southeast Asia

Lee Hwok Aun and Christopher Choong

A PRESSING AND DEFINING ISSUE

Inequality and exclusion are defining problems of our times globally, regionally, nationally. In introducing this book's impetus and formation, it is helpful to passage through these geographic and academic layers. Inequalities of opportunity, well-being, income and wealth have existed in all societies, but the past decade has seen heightened perceptions that globalized capitalist systems enrich the few at the expense of the many. Tellingly, the Millennium Development Goals 2015 specified gender equality while generally focusing on poverty and basic needs, while the Sustainable Development Goals 2030 inscribed reduction of inequality within and among countries as one of the various new goals pursuing equitable distribution of socio-economic benefits.

Alongside burgeoning prosperity, uncertainty and precarity are also growing, fuelling public sentiments and popular discourses surrounding these phenomena. Social discontent arises from local, lived experiences.

Social movements, voters and the general public around the world are signalling for more policies that foster equitable outcomes and bolster incomes at the bottom and middle of the distribution, and that protect the vulnerable and disadvantaged. The COVID-19 pandemic and its economic aftermath have further revealed the ways that existing inequalities can be compounded in crisis times.

The focus has decidedly fallen on disparities within countries. Inequality between countries remains salient; national income persists at low levels in many countries. Nonetheless, inequality is acknowledged as a problem all countries need to address; even if poverty alleviation takes relative precedence, rich-poor disparities and structural exclusion can undermine sustainable growth. Empirical evidence, based on increasingly widespread household income surveys, also find that within-country inequality accounts for the bulk of global household income inequality (Milanovic 2016; Bourguignon 2017). Widening inequality has been recognized as a precursor to the global financial crisis, especially in advanced economies that from the 1990s reversed the inequality reduction achieved from the 1950s through to the 1980s (Piketty 2014; Milanovic 2016; Christiansen and Jensen 2019). The general public also views the problem with increasing gravity. The World Values Survey, which has repeated the inquiry in a consistent sample of countries representing 40 per cent of the world's population, reports a rising share in the past decade that regard inequality as a significant problem warranting policy attention (UNDP 2019).

Global tides of rising inequality, notably in major economies, have momentously shifted attention to the problem, with attendant interest in the comparative experience of countries in managing the distribution of income, wealth, capability and opportunity (Deaton 2017). The zeitgeist has also shone the light on dimensions of inequality beyond summary indicators and survey datasets. Even in countries where income or expenditure inequality has shown an overall decline in survey-based estimates, there may be increased concentration at the top in ways that elude data capture, broadly breeding grievance toward a system perceivably skewed against the masses. UNCTAD's *2012 Trade and Development Report: Inclusive and Balanced Growth* showed rising income inequality, based on the Gini coefficient, was the dominant trend in most regions of the world in the 1980s to the mid-1990s (for which data are available). However, the subsequent period, roughly 1995–2010, saw inequality fall in more Latin American and African countries than the number that registered rising inequality. In developed countries and Eastern Europe and the Commonwealth of Independent States (CIS), inequality increased in the majority but stabilized or declined in a substantial proportion of these areas. In Asia, reported separately according to two expanses—South and West, and Southeast and East—the number of countries experiencing rising inequality and falling income or consumption inequality were even. The problem of skewed wealth distribution—"trickle-up" economics privileging the rich and marginalizing the poor—is globally consequential, but also more difficult to estimate.

Inequality is important and timely as a subject of empirical study, international advocacy and public policy. The next section surveys some of the more influential works of academic scholars and publications of global bodies, and discusses major themes regarding the causes and consequences of inequality. Asia has increasingly been in the spotlight, with Southeast Asia sharing the stage, albeit not in the main glare. A succession of Asian Development Bank publications highlighted how the major economies, containing almost 3 billion people today, recorded rising income inequality from the early 1990s to the late 2000s (ADB 2012; Kanbur, Rhee and Zhuang 2014; Huang, Morgan and Yoshino 2018). Southeast Asian countries appeared in these volumes, most saliently Indonesia due to the concurrence of its size and the increase in inequality across the time period being observed. Mild changes in other regional countries may partly account for their obscurity in these volumes.

Regardless of the magnitude of time trends, inequality and exclusion have been paramount in social, economic and political contexts in Southeast Asia. Indeed, discrepancies between official measurement of income or consumption inequality and perceptions of wealth or income concentration at the top, social exclusion of the masses and oligarchy-dominated systems, reinforce the relevance of studying inequality. At the same time, there remains a scarcity of studies on inequality in Southeast Asia, particularly works engaged in country-focused, in-depth accounting of the distinctive patterns, contexts and policy responses. The lack of coverage of the 2010s renders the subject in need of an update. This book aims to fill these gaps.

VIEWS OF INEQUALITY: GLOBAL AND CONCEPTUAL

Inquiry into inequality has addressed its incidence, causes and consequences. A proliferation of inequality-themed reports by influential international bodies testifies to the currency of the issue (UNCTAD 2012; UNDESA 2014; UNDP 2019). Inequality has featured in policy discourses for decades, particularly in the context of inequality between nations and the extent to which lower income but faster-growing economies are catching up with the high-income economies (UNCTAD 1997). However, the discourse has come to acknowledge the gravity of inequality and its domestic policy implications.

Income and expenditure have been, and continue to be, the primary lenses for examining inequality and exclusion. The places and times this can be studied depend on the availability of data. National household surveys, conducted for the express purpose of gauging the distribution of income, expenditure or living conditions, provide the most direct information source and enable computation of inequality indicators. Many countries lack a long series of national income and expenditure surveys, but such datasets are increasingly prioritized. Household income surveys strive to capture various source of income, enabling estimation of the distribution of market income or private income from wages, self-employment, interest, private property and private transfers, as well as social income from public transfers and social assistance. Gross income and disposable income, correspondingly representing income before and after taxation and transfers, add further layers. Expenditure arguably encapsulates material welfare more directly; such values represent the amount of goods that households are actually consuming.

However, household surveys are also known to under-enumerate incomes at the two tails of the income distribution (Atkinson 2015), resulting in income inequality being understated. New approaches have been introduced to use tax administrative data to estimate top shares (Jenkins 2017) or harmonize both tax administrative data and household surveys to account for missing incomes (Bourguignon 2018; Lustig 2019; Atkinson and Jenkins 2020). The scope of such research, initially circumscribed within advanced economies with more comprehensive and accessible tax returns data, is expanding beyond those circles, to middle-income countries.

Human development is a multidimensional process, encompassing income, health, education, and other aspects related to the enlargement of capabilities and choices. In line with this acknowledgement, which has engendered multidimensional poverty estimation, inequality is also conceived and computed in terms of education and health (UNDESA

2014; UNDP 2019). An interdisciplinary team from the London School of Economics and Political Science, and the School of Oriental and African Studies, University of London and Oxfam has developed a multidimensional inequality framework that is theoretically grounded in Sen's capability approach, extending to domains of participation, influence and voice as well as physical and legal security (AFSEE 2019).

More ground-breaking contemporary research has probed the distribution of wealth, which has momentous and durable effects—but is also much harder to calculate than income and expenditure. The assiduous efforts of Piketty, with notable collaboration of Saez and Zucman, have established wealth inequality as an important and impactful subject of rigorous academic study (Piketty, Saez and Zucman 2018). The methods they introduced revolve around the construction of distributional national accounts, adjusting national accounts with tax administrative data and household surveys. Oxfam's annual spotlight on global wealth concentration, adopting estimations by Credit Suisse, have further projected the issue in the public domain.

Theories addressing the causes of inequality—primarily income and consumption, but also wealth—are vast, but warrant a brief overview here, from three perspectives: economic structure; capability and participation; and ownership and power.

Inequalities derive from differences in productivity and earnings across economic sectors; such structural factors interact with spatial factors, such as urban-rural or regional disparities, or the location of particular resources, including minerals and arable land. Simon Kuznets' seminal work focused on industrialization and urbanization. The concurrence of these developments, and higher productivity and higher wage of industry relative to agriculture, corresponded with rising national inequality for a phase as intersectoral and urban-rural gaps widened, followed by falling inequality due to narrowing gaps within an urbanized and industrialized society. These observations, while not meant to present a predictive model of how inequality unfolds, remain pertinent. New and more complex waves of structural change, differentiating industries by technological level or stratifying service sectors by market power, may generate new dimensions of inequality.

A second set of explanations for inequality draws in socio-economic factors: disparities in capability stratify economic participation, which impact on income potential and can in turn set different households on diverging trajectories, even across generations. Under this broad banner we can subsume schooling, skills and knowledge acquisition, nutrition and healthcare services, and living environments conducive for learning in general. Education positively correlates with employment and earnings, and the distribution of educational attainment translates into the distribution of income. Scarcity of highly educated workers raises the earnings premium that they command and can widen overall income inequality; expansion of the high-skilled and professionally or technically qualified attenuates this earnings premium and narrows income inequality. Beyond enrolment and formal qualifications, quality of schooling also matters—and can be a factor that reproduces or accentuates income inequality, where rich and privileged households which can afford private schooling, supplementary classes, and higher education while poor households have to contend with overcrowded classes, deficient learning environments and lack of access to higher education. Social norms can also weigh in, in the form of prejudice or stigma impeding certain groups' educational advancement, gender biases influencing women's participation in the labour force, or other manifestations.

Third, disparities in socio-economic outcomes stem from disparities in ownership and power. Wealth inequality is invariably larger than income inequality, due to the concurrent characteristics of wealth at both extremes: as an owned stock, it can be accumulated and inherited; unlike income, which cannot be zero for subsistence, it is possible for households to hold no wealth at all. Ownership also provides the means to control commercial decisions and influence public policy. Economic elites typically gain proximity to political power, which they can leverage to their advantage, for instance, by influencing taxation and public spending towards boosting profits rather than providing more and better education and health services. "Power" encompasses other aspects, mainly related to its deficit. Politically disempowered communities lack the capacity to demand more and better schools, health services, infrastructure and connectivity, thus compounding their disadvantage. In wage negotiation, lack of worker representation and bargaining power curtail wage gains, particularly for lower-skilled workers more dependent on collective processes. Legal protection supposedly steps in to mitigate inordinate or immoral exercise of power. The establishment of laws safeguarding equality and fairness, and prohibiting discrimination and exploitation, contribute to reduction of inequality. Lack of such laws can perpetuate inequality and exclusion.

Inequality provokes strong reactions deriving from normative positions, but its consequences warrant a systematic overview as well. We briefly consider three perspectives. First, from a social justice standpoint, inequality undermines fairness in the economic system, particularly if there are structures that entrench privilege, power and wealth, and perpetuate exclusion, disadvantage and poverty. Normatively, this argument in favour of reducing inequality is premised on a view that ability and talent are distributed throughout the population regardless of socio-economic strata, but the privileged enjoy advantages that sustain their status. This perspective confronts a diametrically opposed, market fundamentalist view, which holds that market outcomes reflect marginal product of labour, which in turn derive from ability and effort. Low income thus equates with less ability or less effort. A sense of systemic unfairness and social injustice is underscored by the reality that swathes of a population, despite their strenuous labour, can be inhibited in their opportunity to complete education, attain higher-level qualifications, receive referrals for employment, access credit, and generally enjoy upwardly mobile trajectories. The potential social destabilizing effects of inequality are growing sources of concern, induced by our witness of mass discontent, demoralization or emigration triggered by persistently high inequality and the reproduction of disadvantage across generations.

A second perspective on the ramifications of inequality pertains to power. Problems surrounding "state capture", whether by a political-business interests or oligarchic or dynastic cabals, or systemically through financialization, delinks the real, productive economy from vested interests that prevail on government policy. The concentration of power also allows plutocrats to shape society's perceptions and behaviours, manifestly through the monopolized control of media and technology, which in turn influence electoral outcomes, or contribute to populist incursions (Deaton 2017). Although the zeitgeist of the global elite is to embrace global development, this is often not without expediency, promulgating philanthropy while sustaining free-flowing global finance and clandestine offshore tax havens, thus perpetuating structures of violence and inequality harmful to peripheral countries.

A third perspective broadly encompasses growth and development implications of inequality, particularly viewed through the lens of economic and social sustainability. Multicountry empirical studies find lower inequality associated with *sustained* economic growth (Berg, Ostry and

Zettelmeyer 2012; Berg et al. 2018). This acknowledgement that inequality has adverse effects on growth confounds mainstream views linking lower inequality with lower growth, resting on the argument that redistributive policies, notably progressive taxation, minimum wage and social protection, will imperil growth. Even the International Monetary Fund, however belatedly compared to other international financial institutions, has come to recognize the productive effects of reducing inequality (IMF 2017). Other economic detriments of inequality include aggregate demand deficiency and macroeconomic instability (UNCTAD 2017). Added to these problems are political economic issues expounded by Stiglitz (2013, 2016), including the big business–political establishment nexus that skews the system to favour the rich and suppresses real wage growth, and breakdown of fairness and trust in the system. Inequality also has "pernicious effects" on society, "eroding trust, increasing anxiety and illness, (and) encouraging excessive consumption", according to Wilkinson and Pickett (2009), whose work shows that, among all the social well-being indicators used, the outcomes are worse in more unequal rich countries.

Emphatically, the complexity and multidimensionality of inequality presage a wide and integrated range of policy responses, which merit a brief mention. One salient aspect of reducing inequality pertains to boosting wages and self-employment earnings of workers and households at the bottom and middle of the income distribution, through direct measures such as minimum wage and indirect measures such as skills development, wage bargaining mechanisms, and access to credit. Measures to curb inordinate influence and entrenched privilege of power elites, while exceedingly difficult to execute, are also exceptionally important, particularly to foster more equitable wealth distribution. Disparities in human development, capability and well-being, particularly education and health, demand some form of public mandate and delivery, such that these provisions are accessible to all. As basic access and participation become more universal, differences in quality impact on socio-economic status, and will need increasing attention. Inequality and exclusion framed by space—whether by region or urban-rural setting—or by population group—race, ethnicity, gender, religion, etc.—elicit a wide array of possible actions, from investment and public expenditure allocations, to legislative safeguards for equality, proactive measures targeting population groups, and redistribution across regions and geographic locations. Various policies such as these have been implemented across Southeast Asia.

ASIA AND SOUTHEAST ASIA: FLOURISHES AND GAPS IN THE LITERATURE

Interest in inequality has been mounting in Asia. Empirical evidence of rising inequality jives with the attention in public domains towards upwardly skewed distribution of economic gains and the meteoric rise of Asian millionaires and billionaires. Disparities in economic opportunity and entrenchment of privilege, mirrored in concentration of wealth and influence in the top 1 per cent, particularly resonate in these times, globally and regionally. Southeast Asian nations have broadened access to schooling and maintained relatively low unemployment, but inclusion in the growth process for a majority of the population increasingly depends on quality of education, skills and jobs. Governments across the region are acutely mindful of social expectations that the economic system must deliver benefits to the lower- and middle-income segments, and improve the livelihoods of successive generations. Introduction of minimum wage laws, or upward revision of minimum wage rates, in numerous countries reflected the underlying problem of slow wage growth at the bottom and the increasing expectations on government to respond. These discourses and policy decisions bear emotive resonance, even political expediency, but also derive from realities on the ground.

International and regional bodies took up the issue, notably the Asian Development Bank, World Bank and UNESCAP. The Asian Development Bank's 2012 *Development Outlook*, themed "Confronting Rising Inequality in Asia", and the recently published *Demystifying Rising Inequality in Asia* (Huang, Morgan and Yoshino 2019), have highlighted phenomena in all regions of the continent, including Southeast Asia. These reports, covering the 1990s into the 2000s, find rising inequality in the major developing economies—especially China, India, and Indonesia—which add weight to the subject. The World Bank's 2018 *East Asia and Pacific Regional Report, Riding the Wave: An East Asian Miracle for the 21st Century*, probed questions of inclusive growth and upward mobility, also with reference to most Southeast Asian economies. UNESCAP's 2018 report, *Inequality in Asia and the Pacific*, addressed issues and problems in the context of the 2030 Sustainable Development Goals. Both documents cover important issues—structural change, technology, education, employment, skills premiums, social protection, gender gaps and urban-rural divides—that deserve to be followed up in country-specific detail.

International agencies report the information that national governments provide, which in turn hinges on each country's engagement with national household surveys, the primary source for calculating inequality. Disparities in data availability partly account for the dearth of past research on inequality spanning the region. Some countries have a longer track record of research on poverty and inequality, with the Philippines quite extensively covered even in the 1950s until the 1980s, while Malaysia has consistently published official calculations of the poverty headcount ratio and Gini coefficient in its planning documents since the 1970s (Booth 2019). Flaws in methodology and estimation, as well as different approaches in computing poverty and inequality measures have not only posed problems for country-level analysis but also made cross-country comparisons challenging. However, more data have become available in the past decades, evidenced in the inequality reports.

Southeast Asia shows a mix of trends. By ADB's (2012) account, from the mid-1990s to the late 2000s, income or expenditure inequality grew in Indonesia, along with Lao PDR, while other regional neighbours registered either mildly decreasing inequality (Malaysia, Thailand), or a barely noticeable difference (Cambodia, the Philippines, Vietnam). The report argues for inequality to be confronted vigorously. Left unaddressed and unabated, inequality not only undermines the poverty-reducing impact of economic growth, but also threatens the basis of growth itself. Southeast Asia countries' experiences of moderate changes in inequality were rather overshadowed by the spotlight falling on countries recording rising inequality until about 2010.

Post-2010, the region continues to receive relatively scant attention, despite standing out in some ways. The 2010s have seen most countries in the region steadily reduce income and expenditure disparities. More recent reports, notably UNESCAP (2018), have captured this new unfolding situation. Nonetheless, while inequality has declined, levels remain high, especially in the middle-income to high-income countries, and there appears to be a growing disconnect between the macro data and realities on the ground. Widespread discontent and economic anxiety prevail, even while macroeconomic indicators paint a more buoyant picture.

PROJECT IMPETUS AND APPROACH

Southeast Asia is worth studying not just because of the gaps in the literature; the region distinguishes itself in particular ways lending to potentially fruitful inquiry. Countries of Southeast Asia display a range of income levels and income growth, economic diversification, population size and urbanization rates (Table 1.1). The region's variation in political regimes, with single party states, constitutional monarchies and democracies of various forms, add to the potential mix of insights that can be drawn.

The structural underpinnings of inequality and exclusion, and the relative policy importance of inequality reduction and poverty alleviation, will correspond significantly with economic conditions distinctive to each country. Poverty alleviation is a relatively higher priority in the lower income countries, where swathes of the population lack basic needs (Figure 1.1). The incidence of poverty is higher in lower income countries, as shown by the figures for Cambodia, Myanmar, the Philippines and Vietnam. These figures are based on the poverty headcount ratio, or the proportion of households with income below the national poverty line—which varies by methodology across countries. Across the region, the incidence of poverty has continuously declined.

Lower-income economies, concomitantly experiencing more rapid population growth, face paramount challenges of industrialization and employment growth—with implications on income distribution. The middle- and high-income countries, with urban areas constituting close to or in excess of the population majority, are confronted with a different set of problems, notably deindustrialization, expansion of services, increased demand for social services, and economic growth which has slowed down and must increasingly be productivity-driven. Southeast Asian countries encompass this range of conditions and challenges, and their interconnections with inequality and exclusion.

The relationships between inequality and income/economic development level are less linear and more complex. The Gini index—from 0 to 1, respectively, representing perfect equality and terminal inequality—remains the most widely used general snapshot. However, we can also refer to other indices, or the shares of total income received by particular segments—such as the top 10 per cent or bottom 40 per cent which show, respectively, extent of income concentration in the richest strata, and the share of the poorest masses in national income.

Southeast Asian countries compute inequality based on household surveys of expenditure or income, or both. Among those reporting the Gini coefficient of expenditure, Indonesia traces out an upward trend in inequality from 2000 to 2011, then a plateauing followed by a slight downward movement (Figure 1.2). Among other countries with a longer

TABLE 1.1
Southeast Asian Countries: Economic and Demographic Profile, 2019

	GDP per capita[a]		Share of Total GDP (%)[b]				Population (million)	Urban Population (% total)
	Constant $ PPP (2019)	Annual Growth % (2010–19)	Agri-culture	Industry: manu-facturing	Industry: non-manuf.	Services		
Cambodia	4,389	5.5	20.7	16.3	17.9	38.8	16.5	23.8
Myanmar[c]	5,142	5.7	21.4	24.8	13.2	40.7	53.7	30.6
Lao PDR	7,826	5.5	15.3	7.5	23.4	42.7	7.2	35.6
Vietnam	8,041	5.2	14.0	16.5	18.0	41.6	96.5	36.6
Philippines	8,908	4.6	8.8	18.5	11.7	61.0	108.1	47.1
Indonesia	11,812	4.0	12.7	19.7	19.2	44.2	270.6	56.0
Thailand	18,463	2.8	8.0	25.3	8.1	58.6	69.6	50.7
Malaysia	28,351	3.6	7.3	21.5	16.0	54.2	31.9	76.6
Brunei	62,100	–1.0	1.0	13.6	48.9	38.2	0.4	77.9
Singapore	97,341	2.5	0.0	19.8	4.7	70.4	5.7	100.0

Notes:
a $2017 international dollars purchasing power parity (PPP);
b Sectoral shares of GDP do not necessarily total 100, due to differences in categorization;
c GDP shares for 2018
Source: World Development Indicators.

Introduction: Inequality and Exclusion in Southeast Asia 13

FIGURE 1.1
Poverty Rate: Headcount Ratio, Based on National Poverty Line Income

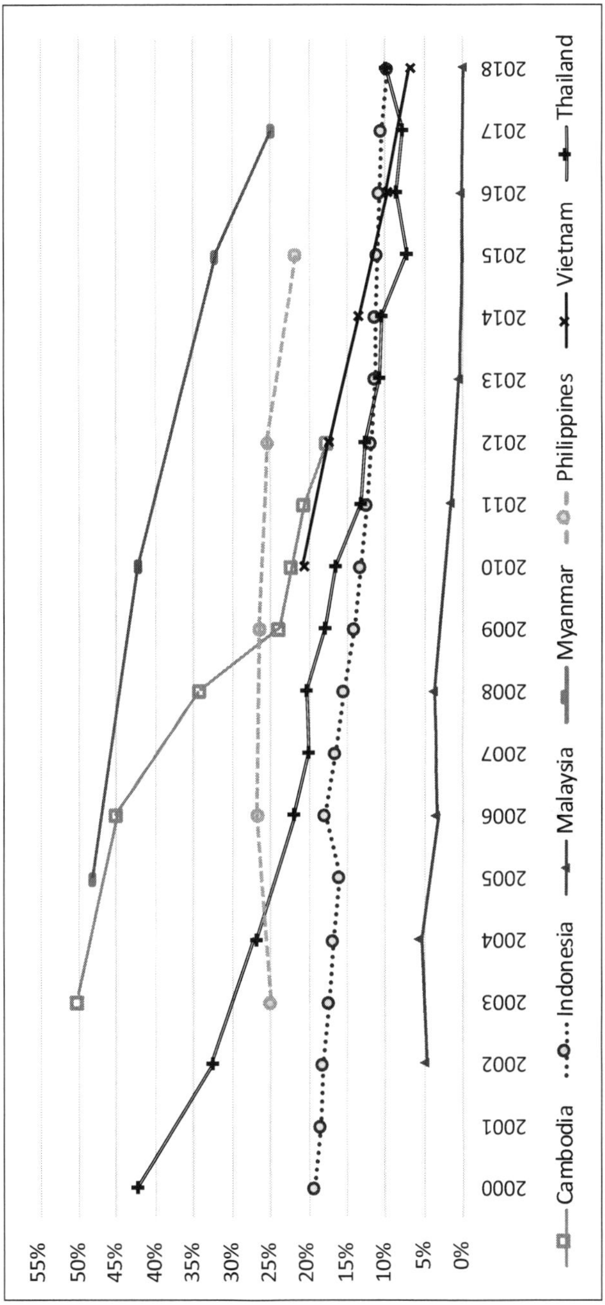

Source: World Development Indicators.

FIGURE 1.2
Gini Coefficient of Household Expenditure

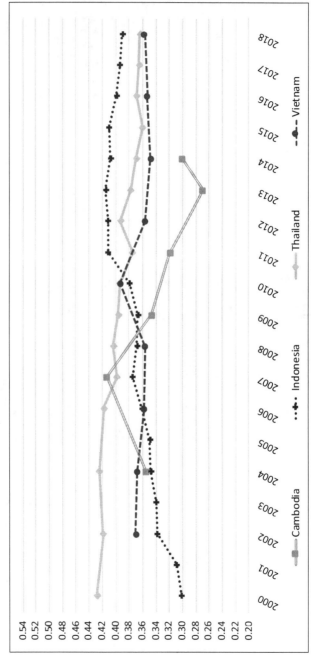

Source: Cambodia (chapter in this volume); Indonesia, Thailand, Vietnam (World Development Indicators).

inequality series, Thailand's shows sustained decline, while Vietnam holds steady. National survey data remain sparse in Cambodia; while the available Gini coefficients are inadequate to draw conclusions about trends, the level is markedly lowest among the four countries. Gini coefficients of household income reflect inequality in Malaysia, the Philippines and Thailand declining over the course of the 2000s until the most recent estimate (Figure 1.3). Singapore records a rising Gini from 2000 to 2007, then a marginal decline and a flatlining. Myanmar's survey data and estimated inequality, like Cambodia's, are rare, insufficient for observing trends, and lower in magnitude. These variations in inequality levels and trends set the stage for a regional country-based volume.

This book is the culmination of a project that started in late 2018. We assembled a team of researchers to contribute case studies on eight Southeast Asian countries: Cambodia, Indonesia, Malaysia, Myanmar, the Philippines, Singapore, Thailand and Vietnam. To optimize our ability to tap into local knowledge, and to access data and possibly documentation in the national language, we selected contributors who are citizens and/or home-based. In recognition of the multidimensionality of inequality and the diverse social science backgrounds of chapter contributors, this book takes a multidisciplinary approach.

The chapters capture differences in level of economic development, differing political imperatives of poverty and inequality, as well as availability of data, across Southeast Asia. Papers were presented and critiqued at an in-house workshop in March 2019, and a public conference in July 2019. A selection of these papers was published in a December 2019 special issue of the *Journal of Southeast Asian Economies*. Paper drafts and the journal articles have been revised for incorporation into this book.

CHAPTER OUTLINES AND THEMES

Each chapter provides an overview—as up to date as possible—of inequality levels and trends. Our primary objective is big picture, empirical analysis of inequality outcomes, rather than narrowly focused and sophisticated statistical exercises. While each paper has been given broad latitude, the scope of each country case is limited by data availability, access and quality. Happily, household surveys have been conducted in all Southeast Asian countries, although as Booth (2019) points out, the quality of these datasets

FIGURE 1.3
Gini Coefficient of Household Income

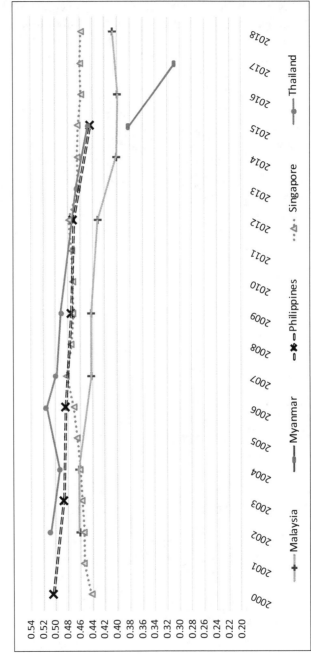

Sources: Malaysia, Philippines, Singapore, Myanmar (respective chapters in this volume); Thailand (World Development Indicators).

varies.[1] In general, we attribute more weight to trends across time within countries than comparisons across countries.

Our inquiry is open to exploring various forms of inequality, although the primary interest and dominant practice references income and expenditure. As it turns out, income or expenditure inequality is covered in all eight countries. In line with economic conditions and policy priorities, the record of poverty alleviation features in the Cambodia, Myanmar, Vietnam and Philippines chapters. Wealth distribution is a nascent field in the region; the Thailand and Singapore chapters shed light on this aspect of inequality. Socio-economic indicators provide some means for assessing the distribution of capability development and more granular details of well-being; education and health inequalities are reported for Thailand, the Philippines, Singapore and Indonesia, and information based on electricity usage supplement our view of Vietnam. Labour participation constitutes a further dimension, and receive some treatment, particularly from the gender angle, in the Malaysia, Myanmar, Indonesia and Philippines chapters.

While examining the state of inequality is our primary objective, we also aspired to engage with the underlying context and causes of inequality, and policy responses.

The authors also discuss salient themes of inequality based on country-specific conditions, contributing authors' interest and expertise, and data availability, such as structural changes and public policies to redress inequality and exclusion, labour market developments, population groups (ethnicity, gender), regional dynamics, and informal economies.

To guide the research and writing of chapters in this volume beyond the documentation of inequality trends, we sought to establish some common ground and broad themes, and remained open to emergent ideas as drafts were written, presented and discussed. The thematic dimensions of inequality can be sorted into four clusters. First, economic structure appears to some extent in all chapters, whether characterized by industrialization and regional agglomeration (Vietnam, Cambodia, Myanmar) or deindustrialization and expansion of services, which also entails linkages across industry and services and stratification within services (Indonesia, Malaysia, Thailand, Singapore). Also pertinent to economic structure are questions surrounding informality and consequent effects on exclusion, which are explored in Cambodia and Myanmar. The second set of inequality dimensions concern spatial inequality and exclusion of geographic areas from the socio-economic mainstream, which are manifest in regional or provincial inequality (Indonesia, the Philippines, Thailand, Vietnam) and urban-rural disparities which are prevalent everywhere but especially taken up in the Cambodia chapter.

Southeast Asia's ethnic diversity and gender dynamics, as well as enduring or emerging class-based inequality and oligarchic power, prompt decisive focus on these dimensions. Our third thematic cluster considers intergroup disparities, related to ethnicity and race in Vietnam and Malaysia, and to gender in Indonesia, Malaysia, Myanmar and Cambodia. With regard to class and power, questions of social stratification and intergenerational transmission of privilege are unpacked in the Philippines and Singapore. The overhanging and contentious issue of oligarchy, or dynastic political power, feature in the Philippines, Indonesia, and Thailand.

As noted earlier, we consider the conditions and contexts of inequality, while generally omitting empirical research on the consequences and applying a light touch on policy responses. Our investigations have enough to handle in focusing on inequality levels and trends. Furthermore, exploration of the consequences of inequality require expanded and more complex methodologies. The wider effects of inequality on society undeniably warrant empirical study but such efforts lie beyond our scope. We do take the cue from the fact that all countries have taken decisive stances to redress inequality, clearly responding to public demands and a general sense that persistent inequality entails considerable social costs. Within the constraints of this project, we deem it reasonable and to proceed into discussion of public policy without delving extensively into the further ramifications on society, but with due acknowledgement of our limited analysis.

National strategies and policies generally correspond with the salient dimensions of inequality that emerge in this book's country studies. All Southeast Asian governments are committed to reducing inequality, whether through a grand policy declaration or measures introduced that clearly aim to foster more equitable distribution. A few specific policy aspects are worth mentioning here. Governance capacity enters the frame in a generic sense, but the immense tasks of promoting equity perhaps demand policy implementation that, more than other policies, demonstrates efficacy and accountability. The chapters on the Philippines and Singapore engage with this issue more substantively. Within country spatial inequalities weigh heavily on most governments in the region, but with different challenges, from the unparalleled redistribution challenges of archipelagic Indonesia and the Philippines, to the perennial problem of overconcentration of wealth and power in Bangkok, and the disparities between regions and states in Malaysia and Vietnam, which partly overlap with ethnicity. For lower-income, industrializing Cambodia and Myanmar, core policy objectives seek to marry employment generation in labour-intensive manufacturing with promotion of agricultural productivity, and to negotiate disparities between formal and informal economies.

Note

1. One way to assess such survey data is to compare the total household income—both wage and profit components—with national accounts, which tally consumption, investment, government expenditure and net exports. In 2013–15, total income from surveys as a percentage of national accounts ranged from 42–43 per cent in Indonesia to 53 per cent in the Philippines, 65–59 per cent in Thailand, 77 per cent in Vietnam, and 126 per cent in Cambodia (Booth 2019).

References

ADB. 2012. *Asian Development Outlook 2012: Confronting Rising Inequality in Asia*. Bangkok: Asian Development Bank.

AFSEE. 2019. *Multidimensional Inequality Framework*. http://sticerd.lse.ac.uk/inequality/the-framework/media/mif-framework.pdf (accessed 29 September 2020).

Atkinson, Anthony B. 2015. *Inequality: What Can Be done?* Cambridge, MA: Harvard University Press.

———, and Stephen P. Jenkins. 2020. "A Different Perspective on the Evolution of UK Income Inequality". *Review of Income and Wealth* 66, no. 2: 253–66.

———, Thomas Piketty, and Emmanuel Saez. 2011. "Top Incomes in the Long Run of History". *Journal of Economic Literature* 49, no. 1: 3–71.

Berg, Andrew, Jonathan D. Ostry, and Jeromin Zettelmeyer. 2012. "What Makes Growth Sustained?". *Journal of Development Economics* 98: 149–66.

———, Jonathan D. Ostry, Charalambos G. Tsangarides, and Yorbol Yakhshilikov. 2018. "Redistribution, Inequality and Growth: New Evidence". *Journal of Economic Growth* 23: 259–305.

Booth, Anne. 2019. "Measuring Poverty and Income Distribution in Southeast Asia". *Asian-Pacific Economic Literature* 33, no. 1: 3–20.

Bourguignon, François. 2017. *The Globalization of Inequality*. Princeton: Princeton University Press.

———. 2018. "Simple Adjustments of Observed Distributions for Missing Income and Missing People". *Journal of Economic Inequality* 16, no. 2: 171–88.

Christiansen, Christian Olaf, and Steven L.B. Jensen. 2019. "Histories of Global Inequality: Introduction". In *Histories of Global Inequality*, edited by Christian Olaf Christiansen and Steven LB Jensen, pp. 1–32. Palgrave Macmillan.

Deaton, Angus. 2017. "How Inequality Works". *Project Syndicate*, 21 December 2017. https://www.project-syndicate.org/onpoint/anatomy-of-inequality-2017-by-angus-deaton-2017-12. (accessed 29 September 2020)

Huang, Bihong, Peter J. Morgan, and Naoyuki Yoshino. 2018. *Demystifying Rising Inequality in Asia*. Tokyo: ADB Institute.

IMF. 2017. *Fiscal Monitor: Tackling Inequality*. Washington, DC: International Monetary Fund.

Jenkins, Stephen P. 2017. "Pareto Models, Top Incomes and Recent Trends in UK Income Inequality". *Economica* 84, no. 334: 261–89.

Kanbur, Ravi, Changyong Rhee, and Juzhong Zhuang. 2014. *Inequality in Asia and the Pacific: Trends, Drivers, and Policy Implications*. Abingdon, Oxon and New York: Routledge and ADB.

Lustig, Nora. 2019. "The Missing Rich in Household Surveys: Causes and Correction Approaches". Commitment to Equity (CEQ) Working Paper Series 75. Tulane University, Department of Economics.

———, Luis Lopez-Calva, and Eduardo Ortiz-Suarez. 2013. "Declining Inequality in Latin America in the 2000s: The Cases of Argentina, Brazil, and Mexico". *World Development* 44: 129–41.

Milanovic, Branko. 2011. *The Haves and the Have-nots: A Brief and Idiosyncratic History of Global Inequality*. New York: Basic Books.

———. 2016. *Global Inequality: A New Approach for the Age of Globalization*. Cambridge: Harvard University Press.

Oxfam. 2017. "An Economy for the 99%". Oxfam Briefing Paper, January 2017. https://www.oxfam.org/sites/www.oxfam.org/files/file_attachments/bp-economy-for-99-percent-160117-en.pdf (accessed 22 October 2018).

Piketty, Thomas. 2014. *Capital in the Twenty-first Century*. Cambridge: Harvard University Press.

———, and Gabriel Zucman. 2014. "Capital Is Back: Wealth-Income Ratios in Rich Countries 1700–2010". *Quarterly Journal of Economics* 129, no. 3: 1255–310.

———, Emmanuel Saez, and Gabriel Zucman. 2018. "Distributional National Accounts: Methods and Estimates for the United States". *Quarterly Journal of Economics* 133, no. 2: 553–609.

Stiglitz, Joseph E. 2013. *The Price of Inequality: How Today's Divided Society Endangers Our Future*. New York: Penguin.

———. 2016. *The Great Divide*. New York: Penguin.

UNCTAD. 1997. *Trade and Development Report 1997: Globalization, Distribution and Growth*. Geneva: United Nations Conference on Trade and Development.
———. 2012. *Trade and Development Report 2012: Policies for Inclusive and Balanced Growth*. Geneva: UNCTAD.
———. 2016. *Trade and Development Report 2016: Structural Transformation for Inclusive and Sustained Growth*. Geneva: UNCTAD.
———. 2017. *Trade and Development Report 2017: Beyond Austerity: Towards a Global New Deal*. Geneva: UNCTAD.
UNDESA. 2014. *Report on World Social Situation 2013: Inequality Matters*. New York: United Nations Department of Economic and Social Affairs.
UNDP. 2019. *Human Development Report 2019: Beyond Income, Beyond Averages, Beyond Today: Inequalities in Human Development in the 21st Century*. New York: UNDP.
UNESCAP. 2018. *Inequality in Asia and the Pacific in the Era of the 2030 Agenda for Sustainable Development*. New York: UN Economic and Social Commission for Asia and the Pacific.
Wilkinson, Richard, and Kate Pickett. 2009. *The Spirit Level: Why Equality is Better for Everyone*. London: Penguin.
World Bank. 2018. *East Asia and Pacific Regional Report, Riding the Wave: An East Asian Miracle for the 21st Century*. Washington, DC: World Bank.

2

CAMBODIA'S EXPERIENCES IN ADDRESSING INEQUALITY

Piseth Keo and Vannarith Chheang

INTRODUCTION

> All human beings are born free and equal in dignity and rights. They are endowed with reason and conscience and should act towards one another in a spirit of brotherhood ... Everyone has the right to take part in the government of his country, directly or through freely chosen representatives ... Everyone has the right to equal access to public service in his country.
>
> *United Nations Universal Declaration of Human Rights (1948)*

The United Nations Universal Declaration of Human Rights stresses that human beings are born free and equal in dignity and rights. Everyone has equal rights to access public services and to take part in the political process and decision-making in their own country. This universal declaration also emphasizes the need for global collective efforts to ensure equal access to social services, free choice of employment, and rights to health and well-being and education, among others. Failing to do so can bring about severe consequences to the economy, society and environment, ranging from economic inefficiency and unsustainable growth to poverty and hunger, social injustice and disparity, and environmental depletion. As a result of this universal call, there has been a sharp reduction in global poverty over the last twenty-five years, in which more than a billion people have been lifted out of poverty (World Bank 2018). This global phenomenon is possible due to global economic growth in Asia, including continental giants China and India.

Despite these achievements, the gains from global economic growth have not been shared equally. The world's richest 1 per cent, numbering 60 million, receive more than 20 per cent of global income, and a select few in the top 0.01 per cent (600,000 individuals, with approximately 1,200 billionaires) have been living extravagant lives (Institute for Policy Studies 2017; Slater 2013). While poverty has declined sharply, inequality has dramatically increased in the same period (Oxfam 2020). Since global resources are finite, resource distribution should be more equal for poverty to be continually reduced, and sustainable growth maintained. Rising inequality erodes the middle class, which is the backbone of society; adversely affects incentives and motivation of workers in sectors that fall behind, thereby lowering labour productivity; hampers investment in human capital because lower income classes do not have access to credit; and, in general, undermines social cohesion (Yap 2013).

In an attempt to reverse the trend of inequality, the United Nations Sustainable Development Goals (SDGs) 2030 commit to leaving no one behind, placing equality at the centre of the national policy-making process, where every individual citizen is included and able to benefit from the fruits of development. SDG Goal 10 is devoted specifically to inequality reduction, while others, including Goal 1 (No Poverty), Goal 2 (Zero Hunger), Goal 3 (Good Health and Well-Being), Goal 4 (Quality Education), Goal 5 (Gender Equality) and Goal 6 (Clean Water and Sanitation), aim to guide national policy formulation and implementation, along with regional and international partnership, towards poverty alleviation, equitable distribution and equality on rights-based principles.

As a member of the United Nations Convention on Sustainable Development, in 2018, Cambodia adopted its national SDGs following the seventeen global goals with the addition of Goal 18 on "Ending the Negative Impacts of Mine/Remnant of War, and Supporting the Victims". The Cambodian SDGs are built on Cambodia's achievements of its Millennium Development Goals (MDGs). On poverty eradication (Goal 1), the poverty rate in Cambodia dropped rapidly from 53.2 per cent in 2004 to 13.5 per cent in 2014 (World Bank 2020a). In addition, other targets including Universal Primary School Enrolment (Goal 2), Infant and Child Mortality Reduction (Goal 4), Maternal Mortality Reduction (Goal 5), Prevention of HIV/AIDS (Goal 6), and Demining (Goal 9) were also attained.

Despite the MDG achievements, poverty and inequality remain pressing issues in Cambodia. Some estimates suggest that a majority of the approximately 4.5 million Cambodian people who escaped poverty since 2007 are on the brink of falling back if economic or natural shocks happen, including changing climate, disease pandemic, crop failure and market fluctuation (World Bank 2020a). Inequalities in access to employment opportunities, education, health and sanitation, public services and decision-making processes can also pose challenges to Cambodia's future development.

The aims of this chapter are to investigate the state of poverty and inequality in Cambodia and to evaluate the country's efforts in addressing these pressing problems. Income data are scarce; Cambodia has historically lacked the resources to conduct regular national household surveys, but such exercises in recent years have provided more empirical grounds to assess income distribution. The record shows steady decline in poverty and low levels of income inequality, which are quite characteristic of low-income countries experiencing steady economic growth and structural change. Beyond the macro summary through the Gini coefficient, more detailed information on income distribution is scarce. Other forms of inequality are also pertinent to the Cambodian situation; focusing on income alone omits other aspects of livelihoods, especially in rural areas where the majority resides. This chapter therefore focuses on other forms of inequality besides income, including living environment, natural resources and access to services, mainly health and education. We also probe dimensions of inequality between groups based on gender, location (urban/rural) and the formal/informal divide.

The chapter starts with an overview of geography, demography, socio-economics and political regime of Cambodia, to familiarize readers with a country infrequently in the spotlight. We then discuss Cambodia's performance on the Human Development Index and various forms of inequality, referring to data sources besides income to unpack disparities based on gender, urban-rural location and formal-informal status. Following this, we focus on rural areas, comprising three quarters of Cambodia's population, and consider how resource-based communities are coping, and how access to public services and outmigration are impacting on socio-economic development. We proceed to evaluate a range of Cambodia's policies on poverty alleviation, social protection, gender mainstreaming, education, health and well-being, and natural resource management, and the effectiveness of such measures in fostering equitable distribution. The chapter concludes with a number of possible policy recommendations that may contribute to sustaining low inequality and increased inclusion in Cambodia.

DEMOGRAPHIC, SOCIO-ECONOMIC AND POLITICAL OVERVIEW

Geographically, Cambodia is located in Southeast Asia, borders Thailand, Laos and Vietnam, and has access to the Gulf of Thailand with a coastline stretching 435 km. The country covers an area of 181,035 square km, which features major rivers, floodplains, coastline, plateaus and mountainous areas. The southwest and northeast parts of the country are covered in plateaus. However, Cambodia's most significant natural landscapes are the Tonle Sap Great Lake, the largest lake in Southeast Asia, and the Mekong River, both of which form a huge basin and floodplain comprising more than 43 per cent of the land area of the country (Sokhem and Sunada 2006). These rivers not only supply food to the majority of the population in the adjacent areas, but in the absence of rain remain the only sources of water supply for irrigation and agricultural purposes. Both of these massive bodies of water also contribute to the export of fish products to the regional and global markets.

Demography

According to the census 2019, Cambodia has an estimated population of 15,288,489 people in 3,341,770 households, with an average household size of 4.6, of which around 76 per cent are recorded as living in rural areas (NIS 2019). The average annual growth rate of the population from 2008 to 2019 is 1.2 per cent, with density of 86 people/square km (NIS 2019). However, in urban areas, population grows at a speedier pace of 3.7 per cent per year (UNFPA 2014). Phnom Penh hosts 1.4 million people or 2.1 million people including its greater metropolitan area (NIS 2019).

Cambodia's unemployment rate is at a relatively low 3.5 per cent. The employment-to-population ratio for the working age population, aged 15–64 years, is 84.2 per cent nationally, but ranges from 74.8 per cent in Phnom Penh to 80.4 per cent in urban areas (excluding the capital city) and 86.6 per cent in rural areas (NIS 2018). This rate exceeds that of Southeast Asian neighbours and reflects the need for the adult population, both men and women, to secure employment largely because wages are too low for sustaining single-income households. Indeed, women comprise the majority of the employed, specifically 51.5 per cent of employment, including paid employment, self-employment and unpaid family workers.

In terms of ethnic composition, the Cambodian population is overwhelmingly Khmer (97 per cent), followed by Cham (2.4 per cent), Chinese (0.2 per cent) and other groups (0.3 per cent), who are mainly indigenous peoples settled in mountainous areas (NIS 2018). The poverty rate among this latter group is considerably higher than the national figure partly because of geographical remoteness, lack of access to public goods and service, as well as social exclusion and inability to fully participate in market activities. One question mark persists over these official ethnic composition data regarding the Vietnamese population. There has not been any data providing precise numbers of ethnic Vietnamese because of the politicization and sensitivity of the Cambodian-Vietnamese ethnic relations. It has been observed that there is a large number of Vietnamese living in Cambodia according to registrations in the official state resident books.[1]

Socio-economic Development

Cambodia has grown its GDP per capita from US$244 in 1993, when Cambodia transformed into a market economy, to US$1,512 in 2018 (UNSD 2020). The economy has diversified, with agriculture contributing 25.3 per cent to total output, manufacturing 32.8 per cent and services 41.9 per cent (CIA 2020). The employment composition differs slightly, with agriculture constituting 37.0 per cent of the total while manufacturing and service sector shares are 26.2 per cent and 36.8 per cent respectively (NIS 2018). The service sector in Phnom Penh is high at 75.7 per cent compared to 65 per cent in other rural areas (NIS 2018).

Cambodia's remarkable economic performance of an average 7.6 per cent per year from 1994 to 2017 is largely driven by political and social stability, and its policies that allow openness of trade and capital flows, and overseas development assistance (OECD 2017). The Cambodian Law on Investment (amended 2003) provides, for instance, preferential trade treatment, which "[a] foreign investor shall not be treated in any discriminatory way by reason only of the investor being a foreign investor, except in respect of ownership of land as set forth in the Land Law (Article 8)", and "incentives and privileges" that qualified investment projects can enjoy, which "shall include the exemption, in whole or in part, of custom duties and taxes" (Article 13) along with exemption of tax on profit for certain period of time. From 1993 to 2019, Cambodia has received foreign direct investment averaging 7.7 per cent of GDP per year (World Bank 2020b). This is one of the highest rates in the world (World Bank 2020b).

Political Regime

Understanding the political regime is crucial for properly interpreting how institutional politics and policy processes work for inclusive and sustainable development in Cambodia. This Southeast Asian state is a constitutional monarchy with a democratic multi-party parliament. The constitution provides for the branches of government—the executive, legislative and judiciary—to independently perform their duties without infringing on the powers of others; all have clear mandates outlined in different legal instruments. In reality, the executive branch has, to some extent, influence over the decision making of the other branches. As a post-conflict country with nascent institutions and weak checks and balances, Cambodia has persistently struggled to rein in corruption, which has in turn hindered law enforcement and policy implementation. The International Labour Organization notes that Cambodia's cash-based economy raises the possibility of corrupt behaviour and estimates that the country loses 10 per cent of GDP due to corruption (ILO 2014). The Cambodian law on anti-corruption was endorsed and entered into force in 2012, and in September 2013, the Cambodian Prime Minister stated that corruption is the greatest challenge facing the country and expressed serious commitment to fight the menace.[2] As yet, however, there is scant evidence of a positive change. In 2013, Cambodia ranked 156 out of 175 countries in Transparency International's Corruption Perceptions Index, while in 2019, it ranked 162 out of 180 countries (Transparency International 2019).

POVERTY AND HUMAN DEVELOPMENT

Cambodia's poverty rate, based on the poverty line of US$1.25 per person per day, has dramatically diminished from 53.2 per cent in 2004 to 13.5 per cent in 2014 (Ministry of Economy and Finance 2019; NIS 2018). This decline of poverty rate was largely due to sustained economic growth exceeding 7 per cent annually between 1995 and 2015. Nevertheless, more than 70 per cent of the population still live with less than US$3 per person per day, which means most of them remain at the margins of the poverty line and are vulnerable to falling back into poverty (ADB and ILO 2015). Recent studies estimate that economic, social and climate shocks will cause the income of around 4.5 million people to drop below the poverty line (World Bank 2020a).

Food poverty, which corresponds with extremely low income and destitute living standards, has largely been resolved in Cambodia. Hunger was known to be a problem in rural and urban areas outside of Phnom Penh, especially prior to 2008. From 2008, the situation improved and there was rapid decline of overall food poverty to an estimated 2.33 per cent nationwide, and virtual eradication in Phnom Penh in 2012. Other urban areas registered a slightly higher food poverty rate of 2.91 per cent (MoP 2014).

In addition to alleviating food poverty, Cambodia has also achieved other targets set in the national MDGs, specifically Universal Primary School Enrolment (Goal 2), Infant and Child Mortality Reduction (Goal 4), Maternal Mortality Reduction (Goal 5), Prevention of HIV/AIDS (Goal 6) and Demining (Goal 9). Fewer children die before they reach their fifth birthday, while the live birth rate dropped from 124 per 1,000 to 35 per 1,000 between 2000 and 2014 (WHO 2016). Additionally, the enrolment rate for primary school increased from 82 per cent to 97 per cent between 1997 and 2016, which is one of the highest in Southeast Asia (MoEYS 2020). However, lower secondary completion rate at 57 per cent in 2017 is lower than the average for lower middle-income countries (World Bank 2020a).

Alongside improvements in the poverty situation, Cambodia has also moved up in the Human Development Index (HDI), a composite measure of income, education and health. Cambodia's score of 0.582 in 2017 marked a significant improvement from 0.364 in 1990, 0.420 in 2000 and 0.537 in 2010. As can be seen in Table 2.1, life expectancy has increased from 53.6

TABLE 2.1
Cambodia Human Development Index

	Life Expectancy at Birth	Expected Years of Schooling	Mean Years of Schooling	GNI Per Capita (2011 PPP$)	HDI Value
1990	53.6	6.7	2.7	933	0.364
1995	55.2	7.1	3.0	1,084	0.387
2000	58.4	7.6	3.2	1,347	0.420
2005	63.1	10.2	3.5	1,889	0.490
2010	66.6	11.0	4.4	2,410	0.537
2015	68.6	11.7	4.7	3,086	0.571
2016	69.0	11.7	4.7	3,246	0.576
2017	69.3	11.7	4.8	3,413	0.582

Source: UNDP (2019).

in 1990 to 69.3 years old in 2017, while the expected years of schooling increased from 6.7 to 11.7 years in the same period. In addition, the Gross National Income (GNI) almost quadrupled in this period. The score puts Cambodia in the medium human development category, ranking 146 out of 189 countries.

Despite Cambodia's improvements in the basic state of health, captured in generic indicators such as life expectancy, critical issues emerge when we consider more specific indicators. The nutritional status of children remains a problem, with 32 per cent of children under five (numbering approximately half a million) classified as stunted, while 10 per cent are classified as wasting (UNICEF 2020; WFP 2020). General dietary shortfall, and specific deficiency in zinc, iodine and B-vitamins, widely inhibit children's ability to grow and develop. These conditions are also detrimental to women, particularly in their reproductive capacity. About 14 per cent of Cambodian women are underweight (WFP 2020). The state of water and sanitation is also seriously lagging. In 2017, about 34 per cent (5.4 million people) of the population did not have access to improved sanitation facilities, while 21 per cent (3.4 million people) lacked access to safe drinking water (World Bank 2020a).

INEQUALITY

Income inequality is relatively low in Cambodia and available evidence suggests a decline in recent years. Calculations of the Gini coefficient based on national socio-economic surveys show an increase from 0.36 in 2004 to 0.41 in 2007, but a subsequent decrease to 0.35 in 2009, 0.32 in 2011 and 0.30 in 2014 (ADB 2014; ADB 2019). These positive developments can be attributed to the progressive distribution of the gains from economic growth and redistributive measures. Consumption per capita for the poorest 40 per cent of the population grew by more than 7 per cent per annum during 2007–14, and support from Overseas Development Assistance (ODA) since 1992 has largely invested in social policies (CRDB-CDC 2019; World Bank 2020a).

Earned income, deriving from wages or self-employment, has increasingly contributed to household income; correspondingly, income from self-employment has contributed less over time. The share of wages and salaries in total household income rose from 41 per cent in 2013 to 53 per cent in 2017, the share of self-employment income dropped from 55 per cent to 42 per cent (NIS 2018). The growing share of income from wage employment and simultaneous decline in income inequality concur with structural change in Cambodia's economy and labour migration patterns, both domestic and overseas. A substantial portion of the underemployed rural labour force has moved from agriculture to better-paying employment in manufacturing and service sectors in Cambodia's towns and cities, or overseas. Of the mobile rural population, 57 per cent relocate domestically to urban areas, predominantly Phnom Penh, while 13 per cent move within rural areas and 31 per cent migrate to other countries (NIS 2018). Among overseas destinations, Thailand is the most popular, followed by the Republic of Korea, Malaysia, Japan and Singapore, where they work in a gamut of economic sectors including fishing, agriculture, livestock, construction, manufacturing and services (MoP 2014; ILO 2019). A majority of migrant workers (82.9 per cent of women and 75.9 per cent of men) send back remittances, which provides a significant support to rural households (MoP 2014).

Policy interventions that boost low wages will also impact inequality reduction. Since 1997, Cambodia has mandated a minimum wage specifically for the garment and footwear industry, the key export sector of the economy. Recently, minimum wage has been increased to US$190 in 2020, which amounts to a more-than-threefold increase since 2012. Figure 2.1 provides an overview of minimum wage rates, which have risen steeply in some years, especially the 28 per cent increase between 2014 and 2015. The increase occurred due to the demand of the workers and

Cambodia's Experiences in Addressing Inequality

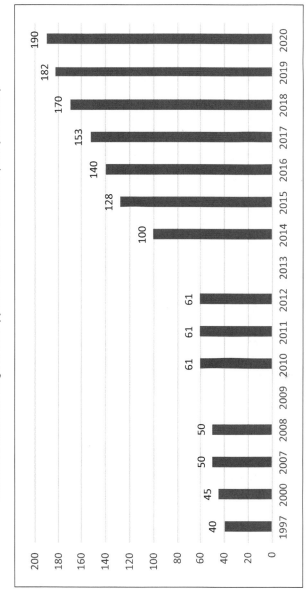

FIGURE 2.1
Cambodia: Minimum Wage in the Apparel and Textile Industries (US$ per month)

Sources: Ministry of Labour and Vocational Training cited in Trading Economics (2020); International Labour Organization (2016).

negotiation among key stakeholders from the government, Association for Garment Manufacturers Association of Cambodia, Cambodian Labour Union Federation and others. The minimum wage is adjusted during the annual meeting held between the Ministry of Labour and Vocational Training, unions and employers' representatives (ILO 2016). The adjustment is based on social and economic criteria agreed among the meeting participants. The wage hikes have increased more frequently in recent years, while it happened only once in the decade preceding 2007 (Shrestha 2019).

Increased minimum wage has largely benefited and improved the well-being and livelihood of women, who have fewer job opportunities and predominantly occupy the garment and footwear industry. This government intervention also arguably helps reduce income inequality between male and female workers in the sector given that the wage levels are publicly known and gender differentiation is prohibited. Since the majority of women remit their salaries home, the benefits from the increased minimum wage extend to rural households and the broader rural economy.

It should be reiterated that minimum wage is confined to the garment and footwear industries. De facto minimum wage also effectively applies to public administration, in view of the fact that the lowest paid workers receive an officially specified wage. However, the policy does not cover informal employment and other formal employment. The informal economy accounts for an estimated 87 per cent of the labour force in a broad range of occupations such as construction workers, tuk-tuk drivers, and staff at restaurants and entertainment outlets like karaoke lounges (THL 2020). While empirical data are lacking, it is reasonable to presume that wages are generally lower, and social protection much weaker, in the informal economy (THL 2020).

Addressing this gap, the Royal Government of Cambodia started a five-year project (2015–19), supported by the European Union, on social insurance for the informal sector, including hired workers and self-employed workers, with a focus on the construction sector for hired workers, and tuk-tuk drivers among the self-employed (THL 2020). The main purpose of the project is to develop evidence-based knowledge and capacity building for key stakeholders towards the eventual integration of informal work into the National Social Security Fund (NSSF), starting with employment injury insurance for construction workers. Participation in the NSSF of the informally employed will need to progress in tandem with the formally employed; only 13 per cent of formal sector workers have registered with the NSSF. It is the responsibility of employers to provide employment injury insurance, which covers medical expenses in any public or private hospital in the case of emergency, and other benefits in the case of death or permanent disabilities. For self-employed and domestic workers, the project is looking into finding proper mechanism to allow them to access benefits that they have not received.

Gender Inequality

Cambodia has made various commitments towards reducing gender inequality. Thanks to the ODA's technical and financial support, and the government's efforts, gender equality and empowerment have been placed on the national priority list. Since 15 October 1992 when the Kingdom of Cambodia ratified the Convention on the Elimination of all Forms of Discrimination against Women (CEDAW), the government has invested signficant efforts to promote women's economic empowerment, access to health services and education, legal protection, and participation in political decision-making. The key legal and policy pillars include Cambodia's National Constitution, National Strategic Development Plan, National Rectangular Strategy, Neary Rattanak (Women as Precious Gem), Cambodian Sustainable Development Goals, and Law on Elections, all of which emphasize women's empowerment and gender equality. Recently, the government has adopted a new policy, termed the "Health Equity Fund", which pays even closer attention to women's well-being (OECD 2017; WHO 2019). The policy supports primary care for female workers, civil servants and armed forces, and provides financial support for female workers and women from poor families during pregnancy with three-month maternity leave, with the payment of 120 per cent of workers' salaries every month in which 50 per cent are paid by the employers, and 70 per cent are from the government's Health Equity Fund.

Looking back at history, Cambodia was a "matriarchal" society in some respects. Women were considered as head in various aspects of life, as evident in the usage of the term "Mae", which indicates "female" connotation, commonly found in family, community, army and public institutions. Such terms as "Mae Krusa" (head of family), "Mae Sahak Kuom" (head of community), "Mae Toep" (general commander), "Mae

Srok" (head of district) and "Mae Krom" (team leader) are commonly found in daily communication.

In current practice, Cambodia is a male-dominated society. Considerable gender disparities persist, notably in education and employment. The literacy rate for women is 78 per cent compared to 87 per cent for men (NIS 2018). Cambodia has made progress in women's tertiary education, especially at the undergraduate level, but has a long way to go in promoting women in postgraduate education. Women's labour force participation rate, at 79 per cent, falls short of the 89 per cent registered for men. Women's employment made up approximately 49 per cent in agriculture, 46 per cent in manufacturing and 46 per cent in services (NIS 2018). In the public sector, female civil servants represent 41 per cent of the total employed, while in manufacturing, 95 per cent are women (NIS 2018). At face value, gender differences in labour participation, in all sectors and industries, are not very wide. However, this does not simply translate into equalizing trends. High labour participation is driven by low household income and the need for dual earners; women often take up insecure and low-paying jobs or self-employment. On the other hand, women benefit disproportionately from minimum wages due to their predominance in the apparel and footwear workforce. In summary, gender equality has been on the top-priority list of the Cambodian government even though there remain many areas for improvement.

URBAN-RURAL DISPARITY

Cambodia is urbanizing, although the majority of its population still lives in rural areas. According to the Cambodia Socio-Economic Survey 2017, the bulk of the total population (76 per cent) lives in rural areas, compared to 84 per cent in 1998 (Table 2.2). The definition of urban and rural areas has changed from time to time, where the government has reclassified certain areas, but the overall national trend of urbanization remains. As highlighted above, according to the Gini index, Cambodia's income and consumption distribution reflects low levels of inequality on a national scale. However, economic growth and development disproportionately benefit urban areas. The average income per capita is US$695 in Phnom Penh, US$602 in other urban areas and US$413 in rural areas. The sources of rural household income are noteworthy. Total income comprises, on average, 53.5 per cent from wages and salary, 5.1 per cent from remittances

TABLE 2.2
Measured or Estimated Population by Residence (in thousands)

Residence	Census 1998	CSES 2004	Census 2008	CSES 2009	CIPS 2013	CSES 2014	CSES 2015	CSES 2016	CSES 2017
Cambodia	11,438 (100%)	12,657	13,396	13,729	14,677	15,184	15,405	15,626	15,848
Urban	1,796	2,388	2,614	2,644	3,146	3,412	3,541	3,670	3,801
Rural	9,642	10,270	10,782	11,085	11,530	11,772	11,865	11,956	12,047

Source: NIS (2018).

and property, and 41.4 per cent from self-employment—which in turn derives from agricultural (17.4 per cent) and non-agricultural (19.9 per cent) activity, and about 4 per cent contributed by "unpaid" family workers (NIS 2018).

Various data sources besides household income shed further light on socio-economic conditions in rural areas. The following subsections provide further elaboration on the various types of disparity between urban and rural areas.

Impact of Development on Resource Dependent Communities

In rural areas of Cambodia, natural resources play pivotal roles for local income, subsistence and livelihoods (NIS 2013). Approximately 72 per cent of the Cambodian labour force is engaged in forestry and hunting in plain areas, Tonle Sap and Mekong rivers, plateaus, mountainous and coastal regions (NIS 2013). Fisheries are similarly important. The country's inland fisheries are among some of the most productive in the world, mainly because of the huge flood plains around the Great Lake, and the Tonle Sap and Mekong rivers. In 2009, inland fisheries provided 390,000 tonnes of fish and employed 420,000 people. Considering the trickle down and multiplier economic effects, this sector impacted roughly 2 million people (FAO 2011). The above numbers become particularly vivid in light of conservative estimates indicating that an average Cambodian consumes 33 kilograms of fish products each year. Some studies suggest an even higher reliance on fisheries with quoted figures of 56 kilograms per person per year in areas with minimal fishing activities and up to 123 kilograms of fish in areas with very intensive activities (FAO 2011). The decline of fish stock driven by overexploitation, habitat destruction, pollution and climate change, among others, can have detrimental effects on the well-being and livelihoods of local people. This may lead to an increase in inequality.

From the early 1990s, when Cambodia transformed its economy from socialist to capitalist and replaced central planning with market-driven processes, the state has viewed natural resources as one of the primary drivers of economic growth. Timber logging, fisheries exploitation, land concessions for economic zones, agricultural projects, hydro-power development, mining, and other forms of extractive industries have all been on the national policy agenda. In 2008, fisheries contributed nearly 12 per cent to Cambodia's GDP, and 21.5 per cent of the goods and services in the agriculture, fisheries, and forestry sectors combined (FAO 2011). As of June 2012, more than 2 million hectares of land have been transferred to about one hundred companies as concessions for intensive and industrial agriculture. According to the government, such concessions are necessary for improving land productivity, creating rural employment and generating state revenue (MAFF 2015; Mohammed, Wang, and Kawaguchi 2013).

These well-intended policies, which aim to make more efficient use of natural resources for national economic growth, do not always produce results as planned. For example, the economic land concession policy that aims to use land more productively was marred by a myriad of reports on forced displacement, forest destruction, ecological changes and biodiversity loss. According to Global Forest Watch (2020) and Tucker (2015), from 2001 to 2019, Cambodia has lost approximately 23,100 square km of tree cover, and in 2013 alone, the country lost 2,800 square km, of which 80 per cent was inside protected areas. Forest loss means the loss of local livelihoods and income sources as well as cultural practices for local people. In 2016, there were at least 1,326 protests from villagers and NGOs against state decisions in Phnom Penh alone, largely due to land conflicts.[3] In addition, the contribution of these land concessions to national coffers is minimal and the scope for profiteering is wide, with the land rental fee of US$5 per hectare. The ministry's figures show that the government has validated a total of 1,178,646 hectares as Economic Land Concessions to 229 companies across the country, collecting a paltry US$6.64 million in rental fees in 2018.[4]

In addition to rapidly depleting forestry resources, Cambodia is also infamous for inland and marine habitat destruction caused by sand dredging, destructive fishing practices, mangrove clearance for timber and shrimp farming, siltation, pollution from urbanization and industrialization, and negative environmental effects of increased tourism (FAO 2011; ILO 2014; Global Witness 2010). These national interventions would disproportionately benefit urban capitalists and be detrimental to rural communities, whose livelihoods and traditional practices depend largely on these natural resources.

State failure to properly manage natural resources can be largely attributed to ineffective state institutions and poor law enforcement. Most institutions are plagued by a shortage of qualified human resources with the necessary skills to fulfil their missions and mandates. In addition, poor governance and corruption are widespread and closely linked to weak law enforcement and poor natural resource management (ILO 2014). Government officers have incentives to take bribes instead of enforcing laws and deliver good public services. This situation is aggravated by low salaries and inadequate financial support for day-to-day operations. Even when those responsible for violations are caught and found guilty, they are often not punished for their misconduct (Milne, Kimchoeun and Sullivan 2015). During the field research conducted by one of the authors in 2014 and 2015, officers from multiple government ministries confirmed that corruption exists and remains one of the most detrimental forces in natural resource management.[5] One of the interviewees at the national level stated that:

> it is difficult to stop officers in charge of enforcing natural resource management law from taking bribes, because they are stationed in the rural areas without financial support for petroleum, food, accommodations and other basic needs. Officers in charge at the national level are aware of the situation, but there is no solution as the annual budget from the state is too small.

The failure of the state to manage environmental and natural resources have detrimentally affected local villagers whose subsistence and livelihoods depend on agricultural land, forests, and surrounding environmental and ecological resources. Forced displacement pushes rural villagers into further exclusion and increases inequality and vulnerability to economic and environmental shocks in an increasingly volatile environment.

Disparity in Access to Public Services

In addition to natural resource issues, rural populations also face obstacles in improving their well-being due to the concentration of health and education services in urban areas, particularly in Phnom Penh. These disparities prevail in both the amount and quality of healthcare and education provisions, affecting the well-being of rural communities and limiting their developmental potential. While 97.6 per cent and 78.5 per cent of the population in Phnom Penh and other urban areas respectively have access to improved water sources, only 58.3 per cent of rural population enjoys the same. The rest of the population in rural areas fetch water from unimproved sources such as ponds, streams, rivers and unprotected dug wells, and 29 per cent of them never treat drinking water (NIS 2018). In 2018, only 67 per cent of rural households have access to improved sanitation facilities. Although this was a marked improvement from 29 per cent in 2010, it starkly contrasts with the urban population that enjoys universal access to sanitation facilities that are fully equipped.

Additionally, urban-rural disparities in health facilities also persist. Each province has one provincial health department managing referral hospitals, health centres and health posts. Located in provincial towns, referral hospitals have capacity to treat 100,000–200,000 patients per year, while health centres can cover 10,000–20,000 people (MIH 2015). Health posts can treat between 2,000 and 3,000 patients, providing mainly primary consultation. Health centres, with eight to eleven health personnel, are located in district towns, while health posts, with no more than two medical staff, serve remote areas 15 kilometres away from the nearest health centre. Medical doctors are concentrated mainly in national and provincial towns, while nurses and midwives are in rural areas, focusing on primary care services. Limited access to health services make life more difficult for rural residents' well-being and livelihoods. Compared to urban medical facilities, assistance provided by rural health centres are limited in terms of the availability of medical supply, drug quality and storage, and the presence of the medical staff.

In education, urban-rural divides are empirically captured in achievement gaps. According to the assessment of the Ministry of Education, Youth and Sport (2018), urban students outperformed rural students in reading by 42 scores, which means that urban students are effectively at least one year ahead of their rural cohort. In other words, grade 10 students in rural areas is roughly on par with grade 9 or lower in urban areas. There are numerous reasons for rural students to fall behind in school, including poor quality teaching and learning, irregular school attendance, inadequate preparation for school, insufficient nutrition and family responsibilities that divert children's attention from schoolwork. While most of the parents in rural areas can understand the value of education, many cannot afford to send their children to school (UNICEF 2020). Urban-rural differences in school attendance rates illustrate the greater challenge of enrolment and completion of school. In 2014, the attendance rate for primary schooling was 97.1 per cent in urban areas and a slightly lower 93.0 per cent in rural areas. The slight gap continued at the lower secondary level, with urban and rural populations, respectively, registering 79.8 per cent and 72.8 per cent attendance rates. However, at upper secondary level, the proportions were 59.1 per cent urban and only 34.3 per cent rural.[6] These disparities in education can have significant impact on the long-term performance and livelihoods of children when they grow up. Some end up living in poverty, their illiteracy consigning them to low-wage jobs.

Impact of Outmigration from Rural Areas

Limited access to public services and opportunities for employment in rural areas lead to outmigration from rural to urban areas. Remittances have been supporting the livelihood of many rural households. However, outmigration has also brought about certain negative impact. One of the current main problems from outmigration is that the elderly and young children are left behind without sufficient support. Old parents who need regular support find it hard to repeatedly turn to other villagers. In some cases, young children have to drop out of school at a very young age in order to support their family. Without education, children are most likely to fall into chronic and intergenerational poverty. Having more jobs and development in the villages can reduce inequality among villagers, and between urban and rural areas.

POLICY INTERVENTIONS

There are numerous policies in place to address both poverty reduction and inequality. Table 2.3 lists some of the key policies along with their origins and objectives.

TABLE 2.3
Cambodia: Policies on Poverty Reduction and Inequality

No.	Policies/Plans	Remarks
1.	Rectangular Strategy Phase IV (2019–23)	Acting as a comprehensive policy framework for formulating the National Strategic Development Plan (2019–23) with clearly defined indicators and time frame for implementation, consistent with the government's sectoral policies.
2.	National Strategic Development Plan (2019–23)	Formulated based on the Rectangular Strategy Phase IV, NSDP provides an overarching framework for national development outlining strategic priorities, including the list of activities, programmes and projects.
3.	Cambodian Sustainable Development Goals 2030 (2016–30)	This is the result of localization of the SDG goals into the Cambodian context. The goals offer both a policy guide and a means of tracking performance—promoting joint decision making and enabling the acceleration of development objectives. It links economic, environmental and social aspects.
4.	National Social Protection Policy Framework (2016–25)	The policy covers both social assistance and social security. This comprehensive approach will provide for a framework linking so that the two systems are complementary. A broad programme of Social Assistance foresees interventions for the poor and most vulnerable people and subsidies from the national revenue such as taxes or overseas development assistance. The Social Security includes programmes and schemes that aim at protecting people from abrupt income decline.
5.	National Population Policy (2016–30)	To enhance and improve the quality of life of the people of Cambodia with unequivocal and explicit emphasis on sustainable development measures and actions. Key sectors are on health, education, social welfare, rural and urban development, agriculture, infrastructure and environment.

6.	National Ageing Policy 2017–30	To ensure that older persons are enabled to fully participate with freedom and dignity for as long as they wish to in family, community, economic, social, religious and political activities; and that younger persons are better equipped with knowledge that enables them to lead a more productive, healthy, active and dignified life in old age.
7.	Neary Rattanak IV: Five-Year Strategic Plan for Gender Equality and Women's Empowerment (2014–18)	Neary Rattanak IV is a policy instrument to foster gender mainstreaming in key government reform programmes. It also reflects the contributions and linkages to the implementation of national plans, policies and targets.
8.	National environmental strategy and action plan (2016–23)	To sustain and consolidate the efforts for the development, protection and conservation of the environment and natural resources by addressing and preventing the loss of natural resources and ecological balance that would compromise the country's ability in achieving sustainable development and livelihoods for the people, in particular for the vulnerable groups—women, children, elderly, ethnic minorities, and the disabled.
9.	National protected areas strategic management framework plan 2017–31	To achieve the most effective, efficient and equitable management of the national protected area system, which eventually contributes to poverty reduction, national economic growth, and sustainable development through conservation and sustainable use of its biological, natural and cultural resources, and other ecosystem services.
10.	2030 Roadmap of Cambodia's SDG 4 (Education)	To ensure that (1) all girls and boys have access to quality early childhood care and education, and pre-primary education, and complete free, equitable and quality basic education (primary and lower-secondary) with relevant and effective learning outcomes; (2) all girls and boys complete upper-secondary education with relevant learning outcomes, and a substantial number of youth have increased access to affordable and quality technical and vocational education; (3) equal

continued on next page

TABLE 2.3 — cont'd

No.	Policies/Plans	Remarks
		access for all women and men to affordable and quality technical, vocational and tertiary education, including university; (4) all youth and adults achieve literacy and numeracy, and learners in all age groups have increased life-long learning opportunities; and (5) governance and management of education system are improved at all levels.
11.	Education strategic plan 2019–23	To ensure inclusive and equitable quality education and promote lifelong learning opportunities for all, and effective leadership and management of education staff at all levels.
12.	Health strategic plan (2016–20)	To ensure that quality health services are geographically and financially accessible and socio-culturally acceptable to all people in Cambodia.
13.	National strategy for rural water supply, sanitation, and hygiene (2011–25)	To ensure that water supply, sanitation and hygiene services are made available to people living in rural areas and the institutional arrangements, financial, human and other resources needed to provide these services.
14.	National Energy Efficiency Policy (2018–35)	To modernize the energy sector that enables economic growth and social inclusiveness, ensures competitiveness of businesses and improves human health, while preserves the valuable natural capital of the country.

The above policies and plans are diverse and multisectoral. Some of the them, namely National Population Policy, National Ageing Policy, National Population Policy and National Social Protection Policy, are designed specifically to support the poor and vulnerable groups. Although Cambodia remains a poor developing country, their policies are fairly progressive compared to numerous developing and developed countries. These policies and plans have set out comprehensive aspirations for fostering sustainable economic growth, food security and poverty reduction, gender inclusiveness and urban-rural disparity reduction.

CONCLUSION AND POLICY RECOMMENDATIONS

With robust and sustained economic growth, reflected in GDP expanding by 7 per cent per year over the last two decades, Cambodia has done relatively well in reducing poverty and achieving its MDGs. The poverty rate dropped significantly from 53.2 per cent to 13.5 per cent between 2004 and 2014. The country reached its MDG targets in universal primary school enrolment, infant and child mortality reduction, maternal mortality reduction, prevention of HIV/AIDs and demining.

On inequality, Cambodia has performed relatively well, registering a Gini coefficient of around 0.30 based on the most recent household survey of 2014, which places it among the least unequal countries in Southeast Asia. The record reflects economic growth that has bolstered disposable income for all, including the poorest segments. In addition, with support from overseas development assistance, the Cambodian government has also introduced policies on minimum wage, social assistance and insurance, gender mainstreaming and ageing population that are key for uplifting the poor and vulnerable groups, and for reducing inequality. To mitigate the fallout of the COVID-19 pandemic and economic downturn, the government introduced intervention to support formal industries, mainly garment and tourism.[7]

Despite the above achievements, there remain challenges, mainly in terms of the formal-informal and rural-urban divide, for Cambodia to address. Starting with the formal-informal sector divide, minimum wage and social security have been limited to only selective sectors namely garments and footwear industries, as well as public administration in which the minimum policy is already applied, leaving other sectors and the informal economy behind. The recent attempt to include the informal economy, especially construction and domestic workers, into the social security scheme face difficulty negotiating the complex nature of the sector.

On rural-urban divides, the benefits from economic growth and development are disproportionately distributed. Wealth and public services are largely concentrated in the urban areas, leaving the rural counterparts with limited access to public services such as health, water, sanitation, education, electricity and transport, and considerably excluding rural residents in political decision-making processes, which eventually have impacts on local livelihoods and development. Outmigration, which is a result of economic disparity, has serious impacts on rural areas. Despite financial support from remittances, changes of household structure have led to the abandonment of many rural areas, leaving ageing population and children behind, who are at risk of increasing inequality, social exclusion, poverty and negative effects of environmental changes. In some cases, national development agenda may proceed at the expense of local environment and livelihoods, which further excludes rural and poor communities.

To address the ongoing challenges, holistic and comprehensive policies and intervention for sustainable and inclusive rural development are required. Cambodia has witnessed a flourishing of numerous development policies and sector-based blueprints in the recent years including (i) Rectangular Strategy Phase IV (2019–23), (ii) National Strategic Development Plan (2019–23), (iii) Cambodian Sustainable Development Goals 2030 (2016–30), (iv) National Social Protection Policy Framework (2016–25), (v) National Population Policy (2016–30), (vi) Neary Ratanak IV: Five-Year Strategic Plan for Gender Equality and Women's Empowerment, (vii) National Environmental Strategy and Action Plan (2016–23) and (viii) National Protected Areas Strategic Management Framework Plan 2017–31, among others.

These policies and plans, while advocating for various interventions for economic development, poverty alleviation, income generation, education, gender empowerment, can be enhanced with a more cohesive and comprehensive approach, with the pivot towards optimizing the utilization of local resources for development and focusing on the people. A proposed new place-based people-centred (PBPC) model can serve as an overarching framework to be incorporated into the national development plan, and sectoral plans including National Development Strategic Plan,

Cambodian Sustainable Development Goals, Tourism Development Strategic Plan and Agriculture Sectoral Strategic Plan (2019–23).

"Place-based" here refers to the development strategy that utilizes endogenous potentialities to allow local places to grow, drawing on natural, physical, financial and human capital available. This strategy is adaptive to socio-cultural and environmental contexts. It applies a holistic and integrated, multisectoral and cross-disciplinary, approach. "People-centred" in this model means putting people at the centre of the development to ensure that everyone equally bears the fruits of the development outcomes. To do so, a bottom-up approach and multi-stakeholder partnerships are needed.

PBPC is an important supplement to the existing government interventions in a way that it provides a platform for coordinating the efforts for sustainable and inclusive development, and rural resilience that are currently fragmented and mostly sector based. Starting with the economic dimension, with numerous potential economic activities, rural areas can act as the centres for food production and consumption of goods, innovative small-medium entrepreneurship, culture and ecology tourism and high-tech industries. These are important for local employment and income generation, as well as help to slow down outmigration and lay a strong foundation for national economic growth for the achievements of the long-term vision.

Second, on the social dimension, PBPC contributes to supporting villagers' happiness and well-being. More ability to earn sufficient income from their land, and opportunity to hold jobs in the villages, will allow villagers to stay close to their family and provide necessary care and support. Children can go to school and enjoy their childhood. One of the main problems from outmigration is that the elderly and young children are left behind without sufficient support, which burdens the old and deprives the young who may drop out of school to support the family. Without education, children are most likely to fall into chronic and intergenerational poverty. However, having more jobs and development in the villages can reduce inequality among villagers, and between urban and rural areas.

Next, on environmental dimension, to ensure sustainability of development activities, PBPC is driven by ecological and environmental-friendly principles that aim to keep the air clean and nature preserved along with man-made spaces. Clean air, non-polluted water and green spaces are essential for healthy and long lives of the villagers. Forests, in particular, provide food and resources for development and play an integral role in ecological processes related to water supply and balancing amidst extreme weather. Numerous activities including forest protection and rehabilitation, fish sanctuary protection, green villages, high-tech incineration and sewerage waste management system are at the core of PBPC.

Finally, human resource development, physical infrastructure construction and digital connectivity brought by PBPC through direct public provision or Public-Private-People-Partnership, lay a strong foundation for rural sustainable and inclusive development and resilience. When shocks such as COVID-19 happen, rural economic activities can remain active, especially in supplying food, and must be enabled to absorb the adverse impacts concentrated in the urban economy. Community support can also be mobilized to help those in need. Better development of rural health infrastructure helps ease the burden on urban infrastructure. Furthermore, better development in rural areas also help solve some of the urban problems including waste management issues, environmental pollution, disease widespread, traffic jam and housing price bubbles.

Cambodia, seeking to catch up with Southeast Asian neighbours and establish a regional presence, sets out multiple and interdependent goals of raising living standards, promoting sustainable development, reducing poverty while enhancing equity and inclusiveness. These challenges are compounded by present global fluidities and uncertainties, and domestic constraints, both economic and political. Nonetheless, the various plans in place present necessary and constructive roadmaps for the country's progress.

Notes

1. Abby Seiff and Chhay Channyda, "Ethnic Vietnamese still adrift in Cambodia", *Phnom Penh Post*, 14 February 2013.
2. Vong Sokheng and Stuart White, "Marathon PM Speech Focuses on Reforms", *Phnom Penh Post*, 26 September 2013.
3. Touch Sokha and Ananth Baliga, "Protest Data for City Don't Add Up", Phnom Penh Post, 25 January 2017.
4. Cheng Sokhorng and Marlowe Hood, "Profit from ELCs 'Doesn't Rectify Ecological Impact'", *Phnom Penh Post*, 8 November 2018.
5. The interviewees include four officers from the national level of the Ministry of Environment and Ministry of Agriculture, Forestry, and Fisheries, one officer

from the Koh Kong Provincial Department of Environment, and five local officers the Ministry of Environment, the Ministry of Agriculture, Forestry, and Fisheries, and the Ministry of Interior.
6. Authors' compilations from UNESCO data (http://data.uis.unesco.org/#).
7. The government grants a monthly allowance of US$40 to each worker working in the garment sector, such as textiles, footwear, travel products and bags. The factories/enterprises shall add US$30 to each worker's allowance (therefore, each worker shall receive US$70 per month in total). The government grants a monthly allowance of US$40 for each worker who works in tourism industry, such as hotels, guesthouses, restaurants, and tourism agents. The tourism enterprises and businesses shall contribute in a voluntary manner based on their capability and in addition to the Royal Government of Cambodia's contribution... The allowance of US$40 from the Royal Government will only apply to the factories, enterprises and businesses that have been permitted to suspend employment contracts by the Ministry of Labor and Vocational Training from 10 April 2020. Furthermore, this allowance shall only apply to the workers who work at the factories, enterprises and businesses in the formal sector and are officially registered with the Ministry of Labor and Vocational Training, the Ministry of Commerce, the Ministry of Tourism, and the General Department of Taxation of the Ministry of Economy and Finance. (Royal Government of Cambodia's Press Release, 7 April 2020).

References

ADB. 2014. *Cambodia: Country Poverty Analysis 2014*. Manila: Asian Development Bank.
———. 2019. *Cambodia, 2019–2023: Inclusive Pathways to a Competitive Economy*. ADB Country Partnership Strategy, October 2019.
——— and ILO. 2015. *Cambodia: Addressing the Skills Gap Employment Diagnostic Study*. Manila: Asian Development Bank and International Labour Organization.
Cambodian Rehabilitation and Development Board, Council for the Development of Cambodia (CRDB-CDC). 2018. *Development Cooperation and Partnership Report*. Phnom Penh: CRDB-CDC.
Central Intelligence Agency (CIA) (website). 2020. "The World Factbook: East Asia/Southeast Asia-Cambodia". 21 October 2020. https://www.cia.gov/library/publications/-the-world-factbook/geos/print_cb.html (accessed 3 November 2020).
Food and Agriculture Organization of the United Nations (FAO). 2011. *National Fisheries Sector Overview: Cambodia*. Rome: FAO.

Global Forest Watch (GFW) (blog). 2020. "Cambodia Deforestation Rate and Statistics". 2020. https://www.globalforestwatch.org/dashboards/country/KHM/ (accessed 2 November 2020).
Global Witness. 2010. *Shifting Sand: How Singapore's Demand for Cambodian Sand Threatens Ecosystems and Undermines Good Governance*. London: Global Witness Inc.
International Labour Organization (ILO). 2014. *Enabling Environment for Sustainable Business*. Geneva: ILO.
———. 2016. "How Is Cambodia's Minimum Wage Adjusted?". *Cambodian Garment and Footwear Sector Bulletin* 3.
———. 2019. "Triangle in ASEAN Programme Quarterly Briefing Note". Bangkok: ILO.
Institute for Policy Studies (IPS). 2017. *Billionaire Bonanza: The Forbes 400 and the Rest of Us*. Washington: IPS.
Milne, Sarah, Pak Kimchoeun, and Michael Sullivan. 2015. "Shackled to Nature? The Post-Conflict State and Its Symbiotic Relationship to Natural Resources". In *Conservation and Development in Cambodia: Exploring Frontiers of Change in Nature, State, and Society*, edited by S. Milne and S. Manhanty. Oxon: Routledge.
Ministry of Health (MIH). 2015. *Health Strategic Plan 2016–2020: Quality, Effective and Equitable Health Services*. Phnom Penh: MIH.
Ministry of Agriculture, Forestry, and Fisheries (MAFF). 2015. *Agricultural Extension Policy*. Phnom Penh: MAFF.
Ministry of Economy and Finance (MEF) (website). 2019. "Recent Macro-economic Indicators (GDP Growth Rate)". 2019. https://www.mef.gov.kh/ (accessed 5 November 2020).
Ministry of Education, Youth, and Sports (MoEYS). 2018. *Education in Cambodia: Findings from Cambodia's Experience in PISA for Development*. Phnom Penh: MoEYS.
——— (website). 2020. "Primary Education". 2020. http://www.moeys.gov.kh/en/primary-education.html#.X6PK11AxU2w (accessed 5 November 2020).
Ministry of Planning (MoP). 2014. *Poverty Alleviation and Approach to an Action Plan: for CMDG-1*. Phnom Penh: MoP.
Mohammed, Essam Y., Shannon Wang, and Garry Kawaguchi. 2013. *Making Growth Green and Inclusive: The Case of Cambodia*. Paris: OECD Publishing.
National Institute of Statistics (NIS). 2013. *Cambodia Socio-Economic Survey*. Phnom Penh: NIS.
———. 2018. *Cambodia Socio-Economic Survey*. Phnom Penh: NIS.
———. 2019. *General Population Census of the Kingdom of Cambodia 2019*. Phnom Penh: NIS.
Organisation for Economic Cooperation and Development (OECD). 2017. *OECD*

Development Pathways: Social Protection System Review of Cambodia. Paris: OECD Publishing.

Oxfam. 2020. "World's Billionaires Have More Wealth than 4.6 Billion People". 20 January 2020. https://www.oxfam.org/en/press-releases/worlds-billionaires-have-more-wealth-46-billion-people (accessed 2 November 2020).

Seiff, Abby, and Chhay Channyda. 2013. "Ethnic Vietnamese Still Adrift in Cambodia". *Phnom Penh Post*, 14 February 2013. https://www.phnompenhpost.com/national/ethnic-vietnamese-still-adrift-cambodia (accessed 2 November 2020).

Slater, Jon. 2013. *The Cost of Inequality: How Wealth and Income Extremes Hurt Us All.* Oxford: Oxfam.

Sokha, Touch, and Ananth Baliga. 2017. "Protest Data for City Don't Add Up". Phnom Penh Post, 25 January 2017. https://www.phnompenhpost.com/national/protest-data-city-dont-add (accessed 5 November 2020).

Sokhem, Pech, and Sunada Kengo. 2006. "The Governance of the Tonle Sap Lake, Cambodia: Integration of Local, National and International Levels". *International Journal of Water Resources Development* 22, no. 3: 399–416.

Sokheng, Vong, and Stuart White. 2013. "Marathon PM Speech Focuses on Reforms". *Phnom Penh Post*, 26 September 2013. https://www.phnompenhpost.com/national/marathon-pm-speech-focuses-reforms (accessed 3 November 2020).

Sokhorng, Cheng, and Marlowe Hood. 2018. "Profit from ELCs 'Doesn't Rectify Ecological Impact'". *Phnom Penh Post*, 8 November 2018. https://www.phnompenhpost.com/business/profit-elcs-doesnt-rectify-ecological-impact (accessed 5 November 2020).

Shrestha, Maheshwor. 2019. *The Impact of Minimum Wage Hikes on Employment and Wages in Cambodia.* World Bank Policy Research Working Paper, No. 8839. Washington, DC: World Bank. https://ssrn.com/abstract=3381978

THL (Finnish Institute of Health and Welfare). 2020. "European Social Protection Systems Programme". 17 September 2020. https://thl.fi/web/thlfi-en/research-and-expertwork/projects-and-programmes/eu-social-protection-systems-programme-eu-sps/partner-countries/cambodia (accessed 2 November 2020).

Trading Economics. 2020. "Cambodia Minimum Wages". 2020. https://tradingeconomics.com/cambodia/minimum-wages (accessed 5 November 2020).

Transparency International. 2019. "Country data: Corruption Perceptions Index". 2020. https://www.transparency.org/en/countries/cambodia (accessed 5 November 2020).

Tucker, Will. 2015: "Lifting the Veil: Deforestation Disguised as Agriculture in Cambodia". Forest Trend (blog). 13 August 2015. https://www.forest-trends.org/blog/lifting-the-veil-deforestation-disguised-as-agriculture-in-cambodia/ (accessed 2 November 2020).

United Nations Children's Fund (UNICEF) (website). 2020. "Cambodia: Health and Nutrition". https://www.unicef.org/cambodia/health-and-nutrition (accessed 5 November 2020).

United Nations Development Programme (UNDP). 2019. Human Development Report 2019: *Inequalities in Human Development in the 21st Century, Briefing Note for Countries on the 2019 Human Development Report, Cambodia*. Phnom Penh: UNDP.

United Nations Population Fund (UNFPA). 2014. *Urbanisation and Its Linkage to Socio-Economic and Environmental Issues*. Phnom Penh: UNFPA.

United Nations Statistics Division (UNSD). 2020. "Per Capita GDP at Current Price: Cambodia". 8 April 2019. http://data.un.org/Data.aspx?q=cambodia&d=SNAAMA&f=grID%3A101%3BcurrID%3AUSD%3BpcFlag%3A1%3BcrID%3A116 (accessed 2 November 2020).

United Nations World Food Programme (WFP). 2020. "Cambodia". 2020. https://www.wfp.org/countries/cambodia (accessed 5 November 2020).

World Bank. 2018. "Decline of Global Extreme Poverty Continues but Has Slowed: World Bank". 19 September 2018. https://www.worldbank.org/en/news/press-release/2018/09/19/decline-of-global-extreme-poverty-continues-but-has-slowed-world-bank (accessed 2 November 2020).

———. 2020a. "The World Bank in Cambodia". https://www.worldbank.org/en/country/cambodia/overview (accessed 2 November 2020).

———. 2020b. "Foreign Direct Investment, Net Inflows (% of GDP)—Cambodia". https://data.worldbank.org/indicator/BX.KLT.DINV.WD.GD.ZS?locations=KH (accessed 2 November 2020).

World Health Organization (WHO). 2019. "Government-Sponsored Cash Transfer Scheme to Benefit Poor Women and Children and Improve Access to Health Services". 27 June 2019. https://www.who.int/cambodia/news/detail/27-06-2019-government-sponsored-cash-transfer-scheme-to-benefit-poor-women-and-children-and-improve-access-to-health-services (accessed 2 November 2020).

Yap, Yosef T. 2013. "Addressing Inequality in East Asia through Regional Integration". ERIA RIN Statement, 2013/03, 2 November 2013. http://www.eria.org/uploads/media/research-networks/3rd-RIN-statement.pdf (accessed 2 November 2013).

3

INEQUALITY AND EXCLUSION IN POST-SOEHARTO INDONESIA

Mohammad Zulfan Tadjoeddin[1]

INTRODUCTION

Rising economic inequalities have been a global concern. Global awareness of the problem was bolstered by the United Nations in its 2005 Report on the World Social Situation: *The Inequality Predicament* (UN 2005). Rising inequality across the globe has also brought the issue to the centre of attention of the world's two leading multilateral organizations, the International Monetary Fund (IMF) and the World Bank, which were previously reluctant to point to inequality directly and rather focused solely on poverty, but are now openly discussing economic inequality and its social and economic consequences.

Since the advent of neoliberal globalization in the early 1980s, within-country inequality has been rising in most countries: in the advanced economies as well as in the developing world. In advanced economies of the Western world, economic inequality has been seen as a contributing factor to the 2008 global financial crisis (GFC) (Rajan 2010; Kumhof, Rancière and Winant 2015), but at the same time the responses to GFC also contributed to the surge in inequality (Klein and Winkler 2019). Rising economic inequality is also fuelling the more recent rise of right-wing populism of white supremacists. With a focus on the West, Piketty (2018) argues that the electoral results of parties with right-wing populist platforms are greater in countries that experienced higher increases in inequality and endured more severe impacts of the GFC—these are well represented by the Trump presidency in the United States and Brexit victory in the United Kingdom. In the developing world too, the rise of right-wing populism as in the case of Hindu-nationalists in India and Islamist-transnationalists in Indonesia, and the consequent polarization of society, can partly be explained by rising economic inequalities.

In the advanced economies, as in the United States and the United Kingdom, the surge in economic inequality has been characterized by the rise of income of the higher income groups while the income of the lower middle class stagnated. Concomitantly, higher income groups' share of national income expands, while the share of lower income groups diminishes. This is captured by the trend of increasing per capita gross domestic product (GDP) over time while median income stagnates, which reflects how the lower middle-income groups have been particularly excluded from the growth process.

Another general phenomenon that is parallel to the global rise in inequality is the diverging trend between productivity and wage. This is akin to declining labour share of income while, by contrast, income accruing to capital increases. The IMF's *World Economic Outlook* (2017) finds that in many countries—among advanced economies as well as the developing world—the share of national income paid to workers has been falling since the 1980s and this has been attributed to rapid progress in technology and global integration (IMF 2017). The report shows a strong association between rising inequality and declining labour income shares. Researchers also link this to economic liberalization reforms, such as privatization, financial sector and labour market deregulations. These reforms and technological developments have seen declines in unionization and labour's bargaining power (Ciminelli, Duval and Furceri 2018).

In this increasingly globalized and integrated world, as a part of the developing world and a key member of the emerging economies, Indonesia seems to display such a global trend. Since the turn of the millennium soon after the late 1990s Asian crisis, economic inequality has been on the rise and labour shares of income have fallen (Tadjoeddin and Chowdhury 2018). Echoing the global trend, in recent years, the country has also witnessed the rise in (Islamic) populism (Hadiz 2016; Kimura 2017; Ali-Fauzi 2018).

Indonesia's post-Asian financial crisis economic development, among others, has been marked by significant increases in economic inequality. During 2000–11, the Gini index, the most popular measure of economic inequality, increased by 32 per cent reaching the record high of 0.41, based on household expenditure.[2] During the period, according to the Palma ratio, an increasingly new popular measure of inequality, expenditure inequality increased by 66 per cent (Yusuf 2014).[3] The Gini index, based on both expenditure and earnings, stabilized at that level for few years and then has started to decline, albeit slowly, since 2015. However, wealth inequality is estimated to be among the highest in the world. This chapter will review the latest trend of economic inequality in Indonesia covering other indicators, such as income/earning and wealth, and discusses related policy discourses. Inequality trends are also placed in the context of Indonesia's economic structure, the regional dynamics of its archipelagic geography, and the country's political economy—including the persistent issue of oligarchy.

The rest of the chapter proceeds as follows. The next section reviews the long-term trend and pattern of inequality in Indonesia. The chapter then looks at the structural and spatial dimensions of inequality and the extent of exclusion since the Asian crisis, followed by a section that discusses consequences of rising inequality and related policy initiatives and discourse. The last section offers a concluding remark.

INEQUALITY IN INDONESIA

Before reviewing the recent rise in economic inequality in Indonesia, one needs to revisit the issue during the pre-Asian financial crisis era of high economic growth (1966–98). After the deep political and economic crises during the height of the Cold War in the mid-1960s, Indonesia was led by General Soeharto with his authoritarian and centralistic New Order regime for the next three decades. After a successful economic stabilization programme in the late 1960s, and liberalization programme beginning in the mid-1980s and lasting until the mid-1990s, Indonesia recorded a period of high economic growth with an average annual growth of around 7 per cent. Roughly three decades of high growth resulted in a rapid decline in the poverty rate (by national poverty line) from over 60 per cent in 1966 to around 11 per cent in 1996, in circumstances that can be characterized as shared prosperity, in light of relatively low and stable inequality. During the period, the Gini of household expenditure hovered at around 0.32 to 0.35. The period also saw rapid convergence of regional income across provinces (Hill 2000). The combination of high growth with stable and low inequality placed Indonesia in the league of East Asian miracle (World Bank 1993). The miracle—high growth and low inequality—was achieved through centralized-authoritarian equalization policies centred on agricultural and rural development as well as investments in basic health and education across the archipelago.

The notion of low and stable inequality during the New Order administration, however, has been questioned as it may not capture the true nature of economic inequality. The Gini index of household expenditure is in fact a conservative measure. Although it reasonably captures welfare differences deriving from actual spending on goods and services, it also tends to underestimate the true level of economic inequality for a number of reasons. *First*, in collecting household expenditure data, the super-rich households tend to be missed out due to difficulties in reaching them during the survey. *Second*, expenditure inequality will always be lower than income inequality due to the smoothing effect of expenditure through savings and borrowings during good and bad times as well as the flow of social assistances from communities or the state during bad times.[4] In most cases, expenditure is only a fraction of income and it has to be noted that the shares of income spent on expenditure tend to be larger when the income is smaller. Indeed, as we explore later, the Gini coefficient of wage distribution, computed from national wage data which became available two decades ago, shows higher inequality levels than expenditure.

Third, assets or wealth inequality in Indonesia has been assessed to be very high. In 1996, during the peak of the New Order economy and just before the Asian crisis, the top ten families in Indonesia controlled close to 60 per cent of the country's market capitalization (Claessens, Djankov, and Lang 1999). This figure was higher than the Philippines, Thailand, Hong Kong, Korea, Singapore, Malaysia, Taiwan and Japan. This trend continues. In 2011, the average wealth of the forty richest Indonesians was the highest in Southeast Asia and their combined wealth amounted to 10.2 per cent of the country's GDP (Winters 2013). Credit Suisse (2016) reports that Indonesia is the fourth most unequal nation in the world, with 49.3 per cent of the nation's wealth controlled by the top 1 per cent of the population. A year later, Oxfam (2017) reported that Indonesia's economic inequality had risen faster than any other country in Southeast Asia, and the country's four richest men had more wealth than the poorest 100 million of their fellow citizens. Furthermore, the Gini index of land holdings based on the agricultural census is around 0.60 (Winoto 2009; Karimi 2014).

Overall Inequality Trend and Political Economic Context

The Asian crisis brought Indonesia's long-term inequality to a historic lowest level in 1999 according to the expenditure Gini index (Figure 3.1). Since then, however, the levels of inequality significantly increased, reaching an historic peak in 2011 at 0.41, stabilized around the figure for a couple of years, then started to decline, albeit slowly, from 2015 onwards. The figure also shows that wage (earnings) inequality has been consistently higher than expenditure inequality.[5] The decline in inequality since 2015 is also shown by the wage Gini index.

The long-term household expenditure Gini index (since 1976) is taken from official publication of the Central Statistical Agency (BPS, or Statistics Indonesia) based on the National Socioeconomic Survey (*Susenas*, or *Survei Sosial Ekonomi Nasional*). The wage/earning Gini index is calculated from the National Labour Force Survey (*Sakernas*, or *Survei Angkatan Kerja Nasional*). Both surveys are administered by the BPS. The wage/earning Gini index is only available since 2001 because of the consistent coverage of earnings data across employment status of self-employed, regular employment and casual employment.

How might we explain the sharp rise of inequality during the first decade of the new millennium? As in the case of elusive quest for growth à la Easterly (2001), rising inequality is a by-product of economic progress and it is difficult to isolate a single factor that is solely responsible for the surge in inequality. However, one may identify several developments that transpired parallel to the rise in inequality.

The first one is the trend of dealignment between productivity and wage, referring to the continued increase in labour productivity measured as real GDP per worker alongside stagnation in real wages in the first decade of the new millennium, as identified by Tadjoeddin (2016). This trend is akin to the declining share of labour income, which as a consequence implies an increase in income accrued to capital. Labour share of income and the

FIGURE 3.1
Long-Term Gini Index, 1976–2019 (Income and Expenditure)

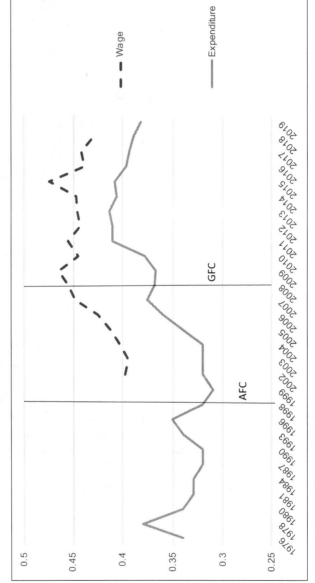

Source: Author's calculation from *Sakernas* (wage Gini) and BPS (expenditure Gini).

wage-labour productivity ratio relate to inequality on similar grounds, corroborated by evidence of negative correlation between labour share of income and Gini index (Figure 3.2). As labour constitutes the majority of population, while only a small minority proportion of the population are the owners of capital, it is understandable that the overall inequality should be on the rise. IMF (2017) confirms such a trend and a relationship at the global level.

The second trend refers to the process of deindustrialization the country has experienced since the beginning of the millennium (Tadjoeddin and Chowdhury 2018). As manufacturing activities are not spread evenly across Indonesian regions and concentrated in Java, one needs to see a disaggregated relationship (across island groups) between manufacturing share and inequality as depicted in Figure 3.3. Java tells a different story than the rest of Indonesia's islands. Across Javanese provinces, the higher share of the manufacturing sector in regional gross domestic product (RGDP) correlates with a lower Gini index. This could possibly mean that reindustrialization may result in declining inequality in Java and this can potentially have a large effect on the overall inequality in the country as around 60 per cent of Indonesia's population live on the island.

The third trend to consider is the low and declining tax to GDP ratio. This is largely due to persistently low tax compliance and pervasive tax evasion among high earners.[6] Furthermore, the situation is made worse by loopholes and inadequacies in tax administration. These point to the failure of tax policy as an instrument of income distribution. While in the early 1990s, Indonesian tax to GDP ratio was the highest in Southeast Asia, recently, in 2017, the country's tax ratio declined to just under 10 per cent, the second lowest in Southeast Asia (Myanmar has the lowest figure).[7] According to the IMF, Indonesia tax ratio is way below the 15 per cent threshold needed to stimulate growth and the figure is much lower than most other middle-income countries.[8] Therefore, addressing the issues of low tax to GDP ratio and tax compliance have been assessed as important elements of key reforms needed to achieve higher growth as well as a means for redistribution.

The fourth trend is the resource boom, referring to the rise of commodity prices globally during the first decade of the millennium. Figure 3.4 shows parallel move of commodity prices and Gini index during the resource boom period. The boom was caused by exceptionally strong resource-intensive growth in China. Between 2003 and 2011, the share of commodities in

FIGURE 3.2
Wage-Productivity Ratio and Gini Index (33 Provinces, 2001–11)

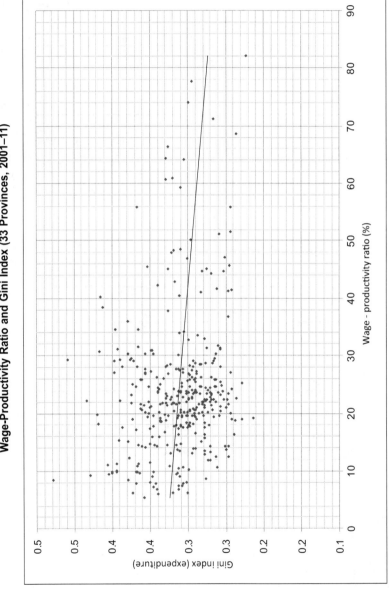

Source: Tadjoeddin and Chowdhury (2018), p. 94.

Inequality and Exclusion in Post-Soeharto Indonesia 59

FIGURE 3.3
Provincial Gini Index and Manufacturing Share (%) of RGDP, 2000–15
By Island Grouping (in brackets, correlation coefficients

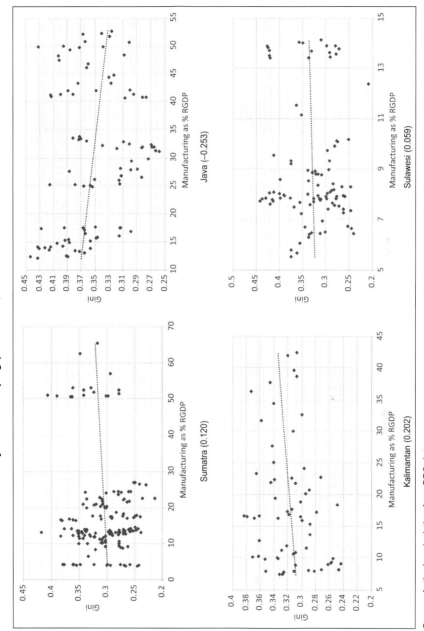

Source: Author's calculation from BPS data.

FIGURE 3.4
Resource Boom: Expenditure Gini Index (Indonesia) and Global Commodity Prices (2010 = 100), 1993–2018

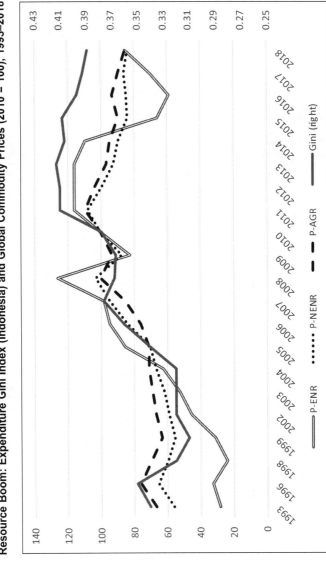

Note: P-ENR = Price of energy commodity, P-NENR = Price of non-energy commodity, P-AGR = Price of agriculture commodity.
Source: World Development Indicators (commodity prices) and BPS (Gini).

total exports rose from 52 per cent to 68 per cent, while the real value of Indonesian goods exports more than doubled during the period (Garnaut 2015). The natural resource boom period has been assessed to be a step backward in the country's industrialization trajectory, with much of the economy driven by consumption-led expansion fuelled by growth in the extractive industries (Wihardja 2016). The resource boom seems to be disproportionately benefiting those at the top of income distribution, as key players in the sector need to be politically connected to have access to the resources. Between-provincial (spatial) inequality does not seem to be affected by the resource boom, as will be explained later, while the overall inequality increases.

The role of the mining (commodity) boom in the overall rise of inequality in Indonesia, however, should not be over-emphasized. While the argument is made based on the fact that the increasing trend of the Gini index during 2001–11 coincided with the rise in commodity prices, the Gini index has not been significantly declining following the sharp drop in commodity prices since 2011. The mining boom was strongly attributed to Kalimantan's economy as the rise in commodity prices corresponds with the increased share of mining in the Island. However, Kalimantan accounts for only 8 per cent the national economy.[9] More importantly, inequality levels and changes over time have been lower in Kalimantan, compared to the national average.

The fifth factor worth considering is the untamed/wild oligarchs (rise of billionaires) in post-crisis Indonesia.[10] As argued by Winters (2011, 2013), the transition experienced by Indonesia in 1998 was not only about the country's important shift from (Soeharto's) dictatorship to electoral democracy as widely known, it was also about the less known transition from "tamed" to "untamed"/wild oligarchic system. This shift coincided with the pattern of stable inequality during most of Soeharto's period to rising inequality in the first decade of post-crisis Indonesia. While Indonesia during the periods of Dutch colonial and Sukarno's rules had elites but not oligarchs, it was during the sultanistic rule of Soeharto that Indonesia's modern oligarchs first arose, originating from a close business alliance between selected Chinese ethnic minorities and the powerful military elites centred on Soeharto. However, Soeharto himself controlled and tamed the oligarchs in making sure that they were in support of New Order development agenda. The oligarchs, however, did not go down with the fall of Soeharto in 1998, but, in fact, survived, flourished and have played key roles in the subsequent democratic processes, for the purpose of defending or growing their wealth. As argued by Robison and Hadiz (2004) and Hadiz and Robison (2013), oligarchs' predatory interests have captured and appropriated Indonesia's new democratic institutions. While many of them were nurtured and incubated during the autocratic New Order, they have reconstituted and reinvented themselves in the new setting of Indonesia's democracy.

Covering the first decade after the democratic transition, Winters (2011) summarizes how wealth in Indonesia was vastly more concentrated in the hands of a few oligarchs than it was before.

> In 2004 Indonesia had about 34,000 people with at least US$1 million in non-home financial assets, 19,000 of whom were Indonesians residing semi-permanently in Singapore. Their ranks grew to 39,000 by 2007, and 43,000 in 2010. Their average wealth in 2010 was US$4.1 million and their combined net worth was about US$177 billion (US$93 billion of which was held offshore in Singapore). Although Indonesia's richest 43,000 citizens represent less than one hundredth of 1 per cent of the population, their total wealth is equal to 25 per cent of the country's GDP (Winters 2011).

Their enduring power and influence in Indonesia's political economy is reflected in exceedingly high wealth inequality which, compounded by capital flight and tax evasion, results in the country's low tax revenue.

SPATIAL AND STRUCTURAL DIMENSIONS OF INEQUALITY

Spatial Dimension of Inequality: New Order

Despite the uneven resource endowment across provinces affecting regional productive capacity, a clear pattern of income convergence, using per capita RGDP measure, across provinces during 1976–96 is observable (Tadjoeddin 2014). In general, poorer provinces grew faster than richer ones over the course of two decades. In this regard, Hill (2000, p. 235) notes, "there is no case of a high-income province growing much faster than the national average, or conversely of a poor province falling sharply behind." A similar pattern during the period is also observable in terms of poverty reductions across provinces, implying that the poverty levels in poorer provinces fell at a much faster rate than in their richer counterparts (Tadjoeddin 2014).

Spatial Dimension of Inequality: Post-Asian Crisis

There was a concern for possible widening of regional disparity in the early periods of decentralization, because of the nature of fiscal decentralization (Suharyo 2002). But the regional income convergence, using per capita RGDP measure, continued after the late 1990s' democratization and decentralization, albeit at a much slower speed, termed as weak convergence (Vidyattama 2013; Hill and Vidyattama 2014).

The above observation is confirmed by the Theil T measure of expenditure inequality, where the overall Theil measure can be decomposed into two components: within-group and between-group inequality. Figure 3.5 shows the Theil measures of expenditure inequality since the turn of the millennium (2000–18). The overall trend according to the Theil T measure of expenditure inequality largely confirms the trend displayed by the Gini index. Our concern here is the decomposition, where there has been no increasing trend of between-province (spatial) inequality shown in the graph. In fact, the between-province Theil index has been declining, albeit slowly, since 2002. If between- and within-province inequalities are transformed into shares of between- and within-province inequalities, one will observe a trend of declining contribution of between-province inequality to the overall inequality. To illustrate, the between-province inequality accounts for about 0.03 out of 0.18 of the Theil index in 2000, compared to much reduced proportion of 0.02 per 0.28 in 2018. This confirms the previous observation on the long-term trend of interregional convergence in Indonesia.

Despite the long-term trend of interregional economic convergence across the large and diverse country, concerns with spatial/regional economic disparity persist, either in the forms of Java and non-Java dichotomy or western and eastern Indonesia differentiation.[11] Such a concern seems to be more influenced by general public perception rather than careful treatment of data, as within-region inequality accounted for the larger proportion of overall inequality. Of course, development policies and projects do not necessarily distinguish these between-region and within-region dynamics. Indeed, both dimensions are intertwined. The strong emphasis of the current administration on infrastructure development initiatives in the remote regions should be seen as political signals of the government's commitments to tackle rising inequality, to spread the development activities across the country and to reduce disparities through increased connectivity.

FIGURE 3.5
Theil T Index of Household Expenditure (Overall, Between and Within Provinces), 2000–18

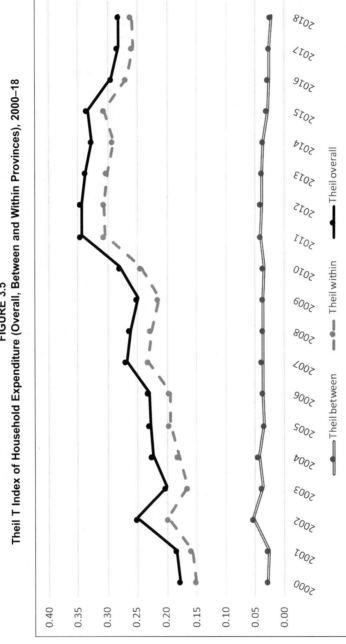

Note: 33 provinces.
Source: Author's calculations from *Susenas*.

Sectoral Inequality

Using the similar Theil T measure of expenditure inequality across nine economic sectors, Figure 3.6 demonstrates the dominant role of within-sector inequality, rather than between-sector. If between- and within-sector inequalities are transformed into the shares of between- and within-sector inequalities, one will certainly observe a trend of declining contribution of between-sector inequality to the overall inequality. The between-sector inequality seems to be largely contributed by occupational inequalities, such as formal versus informal employment, within each sector.

Various Dimensions of Exclusion

Examining earnings data of the workforce from the National Labour Force Survey (*Sakernas*), we look at the extent of exclusion, reflected in wage divergence, in post-crisis Indonesia according to the following dimensions: income groups (higher-lower strata), education (tertiary-secondary-primary), areas of residence (urban-rural), formality of employment (formal-informal), gender (male-female) and persons with disability. To some extent, this follows ESCAP's (2019) study on empowerment and inclusion in Asia and the Pacific that identifies four sources of disadvantage: being located in rural area, having lower education attainment, being female and having (ethnic) minority status. Having more than one attribute of disadvantage will form further-behind groups. Identifying the dimensions of exclusion is important in light of the 2030 Agenda for Sustainable Development that calls to leave no one behind, placing equality at the centre of national policymaking.

First, Figure 3.7 depicts median earnings by income groups, with the top decile as the reference group. Median point is deliberately chosen to see the movement of the person in the middle of the group rather than the average earnings of the group. Palma's grouping of income strata is followed: top 10 per cent, middle 50 per cent (deciles 4 to 9) and bottom 40 per cent. We further extract the lowest decile belonging to the bottom 20 per cent. This division will also allow us to observe the movement of income gaps between top 60 per cent and bottom 40 per cent. The data show a trend of diverging gaps of lower income groups (lower 20 per cent and lower 40 per cent) relative to the higher income group of top 10 per cent in post-crisis period. The middle 50 per cent

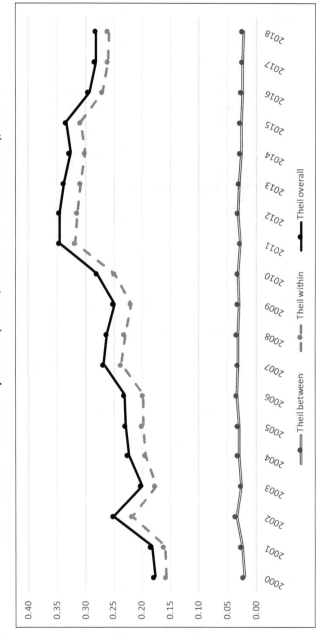

FIGURE 3.6
Theil T Index of Household Expenditure (Overall, Between and Within Sectors), 2000–18

Note: 9 sectors.
Source: Author's calculations from Susenas.

Inequality and Exclusion in Post-Soeharto Indonesia 67

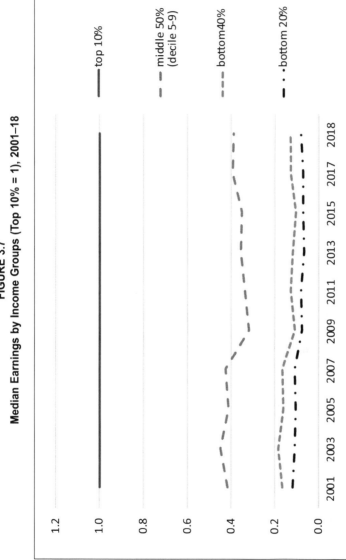

FIGURE 3.7
Median Earnings by Income Groups (Top 10% = 1), 2001–18

Source: Author's calculations from Sakernas.

group (deciles 5 to 9), however, is showing a catching up trend (relative to top 10 per cent group) since 2009 indicating middle-class empowerment. These trends also indicate a diverging trend of median income between the top 60 per cent income strata and the bottom 40 per cent. Such a diverging trend is consistent with ESCAP's (2019) finding in most of countries of Asia and the Pacific.

Second, median earnings by educational groups are depicted in Figure 3.8, with tertiary education level as the reference group. The data indicate weak trends of inclusion since 2009 for workers with primary (or less) and secondary education qualifications. This, however, is an encouraging development. With continual progress in the education sector, the share of workers with primary education qualification is expected to continuously decline, while workers with secondary education qualification form the majority of the workforce. The challenge is, therefore, how to improve their productivity that will eventually result in higher income level.[12] The data also confirm that the tertiary education premium is clear; in 2018, workers with primary and secondary education qualification earn only 37 per cent and 57 per cent of their counterparts equipped with tertiary education credentials. However, it is worth to point out that the tertiary education wage premium declines over the period 2009–18.

Third, Figure 3.9 shows persistent urban-rural divides, in terms of the median earnings of workers residing in rural areas relative to their counterparts living in urban settings. In 2018, median earnings of rural employment were only 72 per cent of their urban counterparts. It is important to note that urbanization, coupled with the rise of metropolitan cities, has been a dominant characteristic of the country's development, and this trend will assuredly continue (Tadjoeddin and Mercer-Blackman 2018). Growth rates of the urban population were consistently higher than the overall rate of population growth: 4.40 per cent versus 1.35 per cent, and 3.33 per cent versus 1.50 per cent for the periods 1990–2000 and 2000–10, respectively (Firman 2016). Hence, even with constant wage gaps, overall inequality may decline due to the increasing share of urban wage earners.

Fourth, based on formal and informal types of employment, the data in post-crisis Indonesia also do not exhibit a trend of inclusion. According to the *Sakernas*, formal employment consists of employer assisted with permanent employees and regular employees, while other employment

FIGURE 3.8
Median Earnings by Education
(Primary, Secondary, Tertiary; Tertiary = 1), 2001–18

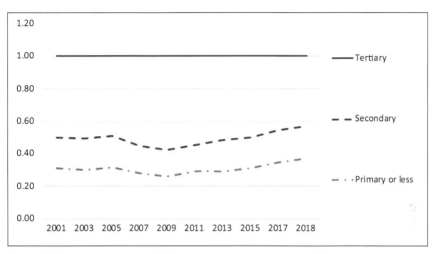

Source: Author's calculations from *Sakernas*.

FIGURE 3.9
Median Earnings by Area (Urban-Rural; Urban = 1), 2001–18

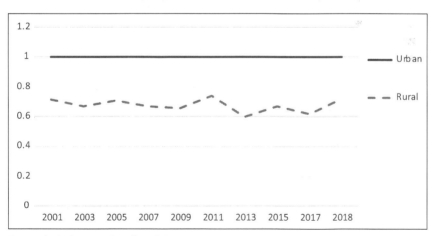

Source: Author's calculations from *Sakernas*.

statuses are classified as informal employment. Since 2001, earnings data have been made constantly available in the *Sakernas* for the following employment statuses: regular employees, casual employees and self-employed. Therefore, in the categories covered by earnings data, the formal employment refers to the regular employees, while informal employment refers to casual employees and self-employed.

In 2018, median earnings of casual employees were less than 60 per cent of their counterparts categorized as regular employees. Further categories of disadvantage can be layered to see how far the "furthest-behind" group is located relative to the reference group. Figure 3.10 shows that, in 2018, median earnings of casual employees who are female with primary (or less) education qualification were less than 30 per cent of median earnings in the formal sector (regular employment) and this furthest-behind group has experienced a trend of exclusion in recent years, at least since 2014. While the share of formal employment (the good quality/decent jobs) was largely stagnant during the first decade of the new millennium, coinciding with the period of sharp rise in economic inequality, it has increased during the second decade of the millennium.

Fifth, based on gender differentiation, there has been no meaningful trend of convergence of male and female median earnings since the turn of the millennium (Figure 3.11). In 2017, female median earnings were only 62 per cent of their male counterparts, the figure declined from 70 per cent in 2015. The furthest-behind group can be identified by adding more categories. In 2017, female employees with primary (or less) education qualification and residing in rural area have only recorded median earnings less than one-third (33 per cent) of median male earnings. The median earnings of the furthest-behind group have relatively declined since 2011, indicating a trend of exclusion.

Finally, we consider people with disabilities, where the paucity of data is a major issue. The questions on disabilities have been included in the labour force survey (*Sakernas*) only since 2016. On that year, Indonesia passed Law No. 8 /2016 as the follow up of the ratification of the UN Convention on the Rights of People with Disabilities in 2011. Through the law, the Indonesian government commits to the eradication of discrimination against people with disabilities and to actively work to support and provide services to them. Following the UN approach, respondents aged 15 and over are asked whether they experience functioning difficulties in seeing, hearing, walking/climbing steps, moving fingers and speaking/communicating.

Inequality and Exclusion in Post-Soeharto Indonesia 71

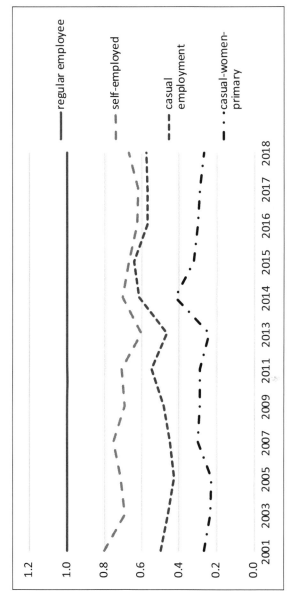

FIGURE 3.10
Median Earnings by Type of Employment (Regular Employee = 1), 2001–18

Source: Author's calculations from Sakernas.

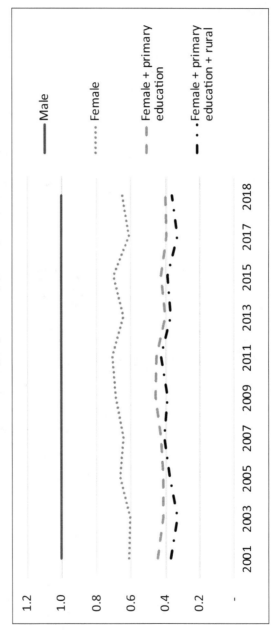

FIGURE 3.11
Median Earnings by Gender (Male = 1), 2001–18

Source: Author's calculations from Sakernas.

Allowed responses are: no difficulty, some (low to medium) difficulty or severe difficulty.

Based on the *Sakernas*, in 2018, it is estimated that 10.6 per cent of the population aged 15 and over have some or severe disability. Median earnings of people with some disability were less than 70 per cent of those with no disability, while the figure for people with severe disability is less than 50 per cent. Data generated from the short time period (2016–18) do not show a trend of inclusion/convergence (Figure 3.12).

In summary, based on the trend of median earnings since the turn of the millennium, there has been no meaningful progress in terms of inclusions of the identified disadvantaged groups. The observation also allows for narrowing down the observation into the furthest-behind groups based on layers of disadvantaged categories. While the above data reflect indicators of outcome (earnings) alongside those dimensions (income groups, educational attainment, gender, location and status of formality), a more fundamental factor to look at is inequality of opportunities. This implies that "all should enjoy equal access to opportunity—that one's chances to succeed in life should not be determined by circumstances beyond an individual's control" (UN 2020, p. 34).

The analysis on exclusion will not be complete without touching the issue of interethnic inequality. However, studies on ethnic inequalities in Indonesia are not widely available. This is probably due to the following two reasons: (i) data on socio-economic variables across ethnic groups in such a large and diverse country are not widely available publicly, and/or (ii) ethnicity-based systematic exclusion is not an issue in the country. Two studies (Suryadarma et al. 2006; Muller 2016) that literally contain the phrase of "ethnic inequalities" in their titles do not identify ethnicity-based exclusion in Indonesia. Suryadarma et al. (2006) finds systematic inequality between urban and rural areas, but not between ethnic groups. However, the economically dominant role of the ethnic Chinese minority in Indonesia has been a source of contentions. The country saw significant anti-Chinese riots in Jakarta, Surakarta and few other cities preceding the fall of Soeharto in 1998 (Tadjoeddin 2014). Anti-Chinese sentiment has been more openly aired in the recent rise of identity politics/religious populism in the country.[13] The case of Indonesian Chinese is arguably a case of market dominant minority, to borrow Chua's (2002) term, alongside Indians in East Africa, Chinese in the Philippines and Whites in Southern Africa. These conditions, if severe and persistent, present the

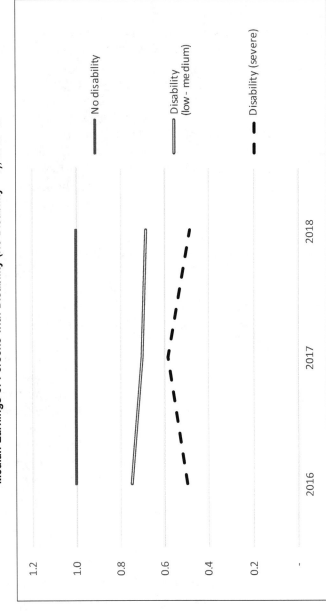

FIGURE 3.12
Median Earnings of Persons with Disability (No Disability = 1), 2016–18

Source: Author's calculations from *Sakernas*.

possibility of the economically dominant minority coming under increased scrutiny and pressure, even discrimination and stigmatization, especially in the wake of rising religious populism.

INEQUALITY: CONSEQUENCES AND RECENT POLICY DISCOURSE

Detrimental consequences of excessive economic inequality at the global level have been well documented as shown by studies produced by world prominent scholars as well as by world leading organizations such as the United Nations, World Bank and the IMF. In Indonesia, too, hard evidence on the negative consequences of higher inequality has been increasingly available. *First*, Yumna et al. (2015) finds that higher inequality will eventually lower economic growth as the study reveals an inverted-U relationship between inequality and economic growth based on across-districts data during 2000–12. *Second*, higher inequality reduces the effect of growth in reducing poverty or in other words inequality reduces the growth-poverty elasticity as argued by Suryadarma et al. (2005) and Yusuf and Warr (2018). *Third*, higher inequality also correlates with higher incidence of violent social conflict as well as violent crime (Tadjoeddin et al. 2020).

Indonesia's development policy has made bold pronouncements on economic inequality; the issue gains salience again as the current Joko Widodo's administration unfolds its second five-year agenda after retaining the presidency in 2019. Rising inequality was identified as one of key factors that weaken the country's economic fundamentals. Therefore, a vision to "develop Indonesia from the periphery" (*membangun Indonesia dari pinggiran*) was adopted as one of the nine development priorities of Joko Widodo's presidency termed as *nawacita* (nine goals). For the first time in history, the administration's medium-term national development plan (RPJMN, or *Rencana Pembangunan Jangka Menengah Nasional* 2014–19) penned a specified target on inequality reduction. The Gini index of household expenditure was set to reach 0.36 by 2019 from the baseline figure in 2014 of 0.41. In the September 2019 round of *Susenas*, which coincided with the end of Joko Widodo's first term in office, expenditure Gini has declined to 0.38. While the Gini index has continuously declined during the period, it is missing the target by 0.02.

The previous medium-term national development plan (RPJMN 2019–14) of the second term of Susilo Bambang Yudhoyono (SBY)'s presidency did not put an emphasis on inequality reduction despite the document being prepared during a period of sharply rising inequality. The focus was still largely confined to social assistance programmes targeted more towards poverty reduction, rather than dealing with rising inequality.

The focus on inequality reduction in the RPJMN (2014–19) centred on expanded amounts of social assistance with more specific targeting and more systematically designed programmes, as well as other development interventions focusing on the bottom 40 per cent of the income strata, covering the informal sector, small and micro enterprises as well as rural and agricultural sectors. The better targeted and expanded social assistance programmes include conditional/unconditional cash transfers, health insurance and educational assistance for the poor, scholarships, subsidized rice and more.[14]

Other development initiatives viewed to have an effect on reducing inequality include the following: First, aggressive regional infrastructure development spread across the country in the form of roads, airports, seaports, agricultural dams and border check points, which seek to develop Indonesia from the periphery. The infrastructure development has multiple aims covering economic growth, interregional connectivity, logistical efficiency as well as strengthening national unity and at the same time, countering the narrative of Java-centric development. The state budget of the current government in 2015 was marked by a significant jump in infrastructure spending. The IDR256 trillion earmarked for infrastructure from the 2015 national budget accounted for a 63 per cent increase from annual infrastructure spending of the final year of SBY's administration. Since then, infrastructure spending has continued to increase. In 2016 budget, the sector's allocation rose by IDR111 trillion, an increase of 41 per cent. During the course of Joko Widodo's five-year term, infrastructure has accounted for an average 17 per cent of total central government spending.[15]

Second, village funds, introduced in 2015, have allocated block grants to more than 80,000 villages (*desa/kelurahan*), the lowest administrative units in Indonesia. This scheme is intended to tackle rural poverty and spread development funds across the country. Each village is given autonomy to determine the use of this funding, which is then formally proposed in an expenditure plan. During 2015–19, a total of IDR257 trillion village funds was disbursed and the funds are projected to increase to IDR400 trillion for next five years till 2024. The village funds adopt the following formula: 77 per cent are allocated evenly to all villages, 20 per cent are allocated proportionally based on number of population, poverty rate and land area, while the remaining 3 per cent are set as additional funds for disadvantaged villages. Between 2015 and 2018, the funding scheme succeeded in the development of 191,600 kilometres of village roads, 58,000 irrigation units, 8,900 village markets and up to 24,000 *posyandu* (*pos pelayanan terpadu*, a monthly clinic for children and pregnant women, providing vaccinations and nutritional supplements).[16] The programme has been viewed by the International Funds for Agricultural Development to be a catalyst for rural transformation through the agriculture sector.[17]

A third major policy concerns land redistribution or land reform, which is believed to be key in maintaining a more equal distribution of income as in the cases of Japan, South Korea and Taiwan. The Indonesian government has planned to provide ownership certificates and long-term leases over land and forests totalling more than 21 million hectares to local communities living within or in surrounding forest areas (Irwan and Nugroho 2018).

In addition, the fourth recent initiative that should have an effect on reducing inequality is the government's strengthening of anti-corruption efforts and public service efficiency through approaches that can be described as non-technocratic. These efforts address the problem of political interests influencing the distribution of budgeted public expenditures, which can have bearing on inequality. Corruption unjustly reallocates funds from the many to benefit the few, skewing income distribution towards the rich, that is clearly an inequality-increasing process. More efficient public services (bureaucratic reform) will maximize the widespread welfare effect of public spending and the overall technocratic approach to tackle rising inequality.

The Problem of Oligarchy

Oligarchic power and its consequences prevail in the contemporary context, although this is, as discussed earlier, a systemic issue with long historical roots. In the post-Soeharto era, the country has made no significant progress in the dismantling of oligarchies, despite repeated presidential commitments to foster people-centred economies, mitigate overconcentration of economic power and combat elite corruption. In fact, in the two decades of democratic era, the relationship between democracy and oligarchy has grown stronger, leading Indonesia to be termed an oligarchic democracy, a variant of illiberal democracy (Winters 2013; Hadiz 2019). As explained earlier, the first generation of modern oligarchs was nurtured during Soeharto's era but at the same time was tamed by him. The fall of Soeharto had untamed the oligarchs, adjusting themselves with the new—and less constrained—democratic arrangements.

As electoral contestations have become increasingly more expensive, the oligarchs have consistently taken more prominent roles during the two-decade-old Indonesian current democracy, primarily since the introduction of direct elections for the president in 2004 and subnational heads in 2005. They control most of political parties and finance the campaign of executive elections at national as well as subnational levels. Not only that, they also control the media, which is important in influencing public discourse in their favour (Tapsell 2017). These have created the so-called dual functions of entrepreneurs or business people in economic as well as political realms, making them the oligarchs. This mirrors the dual functions of the military in the country's security and political affairs (*dwi-fungsi ABRI*) notoriously implemented during the Soeharto's era.

The entrenched power of the oligarchy only gets deeper over time. Hadiz (2017) argued that the oligarchic power is even more entrenched than the growing Islamist populism in the country which only serves as the battle ground of different oligarchic interests. While the defeat of incumbent Basuki Tjahaja Purnama (Ahok) in Jakarta's divisive gubernatorial elections of 2017 and his subsequent imprisonment due to the blasphemy charge marked the peak of Islamic populism in Indonesia, it simply provided a theatre for competing oligarchic interests to exercise power. While Ahok was supported by President Joko Widodo and major ruling parties such as PDI-P and Golkar, Ahok's contender (Anis Baswedan) was backed by Prabowo, Jusuf Kalla, Hary Tanoesoedibjo and Aburizal Bakri, all of whom are oligarchs. With his double minority status for being Chinese and Christian, Ahok was only an intermediate target, the main objective was to topple Joko Widodo's presidency. The oligarchs' alliance with the Islamists is largely pragmatic, rather than ideological (Mietzner 2020). For example, Tanoesoedibjo shifted his alliance to Joko Widodo in the rematch against Prabowo in the 2019 presidential election and, later on, his daughter was appointed to Joko Widodo's cabinet. Even the presidential election has been seen as the main theatre for the battle between competing oligarchic interests (Hadiz 2019; Morse 2019).

One chief consequence of the entrenched oligarchic influence in the Indonesian democracy is the fact that it weakens the country's effort in combating corruption. The systematic weakening of the Indonesia's Corruption Eradication Commission (KPK) through the legislative process in parliament is in fact engineered by political parties that are largely controlled by the oligarchs (*Jakarta Post*, 5 November 2019). Suggestions have been made on how to weaken the oligarchic influence in the Indonesian democracy, one of them is by providing state funding for political parties and electoral campaigns (Mietzner 2007; Reuter 2015). The entrenched oligarchy in Indonesian democracy manifests the trend of oligarchic democracy in many countries, including the United States as highlighted by Winters (2019). Therefore, efforts to substantially dismantle the oligarchic power will have significant implication on efforts to combat (political) corruption; both are closely interlinked and could be considered as non-technocratic approaches to dealing with rising inequality.

CONCLUDING REMARKS

This chapter has reviewed the long-term trend of economic inequality in Indonesia and looked more closely at inequality and exclusion since the country embarked on democratization around two decades ago. In the realm of economic inequality, it has to be noted that there are at least three forms of inequality: consumption, income and wealth. While consumption tends to produce the most conservative figure of economic inequality, inequalities based on income and wealth will produce higher figures respectively. The long-term economic inequality data in Indonesia are based on household expenditure inequality and the Gini index is the most widely used measure.

Economic inequality has been argued to be largely stable and relatively low during the high growth New Order economy during the 1970s to the 1990s. However, inequality sharply increased during the first decade of the millennium reaching a record high in 2011 at 0.41 according to expenditure Gini index. The period of sharply rising inequality corresponded with Indonesia's deindustrialization trend, the divergence between productivity and wage as well as rising commodity prices. Inequality stayed around the figure for couple years, then has started to decline since 2015, where several policy initiatives seem to have contributed to the decline. Despite the most recent trend of slow decline in expenditure inequality, wealth or asset inequality seems to remain high and increasing as shown by wealth shares accrued to the richest people, although this is hampered by data paucity. This points to the fact of persisting oligarchy in the country. Moreover, the data has also consistently pointed to the salience of within-region inequality.

Earnings data from the labour force survey help identify six dimensions of exclusion, or groups relatively excluded from the gains of economic growth: being in the lower income group, residing in rural area, working in informal sector, workers with less educational attainment, women and persons with disability. In general, there has been no meaningful trend of inclusion of the identified groups relative to the reference groups. Indonesia has placed more serious attention to tackle rising inequality, especially conscious of interregional inequality, and has focused on infrastructure and social assistance, but policymakers need to target those potentially excluded groups more seriously and effectively. Extremely high wealth concentration and the entrenched power of Indonesia's oligarchs, alongside low tax revenue which constrains social spending, pose fundamental issues that the country must also address at the systemic level.

Notes

1. I am grateful to the editors, Lee Hwok Aun and Christopher Choong, as well as Anis Chowdhury for helpful comments and suggestions. Thanks to Ridho Al Izzati for calculating the Theil T index. However, I am alone responsible for any remaining shortcomings.
2. A Gini coefficient of 0.4 is regarded as the warning threshold for dangerous levels of inequality, see for example, Chen (2013), Rapoza (2013) and Tobin (2011). The Gini coefficient ranges from 0 representing complete equality (when everyone has the same level of income) to 1 for complete inequality (when one person holds all income).
3. The Palma index is the ratio of the income share of the richest 10 per cent population to the income share of the poorest 40 per cent population (Palma 2011). The Palma index has been assessed to be more relevant for policy-making as it concerns with the particular income segments where inequality is actually located (Cobham, Schlogl, and Sumner 2015).
4. Tadjoeddin (2016) estimates that the overall wage-earning Gini is higher than that of expenditure, on average by 22 per cent, in post-Soeharto Indonesia.

5. In this case, wage (earnings) is the best proxy for income that also covers other sources such as transfer, rent and interest.
6. Various studies have substantiated this argument, among others, see Alstadsæter, Johannesen, and Zucman (2019), and Alventosa and Olcina (2020).
7. World Development Indicators (WDI) database.
8. *Jakarta Post*, 11 October 2018, https://www.thejakartapost.com/academia/2018/10/11/indonesias-low-tax-to-gdp-ratio.html
9. The mining sector plays an important role in the economy of Kalimantan, especially in East Kalimantan, South Kalimantan and Central Kalimantan with mining share in provincial RGDP 41 per cent, 22 per cent and 11 per cent respectively. Across the Indonesian provinces, mining contribution to provincial RGDP is the highest in East Kalimantan.
10. Hadiz and Robison (2013, p. 37) defines oligarchy "as a system of power relations that enables the concentration of wealth and authority and its collective defence."
11. See, for example, *Jakarta Post*, "Jokowi's Java-Centric Development Widening Wealth Gap: INDEF", 21 October 2016; *Antaranews*, "Development Paradigm Changed from Java-Centric to Indonesia-Centric: President", 16 August 2016.
12. Tadjoeddin and Chowdhury (2018) finds that productivity is the most important determinant of workers' earnings in Indonesia's manufacturing sector.
13. See, for example, Juoro (2017); Allard and Da Costa (2017).
14. In 2017, President Joko Widodo's administration allocated more than IDR67 trillion (US$4.75 billion) for social assistance through various programmes. In 2018, the government poured in an additional of IDR11 trillion to the social assistance programs (see *Jakarta Post*, "Socio-Economic Gap Has Closed under Jokowi: INFID", 12 February 2019).
15. "Ahead of the second debate, get the lowdown on infrastructure under Jokowi", *Indonesia at Melbourne* (2019).
16. *Kompas*, "Total Dana Desa 2019–2024 Rp400 Triliun", 2 February 2019.
17. *Antara News*, "IFAD Apresiasi Keberhasilan Program Dana Desa", 14 February 2019.

References

Ali-Fauzi, I. 2018. "Nationalism and Islamic Populism in Indonesia". Heinrich-Boll Stiftung Southeast Asia, 2018. https://th.boell.org/en/2018/05/16/nationalism-and-islamic-populism-indonesia (accessed 1 July 2019).

Allard, Tom, and Agustinus Beo Da Costa. 2017. "Exclusive—Indonesian Islamist Leader Says Ethnic Chinese Wealth Is Next Target". *Reuters*, 13 May 2017. https://www.reuters.com/article/uk-indonesia-politics-cleric-exclusive/

exclusive-indonesian-islamist-leader-says-ethnic-chinese-wealth-is-next-target-idUSKBN18817N (accessed 1 July 2019).

Alstadsæter, A., N. Johannesen, and G. Zucman. 2019. "Tax Evasion and Inequality". *American Economic Review* 109, no. 6: 2073–103.

Alventosa, A., and G. Olcina. 2020. "Tax Compliance and Wealth Inequality". *Applied Economics Letters* 27, no. 11: 899–903.

Antara News, 2016. "Development Paradigm Changed from Java-Centric to Indonesia-Centric: President". 16 August 2016. https://en.antaranews.com/news/106262/development-paradigm-changed-from-java-centric-to-indonesia-centric-president (accessed 1 July 2019).

———. 2019. "IFAD Apresiasi Keberhasilan Program Dana Desa". 14 February 2019. https://www.antaranews.com/berita/798365/ifad-apresiasi-keberhasilan-program-dana-desa (accessed 1 July 2019).

Chen, Y. 2013. "China's 'Above Warning Level' Income Gap Shows Inequality". *Global Times*, 19 January 2013. http://www.globaltimes.cn/content/756786.shtml (accessed 1 July 2019).

Chua, A. 2002. *World on Fire: How Exporting Free Market Democracy Breeds Ethnic Hatred and Global Instability*. New York: Doubleday.

Ciminelli, Gabriele, Romain Duval, and Davide Furceri. 2018. "Employment Protection Deregulation and Labor Shares in Advanced Economies". *IMF Working Paper* 18/186.

Claessens, S., S. Djankov, and L.H.P. Lang. 1999. "Who Controls East Asian Corporations?", *Policy Research Working Paper* No. 2054. Washington, DC: World Bank.

Cobham, A., and A. Sumner. 2013. "Putting the Gini Back in the Bottle? 'The Palma' as a Policy Relevant Measure of Inequality". https://www.kcl.ac.uk/aboutkings/worldwide/initiatives/global/intdev/people/Sumner/Cobham-Sumner-15March2013.pdf (accessed 1 July 2019).

———, L. Schlogl, and A. Sumner. 2015. "Inequality and the Tails: The Palma Proposition and Ratio Revisited". *DESA Working Paper* No. 143. ST/ESA/2015/DWP/143.

Credit Suisse 2016. *Global Wealth Report 2016*. Credit Suisse Research Institute.

Easterly, WR. 2001. *The Elusive Quest for Growth: Economists' Adventures and Misadventures in the Tropics*. Cambridge, MA: MIT Press.

ESCAP. 2019. *Closing the Gap: Empowerment and Inclusion in Asia and the Pacific*. Bangkok: UN ESCAP.

Firman, T. 2016. "Demographic Patterns of Indonesia's Urbanization, 2000–2010: Continuity and Change at the Macro Level". In *Contemporary Demographic Transformations in China, India and Indonesia*, edited by C.Z. Guilmoto and G.W. Jones, pp. 255–69. New York: Springer.

Garnaut, R. 2015. "Indonesia's Resources Boom in International Perspective: Policy

Dilemmas and Options for Continued Strong Growth". *Bulletin of Indonesian Economic Studies* 51, no. 2: 189–212.

Hadiz, V. 2016. *Islamic Populism in Indonesia and the Middle East*. Cambridge: Cambridge University Press.

———. 2017. "The Indonesian Oligarchy's Islamic Turn?". *Australian Institute of International Affairs*. http://www.internationalaffairs.org.au/australianoutlook/indonesian-oligarchys-islamic-turn/ (accessed 8 June 2020).

———. 2019. "Oligarchs, Money and Religion: The Indonesian Elections". *Indonesia at Melbourne*, 2 April 2019. https://indonesiaatmelbourne.unimelb.edu.au/oligarchs-money-and-religion-the-indonesian-elections/ (accessed 8 June 2020).

———, and R. Robison. 2013. "The Political Economy of Oligarchy and the Reorganization of Power in Indonesia". *Indonesia* 96 (October): 35–57.

Hill, H. 2000. *The Indonesian Economy*, 2nd ed. Cambridge: Cambridge University Press.

———, and Y. Vidyattama. 2014. "Hares and Tortoises: Regional Development Dynamics in Indonesia". In *Regional Dynamics in A Decentralized Indonesia*, edited by H. Hill, pp. 68–97. Singapore: Institute of Southeast Asian Studies.

IMF. 2017. *World Economic Outlook* 2017. Washington, DC: International Monetary Fund.

Indonesia at Melbourne. 2019. "Ahead of the Second Debate, Get the Lowdown on Infrastructure under Jokowi", The University of Melbourne, 14 February 2019. https://indonesiaatmelbourne.unimelb.edu.au/ahead-of-the-second-debate-get-the-lowdown-on-infrastructure-under-jokowi/ (accessed 1 July 2019).

Irwan, A., and Y. Nugroho. 2018. "Land Redistribution Key to Reducing Inequality". *Jakarta Post*, 19 September 2018.

Jakarta Post. 2016. "Jokowi's Java-Centric Development Widening Wealth Gap: INDEF". 21 October 2016. https://www.thejakartapost.com/news/2016/10/21/jokowis-java-centric-development-widening-wealth-gap-indef.html (accessed 1 July 2019).

———. 2018. "Indonesia's Low Tax-to-GDP Ratio". Editorial, 11 October 2018. https://www.thejakartapost.com/academia/2018/10/11/indonesias-low-tax-to-gdp-ratio.html (accessed 1 July 2019).

———. 2019a. "Who Killed the KPK?". Editorial, 5 November 2019. https://www.thejakartapost.com/academia/2019/11/05/who-killed-the-kpk.html (accessed 8 June 2020)

———. 2019b. "Socio-Economic Gap Has Closed under Jokowi: INFID". 12 February 2019. https://www.thejakartapost.com/news/2019/02/12/socio-economic-gap-has-closed-under-jokowi-infid.html (accessed 1 July 2019).

Juoro, Umar. 2017. "Why Populist Islam Is Gaining Ground in Indonesia". *Huffington Post*, 22 September 2017. https://www.huffpost.com/entry/indonesia-islamist-populism_b_59c0060ce4b06f9bf04873d1 (accessed 1 July 2019).

Karimi, S. 2014. "Demokrasi, Sistem Pasar dan Redistribusi Kapasitas Produktif" [Democracy, market system and redistribution of productive capacity]. Paper for monthly discussion of the Graduate School, Andalas University, Padang, 15 November 2014.

Kimura, E. 2017. "Populist Politics in Indonesia". East-West Center's *Asia Pacific Bulletin*, 7 December 2017.

Klein, M., and R. Winkler. 2019. "Austerity, Inequality, and Private Debt Overhang". *European Journal of Political Economy* 57, no. 1: 89–106.

Kompas. 2019. "Total Dana Desa 2019-2024 Rp400 Triliun". 2 February 2019. https://nasional.kompas.com/read/2019/02/26/17333511/total-dana-desa-2019-2024-rp-400-triliun?page=all (accessed 1 July 2019).

Kumhof, M., R. Rancière, and P. Winant. 2015. "Inequality, Leverage, and Crises". *American Economic Review* 105, no. 3: 1217–45.

Mietzner, M. 2007. "Party Financing in Post-Soeharto Indonesia: Between State Subsidies and Political Corruption". *Contemporary Southeast Asia* 29, no. 2: 238–63.

———. 2020. "Rival Populisms and the Democratic Crisis in Indonesia: Chauvinists, Islamists and Technocrats". *Australian Journal of International Affairs* 74, no. 4: 420–38.

Morse, I. 2019. "The Natural Resource Oligarchy Funding Indonesia's Election". *The Diplomat*, 11 April 2019. https://thediplomat.com/2019/04/the-natural-resource-oligarchy-funding-indonesias-election/ (accessed 8 June 2020).

Muller, C. 2016. "Ethnic Inequality and Community Activities in Indonesia". *WIDER Working Paper* 2016/170.

OXFAM, 2017. "Towards a More Equal Indonesia". *OXFAM Briefing Paper*, February 2017. https://www.oxfam.org/en/research/towards-more-equal-indonesia (accessed 8 June 2020).

Palma, J.G. 2011. "Homogeneous Middles vs. Heterogeneous Tails, and the End of the 'Inverted-U': It's All About the Share of the Rich". *Development and Change* 42, no. 1: 87–153.

Piketty, T. 2018. "Brahmin Left vs Merchant Right: Rising Inequality and the Changing Structure of Political Conflict (Evidence from France, Britain and the US, 1948–2017)". WID World Working Paper Series No. 2018/7.

Rajan, R. 2010. *Fault Lines*. Princeton, NJ: Princeton University Press.

Rapoza, K. 2013. "The China Miracle: A Rising Wealth Gap". *Forbes*, 20 January 2013. https://www.forbes.com/sites/kenrapoza/2013/01/20/the-china-miracle-a-rising-wealth-gap/#4de54727226a (accessed 1 July 2019).

Reuter, T. 2015. "Political Parties and the Power of Money in Indonesia and Beyond". *TRaNS: Trans-Regional and -National Studies of Southeast Asia* 3, no. 2: 267–88.

Robison, R., and V. Hadiz. 2004. *Reorganizing Power in Indonesia: The Politics of Oligarchy in an Age of Markets*. London and New York: Routledge.

Suharyo, W.I. 2002. "Indonesia's Fiscal Decentralization: A Preliminary Assessment of the First Year Experience". *UNSFIR Working Paper* no. 02/07. Jakarta: UNSFIR.

Suryadarma, D., R.P. Artha, A. Suryahadi, and S. Sumarto. 2005. "A Reassessment of Inequality and Its Role in Poverty Reduction in Indonesia". *SMERU Working Paper*. Jakarta: SMERU Research Institute.

———, W. Widyanti, A. Suryahadi, and S. Sumarto. 2006. "From Access to Income: Regional and Ethnic Inequality in Indonesia". *SMERU Working Paper*. Jakarta: SMERU Research Institute.

Tadjoeddin, M.Z. 2014. *Explaining Collective Violence in Contemporary Indonesia: From Conflict to Cooperation*. London: Palgrave Macmillan.

———. 2016. "Earnings, Productivity and Inequality in Indonesia". *Economic and Labour Relations Review* 27, no. 2: 248–71.

———, and A. Chowdhury. 2018. *Employment and Reindustrialisation in Post Soeharto Indonesia*. London: Palgrave Macmillan.

———, A. Yumna, S.E. Gultom, M.F. Rakhmadi, and A. Suryahadi. 2020. "Inequality and Violent Conflict: New Evidence from Selected Provinces in Post-Soeharto Indonesia". *Journal of the Asia Pacific Economy*. https://doi.org/10.1080/13547860.2020.1773607

———, and V. Mercer-Blackman. 2018. "Urbanization and Labor Productivity in Indonesia". In *Indonesia: Enhancing Productivity Through Quality Jobs*, edited by E. Ginting, C. Manning and K. Taniguchi, pp. 130–69. Manila: Asian Development Bank.

Tapsell, R. 2017. *Media Power in Indonesia: Oligarchs, Citizens and the Digital Revolution*. London: Rowman & Littlefield.

Tobin, D. 2011. "Inequality in China: Rural Poverty Persists as Urban Wealth Balloons". *BBC News*, 29 June 2011. http://www.bbc.co.uk/news/mobile/business-13945072 (accessed 1 July 2019).

UN. 2005. *World Social Situation: The Inequality Predicament*. New York: United Nations.

———. 2020. *World Social Report 2020: Inequality in a Rapidly Changing World*. New York: United Nations' Department of Economic and Social Affairs (DESA).

Vidyattama, Y. 2013. "Regional Convergence and the Role of Neighbourhood Effects in a Decentralised Indonesia". *Bulletin of Indonesian Economic Studies* 49, no. 3: 193–211.

Wihardja, Maria M. 2016. "The Effect of the Commodity Boom on Indonesia's Macroeconomic Fundamentals and Industrial Development". *International Organisations Research Journal* 11, no. 1: 39–54.

Winoto, J. 2009. "Taking Land Policy and Administration in Indonesia to the Next Stage and National Land Agency's Strategic Plan". Paper for Workshop in International Federation of Surveyors' Forum, Washington DC, March 2009.

Winters, J.A. 2011. "Who Will Tame the Oligarchs?". *Inside Indonesia* 104 (Apr–June).
———. 2013. "Oligarchy and Democracy in Indonesia". *Indonesia* 96 (October): 11–33.
———. 2019. "Jeffrey A. Winters on the Rise of Oligarchic Democracy", an interview at *Keen On*, 13 September 2019. https://lithub.com/jeffrey-a-winters-on-the-rise-of-oligarchic-democracy/ (accessed 9 July 2020).
World Bank. 1993. *The East Asian Miracle: Economic Growth and Public Policy*. Washington, DC: World Bank and Oxford University Press.
Yang, L. 2013. "Gini Coefficient Release Highlights China's Resolve to Bridge Wealth Gap". *Xinhuanet*, 21 January 2013. http://en.people.cn/90778/8101702.html (accessed 1 July 2019).
Yumna, A., M.F. Rakhmadi, M.F. Hidayat, S.E. Gultom, and A. Suryahadi. 2015. "Estimating the Impact of Inequality on Growth and Unemployment in Indonesia". *SMERU Working Paper*. Jakarta: SMERU Research Institute.
Yusuf, A.A. 2014. *Has Prosperity Been for All? Revisiting the Trend of Various Dimension of Inequality in Indonesia*. Jakarta, Indonesia: INFID.
———, and P. Warr. 2018. "Anti-Globalisation, Poverty and Inequality in Indonesia". In *Indonesia in the New World: Globalisation, Nationalism and Sovereignty*, edited by A.A. Patunru, M. Pangestu, M.C. Basri, pp. 133–56. Singapore: ISEAS – Yusof Ishak Institute.

4

INEQUALITY AND EXCLUSION IN MALAYSIA
Macro Trends, Labour Market Dynamics and Gender Dimensions

Lee Hwok Aun and Christopher Choong[1]

INEQUALITY IN MALAYSIA: CLEAR PRIORITIES AND UNSETTLED QUESTIONS

Malaysia is generally regarded a success story in reducing income inequality, especially between ethnic groups, while sustaining growth and eradicating poverty over the long term. In recent years, the country has also increased attention to national inequality—particularly, by emphasizing the poorest 40 per cent of households (or B40, for "Bottom 40") as beneficiaries of more inclusive economic growth and social policy—and by addressing gender disparities in opportunity, participation and mobility. The policy priority is premised on an assessment that inequality has remained high, that the lower income segments are being left behind, and that women face barriers to equal participation and remuneration.

Popular discourses on inequality in Malaysia have also, for the past decade and into the present, maintained a broad consensus that inequality has increased, or at least stayed high—with particular emphasis on class-based disparities within ethnic groups. Such diagnoses and outlooks draw on the structural features of Malaysia's political economy, anecdotal observations and public perceptions: masses struggling to cope with cost of living while the fortunes of the elites appear to be burgeoning, concentration of the benefits of growth at the top alongside sluggish employment conditions, and real wage stagnation for the working classes. Official statistics, however, paint an opposite picture of rapidly declining inequality.

This chapter proceeds in three main segments. First, we revisit household income inequality, examining the plausibility of the official account and extracting new insights from the data. The government's calculation of Malaysia's household income Gini coefficient, based on national survey data, has registered a declining trend from 2004 to 2016, far in excess of regional neighbours and even global comparator countries. This is on the back of rapid income growth for the bottom 40 per cent and slower rates of increase for the top 20 per cent. Intraethnic inequalities have reached all-time lows. Perplexingly, inequality rose between 2016 and 2019, based on the latest update. Furthermore, inequality drops precipitously in a few intervals, but these intervals do not correspond with momentous shocks, structural change or policy reforms that can explain the findings.

Second, we provide an overview and critical evaluation of Malaysia's policies geared toward reducing household income inequality, redressing exclusion of low-income households, and narrowing gender gaps, and consider whether the observed patterns correspond with economic structural changes and policy measures. Using published household income statistics, we plot trends based on disaggregations, particularly to draw out some overlooked aspects of interethnic distribution. Disparities are stable on the whole, but have decreased more markedly between the bottom 40 per cent of the bumiputra, Chinese and Indian communities, and inequality levels are lower within urban areas, where interethnic comparisons are most valid and important. While recognizing the continual salience of ethnicity, our primary focus is on more generic and systemic aspects of national inequality, as well as gender dimensions.

We then reference other empirical sources besides the household income survey, which generate alternative inequality estimates, specifically in the realm of earnings, which show moderate change, not steep decline, in recent years. Inequality in personal earnings has remained high, with distribution persistently concentrated in the uppermost strata. Wage growth in skilled occupations has slowed, and the wages of low-skilled occupations have been boosted, but again, these changes do not concur with the official accounts of exceedingly high-income growth for B40 households.

The third main segment of this chapter unpacks the gender wage gap against a backdrop of broad improvements in women's labour force participation and occupational advancement. Despite gender inequality being on the development agenda for many decades—reinforced in the 2019 Budget Speech and the Mid-term Review of the 11th Malaysia Plan (MTR 11MP)—the focus and strategies have always skewed towards women's participation in the workforce without strong links with the gender wage gap and overall inequality discourse (MOF 2018; Malaysia 2018). We refocus the attention on gender aspects of wage inequality, with particular attention to the effects of occupational, life cycle and non-market activities on women's wages.

On the whole, we find inequality patterns that arguably correspond with structural changes in the economy and labour markets, but markedly differ from the official accounts. These two versions derive from data sources that overlap but are not fully comparable. Nonetheless, by our analysis we find more grounds to believe that inequality has moderately changed. Wage-based indicators and data indicate modest changes in inequality, which is difficult to reconcile with the official steep drop in gross household income inequality. We also find that gender inequalities remain salient, despite a narrow national wage gap. Redressing inequality between groups, including ethnicity and gender, will require continual, and more systematic, policy responses.

MACRO PICTURE: DOWNWARD TREND, IMPLAUSIBLE EXTENT

The importance of empirical evidence grows in the current milieu of acute awareness of income and wealth distribution and heightened sentiment especially towards widening inequality. The pattern of inequality in Malaysia in the past three decades marks out two or three periods, depending on the spatial and group-based dimension being observed. The official record of household income inequality, calculated from the household income survey (HIS), provides a consistent data source since 1984

(Figure 4.1). We should note, however, that the Gini coefficient and other inequality indicators prior to 1989 comprised both citizens and non-citizens, but from 1989 onwards includes only Malaysians. The 1980s saw declining inequality, a trend that would arguably hold even if the computation was limited to citizens. While not extensively researched, Malaysia's track record of reduced inequality in the 1980s is generally accepted, concurring as it does with structural changes corresponding with this distributional trend. Urbanization and industrialization spurred mass employment especially in labour-intensive manufacturing, and alongside middle-class expansion, plausibly accounted for the steady decline in inequality.

Inequality drew considerably more attention in the 1990s, prompted by the concurrence of the growth boom with a seeming reversal of the preceding decade's trend of decreasing inequality. The Gini of household income increased between 1989 and 1993, and was sustained at a relatively high level until 1997. Various interpretations were articulated in the literature, deducing plausible explanations for this trend in the national Gini—without further information nor access to microdata (Mat Zin 2008; Ariff 2008; Shari 2000). In the labour market, the benefits of the economic boom were accruing disproportionately to skilled workers, while wage growth for the masses was contained due to influxes of low-skilled migrant labour, and gaps widened between rapidly growing and more technologically advanced manufacturing versus a rather sluggish agriculture sector. Political economy interpretations broadly surmised that professionals and managers, and capitalists and political-business elites, notably the Malay "new rich", were best poised to capture rents from the roaring 1990s—a viewpoint consistent with the sizeable rise in inequality within the bumiputra population (Figure 4.2).

Unfortunately, disaggregated inequality indicators were only disseminated decades later, which raise some questions on the above interpretations. The Gini coefficient within urban areas follows a distinct, and strikingly linear, descent from 1989 to 1997 (Figure 4.1). Many of the explanations for rising inequality derive from structural changes and political economic reconfigurations centred on urban economies. Rising inequality within rural areas from 1992 to 1997 also bypassed contemporaneous attention, and remain difficult to explicate in retrospect. Nevertheless, the inequality uptrend observed in the national Gini was perceivably validated by drawing on broader, sometimes anecdotal, assessments of distributional dynamics in Malaysia, and referring to public

Inequality and Exclusion in Malaysia

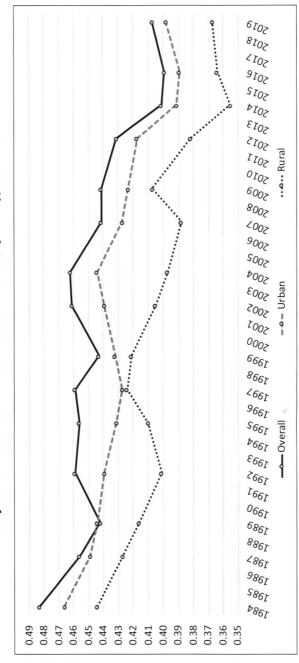

FIGURE 4.1
Malaysia: Gini Coefficient of Gross Household Income, by Area Type, 1984–2019

Source: DOSM (2020).

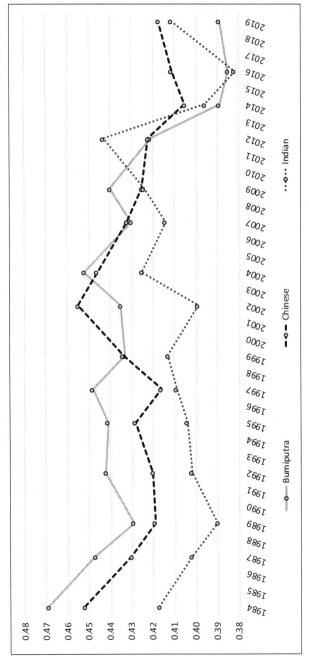

FIGURE 4.2
Gini Coefficient of Gross Household Income, by Ethnicity, 1984–2019

Source: DOSM (2020).

consciousness of economic hardship—more acute among low-income households—and conspicuous consumption and wealth accumulation at the top.

This widely shared perception of rising inequality, and the underlying notion that the lower reaches of society were excluded from the benefits of economic growth, persisted into the next decade. Inequality also received scant mention in academic and policy literature in the 2000s. The New Economic Model (NEM) launched in 2010, aiming to chart a new policy course for Malaysia, declared the B40 as a policy priority, on the grounds of relative exclusion from the growth process: "household income surveys suggest that income growth has been strong only for the top 20 per cent of Malaysian income earners. The bottom 40 per cent of households have experienced the slowest growth of average income, earning less than RM1,500 per month (Malaysian ringgit) in 2008" (NEAC 2010, p. 6). Perplexingly, this assessment ran directly contrary to official statistics showing faster income growth for the B40. From 2004 to 2009, real household income of the B40 actually exceeded that of the Middle 40 (M40) and Top 20 (T20) (Figure 4.3).

Subsequent to the NEM, Malaysia adopted a policy stance that made national inequality a priority, with a focus on the B40. Previously, interethnic inequality received the bulk of attention. However, disconnects persisted between empirical evidence and policy analyses, as well as public perception. The 2010s, after the global financial crisis, has been a decade of pronounced awareness of inequality in Malaysia, as in most of the world. Calculations of income and wealth disparity have flourished, showing rising inequality around the globe—especially runaway growth at the very top and accumulation among the already rich (Atkinson, Piketty and Saez 2011; Piketty 2014; Oxfam 2017).

Popular and policy discourses in Malaysia appear to ride the same wave, propelled by a pervading sense of two phenomena: sluggish earnings growth and widening wealth gaps (Bhattacharjee and Ho 2017). However, minimal evidence was presented to corroborate this policy emphasis. In fact, inequality has continually been reported from one angle: gross household income. The official account of inequality in the 2010s showed a steady decline on the whole, but a precipitous drop between 2012 and 2014 (Figure 4.1).

The magnitude and timing of this drop are immensely implausible, and may be due to changes in estimation method, as discussed in more detail

FIGURE 4.3
Real Annual Average Growth of Gross Household Income, by Income Bracket, 1989–2019

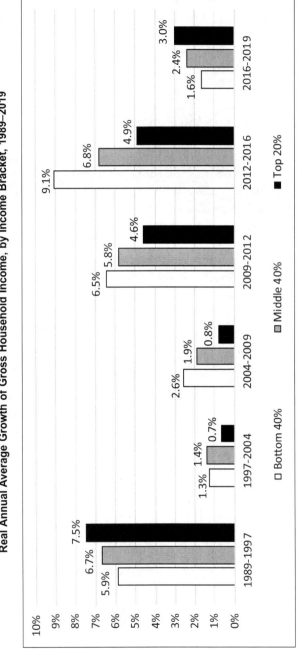

Sources: Lee and Choong (2019), authors' calculations from DOSM (2020).

by Lee and Khalid (2018). The HIS remains the authoritative data source, and the official calculations of household income inequality the definitive reference. However, no labour market change or policy measure emerges, of sufficient scale and abruptness, to account for the trend. Minimum wage was introduced in 2013 and took widespread effect in 2014, but at the rate of RM900–1,000 per month is too low to make a massive dent in overall inequality. For minimum wage to drive the registered decline in inequality, masses of Malaysian workers must have been paid far below the legislated floor prior to that. This is too far-fetched a scenario. One other intervention stands out as a possible contributor to the official decline in inequality: social assistance, specifically the Bantuan Rakyat 1Malaysia (BR1M) cash transfer scheme implemented since 2012. However, while a significant disbursement with immense reach—six million recipients, receiving three lump sums a year—the actual amount on a monthly basis reduces down to a much less sizeable quantum, and the timing of BR1M's pecuniary injection into household revenue, in 2012 and 2016, does not coincide with the major fall in inequality in 2014.

Further implausible results include the pattern of intraethnic inequality—staggeringly, the Gini coefficient among Indian households rises from 1989 to 2012, then plummets back to that starting level within two years, only to rise steeply again between 2016 to 2019 (Figure 4.2). Differentials and volatility of income inequality within states over the 2012–2014–2016–2019 intervals reinforce the view that something is awry in the statistics (Appendix Figure A4.1). The most drastic changes occur in the smaller states, especially Perlis and Terengganu, as shown by shares of national population. Hence, the fall in inequality there does not make a major dent on Malaysia's overall inequality. Nonetheless, these phenomena within states, and variation across states, defy geographic and economic explanation. For instance, Kedah and Perak, two neighbouring states on Peninsular Malaysia's west coast with similar average income and economic profile, record starkly different changes in inequality between 2012 and 2016, with Kedah showing an especially volatile pattern.[2]

On the whole, questions persist over Malaysia's official record of declining household income inequality in recent years, and especially the past decade. Additionally, we remain considerably in the dark about magnitudes and trends in inequality of earnings, which contribute to the bulk of overall household income.

INEQUALITY IN PUBLIC POLICY
Structural and intergroup aspects

Malaysia has continuously sought to reduce income inequality, primarily in an interethnic context. Its long ideological milieu of ethnicity-based politics and eclecticism, without clear positions on the conventional left-right spectrum, continuously engendered a pragmatism, thus embedding a selective adoption of neoliberal practices alongside extensive state intervention and public welfare provisions. Focus on the ethnic dimension was politically imperative, given the constitutional provisions for ethnic preferential policies and underlying political bargains. Addressing ethnic inequality is also socio-economically warranted, in view of the magnitude of interethnic disparity and disadvantages faced by the majority population (Lee 2016, 2021).

With due caveats on the credibility of household income calculations as discussed above, these statistics remain the only nationally representative and across-time reference. On the whole, the proportion of overall inequality attributable to interethnic differences has been halved since 1970 (Ravallion 2020). Within the half century, patterns vary broadly in different phases: Chinese to bumiputra disparities narrowed in the 1980s, rose slightly in the 1990s, then declined more steeply in the 2000s before plateauing in the 2010s (Figure 4.4). The Indian to bumiputra gap is lesser in magnitude but roughly moves in parallel fashion, except for the 1980s when the ratio stayed quite constant. However, there is no available analysis of the contributions of a range of possible factors—educational achievement, occupational mobility, public sector employment—both to evaluate policy implementation and to inform policy formulation going forward. Such analyses would operate more at the personal, rather than household level, with earned income playing a determining role. With rare exceptions such as Milanovic (2006), earnings distribution is largely omitted in Malaysia's policy discourses.

Policy attention and public resources allocated to interethnic inequality have outweighed other dimensions of inequality. Spatial disparities are among the few other dimensions that have been consistently tracked and accorded distinct policy emphasis. This is partly due to the interlinkage with ethnic disparities and the concentration of the majority Malay and bumiputra populations in rural areas and in certain states and regions.

Inequality and Exclusion in Malaysia

FIGURE 4.4
Interethnic and Urban-Rural Household Income Disparities, 1984–2019

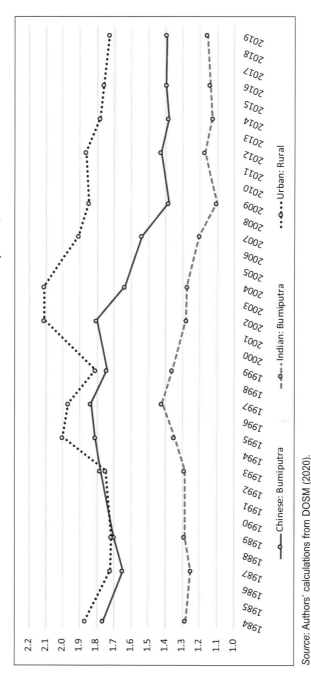

Source: Authors' calculations from DOSM (2020).

As in any economy, urban-rural income gaps persist, and public policies are in place to try to narrow the divide, albeit never achieving full parity. According to official household income figures, the urban-rural gap has grown over some periods, but lessened since the mid-2000s.

The official plotline of interethnic inequality has been confined to national aggregates, but more can be gleaned from the published statistics. Two means of disaggregation shed further light. Jointly accounting for ethnicity and area type, we can compute interethnic income ratios for urban and rural areas separately. This exercise is pertinent, because rural incomes are invariably lower, and the preponderance of bumiputras in the rural population understates the bumiputra national average, concomitantly overstating interethnic gaps. Throughout the 2010s, the Chinese to bumiputra average income ratio of about 1.40 at the national level has corresponded with 1.20 in urban areas, while Indian-bumiputra inequality has held at about 1.20 in rural areas and near parity in urban areas.

Official data disclosures also permit us to observe interethnic disparities within income strata. Mean incomes of the top 20 per cent, middle 40 per cent and bottom 40 per cent of households are reported for the three ethnic groups, from which we can compute intergroup ratios (Figures 4.5A and 4.5B). A few patterns warrant brief comment. Chinese-bumiputra income ratios have been recorded similar levels in all three strata; the T20, M40 and B40 lines generally converge, and all three continuously decline from the 1990s until around 2010. However, from then onwards the magnitude of average inequality continues to decline in the B40 category, but holds constant in the M40 and slightly increases in the T20 (Figure 4.5A). Indian per bumiputra inequality also declines most substantially in the lowest-income B40 category (Figure 4.5B).

These findings derive from relatively faster income growth in the bumiputra B40, which has more steadily closed the gap with B40 counterparts of other groups. Of course, the overall interethnic gap most closely tracks that of the M40, as the segment mirroring the middle. At the same time, T20 interethnic gaps remain relatively larger—and this applies to both urban and rural areas. The underlying factors, and onward implications, of these trends are manifold and do not readily translate into policies favouring the T20. Nonetheless, there are important implications for various pro-bumiputra policies, which reach out in distinct ways to the B40, M40 and T20. We must emphasize that ethnically targeted policies exert

Inequality and Exclusion in Malaysia

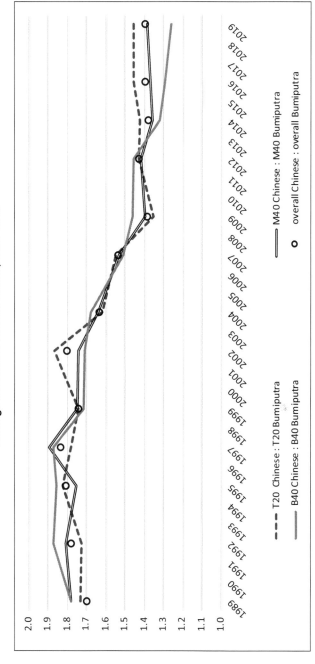

FIGURE 4.5A
Top 20 per cent, Middle 40 per cent and Bottom 40 per cent Chinese to Bumiputra Average Household Income Ratios, 1989–2019

Source: Authors' calculations from DOSM (2020).

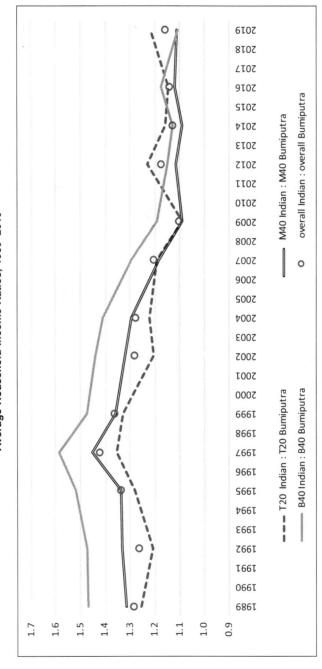

FIGURE 4.5B
Top 20 per cent, Middle 40 per cent and Bottom 40 per cent Indian to Bumiputra Average Household Income Ratios, 1989–2019

Source: Authors' calculations from DOSM (2020).

an indirect effect on income—their primary domain concerns the allocation of socio-economic opportunity, notably in higher education, public sector employment, government contracting, microfinance and business loans. These interventions will have effects on income, but numerous and complex factors also impinge on income distribution (Lee 2021).

The causal links between pro-bumiputra policies and bumiputra household income are not straightforward. Still, we can broadly deduce that interventions mainly benefiting the B40 and M40—saliently, higher education access and sponsorship, public sector jobs, SME support—have played a role in gradually narrowing disparities, especially up to the M40 ceiling. These outcomes reflect policy achievements of bumiputra-targeted programmes as well as universalist and need-based policies such as minimum wage. An imperative next frontier will be to address disadvantage more comprehensively, including among non-Malay bumiputra of Sabah and Sarawak, and Orang Asli indigenous peoples of Peninsular Malaysia, and to broaden participation and develop capability such that policy beneficiaries can acquire more self-reliance.

Wage distribution can be observed, indirectly, by computing disparity ratios from the summary statistics disclosed in the Salaries and Wages Survey Report since 2010. The Salaries and Wages Survey obtains a nationally representative sample across public and private sectors, and the reports deriving from this data source present statistics of Malaysian employees, albeit with a limited range of information. Nonetheless, we gain some insight into the ethnic dimensions which can be juxtaposed against household income statistics discussed above. We must be mindful of differences in content and unit of analysis between individual wages and household income, which includes multiple earners and other income sources besides wages. Interethnic gaps in wages are lesser than that of household income (Figure 4.6). At the same time, the ratios have been stable over the past decade, markedly parallel to the trend in household income. Chinese employees on average earn 20 per cent more than bumiputra counterparts, while the Indian and bumiputra wages are virtually on par. These interethnic gaps are larger among male workers, but smaller among female workers—furthermore, Indian women earn less than bumiputra women. Without access to the raw data, we cannot estimate the determinants of these distribution patterns. However, it is distinctly plausible that the public sector, which on average pays higher than the private sector, and where there is concentration of

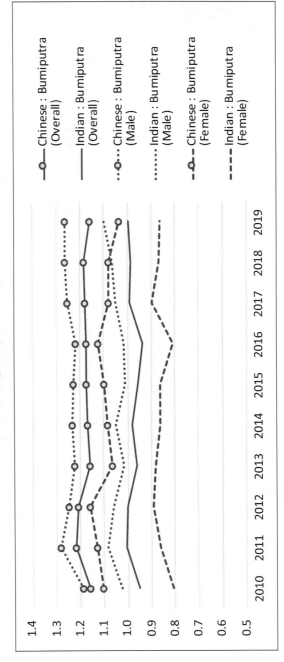

FIGURE 4.6
Interethnic Average Wage Ratios, by Gender, 2010–18

Source: Authors' calculations from DOSM (2019).

bumiputras—especially bumiputra women—contributes significantly to these distributional patterns.

From the mid-2000s, the government promoted regional economic corridors as a new approach to reducing geographic disparities and stimulating new growth poles (Malaysia 2006). As argued by Hutchinson (2017), the new approach sought to leverage on competitive advantages of regions and focused less on redistribution across states. But the reduction of spatial inequalities has been limited by the lack of regional corridor authorities' remit in local developmental matters, while state governments, which crucially hold sway over land use decisions, are limited in revenue and generally too under-resourced to effectively drive growth and innovation. Inequality between Malaysia's states has remained fairly constant in recent years, based on the coefficient of variation of states' average incomes.[3] With reference to the ratio of states' average income to the national average over the period 2009–16, we find most states persistently lagging but with minimal change. The highest income states did not pull away from the rest, but at the same time, no state has shown a robust momentum of catching up with the national average, and Sarawak—the site of one economic corridor—has noticeably fallen further behind (Appendix Figures A4.2 and A4.3).

As noted above, income class-based inequality and exclusion of the B40 have been policy priorities since 2010. This policy shift mainstreamed the B40 as a target beneficiary group, aligned with the centralization of inclusive and sustainable growth on the national agenda. Practically, a number of policies have also been promulgated, notably minimum wage and social transfers. The year 2010 also ushered in a new practice of setting Gini reduction targets. The Tenth Malaysia Plan resolved to lower the Gini from 0.441 in 2009 to 0.420 in 2015 (Malaysia 2010). Most recently, the Mid-term Review of the Eleventh Malaysia Plan, observing that the country has superseded the target—with the Gini put at 0.401 in 2014—proposed 0.385 in 2020 (Malaysia 2018). Within this overarching ambit of reducing inequality, development policies have in recent years also sought to redress the marginalization of certain groups—specifically, ethnic Indians and the Orang Asli indigenous peoples of Peninsular Malaysia. Notably, recent research has shown that intergenerational upward mobility has occurred to a lesser extent among Indian households (Khalid 2014). Public policies have reached out to these groups, such as through the Malaysian Indian Blueprint, saliently with regard to higher education access and participation in commerce. However, it often remains unclear how identity and disadvantage are demarcated as selection criteria, and to what extent the system is more inclusive. For instance, various post-secondary and higher education programmes, while emphasizing the B40 as targeted beneficiaries, remain exclusively accessible to B40 bumiputras.

Indeed, the increased attention to inequality on a national scale, as distinct from inequality between ethnic groups, regions or other categorizations, is only beginning to be manifest in a more systematic way in policy formulation. As noted above, inequality measurements solely report gross household income, lumping together all forms and sources of income, including wages, self-employment earnings, interest, rent and investment income, imputed rent for owner-occupied homes, and transfers from private and public sources. Malaysia's rich data repositories for the most part remain untapped, foregoing potential insights into academically important and policy-relevant questions, most saliently the distribution of household earned income, number of income earners, and the effects of private and public transfers. The HIS can indeed be utilized to estimate wealth inequality, such as Khalid's (2014) imputation of asset-based income flows into stocks. But due to data access constraints, his work also offers one snapshot, not a comparison across time.

Some empirical work and policy discourses have yielded change, albeit on a small scale. Considerable attention and policy advocacy have in recent years centred on the state of Malaysia's progressive taxation—specifically, its modest utilization for redistribution and inequality reduction. Ad hoc investigations, contingent on access to HIS raw data, have calculated net household income inequality to juxtapose against the gross figures—notably finding that, after accounting for taxes and transfers, progressive redistribution in Malaysia effects less reduction in inequality compared to various countries (World Bank 2014).[4] These discourses presaged a small step towards enhancing progressiveness in the 2020 federal government budget, which raised the top marginal tax rate (Choong and Firouz 2020). But it remains to be seen whether these difficult policy efforts will be sustained, particularly with tenuous and unstable political coalitions.

Labour Market Dynamics

Relying on gross household income is symptomatic of the policy omissions and of shortfalls in the country's accounting for deeper structural underpinnings of inequality. The dearth of labour market analyses, including the patterns and determinants of wage and earnings inequality, is a particular lacunae, given that these are the primary sources of household income. In 2019, paid employment (wages and salaries) contributed 61.6 per cent on average to the head of household's gross income, followed by self-employment (17.3 per cent), property and investment (12.9 per cent), and transfers (8.2 per cent) (DOSM 2020). In fact, growth in household heads' earned income in the 2012–16 period was much slower than that of transfers and property and wealth ownership. For the most part, labour market policies take a supply side approach of focusing on skills and cost competitiveness, with considerably less attention to labour demand, deepening of labour market institutions, and strengthening of workers' bargaining power.

A few other sources besides the HIS, which contains earnings data but is effectively inaccessible for research, can be utilized to shed light on inequality within specific scopes. No other datasets enjoy the national representation and sample size of the HIS, but a number of registries or surveys provide some information. Lee and Khalid (2018) derived inequality indicators from Employees Provident Fund accounts. With 6.5 million active members, and the legal mandate for all private sector employees to make EPF contributions at a standard rate based on monthly salary, the catchment of this data source is vast, and its distribution correlates with that of salaries—specifically in the private sector. Estimations of the Gini coefficient show mildly increasing inequality, and a stabilization in 2011–16 (Figure 4.7). Breaking down the distribution into segments, we observe the share of the top 20 per cent and top 1 per cent gradually rising, then plateauing, while that of the middle 40 per cent and bottom 40 per cent decline slightly, then hold steady (Figure 4.8).

Drawing on the Salaries and Wages Survey Reports, we can derive another series of wage inequality proxies. The statistics disclosed only permit us to compute some disparity ratios, not any overall inequality indicator calculated from raw datasets, which are inaccessible. We obtain ratios of average salaries of occupation groups relative to managers, the highest paid category (Figure 4.9A). The wage differentials between managers and occupation groups at the lower end remains stable: low-wage machine operators and craft workers maintain the same differential, constantly earning 25 per cent of managers' mean wage. Interestingly, elementary workers' wages relative to managers' follow

FIGURE 4.7
Gini Coefficient of EPF Savings Accounts (Proxy for Wage Inequality), 2004–18

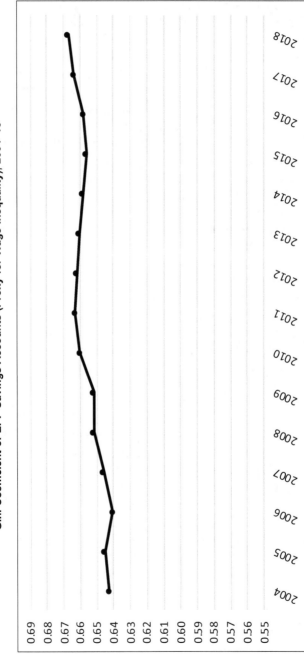

Sources: Lee and Khalid (2018), authors' calculations from EPF (2015–18).

Inequality and Exclusion in Malaysia 107

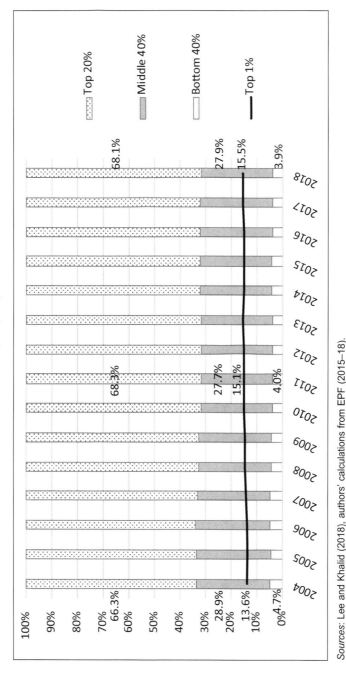

FIGURE 4.8
Share of EPF Savings, by Segment, 2004–18

Sources: Lee and Khalid (2018), authors' calculations from EPF (2015–18).

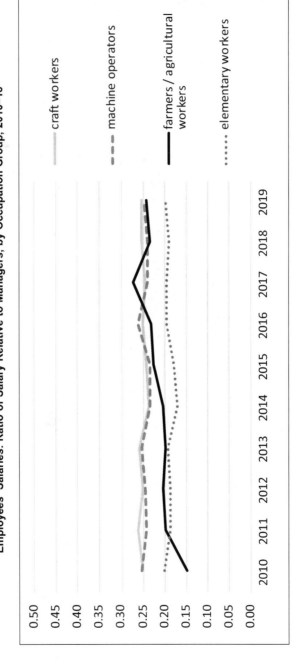

FIGURE 4.9A
Employees' Salaries: Ratio of Salary Relative to Managers, by Occupation Group, 2010–18

Sources: Lee and Choong (2019), authors' calculations from DOSM (2019).

Inequality and Exclusion in Malaysia

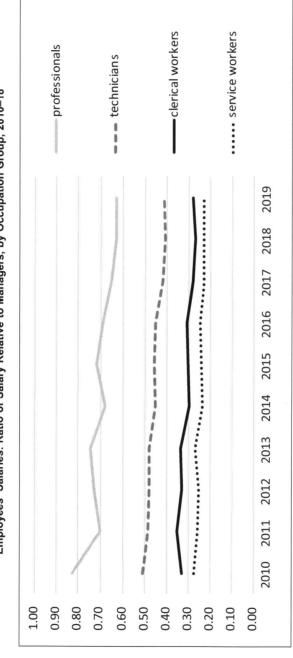

FIGURE 4.9B
Employees' Salaries: Ratio of Salary Relative to Managers, by Occupation Group, 2010–18

Sources: Lee and Choong (2019), authors' calculations from DOSM (2019).

a mild downtrend, then trace out an uptrend from 2014 to 2017. This inflection coincides with the effective introduction of minimum wage. Notably, farmers' and agricultural workers' wages grow relatively faster. Perhaps most strikingly, the wage premium of professionals and technicians, and clerical and service workers, have distinctly and steadily declined (Figure 4.9B).

Although we cannot estimate a summary measure of inequality, these trends in inter-occupational wage inequality possibly correspond with a moderate decline in inequality, given the increasing share of the professional, technician, and service worker categories in total employment. It is highly improbable that inequality has declined steeply, as in the official account of household income.

These wage trends also point to major structural features and socioeconomic developments with possible impacts on wage distribution. First, the relatively slower wage growth in professional and technician occupations, as well as clerical workers, is a matter of concern warranting further analysis and policy response, to unpack underlying factors and to determine the extent to which it stems from burgeoning labour supply of tertiary-educated workers or diminishing quality of graduates. Second, the persistence of low-skilled employment and presence of low-waged migrant workers may constrain wage growth for Malaysian workers in various occupations, notably service workers, craft workers and production workers (assemblers and machine operators in the official classification). These categories likely do not benefit directly from minimum wage enforcement, although they may indirectly gain from ripple effects of wage increases to maintain differentials relative to the wage floor. But they also depend on collective bargaining power, which is structurally weak in Malaysia, largely due to low unionisation, labour contracting and preponderance of migrant workers (Lee 2017). Third, the wages of lowest-paid elementary jobs appear to have been boosted—to which minimum wage has likely made a contribution.

These findings also underscore the importance of policy attention to labour market dynamics. Indeed, the labour market, as the sphere where wage distribution is determined, impacts immensely on earnings inequality—the preponderant component of household income. Labour market participation and remuneration are also central to gender aspects of inequality, to which we turn next.

UNPACKING THE GENDER WAGE GAP

National policies on women can be traced back to the 3rd Malaysia Plan, 1976–80, with the setting up of the National Advisory Council on the Integration of Women in Development in 1976. This was followed by the formulation of the National Policy for Women in 1989. The women's agenda, up until the recent 11th Malaysia Plan (11MP), features female labour force participation as a central part of the policy focus. The government's efforts to advance female labour force participation have focused on incentivizing the market provision of childcare and promoting flexible working arrangements. In addition, the government introduced the 30 per cent target for the participation of women in leadership positions for the public sector since 2004. This was extended to state-owned enterprises, statutory bodies, and public listed companies in the 11MP. A "Back to Work" programme targeted at qualified women was also introduced. In the Mid-Term Review of the 11th Malaysia Plan, the government reinforced the focus on getting more women to return to work by announcing a one-year tax break in 2019 for women who return from a career break. The situation of income of female-headed households can be generated from HIS data, as shown in UNDP (2014) based on the 2009 HIS, but development planning documents have not utilized the survey data in this manner.

Socio-economic development generally progresses in tandem with income growth. Malaysia's remarkable record of women's educational attainment, coupled with economic structural changes, constitute important context for exploration of gender gaps amid data scarcity. Specifically, the growth of the tertiary sector, in tandem with the remarkable rise in female educational attainment, have been generally favourable to women's labour participation and occupational mobility. Between 1995 and 2018, increase in the tertiary sector's share in the economy from 50.5 per cent to 55.6 per cent corresponds with increase in the share of women in the labour force from 34.1 per cent to 38.9 per cent and improvement in women's labour force participation rate from 44.7 per cent to 55.6 per cent. In 2018, 73.6 per cent of women were employed in services, compared to 55.1 per cent of men. Between 2011 and 2018, service industries constituted 78.8 per cent of the net increase in women's employment, compared to 71.5 per cent for men. This is consistent with literature on the U-shaped relationship between economic development and female labour force participation although we have insufficient longitudinal data points to test out the hypothesis for Malaysia (Tansel 2001).

Of course, the incorporation of women in the economy alone is insufficient to drive wage convergence without a rise in female educational attainment that propels women into higher-waged jobs. There are more women than men in both public and private universities in Malaysia. Female-to-male ratios for intake, enrolment, and graduation in public universities have increased continuously, with recent levels shown in Figure 4.10 for the 2010–18 interval. This has translated to a workforce that has a higher number of tertiary-educated women. Across education levels, the share of tertiary-educated women in the female labour force has seen the largest increase of 5.0 percentage points from 31.1 per cent in 2010 to 36.2 per cent in 2018. Women are also increasingly employed in skilled jobs, with the share of skilled women—professionals, technicians and associate professionals—in female employment rising from 17.8 per

FIGURE 4.10
Female:Male Ratio in University Intake, Enrolment and Graduation, 2010 and 2018

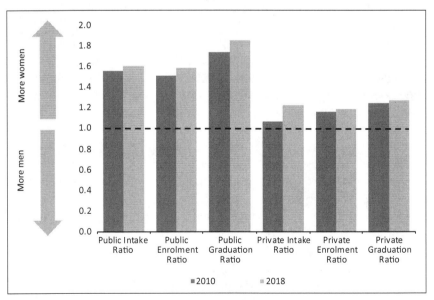

Source: Authors' calculations from Ministry of Higher Education (2011, 2018).

cent in 2010 to 26.0 per cent in 2018, while the men's share increased from 16.5 per cent to 20.7 per cent. Over the same period, the number of female and male skilled workers, respectively, increased 5.3 per cent and 3.4 per cent per year.

The increased demand for women workers brought about by a structural shift in the economy towards the tertiary sector, coupled with the increased supply of tertiary-educated women in the labour force, have advanced women's employment in skilled jobs. Skilled jobs, in turn, tend to be relatively higher-paid jobs; these developmental and structural trends are expected to contribute to gender wage gaps. Improvement in gender wage gaps corresponds with reductions in other gender gaps, notably in labour force participation and employment in skilled jobs categories— professionals and technicians and associate professionals.[5]

Gender wage inequality has not been a policy focus, and it is quite a challenge to evaluate the incidence and magnitude of the phenomenon. The Labour Force Survey Reports, which provide summary statistics through various tabulations, show that, on aggregate, gender wage disparity is low and narrowing (Figure 4.11). The gender wage gap, calculated as the difference between men's wages and women's wages as a percentage of men's wages, declined from 9.0 per cent in 2012 to 6.8 per cent in 2018 if we use mean calculations, and fell from 6.3 per cent to 4.9 per cent based on the median.[6] In absolute terms, women on average earn RM215 less than men in 2018, and RM115 less at the median.

The gender wage gap also varies quite substantially between ethnic groups. Between 2010 and 2018, all the ethnic groups have seen improvements in their gender wage gaps except for Chinese, where the gender wage gap increased from 12.2 per cent in 2010 to 16.1 per cent in 2018. Bumiputra's gender wage gap decreased from 5.5 per cent to 1.7 per cent while Indians decreased from 25.7 per cent to 20.1 per cent in the same period. In terms of level, in 2018, Indians have the highest gender wage gap at 20.1 per cent, followed by Chinese (16.1 per cent) and bumiputra (1.7 per cent). Those classified as "Others" have a gender wage gap of –8.5 per cent, which means that the average wage of female was higher than the average wage of male, a marked improvement from a gender wage gap of 13.6 per cent in 2010.

Another data source gauges male-female wage disparities quite differently. The National Employment Returns (NER) 2018 reports a gender wage gap of 24 per cent for Malaysian private sector employees,

FIGURE 4.11
Malaysian Mean Wage by Gender, and Gender Wage Gap, 2012–18

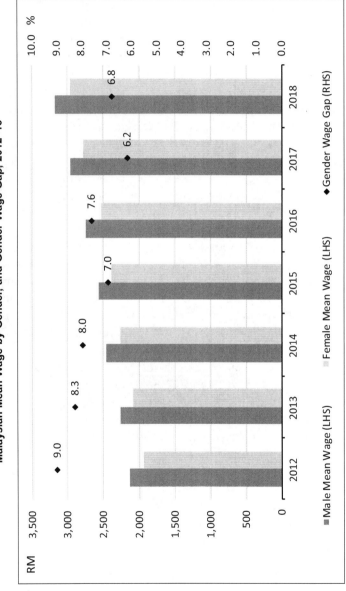

Source: Authors' calculations from DOSM (2012a, 2013b, 2014, 2015b, 2016, 2017b, 2018a).

based on median monthly basic salary (ILMIA 2018). The higher figure could be because the NER uses an establishment approach that includes members living in institutional living quarters in contrast with the Labour Force Survey (LFS) that uses a household approach that only enumerates members living in private living quarters. Including institutional living quarters captures low-waged women working and living in hospitals, hostels, hotels and boarding rooms. In addition, the NER excludes the public sector which tends to have a smaller gender wage gap (Seshan 2013). The civil service has seen a 176 per cent increase in female employment from 1995 to 2015, compared to 32 per cent in male employment, with the largest increase coming from top and professional management positions (MWFCD 2015). A third difference is that the NER only includes basic salary while the LFS includes allowances and overtime payments on top of basic salary. The large number of women employed as clerical workers as well as service and sales workers, whose remunerations are tied more to allowances and overtime payments, could result in a higher gender wage gap when these are excluded from the NER. Due to these sampling and content limitations of the NER, we omit it from the following analysis while concentrating on insights we can derive from the LFS.

Importantly, the LFS Reports provide wage statistics disaggregated by gender, occupation and age groups, from which we can further unpack patterns and trends. These findings also underscore the shortcomings of referencing the aggregated gender wage ratio, which omits different levels of male-female disparity within occupations and cohorts.

Three insights stand out. First, women are concentrated in a set of occupational groups, within which gender wage gaps are relatively lower (Figure 4.12). In 2018, two occupations made up a combined 36.2 per cent of female employees: clerical support workers (24.3 per cent) and technicians and associate professionals (11.8 per cent). These two also register narrower gender wage gaps, i.e., 11.6 per cent, and 10.8 per cent respectively. Professionals have the highest number of female employees (26.5 per cent) and service and sales workers have the third-highest number (20.8 per cent), but in contrast, they have higher gender wage gaps at 20.3 per cent and 26.3 per cent respectively. The other two occupations with relatively lower gender wage gaps are managers (19.2 per cent) and elementary occupations (24.9 per cent)—but they only make up 2.4 per cent and 5.3 per cent of female employees in 2018.

FIGURE 4.12
Malaysian Female Employees (Share of Total Female Employees) and Gender Wage Gaps, by Occupation, 2018

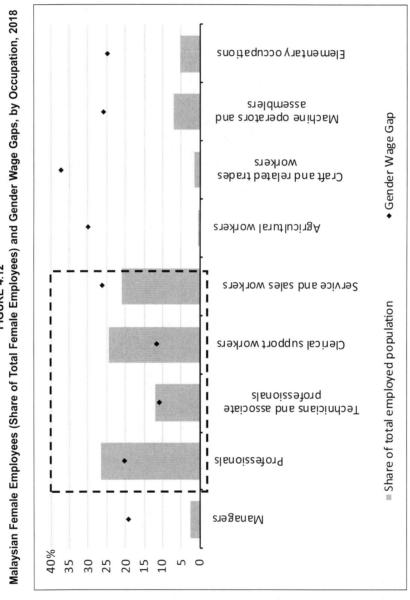

Source: Authors' calculations from DOSM (2018b).

The concentration of women in certain occupational categories could be the result of pre-labour market "gender sorting", resulting from gender bias or self-selection into higher education programmes. Yusof, Alias and Habil (2012), analysing the Ministry of Education's data from 2007 to 2010, provide some evidence of gender bias in the selection of postgraduate programmes in universities. The chapter shows that women are participating more in sciences as well as arts and humanities, and substantially less in technical programmes. Similar research to assess gender sorting in university programmes should be extended to undergraduate studies. In addition, such research should be done at further levels of disaggregation, i.e., two digits and above, for both university programmes and occupational categories. This is because gender sorting is likely to be more acute in certain courses within a programme, translating to concentration of women in certain occupational subgroups within a major occupational category.

Second, the gender wage gap is not distributed evenly across age groups. At the entry level and the first few years, women lag behind men in average wages, but enjoy more favourable terms after gaining some work experience, only to see the relative reward turn against them again as they progress in the childbearing and parenting stages (Figure 4.13). From 2012 to 2018, women in the 25–34 age group either earn more, or only slightly less, than men. The reversal in the gender wage gap generally starts from the 35–39 age group except for the year 2014 where it starts from the 40–44 age group. Moreover, the gender wage gap tends to worsen for women in all subsequent age groups—the anomalies are only for the 60–64 age group in 2016 and 50–54 age group in 2017. This life cycle pattern in gender wage gap overlaps with the life cycle pattern in women's participation in the labour force. The latter generally peaks at the 25–29 age group before decreasing in all subsequent age groups. Synthetic birth cohort analysis,[7] which accounts for both the life cycle effect of labour participation due to age and family considerations and the cohort effect of varying preferences across age groups and each group's share of the population, provides a framework to assess the net effect. It shows that women do return to the labour force in their mid-30s and early 40s but with a wage penalty (KRI 2018b; Goldin and Mitchell 2017; KRI 2019).[8] However, women's labour participation continues to decline by age group on the whole due to stronger cohort effects.

The gender wage gap by age group only partially captures the distribution of female employment across age groups. One way of

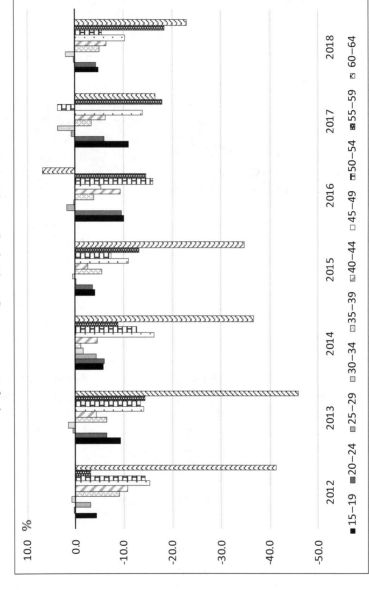

FIGURE 4.13
Employees: Gender Wage Gap, by Age Group, 2012–18

Source: Authors' calculations from DOSM (2012a, 2013b, 2014, 2015b, 2016, 2017b, 2018a).

accounting for this distributional aspect is to construct the wage share gap by life cycle which provides an important indicator of economic power and control.[9] Unlike the wage gap, the wage share gap shows that women lag behind men across age groups. Nonetheless, the wage share gap is still lowest for the 25–29 age group across the years before worsening for all subsequent age groups (Figure 4.14).

This pattern of gender wage gaps reinforces the life cycle narrative that the "turning point" for women happens around the age of 30 which coincides with women's mean age of childbearing[10] (United Nations Population Division 2017). This finding is consistent with existing literature that shows the impact of childbearing and parenting on women's labour force participation, but we have extended this to the remuneration domain (Abdullah et al. 2012; Amin and Rameli 2014; Ismail and Sulaiman 2014). The relatively lesser gender wage share gap among younger cohorts is also consistent with the literature which has found that the returns to education are higher for women while returns to experience and training are higher for men, which perpetuates or compounds the gap for older cohorts (Ismail 2011; Ismail and Jajri 2012; Almeida and Faria 2014).

The "child penalty" that affects the gender wage gap through different routes is undoubtedly intertwined with the "marriage penalty". Labour force statistics by marital status are revealing—the largest gender gap in participation rates is for those in the married group from 2010 to 2018 (Figure 4.15). In the labour force, the number of women in the married group is slightly under two-thirds that of men. In contrast, the number of women who are widowed and divorced is generally double that of men. The same pattern applies to employment numbers, suggesting that marriage, along with childbearing, lower women's participation rate, limit upward advancement especially to managerial positions, thus perpetuating or even exacerbating gender wage gaps. The higher number of women who are widowed and divorced in the labour force could reflect women's higher life expectancy, men's higher likelihood of remarrying, as well as the disproportionate burden that falls on women to support the family after being divorced (Ismail and Poo 2012).

Third, supplementary evidence points to possible increased precarity and vulnerability in the type of jobs for women, raising questions on the quality and sustainability of gender wage convergence. While the expansion of tertiary sector has created more demand for female workers, part of the growth is driven by the rise of new technologies and business models,

FIGURE 4.14
Wage Share Gap, by Age Group, 2012–18

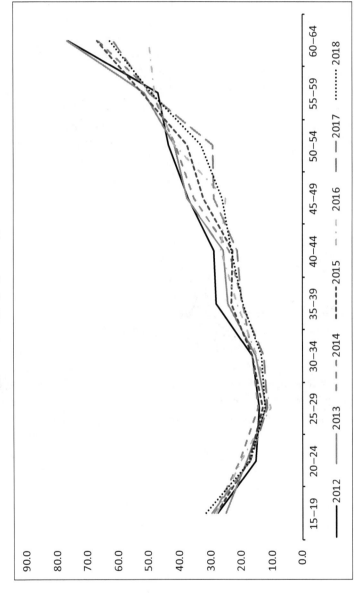

Source: Authors' calculations from DOSM (2012a, 2013b, 2014, 2015b, 2016, 2017b, 2018a).

FIGURE 4.15
Labour Force and Participation Gap, by Marital Status, 2018

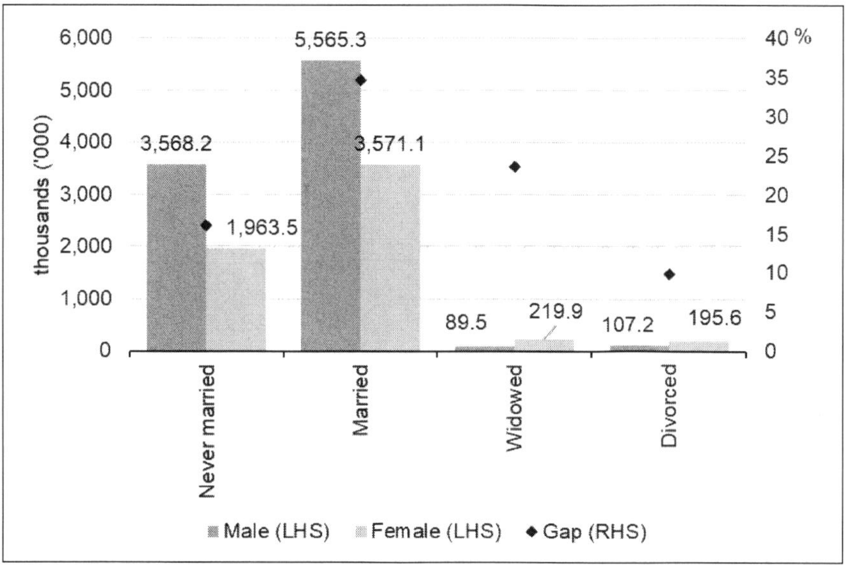

Source: Authors' calculations from DOSM (2018b)

e.g., e-commerce, sharing economy and digital freelancing (KRI 2018a), or what is popularly called the gig economy. Although this has created new opportunities for women who may find these jobs more appealing to cope with both market work and unpaid care work, it has raised pivotal questions on social protection and decent work environment for women. Between 2010 and 2017, women contributed 74.9 per cent of the increase in overall own account workers, a proxy for work insecurity (KRI 2018b). The share of own account workers in total female employment remained relatively stable at between 12.2 and 15.3 per cent from 1998 to 2013, but shot up to 19.5 per cent in 2018.

The rise of female own account workers raises questions on job security, and whether the wage increase comes at the expense of omitted employers' compensation in the form of mandatory old-age savings and social security contributions. However, salaries and wages survey data, from this we estimate wage inequality, exclude own account workers. Nonetheless, women as a proportion of total employees recently fell back

FIGURE 4.16
Share of Employment, by Employment Status, 1998, 2003, 2008, 2013, 2018

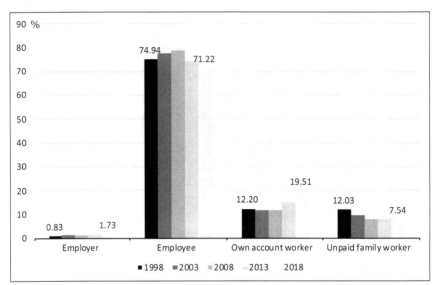

Source: Authors' calculations from DOSM (2012c and 2018b).

to levels of two decades past after a stable period (Figure 4.16). After sustaining at around or above 77 per cent across 2003–12, the women's share dropped to 74.6 per cent in 2013 and 71.2 per cent in 2018, below the 74.9 per cent recorded in 1998. This shift is consistent with a broader trend towards more vulnerable and insecure forms of employment, which reinforces the limitation of using the aggregate gender wage gap to assess gender inequality.

CONCLUSION

Inequality continues to be a top policy priority in Malaysia, and a timely and important subject of inquiry. That inequality has declined is plausible, but questions persist on the country's spectacular official record of the past decade and a half. This chapter unpacked some internal inconsistencies in the official statistical series, alongside the lack of explanation for such a magnitude of change. The series, based on gross household income, departs considerably from other data sources that suggest moderate change in inequality of earnings—the predominant component of household income—which are also arguably more consistent with structural developments in the economy and labour market. Expanding the empirical scope beyond highly aggregated averages, we find that magnitudes and trends of interethnic disparity vary by income bracket, and between urban and rural areas. Empirical analysis and policy discourse on this paramount issue of inequality should be grounded in a firmer, broader and deeper grasp of the situation, particularly for redressing national inequality and uplifting the B40, which have been emphasized for the past decade.

A clarion call emanating from this chapter concerns the need to probe inequality in Malaysia more systematically and rigorously, and to prompt policy attention to earnings distribution—across all the designated priority areas of ethnic, regional and national inequality (Lee 2017). Malaysia's commitment to redressing gender inequality is necessary and timely, but it is also imperative to focus more on labour market dynamics and the gender wage gap, in the context of changing economic structure, expanding education and skills development, and newly emergent forms of employment. Our analysis has also underscored the importance of life cycle dynamics in shaping gender gaps in labour market outcomes. This chapter has offered some insights, but also, and perhaps more importantly, highlighted various under-researched areas that require further academic study and policy discourse.

APPENDIX

APPENDIX FIGURE A4.1
Gini Coefficient of Gross Household Income, by State, Lowest to Highest Average Income (2012 → 2014 → 2016 → 2019)

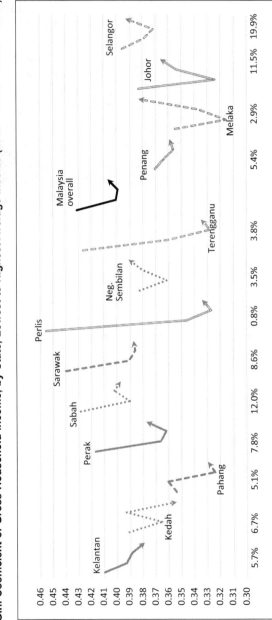

Source: Ministry of Economic Affairs (2019) and DOSM (2017a, 2019).

Inequality and Exclusion in Malaysia

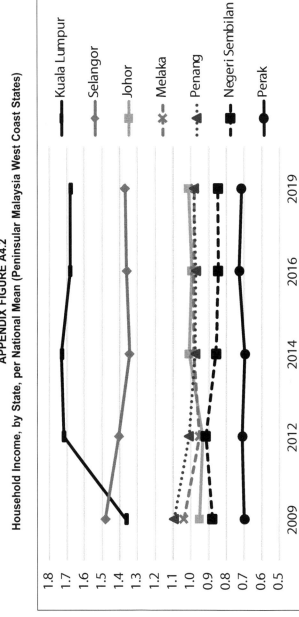

APPENDIX FIGURE A4.2
Household Income, by State, per National Mean (Peninsular Malaysia West Coast States)

Source: Authors calculations from Malaysia (2010) and DOSM (2017a).

APPENDIX FIGURE A4.3
Household Income, by State, per National Mean (Peninsular Malaysia Northern and East Coast States, East Malaysia)

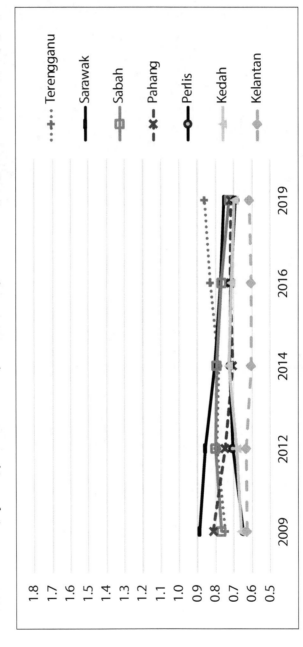

Source: Authors calculations from Malaysia (2010) and DOSM (2017a).

Notes

1. The authors thank participants at the ISEAS – Yusof Ishak Institute workshop on inequality and exclusion in Southeast Asia, 29 March 2019, and its follow-up conference on 25 July 2019, for helpful feedback, and gratefully acknowledge comments and suggestions from Francis Hutchinson, Cassey Lee, Hawati Abdul Hamid and Tan Theng Theng. The usual disclaimer applies.
2. The direction and magnitude of change in Gini coefficients differ across states in other intervals as well, but the variance is much greater in the 2012–16 interval.
3. The coefficient of variation of average household income of Malaysia's thirteen states rises slightly, then holds steady:

2009	2012	2014	2016
0.289	0.326	0.330	0.320

   Authors' calculations from MEA data.
4. Calculation of Gini coefficients based on different income components reveals some interesting patterns. Calculations using the 2014 HIS data reports 0.403 for gross household income, but a surprisingly higher figure of 0.417 for money income (gross income minus imputed rent and other in-kind income). This suggests, counterintuitively, that inclusion of imputed rent and in-kind sources (such as agriculture for own consumption) augments the income of lower income households by a greater margin, compared to higher income households. This is surprising; we would expect the imputed rent of higher income households in owner-occupied homes to be exponentially higher than that of lower income households. It is not conclusive whether there is overcounting of these non-money income sources, or if imputed rent was counted more vigorously in 2014, when the precipitous drop in inequality was recorded. Nonetheless, it is possible that these notional sources have contributed to the implausible downtrend.
5. This categorization follows the Malaysia Standard Classification of Occupations 2008.
6. The 2017 data only includes citizens, hence only citizens data are used for all prior years to maintain consistency.
7. The labour force participation curve provides a snapshot in a particular year for individuals in different age groups but should not be interpreted as individuals moving through the life cycle. To assess participation in different stages of life for similar individuals, we construct synthetic birth cohorts by following individuals in different age groups using multiple labor force surveys. They are "synthetic" because the data is not panel.

8. See Goldin and Mitchell (2017) for further explanation on synthetic birth cohort analysis.
9. The wage share gap is calculated as the difference between women's wage share and men's wage share.
10. The mean age of childbearing is based on the age schedule of age-specific birth rates. It is calculated by taking the sum of age-specific fertility rates weighted by the mid-point of each age group, divided by the sum of the age-specific rates.

References

Abdullah, Norehan, Rahmah Ismail, Zulridah Mohd Noor, and Fariza Ahmad. 2012. "Probability of Working among Married Woman in Malaysia". *Jurnal Ekonomi Malaysia* 46, no. 1: 107–17.

ADB. 2012. *Asian Development Outlook 2012: Confronting Rising Inequality in Asia*. Manila: Asian Development Bank.

Almeida, Rita K., and Marta Faria. 2014. "The Wage Returns to On-The-Job Training: Evidence from Matched Employer-Employee Data". *IZA Journal of Labor and Development* 3, no. 1: 1–33.

Amin, Suhaida Mohd, and Mohd Faizal P. Rameli. 2014. "Fenomena Kekurangan Tenaga Kerja Wanita Berpendidikan dan Berkemahiran di Malaysia". The 9th Malaysian National Economic Conference (PERKEM), Bangi, Universiti Kebangsaan Malaysia (UKM).

Ariff, Muhammed. 2008. "Comment on 'Income Inequality in Malaysia'". *Asian Economic Policy Review* 3, no. 1: 133–34.

Atkinson, Anthony B., Thomas Piketty, and Emmanuel Saez. 2011. "Top Incomes in the Long Run of History". *Journal of Economic Literature* 49, no. 1: 3–71.

Bhattacharjee, Rash Behari, and Samantha Ho. 2017. "Cover Story: The Growing Wealth Gap—A Fate We Can't Afford". *The Edge Malaysia Weekly*, 6 November 2017. https://www.theedgemarkets.com/article/cover-story-growing-wealth-gap-fate-we-cant-afford (accessed 1 August 2019).

Choong, Christopher, and Adam Firouz. 2020. *Social Protection and Fiscal Policy in Malaysia*. Kuala Lumpur: Khazanah Research Institute.

DOSM (Department of Statistics Malaysia). 2012a. *Salaries and Wages Survey Report, Malaysia*. Putrajaya: Department of Statistics Malaysia.

———. 2012b. *The Informal Sector Work Force Survey Report, Malaysia*. Putrajaya: Department of Statistics Malaysia.

———. 2012c. *The Labour Force Survey Report, Malaysia*. Putrajaya: Department of Statistics Malaysia.

———. 2013a. *Household Income and Basic Amenities Survey Report 2012*. Putrajaya: Department of Statistics Malaysia.

———. 2013b. *Salaries and Wages Survey Report, Malaysia.* Putrajaya: Department of Statistics Malaysia.
———. 2013c. *The Informal Sector Work Force Survey Report, Malaysia.* Putrajaya: Department of Statistics Malaysia.
———. 2014. *Salaries and Wages Survey Report, Malaysia.* Putrajaya: Department of Statistics Malaysia.
———. 2015a. *Household Income and Basic Amenities Survey Report 2014.* Putrajaya: Department of Statistics Malaysia.
———. 2015b. *Salaries and Wages Survey Report, Malaysia.* Putrajaya: Department of Statistics Malaysia.
———. 2015c. *The Informal Sector Work Force Survey Report, Malaysia.* Putrajaya: Department of Statistics Malaysia.
———. 2016. *Salaries and Wages Survey Report, Malaysia.* Putrajaya: Department of Statistics Malaysia.
———. 2017a. *Household Income and Basic Amenities Survey Report 2016.* Putrajaya: Department of Statistics Malaysia.
———. 2017b. *Salaries and Wages Survey Report, Malaysia.* Putrajaya: Department of Statistics Malaysia.
———. 2017c. *The Informal Sector Work Force Survey Report, Malaysia.* Putrajaya: Department of Statistics Malaysia.
———. 2017d. *The Labour Force Survey Report, Malaysia.* Putrajaya: Department of Statistics Malaysia.
———. 2018a. *Salaries and Wages Survey Report, Malaysia.* Putrajaya: Department of Statistics Malaysia.
———. 2018b. *The Labour Force Survey Report, Malaysia.* Putrajaya: Department of Statistics Malaysia.
———. 2019. *Labour Force Survey Time Series Statistics by State, 1982–2018.* Putrajaya: Department of Statistics Malaysia.
———. 2020. *Household Income and Basic Amenities Survey 2019 Report.* Putrajaya: Department of Statistics Malaysia.
EPF (Employees Provident Fund). 2015. *Annual Report 2015.* Kuala Lumpur: Employees Provident Fund.
———. 2016. *Annual Report 2016.* Kuala Lumpur: Employees Provident Fund.
———. 2017. *Annual Report 2017.* Kuala Lumpur: Employees Provident Fund.
———. 2018. *Annual Report 2018.* Kuala Lumpur: Employees Provident Fund.
Franck, Anja K. 2012a. "Factors Motivating Women's Informal Micro-Entrepreneurship". *International Journal of Gender and Entrepreneurship* 4, no. 1: 65–78.
———. 2012b. *From Formal Employment to Street Vending: Women's Room to Maneuver and Labor Market Decisions Under Conditions of Export-Orientation.* Gothenburg: University of Gothenburg.

Goldin, Claudia, and Joshua Mitchell. 2017. "The New Life Cycle of Women's Employment: Disappearing Humps, Sagging Middles, Expanding Tops". *Journal of Economic Perspectives* 31, no. 1: 161–82.

Hutchinson, Francis E. 2017. "Evolving Paradigms in Malaysia's Regional Development Policy". *Journal of Southeast Asian Economies* 34, no. 3: 462–87.

Institute of Labour Market Information and Analysis (ILMIA). 2018. *National Employment Returns (NER), 2018*. Putrajaya: Ministry of Human Resources.

Ismail, Rahmah. 2011. "Gender Wage Differentials in the Malaysian Services Sector". *African Journal of Business Management* 5, no. 19: 7781–89.

——, and Poo Bee Tin. 2012. "Globalisation and Labour Supply of Single Female Heads of Households in Malaysia". *Life Science Journal* 9, no. 4: 2750–59.

——, and Idris Jajri. 2012. "Gender Wage Differentials and Discrimination in Malaysian Labour Market". *World Applied Sciences Journal* 19, no. 5: 719–28.

——, and Noorasiah Sulaiman. 2013. "Married Women Labor Supply Decision in Malaysia". *Asian Social Science* 10, no. 3: 221–31.

——, Hazrul Izuan Sahri, and Ferayuliani Yuliyusman. 2015. "Occupational Selectivity Bias and Gender Wage Gap in Malaysian Manufacturing Sector". *Economic Annals-XXI* 3–4, no. 1: 109–12.

Kanbur, Ravi, Changyong Rhee, and Juzhong Zhuang. 2014. *Inequality in Asia and the Pacific: Trends, Drivers, and Policy Implications*. Abingdon: Routledge.

Khalid, Muhammed Abdul. 2014. *The Colour of Inequality: Ethnicity, Class, Income and Wealth in Malaysia*. Petaling Jaya: MPH Group.

KRI (Khazanah Research Institute). 2018a. *Balancing Work and Home*. Kuala Lumpur: Khazanah Research Institute.

——. 2018b. *The State of Households 2018: Different Realities*. Kuala Lumpur: Khazanah Research Institute.

——. 2019. *Time to Care: Gender Inequality, Unpaid Care Work and Time Use Survey*. Kuala Lumpur: Khazanah Research Institute.

Lee, Hwok-Aun. 2016. "Affirmative Action Regime Formation in Malaysia and South Africa". *Journal of Asian and African Studies* 51, no. 5: 511–27.

——. 2017. "Labour Policies and Institutions in the Eleventh Malaysia Plan: Aiming High, Falling Short". *Journal of Southeast Asian Economies* 34, no. 3: 552–70.

——. 2021. *Affirmative Action in Malaysia and South Africa: Preference for Parity*. London and New York: Routledge.

—— and Muhammed Abdul Khalid. 2018. "Is Inequality Really Declining in Malaysia?". *Journal of Contemporary Asia* 50, no. 1: 14–35.

Malaysia. 2006. *The Ninth Malaysia Plan, 2006–2010*. Kuala Lumpur: Government of Malaysia.

——. 2010. *The Tenth Malaysia Plan, 2011–2015*. Kuala Lumpur: Government of Malaysia.

———. 2015. *The Eleventh Malaysia Plan, 2016–2020*. Kuala Lumpur: Government of Malaysia.

———. 2018. *Mid-Term Review of the Eleventh Malaysia Plan, 2016–2020*. Kuala Lumpur: Government of Malaysia.

Mat Zin, Ragayah. 2008. "Income Inequality in Malaysia". *Asian Economic Policy Review* 3, no. 1: 114–32.

Milanovic, Branko. 2006. "Inequality and Determinants of Earnings in Malaysia, 1984–97". *Asian Economic Journal* 20, no. 2: 191–216.

Ministry of Economic Affairs. 2019. *Income and Household Poverty*. http://www.mea.gov.my/ms/sosio-ekonomi/pendapatan-kemiskinan-isi-rumah (accessed 19 March 2019).

MOF (Ministry of Finance). 2017. *Economic Report 2016/2017*. Putrajaya: Ministry of Finance.

———. 2018. *Budget 2019*. Putrajaya: Ministry of Finance.

MOHE (Ministry of Higher Education). 2011. *Perangkaan Pengajian Tinggi Malaysia*. Putrajaya: Ministry of Higher Education.

———. 2017a. *Statistik Pendidikan Tinggi—Chapter 2: Public Universities*. Putrajaya: Ministry of Higher Education.

———. 2017b. *Statistik Pendidikan Tinggi—Chapter 3: Private Higher Education Institutions*. Putrajaya: Ministry of Higher Education.

———. 2018a. *Statistik Pendidikan Tinggi—Chapter 2: Public Universities*. Putrajaya: Ministry of Higher Education.

———. 2018b. *Statistik Pendidikan Tinggi-Chapter 3: Private Higher Education Institutions*. Putrajaya: Ministry of Higher Education.

MWFCD (Ministry of Women, Family and Community Development). 2015. *Statistics on Women, Family and Community*. Putrajaya: Ministry of Women, Family and Community Development.

NEAC (National Economic Advisory Council). 2010. *The New Economic Model—Part 1*. Putrajaya: National Economic Advisory Council.

Oxfam. 2017. *An Economy for the 99%*. Oxfam Briefing Paper, January 2017 https://www.oxfam.org/sites/www.oxfam.org/files/file_attachments/bp-economy-for-99-percent-160117-en.pdf (accessed 22 October 1999).

Pew Research Center. 2013. *Economies of Emerging Markets Better Rated During Difficult Times: Global Downturn Takes Heavy Toll; Inequality Seen as Rising*. 23 May 2013. http://www.pewglobal.org/files/2013/05/Pew-Global-Attitudes-Economic-Report-FINAL-May-23-20131.pdf (accessed 21 June 2014).

Piketty, Thomas. 2014. *Capital in the Twenty-first Century*. Cambridge: Harvard University Press.

Ravallion, Martin. 2020. "Ethnic Inequality and Poverty in Malaysia since May 1969. Part 1: Inequality". *World Development* 134: 0305–750X (available online 7 July 2020, https://doi.org/10.1016/j.worlddev.2020.105040).

Seshan, Ganesh K. 2013. "Public-Private-Sector Employment Decisions and Wage Differentials in Peninsular Malaysia". *Emerging Markets Finance and Trade* 49, no. 5: 163–79.

Shari, Ishak. 2000. "Economic Growth and Income Inequality in Malaysia, 1971–95". *Journal of the Asia-Pacific Economy* 5, no. 1–2: 112–24.

Tan, Peck-Leong, and Geetha Subramaniam. 2013. "Perception of Undergraduates towards Female Labour Force Participation". *Procedia: Social and Behavioral Sciences* 105: 383–90.

———, Muhammad Adidinizar Bin Zia Ahmad Kusairee, and Norlida Abdul Hamid. 2015. "Tertiary Educated Muslim Women's Work Decision". *Journal of Emerging Economies and Islamic Research* 3, no. 2: 1–10.

Tansel, Aysit. 2001. "Economic Development and Female Labor Force Participation in Turkey: Time-Series Evidence and Cross-Province Estimates". ERC Working Papers 0105. Economic Research Center, Middle East Technical University, May 2001.

UNDP (United Nations Development Programme). 2014. *Malaysia Human Development Report 2013*. Kuala Lumpur: United Nations Development Programme.

United Nations Population Division. 2017. "Female Mean Age of Childbearing (years)" World Population Prospects: The 2017 Revision. United Nations, Department of Economic and Social Affairs, 2017. http://data.un.org/Data.aspx?d=PopDiv&f=variableID%3A195 (accessed 29 July 2019).

World Bank. 2014. *Malaysia Economic Monitor December 2014: Middle Class Society*. Washington, DC: World Bank.

———. 2019. *Malaysia Economic Monitor December 2019: Making Ends Meet*. Washington, DC: World Bank.

Yusof, Aminah M., Rose Alinda Alias, and Hadina Habil. 2012. "Stereotyping in Graduate Education: An Insight of Women's Participation in Malaysia". *Journal of e-Learning and Higher Education* 1–9. https://doi.org/10.5171/2012.624177

5

INEQUALITY IN MYANMAR
Structural Change, Policy Outcomes and Gender Dimensions

Ngu Wah Win, Zaw Oo, Jana Rue Glutting, Aung Htun and S. Kanayde

INTRODUCTION

Over the past decade, Myanmar has been undertaking political and economic reforms to reintegrate itself to regional and international economic communities. After years of self-isolation and international sanctions, President U Thein Sein, upon his appointment as the head of state, in his inaugural address on 31 March 2011 openly acknowledged the country's dire situation regarding poverty and unemployment, and initiated an eight-point comprehensive plan for poverty reduction and rural development. U Thein Sein's government introduced and implemented the Framework of Social and Economic Reforms to initiate short-term liberalization and remedy economic isolation of the past while the succeeding government under State Counsellor Daw Aung San Suu Kyi adopted the longer-term Myanmar Sustainable Development Plan. Various efforts at economic and political liberalization since 2011 have boosted foreign investment and private sector involvement in the country, further integrating Myanmar's economy to the ASEAN Economic Community and global markets. These reforms broadly transformed the socialist-oriented state-led economy into a vibrant market economy and generated among the fastest economic growth in the region.[1]

Income inequality is relatively low in Myanmar. Income surveys have been scarce, but the available data generate estimates of relatively lower Gini coefficients than most of its Southeast Asian neighbours. This is not surprising, given its economic structure characterized by agricultural employment and labour-intensive industry; low-income countries around the world similarly tend to register low levels of inequality. In accordance with its developmental needs, Myanmar has focused on poverty and significantly alleviated its incidence, although lack of basic income remains a major challenge. Drawing on multidimensional indicators, we observe substantial inequalities, specifically in health and electrification and in the regional dimension, where disparity between Yangon and other regions persists. Educational attainment and labour participation also impact on inequality, hence we also investigate Myanmar's developments in these areas, where the gender implications are more pronounced. The country's efforts to redress gender imbalance in socio-economic development, from education to employment, have achieved significant progress, reflected in the boost to Myanmar's human development indicators when modified to take into account gender inequality, and in the rapidly growing textiles, clothing and footwear manufacturing sectors that predominantly employ young women. Nonetheless, much remains to be done in promoting gender parity.

What has shaped the emerging trends of inequality in Myanmar? This chapter reviews various aspects of structural changes in the economy since 2011 and analyses how such changes have shaped inequality. Comprehensive policy reforms throughout this period have produced various outcomes, which in turn shaped the equality of access and opportunity such as education, health, nutrition, electricity, and jobs across different social, ethnic and gender groups. These dynamic forces of structural changes and policy outcomes impacted on multiple dimensions of inequality; we will highlight some of their outstanding features. The chapter then focuses on gender, a consequential dimension of distribution in Myanmar, explaining the reasons for the inequality trends and underlying dynamics of male-female gaps.

ECONOMIC REFORM, STRUCTURAL CHANGE AND HUMAN DEVELOPMENT

Unlike its more dynamic neighbours, Myanmar's economy was much less diversified until a decade ago. It remained highly concentrated in the agriculture and natural resources sectors until 2008 when the country was hit with the catastrophic cyclone Nargis that accounted for the loss of over 200,000 lives and US$2 billion worth of damages. The country slowly recovered in the next two years until a new government, instated through the 2010 elections, introduced comprehensive economic reforms in 2011. Structural change to the economy, amid sustained high economic growth, is remarkable (Table 5.1). In the 2000s, the contribution of agriculture to GDP remained close to 50 per cent, while industry comprised well below 20 per cent. However, by 2018, agriculture's share dropped to 25 per cent, and industry's share rapidly rose to 32 per cent, and services grew steadily to 43 per cent. The changing economic structure was significant, given the high share of agriculture sector, accounting for nearly half of GDP and the industry sector accounting for less than 20 per cent of GDP a decade ago.

Like many economies in their early stage of industrialization, Myanmar's emerging industry sector consists of labour-intensive manufacturing and low-technology industries. At this juncture, the country's manufacturing

TABLE 5.1
Growth and Structural Change of Myanmar's Economy

	1980s	1990s	2000s	2007	2012	2017	2018
Real GDP growth							
Agriculture	...	...	8.4	8.6	1.7	1.3	1.3
Industry	...	...	22.6	18.8	8.0	9.4	8.2
Services	...	...	13.4	13.2	12.0	8.3	7.7
Total	1.9	6.1	12.4	12.0	7.3	6.8	6.2
Share in GDP							
Agriculture	50.5	60.1	48.0	43.3	30.6	23.3	24.6
Industry	12.0	9.7	16.8	20.4	32.4	36.3	32.3
Services	37.5	30.3	35.2	36.3	37.0	40.4	43.2
Total	100.0	100.0	100.0	100.0	100.0	100.0	100.0

Source: ADB Key Indicators (various issues).

sector is also dominated by relatively low value-added activities, specifically assembly of the textiles, clothing and footwear (TCF) sector, which employ 57 per cent of the total workforce in the country's twenty industrial zones, followed by leather products and food processing sectors employing 10 per cent and 8 per cent of the workforce, respectively. The industrial zones are also marked by gender imbalance; young migrant female workers constitute 89 per cent of the workforce (Department of Labour 2019). Combined with the workforce outside of the industrial zones, the TCF sector employed 738,000 workers in 2016, equivalent to nearly 50 per cent of formal manufacturing sector employment (ILO 2016). While male workers are employed in the sector, they are often in management positions. Amid the incorporation of Myanmar to the global value chain, this industry is expanding dramatically, and it is projected that the TCF sector may grow to 1.5 million workers in the next five to ten years.

The emergence of labour-intensive TCF manufacturing and its workforce composition translate into some positive outcomes for gender equality, in light of the vast number of jobs for women coupled with lesser wage inequalities between men and women. In 2016, the ILO estimated daily wages for all employees in the TCF sector and found that men tend to earn around 10 per cent more than women. When controlling for other factors such as age, marital status, education, experience, geographic location, subsector, occupation and firm dynamics, women still face a wage gap of nearly 9 per cent. In comparison, the ILO suggested that gender pay disparity is significantly higher in non-TCF industries, where the adjusted earnings of men are around 20 per cent more than for women. Moreover, the male-female earnings gap in Myanmar's TCF sector is comparable to that in Cambodia, the Philippines and Vietnam, and considerably lower than India and Pakistan (ILO 2016). Since the sector is rapidly expanding and economically influential, the positive trends of job generation for women and narrowing wage gaps may serve as important benchmarks for other sectors.

The reforms Myanmar introduced in 2011 not only changed the economic structure of the country but also the ownership of production, as the government slowly transformed state-owned enterprises into corporatized commercial entities or wholly privatized firms. In 2012, the government fully dismantled its control over the exchange rate, privatized transportation, telecommunications and network industries, and reduced import licensing requirements. According to the World Bank, those changes caused real GDP and investment to grow by an annual average of 7.3 per cent and 19.6 per cent respectively between 2010 and 2015. More importantly, during that 5-year span, the number of registered private companies almost doubled, and the number of foreign enterprises permitted under Foreign Investment Law increased 30-fold (World Bank 2018, p. 108).

In 2016, Myanmar was able to go through democratic elections that brought a popular government led by the National League for Democracy (NLD) and party leader Daw Aung San Suu Kyi to the seat of government. While the economy gained momentum from earlier reforms, the government turned its focus to peace building and national reconciliation. The government put energy and resources in organizing a peace process to end deep-rooted conflicts in the country. It also outlined a twelve-point strategy of economic policies; however, the agenda on poverty alleviation was dropped from the list of policy priorities. Major disappointments with the new government emerged since the first-year anniversary of NLD's landslide electoral victory, as high expectations of the public were not met by the slow pace of implementing reforms and poor communication of government policy agenda (Maw 2018).

Myanmar's economy is navigating significant uncertainty and risks at home and abroad. A year after violent upheaval in Rakhine State which led to the forced displacement of over 700,000 refugees to Bangladesh, limited progress has been made in resolving fundamental issues relating to rights, repatriation and recovery. Likewise, there are pockets of instability and armed conflicts in various border areas of the country, causing human displacements and relocations. These conditions of low intensity conflicts and instability have undermined not only economic growth potential but also more equitable generation of economic wealth across various regions of the country.

The 2011 liberalization reforms, coupled with withdrawal of Western sanctions in 2013, provided some boost to economic growth, with real GDP expanding by 8.4 per cent in 2014, 8.0 per cent in 2015 and 7.0 per cent in 2016. However, growth slowed down subsequently, at 5.9 per cent in 2017 and 6.8 per cent in 2018, as the economy lost its initial momentum and experienced reductions in foreign direct investment inflows and export revenues (World Bank 2019). However, structural change proceeds, with the contribution of agriculture to GDP continually shrinking, while the industrial and service sectors have been steadily contributing to the country's growth. It is worth noting that the agriculture sector is by far the largest employer in the country, accounting for around 70 per cent of employment, according to the United Nations Food and Agriculture Organization.

In line with Myanmar's economic record of rapid growth but somewhat uneven gains across different sectors as shown in the Table 5.2, the country's achievements in reducing income poverty and advancing human development have also been substantial—with considerable room for improvement. The human development index (HDI), introduced by the UNDP in 1990, consists of a holistic set of variables such as life longevity, education, and living standards that aim to capture non-income vulnerabilities of poor people. Low levels of development are associated with high levels of poverty and socio-economic disparities, particularly

TABLE 5.2
Myanmar: Share of GDP Contributions by Economic Sectors

Sectors	2005–6	2010–11	2015–16	2016–17	2017–18	2018
Agriculture	50.1	36.9	28.9	27.1	25.8	22.6
Agriculture	40.2	27.9	20.1	18.8	17.7	11.9
Livestock and Fishery	9.5	8.5	8.5	8.2	8.0	10.6
Forestry	0.4	0.4	0.2	0.1	0.1	0.1
Industry	15.3	26.5	30.0	30.9	31.7	29.1
Energy	0.2	0.2	0.2	0.1	0.1	0.3
Mining	0.5	0.8	0.9	1.0	1.0	1.5
Processing and Manufacturing	11.4	19.9	22.1	22.8	23.6	20.7
Electric Power	0.1	1.1	1.3	1.3	1.3	2.0
Construction	3.1	4.6	5.6	5.7	5.6	4.6
Services	34.6	36.7	41.1	41.9	42.6	48.3
Transportation	7.7	11.6	12.6	12.8	12.9	16.4
Communications	0.7	0.8	4.7	4.9	5.1	7.3
Financial Institutions	0.2	0.1	0.4	0.5	0.6	0.9
Social and Admin. Services	1.5	2.3	2.7	2.6	2.6	3.3
Rental and Other Services	1.6	1.9	2.5	2.7	2.8	3.9
Trade	23.0	20.0	18.2	18.4	18.5	16.6

Source: Central Statistical Organization (2019).

in education and health (Coudouel, Hentschel and Wodon 2002; Dollar and Kraay 2002).

When Myanmar's human development is viewed in the context of ASEAN countries, as well as against averages in other developing regions across the world, it becomes clear that there is much room for improvement to reach the 2030 targets. Within ASEAN, Myanmar most closely resembles the much smaller and less naturally endowed countries of Laos and Cambodia, but lags significantly behind Thailand, Malaysia and Vietnam on sustainable development goals (SDG) indicators. Myanmar's poverty rate, estimated at about 25 per cent, exceeds that of its neighbours—based on each country's national poverty lines. Life expectancy is only 66.7 years and the mean years of schooling for adults is only 4.9 years (HDI Statistical Update 2018). On the other hand, Myanmar's performance matches that of other ASEAN nations on some indicators, or modification of indicators that take into account gender parity.

Nonetheless, Myanmar in 2017 was upgraded to the "Medium Human Development" category, ranking 148 globally, in the Human Development Statistical Update Report (2018), a category that includes the majority of the ASEAN member states; namely Cambodia (at 146), Laos (at 139) as well as Vietnam and Indonesia (both at 116) and the Philippines (at 113) (Table 5.3). This upward mobility in the ranking can be attributed to the

TABLE 5.3
Human Development Index (HDI) in Myanmar and Southeast Asia:
Score and Rank, and Gender Inequality Index (GII) Rank, 2017

Country	HDI Score	HDI Ranking	GII Ranking
Singapore	0.932	9	12
Brunei	0.853	39	51
Malaysia	0.802	57	62
Thailand	0.755	83	93
Philippines	0.699	113	97
Indonesia	0.694	116	104
Vietnam	0.694	116	67
Laos	0.601	139	109
Cambodia	0.582	146	116
Myanmar	0.578	148	106

Source: UNDP, Human Development Indices and Indicators: 2018 Statistical Update. New York.

liberalization reform process initiated in 2011, which has paved the way for improvements in living standards.

As HDI measures long-term progress in three basic dimensions of human development—a long and healthy life, access to knowledge and a decent standard of living—Myanmar seemed to be catching up with the rest of the region in all three categories. Table 5.4 reviews Myanmar's progress in each of the HDI indicators. Between 1990 and 2017, Myanmar's life expectancy at birth increased by 8.0 years, mean years of schooling increased by 2.5 years and expected years of schooling increased by 3.9 years. Myanmar's GNI per capita increased by 7.6 per cent annually between 1990 and 2017. In fact, this GNI per capita increase was much faster and higher than many of the Southeast Asian countries, helping Myanmar achieve better income equality than the average of medium HDI countries.

The effects of inequality on human development can be evaluated through a statistical exercise undertaken by UNDP (2019), which derives an Inequality HDI (IHDI) representing the loss of human development due to inequality (Table 5.5). This procedure yields an IHDI of 0.466 for Myanmar, which amounts to an imputed overall loss of 19.4 per cent compared to the HDI of 0.578. Myanmar's HDI loss is comparable to Cambodia's, and midway between the averages of East Asia and Pacific average and of medium HDI countries globally. This exercise is extended to each dimension of the HDI. Interestingly, Myanmar's loss in the income

TABLE 5.4
Myanmar's HDI Trends

	Life Expectancy at Birth	Expected Years of Schooling	Mean Years of Schooling	GNI Per Capita (2011 PPP$)	HDI Value
1990	58.7	6.1	2.4	770	0.358
1995	60.5	7.4	2.7	959	0.398
2000	62.1	7.8	3.1	1,300	0.431
2005	63.6	8.1	3.6	2,264	0.477
2010	65.2	9.2	4.1	3,717	0.530
2015	66.5	9.9	4.9	5,039	0.569
2016	66.6	10.0	4.9	5,282	0.574
2017	66.7	10.0	4.9	5,567	0.578

Source: UNDP (2019).

TABLE 5.5
Myanmar and Selected Countries: Inequality and Human Development Index

	IHDI Value	Overall Loss (%)	Inequality in Life Expectancy at Birth (%)	Inequality in Education (%)	Inequality in Income (%)
Myanmar	0.466	19.4	24.0	26.9	5.8
Cambodia	0.469	19.4	16.0	27.3	14.3
Laos	0.445	26.1	23.1	34.1	20.3
East Asia and the Pacifi	0.619	15.6	10.0	13.1	23.1
Medium HDI Countries	0.483	25.1	20.3	33.1	21.2

Source: UNDP (2019).

dimension is acutely low compared to Laos and Cambodia and the other comparator categories, and the losses in health and education are similar or higher. Specifically, loss of HDI value caused by income inequality was only 5.8 per cent in the case of Myanmar, whereas the average loss in the East Asia and the Pacific was much higher at 23.1 per cent, and Cambodia and Laos at 14.3 per cent and 20.3 per cent respectively (Table 5.5, rightmost column). These findings suggest that inequality in terms of health and education service delivery are causing Myanmar to fall short of its initial human development potential to a greater extent than in other countries. The computations also underscore the importance of evaluating inequality beyond the income dimension.

Another positive aspect of reducing inequality in Myanmar has to do with gender. In general, improvements in HDI over the years benefited both men and women quite evenly. The Gender Development Index (GDI), a ratio of the female to male HDI, is higher in Myanmar than other least developed countries (LDCs) in ASEAN, reflecting a good progress in improving gender equality (Table 5.6). Worldwide, the average HDI value for women (0.705) is 5.9 per cent lower than men (0.749) and much of the gap is due to women's lower income and educational attainment in many countries. The income gap between male and female is much wider in Myanmar, but education is not necessarily the cause as the mean years of schooling for both female and male are almost identical. Compared to other developing countries, households in Myanmar still tend to rely on single income causing persistent male-female wage gap while income inequality across households are declining. Lack of women's empowerment is a critical aspect of gender inequality. While empowerment barriers exist in many forms, it is important to take a closer look at gender inequality particularly in emerging labour markets. As Table 5.6 indicates, women have acquired similar amounts of formal education, but the question is whether women can enter the labour force and participate effectively in newly emerging economic sectors that generate jobs.

The case of Myanmar suggests that approaches to inequality should go beyond income to also consider inequalities in other dimensions that are also important to people's well-being, from health and education to access to public infrastructure and labour market. In fact, the UNDP is currently promoting a more holistic approach to understanding the dynamics of inequality and exclusion, as previous approaches on measures of income such as the Gini coefficient do not provide a comprehensive and timely picture of the state of inequality across countries. The case of Myanmar also suggests that it is important to investigate the causes of income gaps in order to empower women to overcome inequality. In addition, one should also investigate the causes of structural inequality, as rapid economic growth may only improve income but may worsen other attributes of inequality.

Using such a holistic framework, this chapter looks at the structural dimensions of inequality and emerging challenges of labour market transformation, and how these factors may shape different forms of inequality, particularly gender dimensions. In Myanmar, the gap between the rich and poor has been narrowing; however, this positive trend can be less sustainable if its underlying economic structure and emerging labour market do not contribute to reducing other causes of inequality. These "new" inequalities will have long-term consequences, particularly given the rapid technological changes that are already affecting labour markets. Meanwhile, fixing structural barriers takes time and the government may need to address inequality caused by structural conditions.

POVERTY AND INEQUALITY IN MYANMAR: INCOME AND MULTIPLE DIMENSIONS

Income

Different empirical sources report different poverty levels, but all point to a downward trend (Figure 5.1). By the government's account, poverty

TABLE 5.6
Myanmar and Selected Countries: Gender Gaps in HDI Components
(F = female; M = male)

	Life Expectancy at Birth		Expected Years of Schooling		Mean Years of Schooling		GNI Per Capita		HDI Values		F:M Ratio
	F	M	F	M	F	M	F	M	F	M	
Myanmar	69.1	64.4	10.3	9.8	4.9	4.8	3,860	7,355	0.563	0.586	0.959
Cambodia	71.3	67.1	11.2	12.2	3.8	5.6	2,970	3,878	0.553	0.605	0.914
Laos	68.6	65.4	10.9	11.5	4.6	5.7	5,354	6,789	0.579	0.621	0.934
East Asia and the Pacifi	76.7	72.8	13.5	13.2	7.6	8.3	10,689	16,568	0.717	0.750	0.957
Medium HDI Countries	71.1	67.2	12.2	11.8	5.6	7.9	3,673	9,906	0.598	0.680	0.878

Source: UNDP (2019).

FIGURE 5.1
Myanmar: Poverty Incidence under Two Different Methodologies

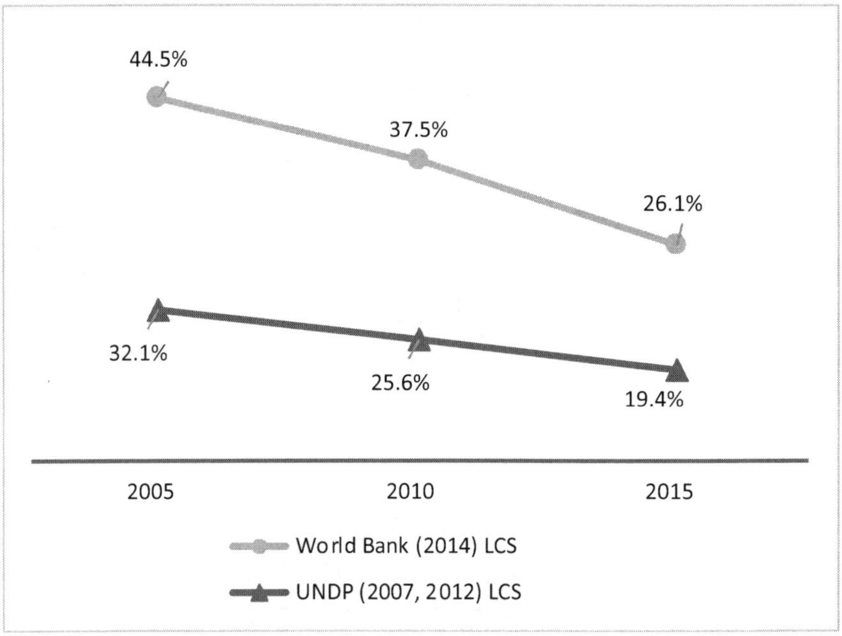

```
44.5%
        37.5%
                26.1%

32.1%
        25.6%
                19.4%

2005    2010    2015

── World Bank (2014) LCS
── UNDP (2007, 2012) LCS
```

Source: World Bank (2015) calculations using the Living Conditions Survey (LCS).

incidence dropped from 48.2 per cent in 2005 to 24.8 per cent in 2017.[2] The World Bank (2017) estimates that income poverty in Myanmar declined from 32.1 per cent in 2004/5 to 25.6 per cent in 2009/10 and further declined to 19.4 per cent in 2015. This series applies a method first proposed by the Government of Myanmar and its development partners in 2007, which is based on living standards from 2004/5 (World Bank 2017). However, in 2015, the World Bank recommended the government to revise the calculation of poverty headcounts using a new method that adjusts for cost of living. According to the new method, Myanmar's headcount poverty declined from 44.0 per cent in 2005 to 26.1 per cent in 2015. Although the new method suggests that Myanmar still experienced high incidence of poverty, the rate of reduction between 2005 and 2015 was quite remarkable at 40 per cent for both methods. On the other hand, one can note that growth in agricultural GDP accounted for only 1 per cent of growth in total GDP for the period 2016–19, suggesting that the reduction of poverty and inequality for 70 per cent of the population who live in rural areas and rely on agriculture income may still experience challenges in terms of catching up with economic growth in urban centres of the country.

On the whole, various reforms undertaken by two governments in the last nine years can be credited for the significant reduction of poverty incidence. However, with one-quarter of the population remaining below the poverty line, Myanmar has a long way to go towards eradicating the problem, which is probably the most serious in Southeast Asia. In Myanmar, poverty incidence is around twice as high in rural than urban areas; rural areas account for almost 85 per cent of total poverty. Myanmar has seven states and seven regions. Ethnic nationality areas where ethnic minorities dominate the population are designated as "states". The term "regions" refers to areas with majority Burman residents. Although poverty incidences are high in ethnic nationality areas such as Chin, Rakhine and Shan states, two central regions account for the highest absolute numbers of those in poverty—Ayeyarwady (19 per cent) and Mandalay (15 per cent) due to their large populations.

Inequality in Myanmar remains at levels comparable to or below those of neighbouring countries such as other LDCs. However, lower inequality may also reflect an LDC-type situation in which a majority of individuals are earning similar incomes, and large numbers are living under or near the poverty line. In other words, a large segment of the population can be equally poor and hence concerned governments should take a more nuanced view on inequality. Indeed, the relatively moderate inequality figures presented in Table 5.7 for Myanmar need to be considered in the broader context of the level of economic development and economic structure, particularly urban and rural differences. Myanmar's demographic profile remains predominantly rural, where 70 per cent of the population resides. Only 30 per cent of the population live in urban areas, where new economic opportunities concentrate and attract migrants to such hubs. These growth centres present higher income and expenditure inequalities, as captured in higher Gini as well as inequality indices of urban areas compared to rural areas shown in Table 5.7 (Thein and Akita 2019). To some extent, these urban income disparities account for most of the total inequality, and such inequality dynamics observed in Myanmar, along the lines of the Kuznets Curve, are similar to other regional countries (World Bank 2017).

TABLE 5.7
Indicators of Inequality in Myanmar, 2015

	National	Urban	Rural
Gini	30.03	31.82	26.34
Theil-0	14.84	16.59	11.52
Theil-1	17.48	32.3	13.43
Bottom 20% share of national income	9.09	8.55	9.93
[a]Ratio of 90th/10th	6.47	7.25	5.24

Note: a. The income earned by individuals at the 90th percentile (those earning more than 90 percent of other workers) compared to the income of individuals at the 10th percentile (those earning higher than the bottom 10 percent).
Source: World Bank (2017).

The economic liberalization reform process that began in 2011 created many jobs, particularly in FDI-based manufacturing operations, and allowed the country to tap into its demographic dividend. However, rapid economic transition since 2011 may have benefited richer households more than low-income households. The available income data suggests that the welfare of the poorest 10 per cent has not changed as markedly as the average household in the country. The relatively moderate levels of inequality in Myanmar also reflect higher concentrations of households with low levels of expenditure, i.e., most individuals live in poverty or near the poverty line. There are some households at the top end of the distribution who show markedly different consumption patterns, in particular their expenditure on higher-value durables. These households live in urban areas, which combined with the large inflow of migrants to such areas explain the high Gini coefficient within urban areas and overall enlarged urban-rural inequality.

It is widely acknowledged that various Southeast Asian countries have been achieving impressive growth rates and received acclaimed attention for poverty reduction efforts associated with robust economic performance in the region, to the extent that it is often assumed that the faster the growth, the more rapid the decline in poverty. However, as Amartya Sen stressed, poverty must be considered as multidimensional (Sen 1980; Alkire and Santos 2010), and should not be equated with higher income alone. Concomitantly, the absence of income poverty does not guarantee the absence of other forms of poverty, such as health, education, personal safety and nutrition.

In the regional context, looking into the multidimensional aspect of poverty, recent studies have found significant regional differences between members (McGillivray, Feeny and Iamsiraroj 2013; Sumarto and Moselle 2015). Moreover, the overall experience of these countries has been of declining income-poverty incidences but increasing non-income inequalities. Such puzzles are driven by weak correlation between income level and human welfare indicators, in particular health and education, signalling the government's inability to translate economic growth into the reduction of multi-dimensional poverty (Yap 2014). The factors facilitating inclusiveness in economic gains are the sectoral composition of a country's growth rates, depth and typology of public investments and public service deliveries, and the quality of governance (McGillivray, Feeny and Iamsiraroj 2013).

Food, Nutrition and Stunting

Access and availability of food system in developing countries are also closely related to the dynamics of inequality. Even if enough food exists in absolute terms to feed the whole population, one cannot assume that it is distributed equally across the country. Access to food at the household level can be different from one household to another, depending on socioeconomic factors that determine the ability of households to either produce their own food or earn enough income to purchase food. Food access also depends on the price of food and its volatility over time, relative to household income. Many developing countries such as Myanmar produce food and even export surplus food products; however, one cannot assume that its whole population has equal access to food.

In Myanmar, the national average incidence of food poverty suggests that access to food varies from region to region. Eleven of the states/regions experience less than half the national food poverty incidence in terms of daily caloric intake. Among them, Chin State experiences two-and-a-half times that of national average, where the residents of Chin State face challenging situations of food security. Two successive rounds of the Integrated Household Living Conditions (IHLCA) surveys undertaken in 2005 and 2009 provided some estimates of the incidence and distribution of food poverty in Myanmar. Recently, newer data such as the prevalence of stunting is available under various health surveys, which serves as indicators of access to food and incidence of food poverty.

In developing countries, the prevalence of stunting is used as a proxy for structural absence of nutrition opportunities for at-risk socio-economic groups or marginalized minorities (Krishna et al. 2018). It has been found that stunting directly influences school attendance rates and future earning potential, further exacerbating existing inequality and widening income and non-income poverty measures (Bloem et al. 2013). Stunting, as the possible outcome of unequal access to nutrition, can be an important issue for food-producing and food-surplus economies such as Myanmar, which produce staples, such as rice, pulses and corn, and export all these commodities to neighbouring economies.

Even though Myanmar is an agriculture-surplus economy with sufficient food availability at the national level, uneven distribution of resources and low investments in diverse agriculture production systems impact on household food security. Myanmar has diverse agro-climatic conditions across the country while staple food such as rice could be grown only in certain regions with good supply of water or rain. Although most regions try to adapt cultivation of various food crops suitable to their own ecological conditions, there are constraints and vulnerabilities in the availability of food, with appropriate quality, supplied through distribution networks within each region.

Myanmar has made progress in promoting food and nutrition security in the past few years, but there are still significant gaps. A few regions, particularly the hilly areas, still face physical and economic hurdles in accessing sufficient, safe and healthy food that meets their dietary and nutritional needs. Under the Myanmar Sustainable Development Plan, it is a key objective of the government of Myanmar to eliminate hunger in the country and ensure that all people in all states and regions have access to sufficient nutritious food to sustain their health, support their work and allow their children to develop their full cognitive and physical potential by 2030.

Another major challenge is food stability in regions that are vulnerable to climate change conditions. Many regions in Myanmar are still not ready to cope with sudden shocks either from economic or climatic crisis as they do not have proper storage systems or alternative logistic infrastructure. More importantly, even the food-surplus regions experience seasonal food insecurity as most regions in the country can grow crops mostly in rainy season. In this regard, many regions in the country experienced various manifestations of food insecurity and instability.

One of such manifestations is stunting, which is a proxy for chronic undernutrition, and overall degree of poverty in the area. According to the 2015–16 Myanmar Demographic and Health Survey conducted by the Ministry of Health and Sports (MOHS 2017), 29 per cent of children under five are stunted, or too short for their age. As Table 5.8 illustrates, stunting is relatively high in Chin, Kayah and Rakhine states, and Ayeyarwady region, which are also the poorest states and regions of Myanmar. High prevalence of stunting in the Ayeyarwady region, a major region of food production known as the "rice bowl" of the country, is a reminder of the vulnerability of the population across the country in terms of food security and stability.

Different access to food between rural and urban regions also continues to exacerbate the inequality between them. Although agriculture is the dominant share of economic activities for the rural population, food poverty in rural areas is much higher than urban areas. This is because of the difference in food availability and economic access to food. In

TABLE 5.8
Myanmar: Stunting Rates in States and Regions, 2015–16

States	Stunting Rates (%)
Chin	41.0
Kayah	39.7
Rakhine	37.5
Shan	36.5
Kachin	36.1
Mon	28.1
Kayin	25.4
Regions	*Stunting Rates (%)*
Ayeyarwady	37.2
Sagaing	26.7
Mandalay	26.1
Magway	25.9
Tanintharyi	25.6
Bago	23.0
Nay Pyi Taw	22.0
Yangon	20.3
National average	25.8

Source: MOHS (2017)

addition, rural areas in Myanmar are also more vulnerable to natural disasters, such as cyclones, landslides, earthquakes and droughts, that not only disrupt food production, but also stability of food stocks in rural areas (WFP 2017).

Public Infrastructure: Electrificatio

Access to energy has recently taken a prominent place in the Sustainable Development Goals (SDG) of the Agenda 2030. SDG number 7 is "to ensure access to affordable, reliable, sustainable, modern energy for all by 2030". While electrification does not guarantee poverty eradication, it can enable pro-poor growth. Conversely, various studies have found a negative impact of the lack of access to electricity on health, improved air quality (Barron and Torero 2017) and improved children's nutrition (Fujii, Shonchoy, and Xu 2018). Other studies have found similar negative impact of poor electrification on the educational attainment of young children, particularly girls' education (Khandker et al. 2009; Utama et al. 2011).

Thus, unequal electrification rates not only exacerbate persisting spatial inequalities, they can compound non-income-related inequalities. Among the ASEAN members, Myanmar is the country with the lowest electricity penetration in the region, according to the ASEAN Centre for Energy (Gnanasagaran 2018). In Myanmar, inequality within the country in access to electricity is stark. The countrywide electrification rate is 36.1 per cent, but there is substantial variation: Yangon has an electrification rate of almost 78 per cent, while Rakhine State has the lowest average of 6 per cent (MOEEP 2011).[3] Diesel-powered generators are used despite being a high-cost alternative. In addition, most rural households rely on burning biomass to cover their energy needs (Dobermann 2016) and their ability to utilize energy is diminishing with rapid rate of deforestation.

Regional inequality in terms of access to electricity is extreme, particularly heightened in Chin, Kayin, Ayeyarwady, Tanintharyi and Rakhine states (Table 5.9). The Ministry of Energy and Electricity Power (MOEEP) estimates of the expansion of electrification coverage also show a protracted time frame in addressing the coverage gap. While the government has vouched to prioritize rural areas further away from the national grid line, the indicative plans show that the government is prioritizing further electrification of urban areas within the regions.[4]

TABLE 5.9
Myanmar: Electrification Rates Across State and Region

Region	Total Number of Households	Households Electrified up to September 2017 — Number of Households	Households Electrified up to September 2017 — Percentage of Total
Kachin	269,365	130,926	48.4
Kayah	57,274	44,283	77.3
Kayin	308,041	63,320	20.6
Chin	91,121	19,483	21.4
Mon	422,612	194,432	46.0
Rakhine	459,772	74,408	16.2
Shan	1,169,569	347,317	29.7
Nay Pyi Taw	262,253	135,183	51.6
Sagaing	1,096,857	356,639	32.5
Bago	1,142,974	413,447	36.2
Magway	919,777	230,024	25.0
Ayeyarwady	1,488,983	239,276	16.1
Tanintharyi	283,099	29,161	10.3
Yangon	1,582,944	1,285,580	81.2
Mandalay	1,323,191	687,985	52.0
Total	10,877,832	4,250,834	39.1

Source: MOEE (2018).

Unequal access to electricity has a major impact on the rate of socio-economic development in various regions in Myanmar, particularly in educational progress, healthcare provision, and household livelihoods in general. Children of electrified households may have better chance to attain higher education. Lack of access to electricity can have many negative consequences for women who are responsible for household chores, where women in non-electrified areas have to spend significant amount of time for finding fuelwood while suffering from polluted air during long hours of cooking. Within the electrified regions of the country, urban areas usually obtain access to electricity earlier and faster than rural areas. This is evident even in the metropolitan Yangon city area, where rural and satellite towns near the city are not yet electrified, suggesting that access to electricity can worsen the inequality among the communities living in the same region.

INEQUALITIES IN EDUCATION AND EMPLOYMENT

Higher Education

National cohesion, and inclusive education, at all levels, including higher education, is both an opportunity and a challenge for many developing countries. The national educational policies of Asian and Southeast Asian nations support the view that inclusive higher education is justified on both productive and equity grounds. As observed by the ADB (2012, p. 1), "Any higher education system that fails to cultivate the breadth of talent in society—men and women, rural and urban, rich and poor—is sacrificing both quality and efficiency." Further evidence also suggests that the risks of failing to pursue inclusive education policies can result in lower growth and higher inequalities; and rising absolute income and consumption gaps between the richest and poorest quintiles could trigger social and economic tensions and, in extreme forms, armed conflict (Ali and Zhuang 2007).

In many developing countries, greater inequality can be found in secondary and tertiary education, as educational investment decisions are driven by the increasing skills premium and returns on human capital (Yap 2014). With greater economic and market liberalization, individuals with higher educational attainment and skill endowment are able to benefit more, further exacerbating income and opportunity inequalities (Buasuwan and Suebnusorn 2016). Buasuwan and Suebnusorn (2016) find that, although there is a declining trend of tertiary educational inequality among East Asian countries, Myanmar and Cambodia are the regional laggards when it comes to access to higher education. Among Southeast Asian countries, gender disparity with regards to access to tertiary education, including Myanmar, appears to favour women, with the notable exception of Cambodia.

One of the urgent problems of any modern society is the accessibility and quality of higher education for various population groups. The vast disparities in college attendance and graduation rates between students in different parts of Myanmar has been a decades-long concern for the authorities. The previous military government set up several higher education institutions (HEIs) in regions that previously did have colleges and universities. In the government's view, higher education was the solution to inequality, but the impact of broadened access to higher education remains to be seen.

HEIs are predominantly located in the two main urban areas, Yangon and Mandalay (Table 5.10). Successive governments have justified this concentration because the cities also important economic growth poles. Regional population is another factor in education investment. However, the distribution of HEIs in the regions beyond the major cities does not clearly correspond with demographic or socio-economic factors. Indeed, certain areas such as Ayeyarwady region and Rakhine and Mon states have disproportionately fewer numbers of HEIs similar to regions and states that have even fewer population.

Labour Market Structures

The structure of the labour market has a significant impact on household income and welfare. As Myanmar embraced foreign direct investment in the manufacturing and industry sector, there was a major shift in labour force from agriculture to manufacturing and service sectors. The structure of the labour market, as a main source of disposable income, and the quantity

TABLE 5.10
Myanmar: Relative Distribution of Higher Education Institutions (HEIs) per capita (per cent)

	No. of HEIs (% of Total)	Population (% of Total)	Ratio of % (HEI per Population)
Ayeyarwady	7	12.0	0.58
Kachin	5	3.3	1.52
Kayah	2	0.6	3.33
Chin	2	0.9	2.22
Kayin	3	3.1	0.97
Mon	2	4.0	0.50
Rakhine	3	6.2	0.48
Shan	9	11.3	0.80
Sagaing	8	10.3	0.78
Tanintharyi	4	2.7	1.48
Bago	5	9.5	0.53
Magway	7	7.6	0.92
Mandalay	22	12.0	1.83
Yangon	21	14.3	1.47

Source: CESR (2012) and Census (2014).

and quality of employment opportunities, impact on income distribution. In particular, persistence of precarious forms of work, such as temporary workers, part-time seasonal workers or self-employed rural farm workers, perpetuate low earnings and economic insecurity. Additionally, economic liberalization has enabled certain industries to offer employment to specific population groups within the economy, e.g., high female employment in the garment sector, while construction remains a male-dominated industry. Segmented labour markets, with sector-based barriers to entry, also cause inequalities in employment opportunity (Van der Meulen Rodgers and Zveglich 2012). It is widely acknowledged that women contribute greatly to economic well-being through unpaid work, childcare and household chores, hence, their ability to participate in the labour market is limited due to these types of unpaid work.

Myanmar's labour force participation rate (LFPR) varies within the country—and how it compares to other countries depends on the data source. The LFPR is regarded as lower than expected, given the country's income per capita (ILO 2018), and at 61.2 per cent by some estimates, is lower than the ASEAN regional average of 63.4 per cent (Mahbubani and Severino 2018). Other sources put the LFPR for the union of Myanmar at closer to 67 per cent, in 2014, and also shed light on substantial differences across regions and states (Figure 5.2). The higher LFPRs in some regions can be partly attributed to household work and farm work, which again, are particularly relevant for women, but agricultural employment entails seasonality in job availability and income. Political and geographic factors also weigh in. Rakhine State, recently embroiled in conflicts, has the lowest rate while Shan State, closer to lucrative border trade markets with China and Thailand, has the highest.

The labour force participation rates could further rise due to the country's young population and proactive policies in encouraging more women to enter the labour market. However, the relationship between women's participation in the labour force and development is complex in Myanmar, and low participation does not necessarily reflect the actual contributions of women to the economy, given their work in the domestic and informal sectors that are generally omitted from national income accounting. Besides labour participation, it is also important for policy to improve working conditions, since most women are now engaging in low-skill and low-wage sectors.

FIGURE 5.2
Myanmar: Labour Force Participation Rates across State and Regions, 2014

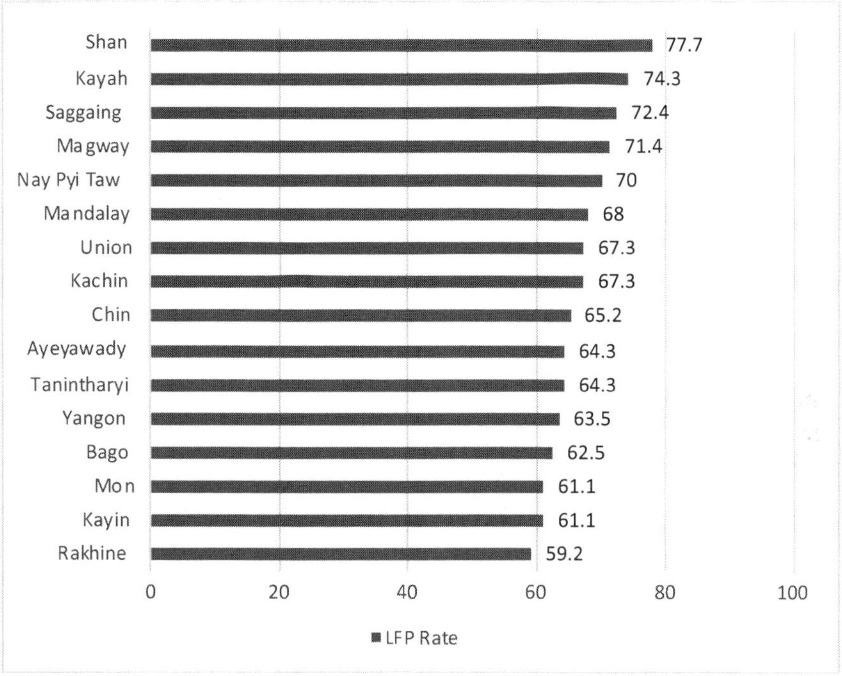

State/Region	LFP Rate
Shan	77.7
Kayah	74.3
Saggaing	72.4
Magway	71.4
Nay Pyi Taw	70
Mandalay	68
Union	67.3
Kachin	67.3
Chin	65.2
Ayeyawady	64.3
Tanintharyi	64.3
Yangon	63.5
Bago	62.5
Mon	61.1
Kayin	61.1
Rakhine	59.2

Source: Labour Force Survey (2015).

GENDER DIMENSIONS OF INEQUALITY

Schooling and Education

Gender patterns of schooling enrolment in Myanmar deserve special attention. At the primary level, female enrolment ratio is slightly lower than the male. However, girls' enrolment at the secondary level surpassed boys'—by a sizeable margin at the high school level. In higher education admissions, in general arts and sciences universities and colleges as well as professional institutes such as medicine, nursing and engineering, the share of women has continuously risen, although the ratio of female students in government technical institutes remains low. Overall, female attainments in education in Myanmar exceeds male attainment, although the country has yet to achieve gender parity in basic literacy. Table 5.11 shows the ratio of female-to-male students at each level of education in Myanmar. However, this advantage of educational attainments does not readily translate into labour force participation, as noted earlier and discussed further in the next section.

In Myanmar, gender differences are more marked when we look at labour market participation. As presented earlier, the education sector workforce is overwhelmingly women while 90 per cent of plant and machine operators are men, reflecting an inherent cultural stereotyping. As of 2015, 31 per cent of employees are women, similar to the average lower-middle income countries, yet slightly below the East Asia-Pacific average. It is reported that only half of the women (50.5 per cent) are in the labour force, compared to 85.6 per cent of men. Three quarters of women outside the labour force are engaged in unpaid household work and 60 per cent of (informal) micro enterprises in Myanmar have female workers (MoLIP 2017a, 2017b).

Gender Division of Labour

This subsection provides a closer examination of the gender division of labour alluded to earlier. Persisting traditional beliefs about the nature and social value of gender differences in competencies and traits play a

TABLE 5.11
Myanmar: Female Students as Percentage of Total Enrolment, by Level of Education

Education Level	2012/13	2013/14	2014/15	2015/16	2016/17
Primary school	49.0	49.0	49.0	48.8	48.9
Middle school	50.6	51.0	50.9	51.2	51.2
High school	54.0	55.0	55.4	55.6	55.2
Professional institutions	75.6	75.8	73.1		70.4
Arts and science universities	58.7	58.6	63.3		83.0
Associateship government technical institute	46.7			39.5	36.6
State agricultural institute	42.0	43.0	48.0	39.0	45.0
Government technical high school	37.0	31.0	29.8	35.5	27.9

Source: Department of Labour (2018).

part; women are regarded as intrinsically more appropriate candidates for certain occupations. Gender stereotypes are inculcated by parental and societal expectations, but some policies reinforce them. HEIs in Myanmar maintain gender quotas for specific studies, for instance 20/80 for forestry major, favouring men. In engineering subjects, mechanical engineering majors are only open for men while nursing is almost exclusively female. Some fields have a 50/50 quota, such as computer studies. Since admissions to these majors are often decided by the students' grades achieved at the high school graduating matriculation exam, where girls are achieving higher grades, boys are now allowed to enter into these competitive majors with lower passing marks than girls (ADB 2016). These quotas to boost male enrolment are often argued on the basis of gender equality.

The gender division of labour across economic sectors is strikingly reflected in the Labour Force Surveys conducted by the Ministry of Labour and Population (Figure 5.3). Women constituted exceedingly high proportion of workers, of 81 per cent, 78 per cent, 70 per cent and 68 per cent, respectively, in education, health and social service, garment, and financial sectors. In contrast, male labour dominates in transportation, fisheries and construction, where they account for 93 per cent, 91 per cent and 86 per cent of total labour. Another example of gender division of labour can be found in the financial sector, which is mainly composed of commercial banking, and it relies on bank tellers physically interacting with customers. For this reason, nearly 60 per cent of workers are women. Similar dynamics occur in the wholesale and retail sector (55.4 per cent). Agriculture and food processing workforces have quite even numbers of women and men.

Data on the teaching profession underscore the labour force profile just presented. According to UNESCO Institute of Statistics, Myanmar has the highest ratio of female participation in higher education institutions in the world. All levels of higher education and basic education institutions have consistently high ratios of female teachers (Table 5.12). While gender disparities in school attendance at basic education level are minimal, it is only after high school where male students between 15 and 20 years old register lower university attendance rates. According to the Comprehensive Education Sector Review (CESR) conducted by the government with support from multilateral donors in 2012, female students represents 60 per cent of all higher education students and more strikingly, 82.6 per cent of all academic staff members. CESR recommended that the government

FIGURE 5.3
Myanmar: Gender Division of Labour by Economic Sector, 2015

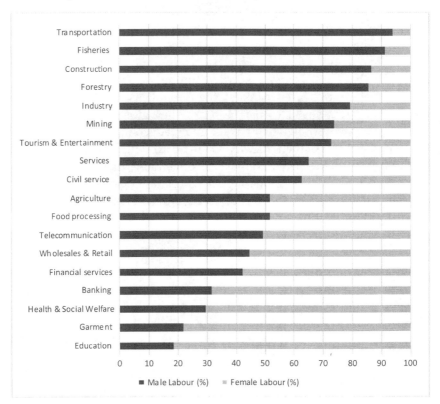

Source: Labour Force Survey (2015); authors' calculations.

investigate systematically the reasons for this gender disparity. However, the most likely contributing factors seemed to be the lower level of wages in the education sector compared to other professions, that men are more able to find employment at an earlier age than women, and that women are more likely to pursue a career as a teacher, and hence must continue their studies at a HEI. Cultural factors have also been offered as an explanation as the education profession provides job stability and social status for educated women, that they prefer to work in the sector even though the wages are relatively low.

TABLE 5.12
Myanmar: Women Staff in Basic Education Sector (Number and Percentage of Total)

	Area	Staff	2005–6		2010–11		2015–16		2017–18	
Primary assistant teacher	Union	Total	90,358		97,156		154,380		172,961	
		Women	79,941	88%	85,981	88%	130,967	85%	143,499	83%
	Urban	Total	20,886		19,994		22,776		23,517	
		Women	19,973	96%	19,310	97%	21,873	96%	22,528	96%
	Rural	Total	69,472		77,162		131,604		149,444	
		Women	59,968	86%	66,671	86%	109,094	83%	120,971	81%
Junior assistant teacher	Union	Total	99,604		114,220		142,782		145,226	
		Women	85,136	85%	100,186	88%	128,642	90%	131,496	91%
	Urban	Total	45,798		46,433		48,079		45,776	
		Women	41,016	90%	42,711	92%	45,231	94%	43,524	95%
	Rural	Total	53,806		67,787		94,703		99,450	
		Women	44,120	82%	57,475	85%	83,411	88%	87,972	88%
Senior assistant teacher	Union	Total	20,987		26,500		39,031		40,117	
		Women	16,501	79%	22,000	83%	31,963	82%	33,179	83%
	Urban	Total	13,604		15,125		17,327		17,170	
		Women	11,024	81%	12,840	85%	15,286	88%	15,233	89%
	Rural	Total	7,383		11,375		21,704		22,947	
		Women	5,477	74%	9,160	81%	16,677	77%	17,946	78%

Source: Central Statistical Organization (2019).

Another interesting phenomenon found in these female-dominated sectors is the clearly perceivable glass ceiling for the advancement of women to organizational leadership positions within the higher education sector. Although female faculty members represent over 80 per cent of all positions from tutors to professors and heads of departments, a majority of university rectors are men. The same pattern can be found at the basic education level. Nearly 40 per cent of headmasters of primary, middle and high schools are men although 80 per cent of teachers at any levels are women. Presently, at the Ministry of Education, all nine director generals, the most senior official at various departments under the ministry, are men despite most of the staff being women (Ministry of Education 2019). These patterns suggest that certain conditions are holding back women from assuming top positions in the education sector or there are unseen yet unbreakable barriers that keep women from rising to the upper rungs of leadership position regardless of their qualifications or achievements.

Gender Wage Inequality

Globally, the gender inequality in wages is estimated to be at 22.9 per cent. Furthermore, it is estimated to further widen for higher-educated women compared to similarly qualified men (ILO 2015). Such disparities are exacerbated among women from minority groups and are persistent even in gender segregated occupations (Terada-Hagiwara, Camingue-Romance, and Zveglich 2018). Various country studies consistently show that the gender wage gaps remain even after controlling for gender differences in qualifications and type of work (Blau and Kahn 2003; Weichselbaumer and Winter-Ebmer 2005). Having more children is found to widen the gender wage gap, a phenomenon that may be more pertinent for developing countries.

Wage gaps reflect systemic gender inequalities in upward occupational mobility and possibly gender wage discrimination—as also described above with reference to education (Figure 5.4). We consider between-sector and within-sector effects. Wage gaps between the most gender-defined sectors impact on gender wage inequality. Feminized sectors such as garment and footwear, on average, pay less than male-dominated sectors such as construction sector. In both sectors, the majority of workers have low education levels.

Inequality in Myanmar

FIGURE 5.4
Myanmar: Average Daily Wage Rate by Economic Sector, Per Civil Service, 2015

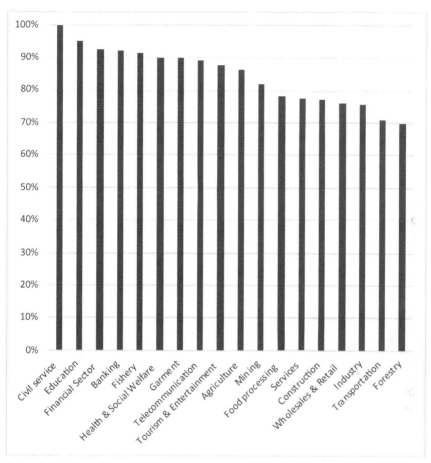

Source: Labour Force Survey (2015); authors' calculations.

There is a clear wage gap between male and female workers within all economic sectors. The public sector is an exception here; the government sets wage scales and as a result, there is gender parity on average. We should note that the statistics in Figure 5.4 denote daily wages; given the likelihood that women work fewer hours, gender gaps in monthly wages are likely to be wider—but the incidence and magnitude will vary by sector. In the private sector, wage gaps are observed in the sectors where female workers clearly dominate such as banking, finance, and health and social sectors. Among the moderately feminized sectors, some such as wholesale and retail trade pay male workers slightly higher than female workers, on average. One anecdotal explanation is that male workers, who are assumed to be more capable of multitasking, are favoured when it comes to appointment in supervisory roles or job rotations, whereas female workers are kept in routine, manual jobs. This disparity stands out even more in the newer industries predominantly staffed by women, such as the garment sector. Taking a more detailed look at this sector, we found what men, who are employed mainly as security guards, truckers and manual workers, tend to receive higher salaries than women counterparts.

There is a wage gap within male-dominated sectors, also driven by women mainly occupying lower-paying positions. With the decline of the agriculture sector, more rural women took up traditional male jobs in rural agriculture such as "forestry," and some women—but declining numbers—are engaged in agro-forestry sectors such as rubber plantation. Rubber plantation jobs are still primitive and have no adoption of modern technology. There is a large gender wage gap in agro-forestry establishments where women engaging in traditionally male jobs are paid less.

In concluding this section on gender, broader initiatives to summarize gender inequality in cross-country perspective, complementing the gender inequality index referenced earlier, are worth a brief note. Specifically, the World Economic Forum's publication on the Global Gender Gap Index included Myanmar for the first time in 2017, during which the country was ranked 83rd among 144 countries (Table 5.13). However, Myanmar dropped to the 114th position in 2020. Within three years, the rank dropped because

TABLE 5.13
Myanmar's Position in Global Gender Gap Rankings

	2017	2020
Global Gender Gap Rank	83	114
Economic participation and opportunity	26	102
Educational attainment	95	99
Health and survival	66	57
Political empowerment	132	133

Source: WEF (2019).

all four indicators, except for health and survival, suggest worsening gender gaps, or relatively slower progress compared to other countries. Myanmar's gender gap in economic opportunity had a huge drop from 26th to 102nd position, suggesting that women workers and entrepreneurs faced great challenges during the last three years. Meanwhile, political empowerment for women remains low: low representation of female legislators, absence of female cabinet ministers and heads of government institutions; and this is a priority area to address.

CONCLUSION

Myanmar has experienced a great deal of change in economic life following the comprehensive liberalization and reform measures in 2011. As a result, there is a profound impact on inequality through structural changes in the economy which in turn also shaped the country's labour markets. There is a consistent decline in the agriculture sector's share of GDP and employment, concurrent with growing shares of services and manufacturing industries. These shifts correspond with an overall decline of inequality in the country. However, inequality within urban areas exceeds inequality within rural areas. Former rural agriculture workers have migrated to cities, taking up low-paying jobs in labour-intensive manufacturing and service jobs, while middle- and high-paying jobs have grown in the urban commercial centres. Urban-rural divides also endure, not just in income but also in public provisions such as electrification and higher education.

The ongoing structural change and labour mobility also affected gender in terms of equality of access, opportunity and outcomes. Myanmar has considerably progressed in equalizing access to public services such as health and education. In fact, there is an outstanding achievement in terms of gender equality of access to education, such that female students outnumber male counterparts at all levels of education except at primary schooling, where the gender gap is negligible. Gender differences in higher education majors and specializations continue, in some ways as a direct result of policies and quotas. On the whole, educational attainment and structural change of the economy enhance labour force participation and job opportunities for women. Among the employment success stories such as garment industry that employs nearly 700,000 workers, of which 80 per cent are women.

However, gender gaps in upward mobility and wages persist: women earn lower than men across all economic activities in the private sector. The public sector has ensured equal wages for women and men, on average. We have discussed between-sector and within-sector factors related to gender wage gaps, which pose several policy implications for the Myanmar government. Our analysis suggests that it is not enough for the government to just ensure that there are policies, particularly through the Ministry of Education in offering equal access and opportunity to education. Beyond targets for gender parity in enrolment and attainment, there is a need to ensure that women and girls in both rural and urban labour markets have equal opportunity to work and earn without any discrimination against their gender. The continuing challenges of gender inequality in Myanmar are forcefully demonstrated in the education sector, where women dominate in staffing, but few enjoy upward mobility to decision-making positions. Clearly, more detailed analysis of the causes and consequences of these challenges, which lie beyond the scope of this chapter, should be further examined.

Notes

1. Asian Development Bank, "What's the Fastest Growing Country in Asia? Surprise! It's Myanmar", 14 April 2016, Further reading at https://www.adb.org/news/features/whats-fastest-growing-country-asia-surprise-its-myanmar
2. Speech by H.E. U Kyaw Tint Swe, Minister for the Office of State Counsellor to the 74th Sessions of the United Nations General Assembly, 28 September 2019.
3. Given the large difference between Yangon electrification rates and the rest of states and regions, to compute the national average, Yangon can be considered an outlier.
4. Aung Shin, "World Bank Approves $400m Electrification Loan", *Myanmar Times*, 18 September 2015.

References

ADB (Asian Development Bank). Various years. *Key Indicators for Asia and the Pacific*. Manila: Asian Development Bank.
———. 2012. *Counting the Cost. Financing Higher Education for Inclusive Growth in Asia*. Manila: ADB.
———. 2016. *Gender Equality and Women's Rights in Myanmar: A Situation Analysis*. Manila: ADB.

Ali, I., and J. Zhuang. 2007. "Inclusive Growth Toward a Prosperous Asia: Policy Implications". ERD Working Paper No. 97. Manila: ADB.

Alkire, S., and M. E. Santos. 2010. *Acute Multidimensional Poverty: A New Index for Developing Countries.* United Nations Development Programme Human Development Report Office Background Paper, 2010/11)

Amalia, S., and R. Yudaruddin. 2017. "Female Labour Force Participation and Economic Development in Southeast Asia". In Mulawarman International Conference on Economics and Business (MICEB 2017). Atlantis Press.

ASEAN Centre for Energy. 2015. *ASEAN Plan of Action for Energy Cooperation (APAEC).* Jakarta, Indonesia.

Barron, M., and M. Torero. 2017. "Household Electrification and Indoor Air Pollution". *Journal of Environmental Economics and Management* 86: 81–92.

Blau, F.D., and L.M. Kahn. 2003. "Understanding International Differences in the Gender Pay Gap". *Journal of Labor Economics* 21, no. 1: 106–44.

Bloem, M., S. de Pee, T. Hop, N. Khan, A. Laillou, Minarto, R. Moench-Pfanner, D. Soekarjo, Soekirman, J. Solon, C. Theary, and E. Wasantwisut. 2013. "Key Strategies to Further Reduce Stunting in Southeast Asia: Lessons from the ASEAN Countries Workshop". *Food and Nutrition Bulletin* 34 (2_suppl 1): S8–S16.

Buasuwan, P., and W. Suebnusorn. 2016. "Higher Education Inequality in East and Southeast Asia". In *Palgrave Handbook of Asia Pacific Higher Education*, edited by Christopher S. Collins, Molly N.N. Lee, John N. Hawkins and Deane E. Neubauer, pp. 297–314. New York: Palgrave Macmillan.

Coudouel, A., J.S. Hentschel, and Q.T. Wodon. 2002. "Poverty Measurement and Analysis". World Bank Poverty Reduction Strategy Papers Sourcebook. Washington, DC: World Bank.

Cunningham, W. and R. Munoz. 2018. *Myanmar's Future Jobs: Embracing Modernity.* Washington, D.C.: World Bank.

Dapice, David O., Tomas J. Vallely, Ben Wilkinson, and Michael J. Montesano. 2010. "Revitalizing Agriculture in Myanmar: Breaking Down Barriers, Building a Framework for Growth." Ash Center for Democratic Governance and Innovation Occasional Paper.

Department of Labour. Various years. *Labour Force Statistics (LFS).* Nay Pyi Taw: Department of Labour.

———. 2018. *Handbook on Human Resource Development Indicators.* Nay Pyi Taw: Department of Labour.

Dobermann, T. 2016. "Energy in Myanmar". IGC Note, June 2016, International Growth Centre Myanmar.

Dollar, D., and A. Kraay. 2002. "Growth Is Good for the Poor". *Journal of Economic Growth* 7: 195–225.

Elborgh-Woytek, K., M. Newiak, K. Kochhar, S. Fabrizio, K. Kpodar, P. Wingender, B. Clements and M.G. Schwartz. 2013. "Women, Work, and the Economy:

Macroeconomic Gains from Gender Equity". International Monetary Fund Staff Discussion Note SDN/13/10, September 2013.

Fujii, T., Shonchoy, A.S., and Xu, S. 2018. "Impact of Electrification on Children's Nutritional Status in Rural Bangladesh". *World Development* 102: 315–30.

Gnanasagaran, A. 2018. "Electrifying Rural ASEAN". *The ASEAN Post*, 4 January 2018. https://theaseanpost.com/article/electrifying-rural-asean (accessed 7 February 2020).

Guelich, U., and S.R. Xavier. 2017. "Women's Entrepreneurship within the ASEAN Economic Community: Challenges and Opportunities". *Entrepreneurial Ecosystems and Growth of Women's Entrepreneurship: A Comparative Analysis*, edited by Tatiana S. Manolova, Candida G. Brush, Linda F. Edelman, Alicia Robb and Friederike Welter, pp. 15–43. Chelthenham: Edward Elgar.

ILO (International Labour Organization). 2015. *Global Wage Report 2014/15*. Geneva: International Labour Organization.

———. 2018. *Asia-Pacific Employment and Social Outlook 2018: Advancing Decent Work for Sustainable Development*. Bangkok: ILO.

Khandker, S., Z. Bakht, and G.B. Koolwal. 2009. "The Poverty Impact of Rural Roads: Evidence from Bangladesh". *Economic Development and Cultural Change* 57, issue 4: 685–722.

Krishna, A., I. Mejía Guevara, M. McGovern, V.M. Aguayo, and S.V. Subramanian. 2018. "Trends in Inequalities in Child Stunting in South Asia". *Maternal & Child Nutrition* 14: e12517.

Leuze, K., and S. Strauß. 2016. "Why Do Occupations Dominated by Women Pay Less? How 'Female-Typical' Work Tasks and Working-Time Arrangements Affect the Gender Wage Gap Among Higher Education Graduates". *Work, Employment and Society* 30, no. 5: 802–20.

Mahbubani, K., and R. Severino. 2018. *ASEAN: The Way Forward*. McKinsey & Co.

Maw, Aka Kyaw Min. 2018. "Stability and Expectations: Economic Reform and the NLD Government". *Southeast Asian Affairs 2018*, edited by Malcolm Cook and Daljit Singh. Singapore: ISEAS – Yusof Ishak Institute.

McGillivray, Mark, Simon Feeny, and Sasi Iamsiraroj. 2013. "Understanding the ASEAN Development Gaps". In *Narrowing the Development Gap in ASEAN: Drivers and Policy Options*, edited by Mark McGillivray and David Carpenter, pp. 21–64. London and New York: Routledge.

MOEEP. 2011 and 2018. *Myanmar Electrification Rate*. Nay Pyi Taw: Ministry of Energy and Electricity Power.

MOHS. 2017. *Myanmar Demographic and Health Statistics*. Nay Pyi Taw: Ministry of Health and Sport.

MoLIP. 2017a. *The 2014 Myanmar Population and Housing Census: Thematic Report on Education*. Nay Pyi Taw: Ministry of Labour, Immigration and Population.

———. 2017b. *The 2014 Myanmar Population and Housing Census: Thematic Report on Migration and Urbanization*. Nay Pyi Taw: Ministry of Labour, Immigration and Population.

Oelz, M., and U. Rani. 2015. "Domestic Work, Wages, and Gender Equality: Lessons from Developing Countries". Gender, Diversity and Equality Branch Working Paper No. 5/2015. Geneva: ILO.

Orbeta Jr, A., and K.G. Gonzales. 2013. "Managing International Labor Migration in ASEAN: Themes from a Six-Country Study". PIDS Discussion Paper Series No. 2013-26. Philippine Institute for Development Studies.

Sachs, C.E. 2018. *Gendered Fields: Rural Women, Agriculture, and Environment*. New York and London: Routledge.

Sauré, P., and H. Zoabi. 2011. "International Trade, the Gender Gap, Fertility and Growth". Unpublished manuscript.

Sen, A. 1980. "Equality of What?". In *Tanner Lectures on Human Values*, edited by S. McMurrin. Cambridge: Cambridge University Press.

Shin, Aung. 2015. "World Bank Approves $400m Electrification Loan". *Myanmar Times*, 18 September 2015. https://www.mmtimes.com/business/16556-world-bank-approves-400m-electrification-loan.html (accessed 8 February 2020).

Shittu, W.O., and N. Abdullah. 2019. "Fertility, Education, and Female Labour Participation: Dynamic Panel Analysis of ASEAN-7 Countries". *International Journal of Social Economics* 46, no. 1: 66–82.

Sumarto, S., and S. Moselle. 2015. "Addressing Poverty and Vulnerability in ASEAN: An Analysis of Measures and Implications Going Forward". ERIA Discussion Paper Series 2015-63, September 2015.

Terada-Hagiwara, A., S.F. Camingue-Romance, and J.E. Zveglich Jr. 2018. "Gender Pay Gap: A Macro Perspective". ADB Economics Working Paper Series No. 538. Manila: Asian Development Bank.

Testaverde, M., H. Moroz, C.H. Hollweg, and A. Schmillen. 2017. *Migrating to Opportunity Overcoming Barriers to Labor Mobility in Southeast Asia*. Washington, DC: World Bank.

Thein, A.T.Z., and T. Akita. 2019. "Education and Expenditure Inequality in Myanmar: An Analysis with the 2006 and 2012 Household Income and Expenditure Survey in an Urban and Rural Setting". *Regional Science Policy and Practice* 11, no. 1: 55–70.

UNDESA. 2015. *Trends in International Migrant Stock: The 2015 Revision*. New York: United Nations Department of Economic and Social Affairs.

UNDP. 2019. *Human Development Indices and Indicators: 2018 Statistical Update Briefing note for Countries on the 2018 Statistical Update – Myanmar*. Yangon: UNDP. http://hdr.undp.org/sites/all/themes/hdr_theme/country-notes/MMR.pdf

Utama, N.A., K.N. Ishihara, Q. Zhang, and T. Tezuka. 2011. "2050 ASEAN Electricity Demand: Case Study in Indonesia and Cambodia". In *Zero-Carbon Energy Kyoto 2010*, edited by Takeshi Yao, pp. 32–39. Tokyo: Springer.

Van der Meulen Rodgers, Y., and J.E. Zveglich, Jr. 2012. "Inclusive Growth and Gender Inequality in Asia's Labour Markets". ADB Economics Working Paper Series, Manila.

Weichselbaumer, D., and R. Winter-Ebmer 2005. "A Meta-Analysis of the International Gender Wage Gap". *Journal of Economic Surveys* 19, no. 3: 479–511.

World Bank. 2017. *Selected Poverty Related Indicators.* Yangon: World Bank.

———. 2018. *Myanmar's Future Jobs: Embracing Modernity.* Yangon: World Bank.

———. 2019. "Poverty Report- Myanmar Living Conditions Survey 2017. https://openknowledge.worldbank.org/bitstream/handle/10986/30400/129754-4-9-2018-14-36-21-MyanmarFutureJobsMainReportfinal.pdf?sequence=1

WEF (World Economic Forum). 2019. *Global Gender Gap Report 2020.* Geneva: World Economic Forum.

WFP (World Food Programme). 2017. *Food Security Assessment in the Northern Part of Rakhine State.* Yangon: World Food Programme.

Yap, Y.T. 2014. "Addressing Inequality in Southeast Asia through Regional Economic Integration". Unpublished paper, Institute of Developing Economies (IDE-JETRO).

6

STRUCTURAL INEQUALITY IN THE PHILIPPINES
Oligarchy, Economic Transformation and Current Challenges to Development

Philip Arnold Tuaño and Jerik Cruz[1]

INTRODUCTION

The recent performance of the Philippine economy poses a number of conundrums for analysts of growth and development. Regarded as the "sick man of Asia" since its mid-1980s debt crisis (Balisacan 2015), the country's economic prospects until onset of the global COVID-19 pandemic have dramatically improved over the past decade, catapulting the economy to the ranks of Asia's leading growth performers, and onto several lists of promising emerging economies such as Goldman Sachs's "Next-Eleven", Turner Investment Partners' "TIMPs" (Turkey, Indonesia, Malaysia, Philippines), and *Time* magazine's "PINEs" (Philippines, Indonesia, Nigeria, and Ethiopia). Nevertheless, parallel to this economic resurgence, deep-seated challenges of structural poverty and marginalization have persisted, with the country's record in reducing poverty and inequality, generating quality employment, and promoting social mobility, having been disappointing. More troublingly, there is growing evidence that wealth inequality has risen, even while the social mobility prospects of most of the population have been hampered by entrenched forms of social and economic insecurity. These, in turn, have elicited concern from observers about the "exclusive" and even "oligarchic" character of the Philippine economy, which have yet to be decisively tackled by policymakers and the country's political leadership (Habito 2012; Teehankee 2017).

Underlying these dynamics are political and economic systems that in the case of the Philippines have undergone extended transformations over the past few decades. In line with growing concern on rising domestic inequalities as well as entrenched obstacles towards achieving inclusive growth (Albert, Dumagan and Martinez 2015; Albert and Raymundo 2015), this chapter aims to situate inequality trends in the country amidst transformations in the Philippines' political economy since the return to democracy in the mid-1980s—focusing on the contribution of structural and institutional change on the distribution of wealth and incomes, as well as social mobility. Starting with an overview of these transformations in the next section, we survey more specific trends in inequality and exclusion, and examine the factors that have driven such processes. In so doing, we stress the underlying political economy constraints that have impeded significant advances in the Philippines' efforts to address inequality and exclusion, and attest to how incoherencies in the country's response to the COVID-19 pandemic are linked to these structural issues.

THE PHILIPPINE POLITICAL ECONOMY SINCE THE 1980s

Once regarded as a leading Asian example of the "Third Wave" of democratization (Huntington 1991), the Philippines has witnessed a series of sea-changes in its political and economic landscape. In the aftermath of the 1986 People Power Revolution, which ended the twenty-one-year regime of Ferdinand Marcos, elites alienated by the dictatorship reinstalled a political system highly reminiscent of pre-Marcos liberal democracy: competitive elections and civil liberties were restored, while substantial powers and privileges were retained in the institution of the presidency (e.g., budgetary and appointment powers). Meanwhile, through the passage of the 1991 Local Government Code, an entire continuum of governance functions, including in local administration, planning, revenue-raising and development promotion were downscaled from the national towards provincial, municipal/city, and village levels (Porio 2012), even as one of the most active and expansive civil society sectors in the Asia-Pacific was able to secure greater policymaking influence through innovations in participatory and accountable governance, such as the adoption of a "party-list" system of proportional representation for marginalized and under-represented sectors (Clarke 1998; Magadia 2003; Quimpo 2008).

More than thirty years onwards, however, the pursuit of more substantive political empowerment has proven elusive. In the absence of an effective political party system, the return to electoral democracy has mostly seen the re-emergence of family-based, rentierist competition for public office, oriented towards an "anarchy of particularistic demands and particularistic actions" (Hutchcroft 1998; McCoy 2009). Labelled variously as "elite democracy" (Bello and Gershman 1990; Timberman 1991; Quimpo 2008) and "oligarchical democracy" (Hutchison 1993; Sidel 2014), the political landscape has experienced a disproportionate concentration of elected political offices in less than two hundred families—reportedly one of the highest levels of dynastic concentration among functioning democracies worldwide (Rivera 2016).

Among all Congresses elected since 1987 (Table 6.1), no Lower Houses elected have had less than six in ten officials from political dynasties, though by the 17th Congress in 2016, this percentage had risen to 78 per cent of district legislators. Dynastic dominance is even more pronounced among local government units (LGUs), where electoral competition can be less than nationally, and where issues of poor public service delivery, corruption, coordination failures, low implementation capacity, and lacklustre development outcomes are especially entrenched (ADB 2007a; ADB 2009). According to recent figures, for instance, 81 per cent of provincial governors and 69 per cent of mayors elected across the country in 2016 were from such political families (Mendoza 2018).

This chequered record in the political order has been accompanied by similar advances and difficulties in the economy. Burdened by a cronyism-ridden, mismanaged economy ravaged in the mid-1980s by its worst recession in the post-war era (Dohner and Intal 1989), successive administrations have facilitated a tectonic shift away from the opportunistic interventionism of the Marcos years. Indeed, since the country's debt

TABLE 6.1
Political Dynasties in Selected Philippine Congresses

House of Representatives	Share of Representatives with Relatives in Elective Offic
8th (1987–92)	62%
9th (1992–95)	64%
11th (1998–2001)	62%
12th (2001–4)	61%
15th (2010–13)	68%
16th (2013–16)	75%
17th (2016–19)	78%

Source: PCIJ (2007), Mendoza et al. (2012), Mendoza et al. (2019).

crisis, the Philippines was among the first recipient countries of World Bank structural adjustment programs (Broad 1981), which compelled it to undertake the most ambitious tariff reductions among ASEAN member states from 1978 to 1996[2] (Paderon 2017) and embark on some of the most ambitious privatization ventures in the world in the 1990s (Bello et al. 2005). The country also opened several sectors once reserved for government for private sector participation (including in air transport, water services, telecommunications, and power), and figured among the global pioneers of the private sector-led development of special economic zones and free trade zones (McKay 2006). Hence, from the patrimonialism and "immiserating growth" patterns of the Marcos regime (Boyce 1993), the country now boasts an economic policy paradigm that is among the most market-oriented within the region (Bello et al. 2014; Montes and Cruz 2020). While such market reforms offered one pathway for the Philippine economy to respond to its post-dictatorship stagnation in the late 1980s and 1990s, the country today still grapples with the long-term implications of adjustment, ranging from issues related to the economy's "premature deindustrialization" (Rodrik 2015; Daway and Fabella 2015), as well as the prominence of family-linked conglomerates over the commanding heights of its economy.

Figure 6.1 presents the broad contours of the economy's structural transformation. From being one of the more industry-focused economies in the region in the 1980s, the Philippines in 2015 has transitioned into a low-end services economy, buoyed by the expansion of its retail, leisure, property development, utilities, and social services subsectors—which

Structural Inequality in the Philippines 173

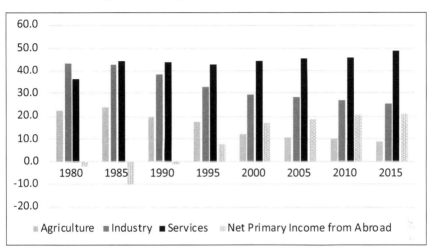

FIGURE 6.1
Philippines: GDP by Sector, 1998–2015 (% Total GDP)

Source: Philippine Statistics Authority (2019a).

has, in turn, been driven by a dramatic increase in remittances from overseas Filipino workers (i.e., a significant increase in the Net Primary Income from Abroad account) (Action for Economic Reforms 2014; Raquiza 2018). More recently, the trade-in-services sector has also become a major contributor to growth, driven by the information technology–business process outsourcing (IT-BPO) revolution of the 2000s as well as the sustained expansion of the tourism economy (Mitra 2013). By contrast, industry and agriculture have substantially declined in terms of their GDP shares in the intervening years, with agriculture contributing less than ten per cent to GDP by 2015.

The focus of Philippine big business activities has reflected these broader structural trends (Figure 6.2): while large family-owned companies in Indonesia, Malaysia and Thailand are also more concentrated in the services sector than in industry, Philippine conglomerates feature the most pronounced case of this trend in the ASEAN region. In 2016, 61.9 per cent of the market capitalization of three of the largest Philippine business groups (i.e., the Ayala, Gokongwei and the Sy groups) were concentrated in the services sector, compared to only 37.8 per cent for industry. Rather than the historical norm of manufacturing and export agriculture until

FIGURE 6.2
Selected Southeast Asian Countries: Market Capitalization of Family-Owned Conglomerates, by Sector (% Total Capitalization)

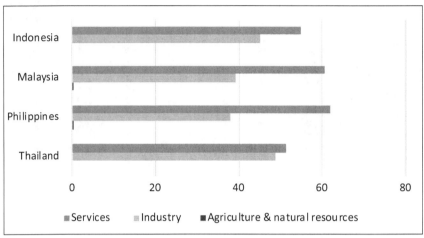

Source: Mendoza, Arbo and Cruz (2019).

the 1980s, the largest conglomerates in the country are now primarily engaged in construction, energy and power generation, education and healthcare, retail, real estate, utilities, BPO (especially through IT centre creation), gaming and tourism, and financial services (Raquiza 2014; Mendoza, Arbo and Cruz 2018). Comparably, the business interests of many politicians in the country have shifted to urban property development, rather than large-scale rural landownership and export agriculture which was arguably the leading wealth accumulation strategy among political elites until the adjustment period (Krinks 2002; Bello et al. 2014). From the "landlord-dominated" legislatures of the late 1980s and early 1990s, more than half of all congresspersons were found to have had substantial interests in construction and real estate by the 12th Congress in 2001, and accounting for dummy companies and nominee accounts has been found to bump the share of such legislators up to 70 per cent (Coronel et al. 2007; Clarke 2013).

This same trend has been manifested in the country's employment structure. According to Figure 6.3, while the total number of employed individuals in the economy has steadily expanded, the number of workers

FIGURE 6.3
Philippines: Total Employment, by Economic Sector (thousands), 1995–2017

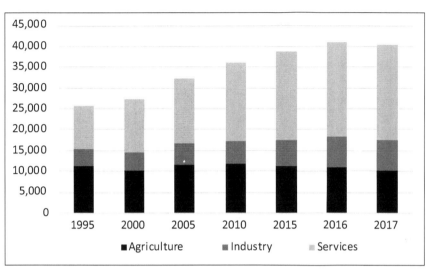

Source: Philippine Statistics Authority (2019b).

in the agriculture and industry sectors has lingered at practically the same level in the last twenty years. Instead, the lion's share of employment growth has occurred in the services sector, with the tourism/food services and IT-BPO sub-sectors being the more recent drivers of job creation (Ang et al. 2019). Unfortunately, this transition to a services-oriented economy has not been paralleled with substantial improvements in sectoral labour productivity. Consistently, from 1995 to 2015 (Figure 6.4), labour productivity within the services sector barely exceeded that of the economy's in general, whereas labour productivity in industry was nearly double that of services, and more than six times that of agriculture—which not only lagged behind other sectors, but hardly grew over that two-decade period. Such developments epitomize how the Philippine economy continues to face difficulties in graduating towards higher end, higher productivity activities, which have had critical implications in efforts to address the country's poverty, employment, and inequality challenges.

Growth has dramatically accelerated since the mid-2000s, and from 2012 until the onset of the COVID-19 pandemic in 2020 the Philippines has been fêted as a "rising tiger" (Konishi 2013), a "break-out nation"

FIGURE 6.4
Philippines: Sectoral Labour Productivity, Nominal Pesos per Worker, 1995–2015

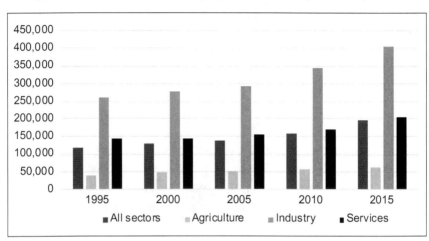

Source: Philippine Statistics Authority (2019b).

(Sharma 2013), and as one of the best economic performers in the region (World Bank 2018a). Despite this, the country's record in promoting decent employment growth as well as poverty and inequality reduction has been dismal. Employment generation has been sluggish, averaging only around 2.2 per cent in the 2010–18 period compared to average GDP growth rates of well over 6 per cent. Moreover, a majority of newly created jobs have tended to be precarious, low-skilled, and low-wage in nature (ILO 2017). In fact, the World Bank has suggested in 2018 that "poor-quality jobs (or "in-work poverty"), rather than unemployment, now constitutes the key challenge for government to reduce poverty" (World Bank 2018b). Partly due to the lacklustre creation of decent jobs, the proportion of poor individuals among the population only reduced marginally from 26.6 per cent in 2006 to 21.6 per cent in 2015 (Figure 6.5).

The country's underwhelming record in employment generation and poverty alleviation also raises critical questions concerning the distribution of the dividends of growth between capital and labour. While the annual net incomes of firms listed in the Philippine Stock Exchange increased by 259 per cent, from 2006 (PhP161.6 billion) to 2015 (PhP580.15 billion), that of average households increased by a far more modest 43.4 per cent during the same period (Cruz 2019).[3] Similarly, the increase in the net

FIGURE 6.5
Philippines: Poor and Subsistence-Poor Individuals, Millions and Percentage of Population, 1991–2015

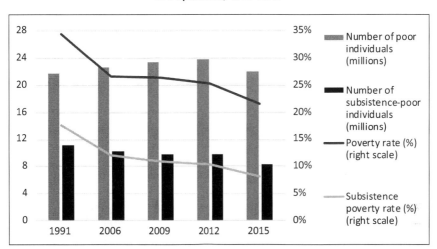

Note: The Philippine Statistics Authority has released the 2018 poverty incidence figures as of this writing but these are not compatible with the data presented.
Source: Philippine Statistics Authority (2019c).

worth of the fifty richest Filipinos in 2016 has been calculated to account for as much as 24 per cent or one-fourth of national GDP growth (dela Paz and Schnabel 2017). Indicatively, these growth dynamics have been taken as evidence of the country's enduring "oligarchic economy" as well as systematic "corporate malpractices" ranging from "unfair labour practices, environmental degradation, service/product quality/safety issues, delayed supplier payments, tax evasion, and anti-competitive practices" (Habito 2012; Teehankee 2017).

Like other countries around the globe, the Philippines has been severely impacted by the ongoing COVID-19 pandemic that has engulfed the world since early 2020. As at the time of writing, growth performance is expected to be the worst since the country's debt crisis in the 1980s (National Economic and Development Authority 2020; World Bank 2020); most analysts are expecting the country's recovery only in late 2021. Conservative estimates put the number of Filipinos out of work at 1 million due to government-mandated lockdowns; it is worth noting that more than 11 million out of 18 million workers in the main island region of Luzon are casual or temporary workers (Muyrong 2020). Many of these workers (close to 4 million) are employed in the micro and small enterprise sector, as well as the retail and transportation sectors, which have been significantly affected by the crisis; of the two sectors, only the food retail business were allowed by the government to operate during the April to May Luzon shutdown (Macaraeg 2020). There is little doubt that the impact of the pandemic will have a severe and lasting toll on the country's efforts to reduce poverty and promote gainful employment.

SOCIAL AND ECONOMIC INEQUALITY: PERSISTING CHALLENGES

Income and Employment Inequality

In recent decades, there has been a multiplication of policy efforts to redress the country's entrenched social and economic inequities. Immediately after the transition to democracy, the government attempted a policy shift towards agricultural development, where the ranks of the poor continue to be concentrated, and in line with this created and provided for the extended implementation of a wide-ranging agrarian reform programme. In the 1990s, Congress likewise passed a series of "affirmative action" laws—i.e., the Urban Development and Housing Act for addressing issues of the urban poor sector, the Fisheries Code for addressing the issues of artisanal fisherfolk—designed to increase access to economic and social opportunities among marginalized sectors through asset reforms and other interventions. In the same vein, institutional mechanisms were established to allow greater participation of civil society in national and local governance, such as through the creation of local development councils among LGUs, as well as dedicated national institutions (e.g., the National Commission for Indigenous Peoples, the Presidential Commission for the Urban Poor) (Clark 1998; ADB 2009).

Despite these efforts, income inequality, as measured by the Gini coefficient, remains high by regional standards and has, in fact, risen between 1991 and 2015 in rural areas (Figure 6.6). The rising tide of rural income inequality can largely be explained by the weak growth of employment opportunities in agriculture, which in turn derives from the poor levels of output and productivity growth in the sector. Annual value-added growth in agriculture has never exceeded 3 per cent, mainly

Structural Inequality in the Philippines

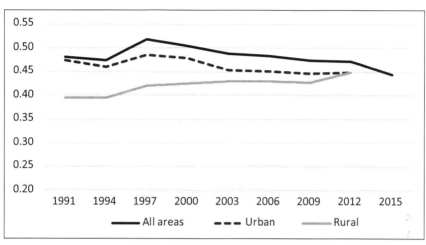

FIGURE 6.6
Philippines: Gini Index, National, Urban and Rural, 1991–2015

Source: Philippine Statistics Authority (various years).

on account of low investments in the sector amidst post-adjustment fiscal constraints. Further compounding such underinvestment have been poorly functioning land markets, stagnant rural education levels, and the presence of elites fixated on accumulating land, while failing to invest in growth-enhancing technology and broader access to social services (Briones 2013).

Even more broadly, the lack of significant progress in reducing income inequality mirrors disparities in the Philippine economy's growth process. Indeed, the majority of economic growth has unfolded in the Greater Manila (NCR, Central Luzon and Calabarzon) region, which significantly increased its share of GDP to 63 per cent in 2018 from 55.5 per cent in 2002 (Table 6.2). This reflects the disproportionately high concentration of services and manufacturing activities within the Greater Manila region, which in 2017 accounted for 68.5 per cent of all gross value-added in the services sector nationwide, and 72.7 per cent of industry (PSA 2018). Meanwhile, other regions' contribution to GDP have mostly diminished—including in regions with significant metropolitan areas such as in Central Visayas (Metro Cebu), Davao (Metro Davao), and Northern Mindanao (Metro Cagayan de Oro). The uneven distribution of growth is also reflected in recalcitrant inequality levels within regions (Figure 6.7): Gini coefficients across the

TABLE 6.2
Philippines: Regional Contribution to Gross Regional Domestic Product, 2002 and 2018

Region	2002	2018	Difference
Mega Metro Manila	55.5%	61.6%	6.1%
CAR, Ilocos and Cagayan Valley	7.3%	6.6%	−0.6%
MIMAROPA and Bicol	4.7%	3.7%	−1.0%
Visayas	15.9%	12.9%	−3.0%
Mindanao	16.6%	15.2%	−1.4%

Note: Mega Metro Manila includes the regions of Metro Manila, Cagayan Valley and Calabarzon regions.
Source: Authors' calculations from Philippine Statistics Authority.

FIGURE 6.7
Philippines: Gini Index, by Politico-Administrative Region, 1997 and 2015

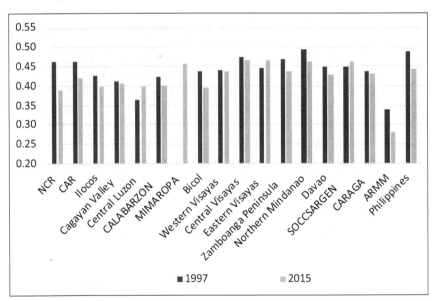

Note: 1997 Southern Tagalog Gini index is inputted as the Calabarzon index.
Source: Philippine Statistics Authority (various years).

1997 to 2015 interval indicate either no significant improvement, except for Metropolitan Manila (NCR), the Cordillera Autonomous Region (CAR), and the Autonomous Region for Muslim Mindanao (ARMM).

Related to spatial disparities are those pertaining to employment. In line with the country's structural transformation, labour market segmentation between formal, permanent and well-paid versus casual, informal, and insecure jobs, has become an even more pronounced feature of the country's employment landscape. From 2000 to 2015 (see Table 6.3), the share of services employment grew at the expense of agriculture, translating into an expansion of formal wage and salary workers, and a decline in the prevalence of informal self-employed and unpaid family workers. However, while increasing formal employment has presented a pathway out of poverty for many, low access to secure jobs in services has persisted. Just as with employment figures, underemployment shares have likewise shifted from agriculture to services, and from unpaid family workers and self-employed workers towards formal wage and salary workers (Table 6.3). Indicatively, these trends reinforce findings from recent World Bank studies of the Philippine labour markets (2013; 2016; 2018) concerning how much of the jobs which has been generated throughout the country's recent boom have remained "precarious and low-paying", with around 30 per cent of workers earning less than two-thirds the minimum wage.

Wealth and Land Inequality

Compared to divides in income and employment, wealth and property inequality are harder to measure. While under certain assumptions, property and financial wealth can be crudely estimated from household surveys utilizing income and expenditure categories, there are problems in undertaking such calculations, the most prominent of which is the fact that the families with very high incomes are underrepresented in these surveys. Proxies are therefore presented for land and financial inequality in Figures 6.8 and 6.9, respectively. Here, the Gini coefficient of land inequality is measured in terms of inequality in operational landholdings as measured from the various years of the Census of Agriculture. From 1960 to the 2010s, the land Gini seems to have been increased to 0.53–0.57, despite the implementation of several land reform programmes through the decades.

Financial measures of wealth inequality remain quite sparse, though data from the Philippine Central Bank provides evidence that financial

TABLE 6.3
Philippines: Share of Employment and Underemployment by Economic Sector and Class of Worker (%)

	2000	2005	2010	2015
Employment				
Sector				
Agriculture	37%	36%	33%	29%
Industry	16%	16%	15%	16%
Services	47%	48%	52%	55%
Class of Worker				
Wage and Salary Workers	51%	50%	54%	59%
Employers	5%	5%	4%	3%
Self-employed	32%	33%	30%	28%
Unpaid Family Workers	12%	12%	12%	10%
Underemployment				
Sector				
Agriculture	45%	46%	45%	40%
Industry	17%	16%	15%	18%
Services	39%	38%	39%	42%
Class of Worker				
Wage and Salary Workers	50%	48%	51%	56%
Employers	4%	4%	3%	2%
Self-employed	34%	36%	34%	32%
Unpaid Family Workers	12%	11%	12%	9%

Source: Philippine Statistics Authority (2019b) and Ang et al. (2019).

wealth inequality has widened. Already, 2003 household survey data indicates that the Gini coefficient of savings was around 0.57, slightly higher than that of the Gini based on incomes (Philippine Human Development Network 2019). Yet more recently, as shown by Figure 6.9, which displays the total amount of savings deposit accounts in financial institutions across the country, the share of the largest 0.6 per cent of savings accounts increased its share by roughly 7 percentage points (from 57.4 per cent to 64.7 per cent) at the expense of that of the bottom 99.4 per cent in a span of only four years (2012 to 2016). However, it should be noted that possession of bank accounts and most formal financial services remains typically out of reach for most Filipinos, with a 2014 Consumer Finance Survey of the Central Bank finding that as much as 86 per cent of Filipino

Structural Inequality in the Philippines 183

FIGURE 6.8
Philippines: Gini of Land Ownership, 1960–2012

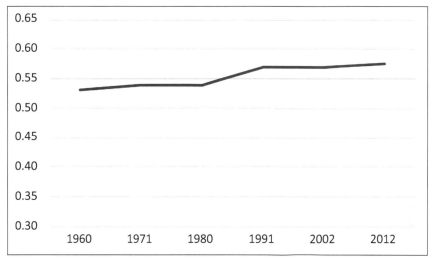

Source: Lanzona (2018).

FIGURE 6.9
Philippines: Share of Savings Deposits, 2012, 2016 and 2019

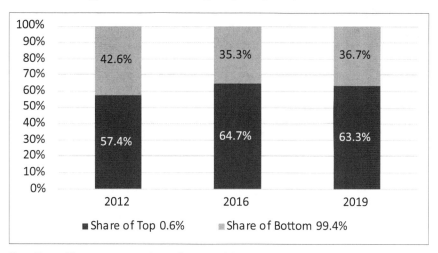

Note: Top and bottom savers are based from the BSP data.
Source: Authors' computations from the Bangko Sentral ng Pilipinas (BSP) (2019).

households did not have any deposit account (BSP 2017). This suggests that the patterns shown in Figure 6.9 may only be a conservative estimate of growing disparities in financial wealth.

Inequality in Education and Health

Throughout the post-Marcos era, the Philippine government has managed to increase its allocation of resources in education and other social services, with a priority to education spending having been enshrined in the country's 1987 Constitution. Yet despite such expanded human capital investments, accessibility and quality issues across income strata have remained pressing concerns. For one, while overall trends in education inequality suggest appreciable advances in reducing educational disparities, with the schooling Gini coefficients having decreased from 0.268 in 1993 to 0.238 in 2013 (Figure 6.10), the picture is more mixed once education attainment levels are considered. Indeed, data in Table 6.4 reveals that among youth in the lowest income decile, almost one out of two individuals only had primary schooling in 1998, although this slightly improved to roughly 40 per cent by 2013. By comparison, only in the highest income

FIGURE 6.10
Philippines: Gini of Educational Attainment (Years of Schooling for Population 15 Years or Older), 1993–2013

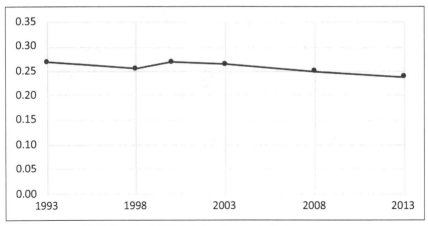

Source: Lanzona (2018), from the World Bank Development Indicators.

TABLE 6.4
Philippines: Proportion of 15–24-year-olds by Education Level and Income Decile, 1998 and 2013

	Highest Level of Education, 1998			Highest Level of Education, 2013		
Decile	Some or Completed Primary	Some or Completed Secondary	Some or Completed Tertiary	Some or Completed Primary	Some or Completed Secondary	Some or Completed Tertiary
First (Poorest)	48.4%	41.9%	9.1%	39.4%	53.2%	6.3%
Second	39.9%	51.4%	7.3%	28.2%	58.5%	11.5%
Third	35.3%	52.1%	11.9%	24.1%	58.8%	15.5%
Fourth	29.8%	53.3%	15.2%	19.8%	59.2%	18.1%
Fifth	23.9%	53.6%	20.6%	16.4%	57.3%	23.0%
Sixth	19.7%	56.6%	21.5%	14.5%	51.9%	30.2%
Seventh	15.1%	50.2%	31.8%	12.4%	49.8%	33.5%
Eighth	12.7%	49.2%	35.1%	7.8%	40.9%	45.1%
Ninth	7.5%	44.4%	44.7%	3.5%	36.9%	52.1%
Tenth (Richest)	3.6%	32.7%	59.6%	2.5%	22.6%	68.7%

Source: Tan and Siriban (2016). Basic data from the Annual Poverty Indicators Survey, 1998 and 2013 rounds.

decile in 1998, and the two highest income deciles in 2013, did a majority of these individuals reach at least tertiary education levels. Thus, though there have been improvements in education attainment across deciles, a significant share of individuals, especially among lower-income households, continue to lack full and consistent access to secondary as well as tertiary levels of education.

Such inequalities in education are partly rooted in the education expenses that households must bear in spite of government support (Tan and Siriban 2016). These expenses typically range from school fees, to the cost of learning materials, extra clothing and living expenses, school activities and transportation. Hence, while public education at all levels in the country is highly subsidized, the educational attainment of lower income groups is considerably limited to elementary and high school levels, since the additional expenses that households must spend for public education are most pronounced at the tertiary level. This is because public universities and colleges and local government universities and colleges are generally located in central cities, while poorer households are situated in more rural, far-flung municipalities. Yet beyond such accessibility problems, acute shortages, especially in basic education, still need to be addressed. David and Albert (2012) identify the most critical needs in primary schooling as involving the lack of nearby school facilities, shortages of teachers and teacher trainings, as well as a lack of learning materials.

Even more pronounced than disparities in education, however, are inequalities in health services and outcomes. On one hand, the Philippine health system suffers from a variety of problem that have weakened its ability to address gaps in health access. Especially prominent have been the fragmentation of the health delivery and financing system due to devolution of the public health system in 1991, as well as the poor ability of the health sector to recruit, train and maintain a skilled health workforce, including managers of the increasingly-complex health system (UPSE HPDP 2017). Against World Health Organization recommendations to countries of retaining a doctor-to-population ratio of 1:1000, the country's public health system reported a physician ratio above 1:30,000 (Table 6.5), which has even further deteriorated between 2013 and 2018. Particularly alarming were the public doctor-to-population ratios in Region 11 (the Davao region) and ARMM (the Muslim Mindanao region), which exceeded a 1:60,000 figure in 2018, even as the ratio in NCR and CAR (the Cordillera region) approximated 1:20,000. Similar, though less severe, asymmetries can also be observed with regard to ratios for nurses, with ARMM again suffering from the most pronounced health human resource difficulties. Finally, a third major challenge has also related to the issue of health financing as lower income deciles pay a substantial amount out-of-pocket to defray

TABLE 6.5
Philippines: Population for Each Type of Government Health Professionals, 2013 vs. 2018, Selected Regions

	Government Physicians		Government Nurses	
	2013	2018	2013	2018
Philippines	32,244	33,909	17,188	17,769
Metro Manila	19,896	20,519	13,623	13,308
Cordilleras	19,052	19,182	11,643	11,080
Davao Region	63,836	65,986	32,361	33,861
ARMM	48,036	61,387	21,977	41,545

Source: Field Health Service Information System, Department of Health.

their health costs. To this end, a study by Racelis et al. (2016) has noted that households in the lower three-fifths of household income groups pay as much as 40 per cent of hospitalization expenses.

Not surprisingly, these health system issues have led to corresponding inequalities in health outcomes. One striking example can be observed in large gaps in mortality rates among infants and children (Table 6.6), despite absolute improvements across most income brackets. In 2017, infant mortality rates among those in the lowest wealth quintile were more than three times that of the highest wealth quintile—a widening of gap relative to 2003 levels. A similar trend manifested for under-five mortality rates, with the rate of the poorest quintile moving from roughly three times to almost four times of the richest quintile. In turn, part of these disparities is driven by gaps in access to adequate maternal and childcare, nutrition and feeding practices and immunization services. As a result, the Philippines has one of the highest levels of child stunting and malnutrition in the world. According to Herrin (2016), this has been attributed to many factors including vitamin and micronutrient deficiency among the young, poor maternal health and child-feeding practices, and lack of immediate treatment of infections, including diarrhoea. The proportion of children below five years in the lowest wealth quintile who suffer from being underweight is almost four times that of those in the highest wealth quintile; the proportions for stunting are three and a half times, and for wasting, 50 per cent more. Table 6.7 shows differences in nutrition among different wealth groups.

Gender Inequality and Socio-economic Exclusion

In addition to the aforementioned inequalities, women and other social groups are also confronted by various forms of exclusion. To be sure, employed women have higher average wages in the manufacturing and service sectors (but not in the agricultural sector), while women-headed households face lower levels of poverty incidence compared to male-headed ones (ADB 2007b; David, Albert and Vizmanos 2018; Philippine Statistics Authority 2016). However, labour force participation of women is lower, and the proportion of women in the informal sector (exemplified by female unpaid family workers) is much higher. Moreover, despite the enactment of a progressive set of laws favouring women and child rights in the country, there are still problems in the execution of protection policies

TABLE 6.6
Philippines: Selected Infant and Child Mortality Rates, per 1,000 Infants/Children, 2003 and 2017

Wealth Quintile	2003 Neonatal Mortality	2003 Post-neonatal Mortality	2003 Infant Mortality	2003 Child Mortality	2003 Under-5 Mortality	2017 Neonatal Mortality	2017 Post-neonatal Mortality	2017 Infant Mortality	2017 Child Mortality	2017 Under-5 Mortality
Lowest	21	21	42	25	66	18	13	31	12	42
Second	19	13	32	15	47	17	6	23	7	29
Third	15	10	26	6	32	15	12	26	5	31
Fourth	15	7	22	4	26	6	5	11	2	12
Highest	13	6	19	1	21	8	2	9	2	11
Average	17	13	30	12	42	14	7	21	6	27

Source: National Demographic and Health Survey, Philippines, 2003 and 2017 rounds.

TABLE 6.7
Philippines: Proportion of Children Below Five Years of Age Stunted, Underweight and Wasted, 2013 and 2015, by Wealth Quintile

Wealth Quintile	Stunted 2013	Stunted 2015	Underweight 2013	Underweight 2015	Wasted 2013	Wasted 2015
Lowest	44.8	49.7	29.8	31.9	9.5	8.1
Second	35.9	38.9	23.4	25.5	7.3	7.8
Middle	28.5	31.7	19	21.3	8.3	7.3
Fourth	20.4	22.0	12.8	13.5	7.8	5.9
Highest	13.3	14.7	8.6	8.6	5.4	5.7

Notes: Stunting is defined as the condition of children whose height for age is below minus two standard deviations from the median of the WHO Child Growth Standards. Wasting is defined as the condition of children whose weight for height is below minus two standard deviations from the median of the WHO standards. Underweight is the condition in which children's weight for age is below minus two standard three deviations from the median of the WHO standards.
Source: Food and Nutrition Research Institute, 2013 National Nutrition Survey and 2015 Updating Nutrition Survey.

for these sectors. For instance, the proportion of women experiencing gender-based violence still remains high (at around a fifth of all women), with one in twenty women having experienced violence while pregnant (PSA 2013).

Senior citizens and persons with disabilities (PWDs), together with children, youth, and victims of disasters and calamities, also experience high levels of social vulnerability. The elderly, defined as those over the age of sixty, typically face issues in home care with diminishing numbers of traditional caretakers (either entering the labour force domestically or abroad in search of better earnings) (Ogena, 2006); they also confront increasing costs of healthcare even as many senior citizens have struggled with low lifetime savings and inadequate pensions. Likewise, PWDs, who numbered 1.4 million in 2017 (Philippine Institute of Development Studies 2017), have contended with systematic disadvantages in terms of access to health facilities, exclusion from the labour force and lack of training due to their physical condition, and the relatively higher level of school drop-out rates.

Occupationally, smallholder farmers (especially corn and coconut growers), artisanal fisherfolk and the indigenous peoples[4] have been arguably the most economically marginalized sectors in the country. Around a third of individuals living in the rural areas live below the poverty line

(Philippine Statistics Authority 2015); moreover, agricultural households are generally deprived of basic amenities, including water, electricity and transport equipment (Reyes et al. 2012). Meanwhile, in the urban areas, informal settlers and home-based workers still live very precariously, with households in these sectors normally dwelling in makeshift homes in high risk-prone areas such as canals, sea walls and river embankments. Significantly, urban poor households are particularly affected by increasing flexibility in Philippine labour markets (Ofreneo 2013).

INCOME INEQUALITY AND SOCIO-ECONOMIC MOBILITY

The changing landscape of development in the Philippines calls for a new framework to accommodate its growing range of socio-economic challenges. One important dimension of a new framework is positive socio-economic mobility (i.e., the ability or opportunity afforded to persons and households to move to better socio-economic positions). The significance of movement among households is underscored by going beyond the dichotomy of poor vs non-poor towards examining the entire social distribution of income or expenditure. This is done in Table 6.8, which shows the changing proportion of households in different expenditure classes from 1997 to 2015. Households are classified here by expenditure

TABLE 6.8
Philippines: Households by Expenditure Class, 1997–2015 (as Percentage of Total Households)

Expenditure Class[a]	1997	2000	2003	2006	2009	2012	2015
Very poor	16.39	18.41	16.84	16.45	11.98	13.11	9.61
Poor	23.92	24.67	23.17	24.22	24.47	24.50	23.34
Vulnerable	27.63	26.8	27.60	26.84	29.42	28.96	30.59
Economically secure	26.82	25.1	27.14	27.07	28.27	27.88	30.83
Upper-middle class	4.84	4.67	5.06	5.23	5.65	5.35	5.42
Top class	0.40	0.35	0.20	0.20	0.21	0.20	0.21

Note: a. Figures may not add up to 100 per cent due to rounding. Daily per-capita expenditure of (a) extremely poor: $1.9 or less; (b) poor: ($1.9, $3.1); (c) vulnerable: [$3.1, $5.5); (d) economically secure: [$5.5, $15); (e) upper middle class ($15, $50); and (f) top class $50 or more.
Source: Philippine Human Development Network [2019] from the Family Income and Expenditure Survey, various years.

classes instead of income, since expenditure or consumption is generally held to better reflect households' standard of living, while capturing the household's ability to mobilize other financial resources besides income (e.g., savings, remittances, etc.).[5]

How have the sizes of these "classes" fared through time? As a share of all households, the "very poor" class first increased in share then began to decline from about 2000 onwards, with significant reductions in 2006–9 and again in 2012–15 (Table 6.8). Meanwhile, households in the narrow "poor" category have taken up a somewhat constant share at 23–24 per cent of all families throughout the period. At the same time, there was an increasing proportion of the vulnerable and economically secure categories, while the upper-middle class also expanded slightly. The proportion in the top expenditure category however was halved from 0.40 per cent to 0.21 per cent during the entire 1997–2015 period.

Nevertheless, compared to other Southeast Asian countries, the increase in those who are in the middle class has been slow (Figures 6.11 and 6.12). While the proportion of the poor in the country was lower compared to China, Indonesia and Vietnam in the 1980s and 1990s, these countries have caught up with, or have already surpassed, the Philippines' record in reducing poverty. The opposite has been true for the proportion of the population who are in the middle class: though the Philippines in the 1980s and 1990s harboured a larger middle-class share than China, Indonesia, and Vietnam, all these countries have either outstripped the Philippines (i.e., China, Vietnam) or were in the process of eventually doing so (i.e., Indonesia).

EXPLAINING POVERTY AND INEQUALITY: TECHNICAL FACTORS

There is no question that appreciable advances have materialized in the Philippines' poverty and inequality record since the democratic transition. Income inequality has declined in important measures (e.g., the national Gini index, income/consumption ratios), while there has been some expansion of the middle and working classes. Driving these gains have been several long-term structural trends in the country. On one hand, steady growth in remittances from overseas Filipinos, and the more recent expansion of the IT-BPO sector have been a common pathway for lower-income households to enter into the ranks of the growing middle class.

FIGURE 6.11
Selected Southeast Asian Countries and China: Proportion of Poor Households to Total (%), 1985–2015

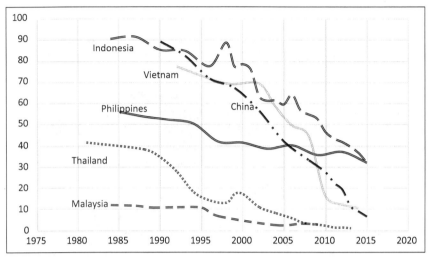

Source: Philippine Human Development Network (2019) from the World Bank PovCalNet.

FIGURE 6.12
Selected Southeast Asian Countries and China: Proportion of Middle-Class Households to Total (%), 1985–2015

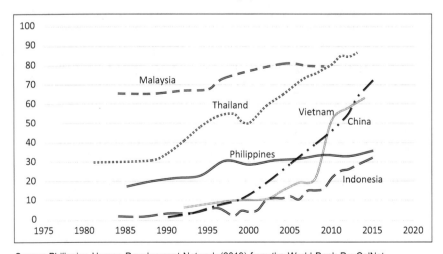

Source: Philippine Human Development Network (2019) from the World Bank PovCalNet.

Slight improvements in the public finances of the Philippine government, owing to fiscal reforms starting in the mid-2000s, have also afforded expanded levels of social spending, such as in pre-school, primary and secondary education, as well as in national health insurance, which has especially redounded to the benefit of vulnerable and the lower middle-income groups (i Terme 2014). These, along with intensified demand for skilled labour, have driven rising wages in certain segments of the economy (e.g., food processing, communications, finance, business services).

Yet compared to other Asian countries, progress in advancing poverty reduction and social mobility has remained unimpressive overall—with the growth of the secure middle class being among the slowest by regional standards, even as certain forms of inequality have widened (e.g., rural income, land ownership, financial assets). Undergirding these challenges have been a confluence of interconnected conditions, which can be distinguished as owing to either *technical* or *political economy* factors (Bernstein, Crow and Johnson 1992; Green and Hulme 2005). Technical factors concern largely exogenous conditions and constraints on domestic development processes affecting poverty, inequality and welfare outcomes. Specifically, these set of factors contribute to entrenching poverty and inequality by serving to leave the poor *excluded* from opportunities for wealth/income creation and social mobility within the mainstream market economy.

Economic Structure and Job Generation Trends

The Philippine economy has experienced unfavourable structural transformation in the past few decades, with industry having been "hollowed-out", while agriculture has remained depressed in terms of sectoral and productivity growth (Aldaba 2013b, 2014; Action for Economic Reforms 2014; Ofreneo 2013b; Usui 2012). Accordingly, the low-end services sector has become the economy's major employment "sink", absorbing the exodus of labour from the countryside into major economic centres, as well as the general tide of labour force expansion. As has already been explained, this shift in the country's economic structure has proven suboptimal in generating higher-quality, decent employment opportunities.

Promoting the resurgence of the manufacturing sector has been the focus of increasing policy efforts in recent years, with the formulation of a Comprehensive National Industrial Strategy in 2012 being a milestone (Aldaba 2013a; Llanto and Ortiz 2015)—yet comparable initiatives have yet to be undertaken for the agricultural sector. Indeed, despite the passage of the Agriculture and Fisheries Modernization Act in 1997, meant to address the sector's dismal state, sustained investment in the rural economy and substantial increases in productivity among small farmers and artisanal fisherfolk have not been realized. These agricultural dilemmas have been attributed to an entire suite of factors, ranging from the impacts of trade liberalization, weak public investment, government failures in providing sectoral support and infrastructure, as well as the capture of the agricultural sector by landed and mercantile elites (Bello et al. 2005, 2014; Lopez 2009; Tauli-Corpuz, Sidchogan-Bati, and Jim Maza 2006; Aldaba 2013a; Usui 2012).

Geography, Infrastructure and Connectivity

The archipelagic nature of the Philippines' geography presents the country with major connectivity, market access, and service delivery issues, especially for the poor and vulnerable. A decomposition exercise, conducted in conjunction with the 2012/2013 report of the Philippine Human Development Network, estimated that geographic factors, including climate type, slope, elevation, sea access/landlocked status, explains between 25 per cent to 47 per cent of the interprovince variations in socio-economic outcomes, such as life expectancy, years in schooling, per capita outcomes and the provincial human development index (HDI).[6] While the aforementioned estimates have not yet controlled for institutional and policy factors, they nonetheless imply that geographical conditions also have effects on socio-economic outcomes across areas.

Effective infrastructure investments, as well as transport and communications connectivity, are vital to overcoming such forms of spatial exclusion and improving the delivery of public and social services across provinces and localities. Yet with regards to transport infrastructure, the Philippines still lags significantly behind its neighbours in ASEAN in terms of quality infrastructure, such as roads. For instance, while 5.6 per cent the country's road networks were still unpaved as of 2017, only 42 per cent of the total road network were determined to be in "good" condition (DPWH 2017). In turn, such infrastructure gaps and consequent higher transaction costs exacerbate difficulties among the poor and near-poor, especially in more isolated rural areas, in acquiring and selling products/services, while also limiting their choices and saddling them with higher market prices due to the role of traders and middlemen (UNDP 2008; Briones 2019).

Human Capital and Labour Market Gaps

Educational attainment has improved substantially in recent years: school enrolment in the secondary level increased from 59 per cent in 2005 to 66 per cent in 2015, and the share of Filipino 25-year olds and above who have completed secondary education have risen from 65 per cent in 2008 to 70 per cent in 2013 (World Bank n.d.). Nonetheless, gaps persist in the working-age population's possession of adequate educational qualifications. In 2017, 22 per cent of Filipino youth (i.e. between 15 and 24 years old) were neither in employment, education, or training (NEET), with females nearly doubling the number of men in this group (ILO 2017). Likewise, more than a quarter of those school aged children in the poorest fifth decile have been out of school. In the long term, this could spell major challenges in the job prospects of a major segment of the future labour force.

Even individuals with sufficient qualifications experience challenges. Strikingly, unemployment has been higher among individuals with tertiary and post-secondary education, hovering around 9 per cent from 2005 to 2015, whereas those without schooling or with only primary school completion was below 3 per cent. One symptom of this "job-skill mismatch" dilemma has been the proliferation of "hard-to-fill" positions owing to the lack of adequate competencies among job applicants: as of 2016, nearly half (47.2 per cent) of all such vacancies have reportedly encountered staffing challenges due to the deficient experience and competencies among job applicants, a substantial increase from 2010 levels when such difficulties accounted for less than 40 per cent of recruitment difficulties (cf. ILO 2017; PSA 2017b). At the same time, social protection schemes for workers such as unemployment insurance, unemployment assistance, severance pay, unemployment insurance savings accounts, and public works programs are fragmented and have only had a weak impact on the labour market (Esguerra 2016; Diokno-Sicat and Mariano 2018; Reyes et al. 2012).

Poor Enabling Environment for MSMEs and Small Producers

The Philippines is well documented to experience challenges in the business environment, ranking only 113th of 190 countries in the World Bank's 2018 Doing Business report (World Bank 2018c). Yet such challenges are even more pronounced among the enterprises and livelihood organizations among micro, small, and medium enterprises. For instance, from 1995 to 2006, the share of small (9.1 per cent to 8.8 per cent) and medium (1.0 per cent to 0.9 per cent) enterprises in manufacturing slightly decreased. The failure of Philippine small and medium enterprises (SMEs) to expand is reflective of sustained challenges that this sector has faced on growth and market entry, even amidst increased competition from foreign imports, such as difficulty in accessing finance, difficulties in dealing with the government bureaucracy, poor infrastructure, and weak linkages with large domestic and multinational firms (Aldaba 2013a, 2014).

Credit, to take only one example, has long been known to be a critical development constraint for the SME sector (ADB 2007a). Based on a 2011 business survey, bank credit was found to comprise only 11 to 21 per cent of the capital funding of SMEs in the Philippines, well below the 30 per cent benchmark observed in other countries like Thailand and India (c.f. Briones 2016). Just as striking have been the findings of the Bangko Sentral ng Pilipinas (BSP)'s Consumer Finance Survey that only 14 per cent of Filipinos were in possession of bank accounts (BSP 2014). This lack of accessible credit compels lower-income, vulnerable groups to borrow instead from informal, unregulated lenders, exposing them to risks of usury. In the Philippines and elsewhere, moneylenders have often been documented to prey on poor households amidst bad shocks (Fafchamps and Gubert 2004).

EXPLAINING POVERTY AND INEQUALITY: POLITICAL ECONOMY FACTORS

Beyond technical factors, political economy processes also loom large in explaining current inequality and social mobility trends. Spanning factors that involve relational dynamics and strategic interactions between various economic actors and players, these drivers tend to contribute to persistent poverty and inequality by reinforcing the "adverse incorporation" of the poor and vulnerable in production, market, and institutional processes (Hickey and du Toit 2007). Clearly, many of the inequalities across different dimensions, including education, health and welfare, as noted in the earlier section, have their roots also in the lack of access of marginalized households to public programmes, which is in turn rooted in the lack of political participation of these households and groups in the country.

Market Power, Patronage, and Political Dynasties

While the Philippine economy has been significantly liberalized and deregulated since the 1980s, insufficiently competitive market structures, and rentierist business dynamics have critically impeded more inclusive development processes in the country. Amid the economic disruptions that the country's trade liberalization has imposed on employment and sectoral performance (Action for Economic Reform 2014; Bello et al. 2005, 2014; Lopez 2009; Ofreneo 2013; Serrano 2008; Tauli-Corpuz, Sidchogan-Bati and Maza 2006), tariff reductions appear to have facilitated a shift in accumulation and employment activities towards more protected and lower-value sectors (e.g., services, non-manufacturing industry) where wage inequality tends to be high to begin with (Aldaba 2012).

This shift has been especially marked for the Philippines' large-scale conglomerates, which amid trade liberalization in agriculture and manufacturing, coupled with the existence of provisions in the 1987 Constitution limiting full foreign participation in certain segments of the Philippine economy (e.g., property development, utilities and finance), have insulated themselves from increased foreign competition by venturing into non-tradeable sectors where new opportunities for private sector participation have either been opened up by market reforms (e.g., energy, water, telecommunications and airlines), as well as increasing consumption by overseas Filipino workers (e.g., retail and property development) (Raquiza 2014; Bello et al. 2014). For the most part, this has allowed Philippine big business to adjust to liberalization by venturing into protected, rent-rich areas, which harbour less potential to drive inequality- and poverty-reducing growth (Mendoza, Arbo and Cruz 2019).

At present, most of the commanding heights of the Philippine economy are dominated by the aforementioned conglomerates, who are typically engaged in limited "conglopolistic" competition (Fabella 2016) in sectors with weak regulators. This likewise underscores broader challenges concerning flawed market structures in the country: for instance, upon being set up in 2017, the Philippine Competition Commission had received no less than twenty-six queries and complaints against anti-competitive practices in various industries in manufacturing, agriculture, and public services (Salaverria 2017). In the rice sector, for example, trading cartels have been documented to generate artificial shortages in rice supply—thus raising consumer prices, while keeping farm-gate prices low (Intal and Garcia 2005).

Linked to the lack of market competition has been the lack of substantive competition in the political sphere, manifested most prominently in the problem of political dynasties. Indeed, the ubiquity of clan dominance in politics as well as patronage relations in governance, have tended to skew economic and political institutions to favour and protect the private interests of elites, whether in terms of dynastic control of political offices, rent-seeking, and political appointments in the bureaucracy, regulatory capture, as well as arbitrary political interference in business and development programs (Hutchcroft 1998; Krinks 2002; World Bank 2013; Mendoza, Arbo and Cruz 2017). Empirical research has confirmed the linkage between political dynasties and poverty, with Beja et al. (2016) finding that the presence of dynasties has a negative effect on socio-economic outcomes in jurisdictions outside of Luzon island. In particular, when coterminous or "fat" dynasties[7] dominate key elective positions in local government, incentives to respond programmatically to citizens' demands for services and uphold accountability norms in the management of public resources may be weakened, given the lower degree of political competition and checks-and-balances that they confront relative to non-dynastic ones (Albert et al. 2015).

Indeed, there is increasing evidence that the presence of coterminous dynasties adversely affects the provision of services that have been devolved for delivery by local governments. As pointed out by Diokno and Maddawin (2018) in a review of the literature and evidence on Philippine decentralization, local governments controlled by dynasties are more likely to distort the provision of goods and services in rentierist directions, whether in terms of allocating resources in areas/projects that are prone to corruption (e.g., infrastructure and public works) or susceptible to clientelist realignment (e.g., health and social welfare services, temporary local government jobs). Recent empirical analyses of public expenditure patterns among all Philippine cities have confirmed that the presence of coterminous dynasties has similar effects on local spending patterns as increases in unconditional fiscal transfers, which are known to be prone to accountability issues (Cruz 2020). Under such conditions of state capture, the impact of public sector interventions to promote inclusive development have generally been diluted, due to the underlying rentierist political economy and its repercussions on the institutional quality of governance.

Policy Regime Incoherence and Weak State Capacity

Since the late 1980s, the Philippines has been noteworthy in terms of the thoroughness with which it has pursued a pro-liberalization policy agenda, and with which it has reined in the strategic role of government in shaping the development of the economy. With the ousting of the Marcos government in 1986, however, state intervention to prop domestic industry was soon viewed as epitomizing the cronyism of the Marcos years, justifying a systematic break with extensive government involvement in the economy and industrial development (Aldaba 2013a; Action for Economic Reforms 2014). Thus, apart from the pursuit of trade liberalization, state monopolies in key sectors (e.g., fertilizer and sugar) were dismantled, programmatic state support to domestic industries (e.g., Marcos' eleven major import substitution industrialization (ISI) projects in intermediate goods production) were abandoned, while major reforms were undertaken in the country's investment regimes to significantly expand the scope for participation by foreign firms and to promote neutrality in the treatment of investment from different sources (Raquiza 2012; Llanto and Ortiz 2015; Bello et al. 2014).

Unfortunately, this abandonment of public sector-led efforts for steering economic development has produced mixed results. While major flaws in Marcos-era interventionism, such as the large-scale mismanagement of the country's economic resources, the penalization of exports, and the artificial cheapening of capital among domestic industries have been avoided (Medalla 1998), market-oriented reforms, coupled with an extended period of debt repayment and fiscal austerity, have been unable to address critical development constraints in the provision of critical inputs necessary for industrial deepening, such as in infrastructure and logistics, industrial peace, buoyant consumer markets, and stable and non-corrupt governance (Aldaba 2006; Bello et al. 2014), and have thus failed to avert the premature deindustrialization of the economy. Similarly, though it is true that a number of investment-oriented agencies (e.g., the Philippine Economic Zone Authority), have been built up in terms of their capacity to firewall investor and business activities from arbitrary governance dynamics, such apparatuses have yet to deliver significantly upon several industrial policy goals, due to their institutional isolation from the rest of their bureaucracy, as well as their potential for policy incoherence with a substantive industrial development framework (Manasan 2013).

On a similar note, the capacity of the government to ensure that it can effectively regulate economic sectors and market players within them has been handicapped by a weak bureaucracy, subpar effectiveness to extract fiscal resources for development, and the lack of institutional capabilities to implement development programs. Monsod (2008/9) noted that the quality of higher-level civil servants (administrative and highly technical) have decreased in the 1990s and 2000s given low civil service pay up until the mid-2010s, inequities in the internal public sector compensation due to compressed salary schedules, and weak monitoring and performance mechanisms. Likewise, in spite of improvements in recent years, such as the passage of excise tax hikes in alcohol and tobacco products in 2012, and major tax reforms in 2017, total government revenue remains low compared to other Asian countries (Larrson, 2013; Manasan 2013). Such limited fiscal space and constraints in allocating budgetary resources significantly compounds government's "structural bottlenecks" in ensuring the effective delivery of critical social and economic development programs.

The shift towards a liberalized policy regime has also consigned redistributive and anti-poverty programmes to residual status. Indeed, as a legacy of social justice clauses in the 1987 Constitution, a spectrum of asset reform laws and programmes benefiting the poorest economic sectors (e.g., land reform for farmers, and ancestral domain titling for indigenous communities) were established in the 1990s, while official anti-poverty structures were institutionalized, including the National Anti-Poverty Commission in 1998. However, the general direction of economic reforms, coupled with the continuing influence of land-based elites, have directly conflicted with the effective implementation of these programmes. Not only were redistribution-focused agencies usually deprived of significant budgets and personnel in most administrations (e.g., the Department of Agrarian Reform and the National Housing Authority), economic pressures unleashed by market reform, such as import competition in agriculture, accelerating urban property development, and the removal of restrictions on foreign mining, served to undermine investments and initiatives undertaken by such programmes (Bello et al. 2014). Further compounding these contradicting trends have been institutional constraints, such as weak targeting, poor interagency coordination, the politicization of programmes along clientelist lines, quick staff turnover, and the absence of a professional "core" of bureaucrats among anti-poverty programmes (ADB 2009).

The entry of the reformist Aquino administration into power in 2010 brought some hope that there would be substantial policy momentum towards addressing entrenched poverty and inequality challenges. While the government has since launched several major initiatives, including the expansion of a widely lauded conditional cash transfer programme, the development of universal education and health programmes, and strengthened participation in the governance processes, including implementation of the "Bottom-Up Budgeting" process (i.e., programme that allows civil society groups to identify programmes and projects that could be funded from the national budget), more difficult structural and institutional reforms (e.g., land reform and land-use policies, labour market reforms and public finance reforms) have yet to be fully implemented. The present Duterte administration has essentially inherited this same set of social policies and coupled it with a greater focus on infrastructure spending (Diokno 2017). Yet the space for more inclusive and participatory governance in the new government has seemingly become more restricted, given its contentious focus on undertaking a "war on drugs" (with adverse effects on the poor), as well as its broader assault on civil rights and freedoms.

Most recently, weaknesses in state capacities to address the needs of the poor and vulnerable can also be glimpsed in the government response to the social effects of the COVID-19 pandemic. While the government has been lauded for its quick response to the provision of cash grants to vulnerable households and unemployed workers, several weeks into the programme, assistance still had yet to reach half of its targeted households and the labour ministry still has to respond to thousands of applications for relief of displaced workers (Nicholls 2020). With regards to the health system, the University of the Philippines (2020) has also noted the weak capacity of the health facilities to absorb those affected by the COVID-19 pandemic despite the imposition of lockdowns across the Philippines, due to the lack of hospital infrastructure, adequate equipment, and medical personnel.

CONCLUSION AND POLICY RECOMMENDATIONS

In the past thirty years, the Philippine political economy has undergone a historic transformation: confronted by severe recession at the end of the Marcos dictatorship, democratic institutions have been restored, even while the economy has been restructured into one of the most market-oriented in the region. While the reconfiguration of the economy has allowed for gains in addressing the country's poverty, inequality, and development challenges, the pace of improvement has been disappointing given the country's accelerating growth record. The structure and patterns of growth, though benefiting low-income and vulnerable demographics, have not been able to generate similar broad-based developmental dividends as with the country's neighbours in the Asia-Pacific. Despite some improvements, the level of overall income inequality remains high, even as the growth in the middle class has been slow. Worse, land and financial wealth inequalities have widened, with little sign of abating.

The drivers of this lacklustre poverty and inequality reduction record throughout the post-dictatorship period can be attributed to several factors. Certainly, technical factors loom large: the country's transition from an industry-led to a low-end services-focused economy, as well as the precarious, insecure working conditions of a significant share of the population, have been critical in explaining the lack of expansive and secure pathways into the middle class. Across sectors, issues of underinvestment in infrastructure, substandard provision of productivity-enhancing goods and services (including for human capital formation), and unfavourable business and labour market environments, have impeded advancement to higher value-adding activities and value-chain segments—though these challenges may be most severe in the case of agriculture. All these factors have resulted in a less than favourable performance in terms of the country's socio-economic mobility record compared to its ASEAN neighbours.

But no less decisive, and in numerous cases underlying many of the same factors, are political economy dynamics concerning the dominance of rentierist elites over the commanding heights of government and the economy. In particular, the restoration of political dynasties over the formal political arena at national and local levels, and the truncation of the capacity of the Philippine state to act as an effective development and regulatory player amidst the much-expanded role of family-linked conglomerates in the economy, have substantially curbed the capacity of non-oligarchic groups, market players, and social formations, to assert more inclusive democratization and development policy regimes. While much of this post-dictatorship order remains "contested" by reformist groups and administrations, who have occasionally secured governance and redistributive advances throughout the years (Quimpo 2008; Thompson 2010; Sidel 2014), the oligarchic complexion of the Philippines' contemporary political economy has yet to experience any comparable challenge similar to what prevailed towards the end of the Marcos period.

The following represent several of the most pressing policy priorities for the Philippines to achieve sustainable and equitable development, while also addressing impacts of the COVID-19 pandemic:

- *Strengthening access to education:* Despite improvements in recent years, large gaps in education inequality at the tertiary level persist—given that the government has not fully addressed gaps in basic education. To this end, additional budgetary resources should be provided by the government to ensure that primary and secondary school aged children have access to adequate classrooms and school facilities; basic education should not suffer from shortages of teachers, learning materials and other teaching equipment, while teacher training should address gaps in teaching competencies. Improving administrative systems, including by providing resources to local school leaders to address maintenance and operating issues, and strengthening accountability to address poor performance would therefore be important.

  At the higher education level, while the Universal Access to Quality Tertiary Education Act of 2017 provides for free tuition and fees in state universities and colleges, out-of-pocket costs continue to be prohibitive for the poor and vulnerable. For this reason, more resources could be redirected to subsidizing their needs. Strengthening technical and vocational education may also be an option especially for those in the lower and lower middle classes.
- *Improve access to health services:* The COVID-19 pandemic has brought to fore the low capacity of the public health system, as well as inequities

in access to health services. As with education, it is important to increase resources allocated for health, especially in the creation of well-equipped health facilities and the availability of health human resources in less urbanized settings. Given the decentralized state of health service provision in the country, however, national government could strengthen the delivery of local health services by providing performance incentives for improved health provision in intergovernmental grants, if not revisiting the decentralization framework to better harmonize the quality of public health services.

In spite of the existence of a National Health Insurance Program and a significant expansion of coverage since 2012 among poor households, a recent study by the UPEcon Health Policy Development Program (2014) shows that out of pocket payments continue to be the largest source of health financing. To address this, health insurance premium ceilings can be raised while rates are lowered to increase contributions from high-income households, even as subsidies can be provided to the poor for medicines and other costs.

- *Supporting smallholder agriculture:* The poorest households continue to be concentrated in agriculture, and usually remain cut off from government support services, such as credit, rural infrastructure, marketing support and other extension services. This remains the case even for marginal and upland farmers who have already have access to land due to the government's agrarian reform program.

  Apart from promoting better access to support services, significant investments in research is necessary in order to help smallholders produce and shift to higher value-added products. Similarly, land markets must also be restructured in order to increase the efficiency of small landownership through a progressive land tax and/or the imposition of higher taxes on abandoned and idle lands.

- *Expanding employment in industry:* as previously mentioned, the Philippine economy has undergone premature deindustrialization, even as labour productivity remains highest among industrial sectors. Similarly, much of the country's lacklustre record in reducing poverty and expanding its middle class can be traced to the stagnation of its industrial sector relative to its neighbouring countries. While the Philippine government has sustained an industrial policy programme since the early 2010s, there remains space for further reforms to strengthen government's tools for fostering industrial development

(e.g., fiscal incentives reform), even as other critical inputs for more rapid industrial growth, such as infrastructure and efficient logistics, remain lacking. Addressing these gaps in the country's industrialization process is instrumental for augmenting patterns of inclusive growth.
- *Strengthening decent employment:* A 2016 report by the World Bank (2016) stresses the importance of undertaking improvements in the labour market, including the expansion of employment protection policies by encouraging formalization of enterprises, strengthening coordination of training programmes undertaken by different government agencies and expanding coverage to less educated youth and expanding the scope of public works programmes in areas with high levels of underemployment. At the same time, there is a need to integrate the different employment programmes with the social protection programmes, and to expand the programmes that deepen skills of workers and improve their long-term employment prospects.
- *Expanding unemployment insurance and social protection:* Compared to heavy-handed approaches towards labour flexibility (e.g., proposals to legislate the abolition of temporary employment contracts), Esguerra (2016) has suggested that mechanisms for risk sharing, including unemployment insurance, unemployment assistance, severance pay, unemployment insurance savings accounts, and public works, be also examined by the government as proposals to support the vulnerable sector.

Expanding social protection systems to minimize the impacts of the variety of risks that the poor and the vulnerable face are especially important. In particular, a recent World Bank review (2018a) of social protection programmes show that much effort still needs to be undertaken to align social insurance systems with the needs of informal workers. The presence of a system to strengthen the social registry of households, not only to include the poor who are present in the National Household Targeting System Poverty Reduction of the government's social welfare ministry but also the vulnerable and the middle class would also be critical. As the effects of the COVID-19 pandemic underscore the need for strong institutional mechanisms to protect vulnerable households from downward spirals. On this same note, increasing access to emergency food programmes and community-based workfare and social fund projects are of increasing importance, as studies have shown that increases in food and income poverty follow rainfall spikes (Safir, Piza and Skoufias 2013; Bayudan-Dacuycuy 2016).

- *Improving local governance:* while the Philippines' local government code has been lauded as a milestone piece of legislation, and one of the most prominent decentralization reforms in Southeast Asia, improvements in local governance have remained uneven due to imperfections in the law. Ambiguities in the delineation of functions have typically led to problems of unfunded mandates; provincial and municipal local governments are disadvantaged in the allocation of resources relative to cities; and the intergovernmental fiscal framework installs a variety of perverse incentives that underpin poor service delivery and a trend among LGUs to ineffectively use, if not outright misuse, public resources. Though islands of good local governance have emerged, these challenges underscore the need for revisiting the local governance framework, which will be of critical importance given LGUs' frontline role in poverty reduction and development efforts.
- *Political reforms and participatory governance:* Given the pervasiveness of dynasties in the country's political system, and their deleterious impacts on development outcomes and service delivery, reforms are necessary to increase electoral competition. This can include legislation that revisits the banning of political dynasties (a clause in the 1987 Constitution that has not been acted upon), checks and balances on elected officials especially in appointing bureaucrats in the civil service, as well as measures to strengthen the role of programmatic political parties. Such reforms can also be completed by ensuring greater participation of social groups in politics and governance processes, such as by reforming the Philippines' party-list law and strengthening the inclusion of the civil society organizations and marginalized sectors in local development councils.

As of writing, the economic and social effects of the coronavirus pandemic are still unknown for the long term, but they have already put immense strain on the economy, most especially for poor and vulnerable households. As with during the Asian Financial Crisis of 1997–98 (Tabunda and Albert 2002), there is a substantial risk of declining output, rising unemployment, and increasing immiseration which could erase much of the gains in poverty and social mobility in recent years. Once the immediate public health crisis caused by the pandemic is resolved, redoubled efforts to reduce inequalities across welfare dimensions, including income, education and health, land and financial assets, and to improve social mobility will be essential to tackling the challenges discussed throughout this chapter.

Notes

1. The authors would like to thank Lee Hwok Aun and Christopher Choong who shepherded the project on Inequality and Exclusion in Southeast Asia, supported by the ISEAS – Yusof Ishak Institute, Singapore, and the Konrad Adenauer Stiftung, under which this research was undertaken and also participants of the various workshops undertaken by the project for useful comments and suggestions. The authors, however, take responsibility for any errors.
2. While Singapore (0.04 per cent), Brunei (4 per cent) and Malaysia (8 per cent) had the lowest tariff levels among ASEAN countries by 1996, the Philippines nonetheless made the biggest strides towards tariff reduction among ASEAN member states, declining by 31 percentage points from 1978 (44 per cent) to 1996 (13 per cent). The next most significant reduction during this period occurred in Indonesia, which, by comparison, decreased by 21 percentage points (33 per cent to 12 per cent) (Paderon 2017).
3. There is very little information on dividend ownership available in the Philippines which can help identify whether the difference in growth rates of firm incomes and household incomes is more an indication that a large portion of the earnings are retained and not distributed to households as dividends. The BSP 2019 Financial Inclusion Survey (Bangko Sentral ng Pilipinas 2019) notes that 55 per cent of the "ABC" population, i.e., those in the upper- and middle-income categories, own investments, including dividends, but only 16 per cent of the "E" population, i.e., the poorest households, are able to undertake these savings.
4. Indigenous peoples refer to a "group of people or homogenous societies identified by self-ascription and ascription by others, who have continuously lived as organized community on communally bounded and defined territory, and who have, under claims of ownership since time immemorial, occupied, possessed and utilized such territories, sharing common bonds of language, customs, traditions and other distinctive cultural traits, or who have, through resistance to political, social and cultural inroads of colonization, nonindigenous religions and cultures, became historically differentiated from the majority of Filipinos" (Republic Act 8371, Government of the Philippines, 1997). These are

primarily ethnolinguistic groups which were fully or partially isolated during the Spanish and American colonial periods in Philippine history. They comprise approximately 8 to 10 per cent of the total Philippine population.
5. The "middle class" socio-economic category is defined based on expenditure thresholds adopts the thresholds from World Bank (2018c). The World Bank defines the different categories according to the per capita expenditures; these categories include the following: extremely poor (daily per capita expenditure is less than or equal to US$1.9), poor (between US$1.90 and US$3.10), vulnerable (between $3.10 to $5.50), economically secure (between $5.50 to $15), upper middle class (between $15 to $50) and top ($50 or more). Middle class in Figure 6.12 is the combined shares of the economically secure and upper middle categories. The shares are calculated using the World Bank PovcalNet http://iresearch.worldbank.org/PovcalNet/introduction.aspx; the shares for each category in each country are calculated using a constant purchasing power parity index for the 2011 base year.
6. See the Philippine Human Development Network (2013) for details of the decomposition exercise. The publication has noted that consideration should be given to the spatial dependence in interprovincial incomes and development outcomes, and these outcomes experience strong "neighbourhood effects," or areas closer together have a direct or indirect effect on each other's outcomes.
7. According to Mendoza (2018), "fat" political dynasties are characterized by two or more individuals belonging to the same family by blood or marital affiliation who are holding a major political post at the local level (e.g., provincial governor, vice-governor or councillor, or congressional representative or city mayor or vice mayor) simultaneously. This is in contrast with "thin" dynasties, in which family members hold political office consecutively, i.e., there is only one member of a family holding office at a single time).

References

Action for Economic Reforms – Industrial Policy Team. 2014. *An Industrial Policy for the Philippines: Correcting Decades of Error*. Quezon City: Action for Economic Reforms.

ADB. 2007a. *Philippines: Critical Development Constraints*. Mandaluyong City: Asian Development Bank.

———. 2007b. *Paradox and Promise in the Philippines: A Joint Country Gender Assessment*. Mandaluyong City: Asian Development Bank, Canadian International Development Agency, European Commission, National Commission on the Role of Filipino Women, United Nations Children's Fund, United Nations Development Fund for Women, United Nations Population Fund.

———. 2009. *Poverty in the Philippines: Causes, Constraints and Opportunities*. Mandaluyong City: ADB.

Albert, Jose Ramon, Jesus Dumagan, and Arturo Martinez, Jr. 2015. "Inequalities in Income, Labour, and Education: The Challenge of Inclusive Growth". Discussion Paper 2015-01, Philippine Institute for Development Studies. Makati City: Philippine Institute for Development Studies.

———, and Martin Joseph Raymundo. 2015. "Why Inequality Matters in Poverty Reduction and Why the Middle Class Needs Policy Attention". Discussion Paper 2015-55, Philippine Institute for Development Studies. Makati City: Philippine Institute for Development Studies.

———, Ronald Mendoza, David Yap, and Jan Frederick Cruz. 2015. "Regulating Political Dynasties Toward a More Inclusive Society". Policy Note 2015-14. Makati City: Philippine Institute for Development Studies.

Aldaba, Rafaelita. 2006. "FDI Investment Incentive System and FDI Inflows: The Philippine Experience". Discussion Papers Series No. 2006-20, Philippine Institute for Development Studies. Makati City: Philippine Institute for Development Studies.

———. 2012. "Surviving Trade Liberalization in Philippine Manufacturing". Discussion Paper No. 2012-10, Philippine Institute for Development Studies. Makati City: Philippine Institute for Development Studies.

———. 2013a. "Twenty Years after Philippine Trade Liberalization and Industrialization: What Has Happened and Where Do We Go from Here". Discussion Paper Series No. 2013-21, Philippine Institute for Development Studies. Makati City: Philippine Institute for Development Studies.

———. 2013b. "Impact of Trade Liberalization on Wage Skill Premium in Philippine Manufacturing". Discussion Paper Series No. 2013-25, Philippine Institute for Development Studies. Makati City: Philippine Institute for Development Studies.

———. 2014. "The Philippine Manufacturing Industry Roadmap: Agenda for New Industrial Policy, High Productivity Jobs, and Inclusive Growth". Discussion Paper Series No. 2014-32, Philippine Institute for Development Studies. Makati City: Philippine Institute for Development Studies.

Ang, Alvin, Bryan Balco, Jerik Cruz, and Natalie Custodio. 2019. *The Impact of Trade on Employment: A Philippine Country Report*. Manila: International Labour Organization.

Arguelles, Cleve V. 2017. "Grounding Populism: Perspectives from Populist Publics". MA dissertation, Central European University, Budapest.

Balisacan, Arsenio. 2015. "The State of the Philippine Economy". Ayala-UPSE Forum, Intercontinental Manila, Makati City, 29 January 2015.

Bangko Sentral ng Pilipinas. 2014. "Consumer Finance Survey 2014". Department of Economic Statistics, BSP. Manila: BSP.

———. 2017. *2017 Annual Report: Sustaining the Growth Momentum*. Manila: BSP.
Bayudan-Dacuycuy, Connie. 2016. *Weather Events and Welfare in the Philippine Households*. Discussion Paper Series No. 2016-34, Philippine Institute of Development Studies.
Beja Jr., Edsel, R. Mendoza, Victor Venida, and David Yap. 2012. "Inequality in Democracy: Insights from an Empirical Analysis of Political Dynasties in the 15th Philippine Congress". MPRA Paper No. 40104. Munich: Munich Personal RePEc Archive.
Bello, Walden, and John Gershman. 1990. "Democratization and Stabilization in the Philippines". *Critical Sociology* 17, no. 1: 35–56.
———, Marissa De Guzman, Mary Lou Malig, and Herbert Docena. 2005. *The Anti-Development State: The Political Economy of Permanent Crisis in the Philippines*. London: Zed Books.
———, Kenneth Cardenas, Jerome Patrick Cruz, Alinaya Fabros, Mary Ann Manahan, Clarissa Militante, Joseph Purugganan, and Jenina Joy Chavez. 2014. *State of Fragmentation: The Philippines in Transition*. Manila: Friedrich Ebert Stiftung and Focus on the Global South.
Bernstein, Henry, Ben Crow, and Hazel Johnson, eds. 1992. *Rural Livelihoods: Crises and Responses*. Oxford: Oxford University Press.
Boyce, James. 1993. *The Philippines: The Political Economy of Growth and Impoverishment in the Marcos Era*. Honolulu: University of Hawaii Press.
Briones, Roehlano. 2013. "Agriculture, Rural Employment, and Inclusive Growth". Discussion Paper Series No. 2013-39, Philippine Institute of Development Studies. Makati City: Philippine Institute for Development Studies.
———. 2016. "Growing Inclusive Businesses in the Philippines: The Government Policies and Programs". Discussion Paper 2016-06, Philippine Institute for Development Studies. Makati City: Philippine Institute for Development Studies.
———. 2019. "Competition in the Rice Industry: An Issues Paper". PCC Issues Paper No. 1, Series of 2019, Philippine Competition Commission. Quezon City: Philippine Competition Commission.
Broad, Robin. 1981. "New Directions at World Bank: Philippines as Guinea Pig". *Economic and Political Weekly* 16, no. 47: 1919–22.
Clarke, Gerald. 1998. *The Politics of NGOs in South-East Asia: Participation and Protest in the Philippines*. London: Routledge.
Clarke, Gerard. 2013. *Civil Society in the Philippines: Theoretical, Methodological and Policy Debates*. London: Routledge.
Coronel, Sheila, Yvonne T. Chua, Luz Rimban, and Booma B. Cruz. 2007. *The Rulemakers: How the Wealthy and the Well-Born Dominate Congress*. Manila: Anvil Publishing.
Cruz, Jerik. 2019. "Conglomerates and Inclusive Markets: Building a Market

Innovation Ecosystem". Ateneo School of Government, Aruga Hotel, Makati City, 6 February 2019.

———. 2020. "Fiscal Contracts and Local Public Services: Evidence from Philippine Cities". Working Paper No. 2020-05. ADMU Econ-ACERD Working Paper Series. Quezon City: Ateneo de Manila University Department of Economics.

Curato, Nicole. 2017. *A Duterte Reader: Critical Essays on Rodrigo Duterte's Early Presidency*. Quezon City: Ateneo de Manila Press.

David, Clarissa, and Jose Ramon Albert. 2012. "Recent Trends in Out of School Children in the Philippines". Discussion Paper 2012-07, Philippine Institute for Development Studies.

———, Jose Ramon Albert, and Jana Flor Vizmanos. 2018. "Sustainable Development Goal 5: How Does the Philippines Fare in Gender Equality". Research Paper Series No. 2018-04, Philippine Institute for Development Studies. Makati City: Philippine Institute for Development Studies.

Daway, Sarah, and Raul Fabella. 2015. "Development Progeria and the Rodrik Hypothesis". *Philippine Review of Economics* 52, no. 2: 84–99.

dela Paz, C., and C. Schnabel. 2017. "Wealth of 50 Filipinos Account for 24% of PH's 2016 GDP". *Rappler*, 25 August 2017. https://www.rappler.com/business/179857-henry-sy-forbes-richest-philippines-2017 (accessed 10 May 2019).

Department of Public Works and Highways. 2017. *National Roads and Bridges 2017 Inventory*. Department of Public Works and Highways. http://www.dpwh.gov.ph/dpwh/2017%20DPWH%20Road%20and%20Bridge%20Inventory/index.htm (accessed 10 May 2019).

Diokno, Benjamin. 2017. "Financing the Philippine Golden Age of Infrastructure". *BusinessWorld*. 1 June 2017. http://www.bworldonline.com/content.php?section=Opinion&title=financing-the-philippine-golden-age-of-infrastructure&id=146039 (accessed 10 May 2019).

Diokno-Sicat, Justine, and Ricxie Maddawin. 2018. "A Survey of Literature on Philippine Decentralization". Discussion Paper 2018-23. Quezon City: Philippine Institute for Development Studies.

Dohner, Robert, and Ponciano Intal. 1989. "The Marcos Legacy: Economic Policy and Foreign Debt in the Philippines". In *Developing Country Debt and Economic Performance, Volume 3: Country Studies—Indonesia, Korea, Philippines, Turkey*, edited by J. Sachs and S. Collins. Chicago: University of Chicago Press.

Esguerra, Emmanuel. 2016. "Ending 'Endo'—Larger Issues". Per Se, School of Economics, University of the Philippines. 23 November 2016. https://www.econ.upd.edu.ph/perse/?p=5734 (accessed 10 April 2020).

Fabella, Raul. 2016. "Conglopolistic Competition in Small Emerging Economies: When Large and Diversified is Beautiful". Discussion Paper 2016-05, School of Economics, University of the Philippines. Quezon City: UPSE.

Fafchamps, Marcel, and Flore Gubert. 2004. "The Formation of Risk Sharing Networks". *Economic Development and Cultural Change* 55, no. 4: 633–67.
Food and Nutrition Research Institute. 2003. *National Nutrition Survey*. Taguig: FNRI-DOST.
———. 2005. *Updating National Nutrition Survey*. Taguig: FNRI-DOST.
Green, Maia, and David Hulme. 2005. "From Correlates and Characteristics to Causes: Thinking About Poverty from a Chronic Poverty Perspective". *World Development* 33, no. 6: 867–79.
Habito, Cielito. 2012. "Economic Growth for All". *Philippine Daily Inquirer*, 25 June 2012. https://opinion.inquirer.net/31439/economic-growth-for-all (accessed 10 May 2019).
Herrin, Alejandro. 2016. "Putting Prevention of Childhood Stunting into the Forefront of the Nutrition Agenda: A Nutrition Sector Review". Discussion Paper 2016-21, Philippine Institute for Development Studies. Quezon City: Philippine Institute for Development Studies.
Heydarian, Richard. 2018. *The Rise of Duterte: A Populist Revolt against Elite Democracy*. London: Palgrave: Macmillan.
Hickey, Samuel, and Andreis du Toit. 2007. "Adverse Incorporation, Social Exclusion and Chronic Poverty". Working Paper 81, Chronic Poverty Research Center. Manchester: CPRC.
Huntington, Samuel. 1991. "Democracy's Third Wave". *Journal of Democracy* 2, no. 2: 12–34.
Hutchcroft, Paul. 1998. *Booty Capitalism: The Politics of Banking in the Philippines*. Ithaca, NY: Cornell University Press.
Hutchison, Jane. 1993. "Class and State Power in the Philippines". In *Southeast Asia in the 1990s: Authoritarianism, Democracy and Capitalism*, edited by Kevin Hewison, Richard Robison and Garry Rodan. St. Leonards, Australia: Allen and Unwin.
i Terme, Rosa Maria Alonso. 2015. "What Prevents the Philippines from Undertaking Tax Reform? A Story of the Unravelling State". ICTD Working Paper 16, International Center for Tax and Development. Sussex: ICTD.
Intal Jr., Ponciano, and Marissa Garcia. 2005. "Rice and Philippine Politics". Discussion Paper Series 2005-13, Philippine Institute for Development Studies. Makati City: Philippine Institute for Development Studies.
International Labour Organization. 2017. *Decent Work Country Diagnostics: Philippines 2017*. Manila: ILO.
Krinks, Peter. 2002. *The Economy of the Philippines: Elites, Inequalities and Economic Restructuring*. London: Routledge.
Konishi, Motoo, 2013. "Press Statement of Motoo Konishi, Co-Chair Philippines Development Forum". Philippine Development Forum, 5 February 2013.
Lanzona, Leonardo. 2018. "Understanding the Linkages between Land and Income

Inequality". Unpublished paper for the Philippine Human Development Network, Quezon City.

Larsson, Tomas. 2013. "The Strong and the Weak: Ups and Downs of State Capacity in Southeast Asia". *Asian Politics & Policy* 5, no. 3: 337–58.

Llanto, Gilberto M., and Ma. Kristina Ortiz. 2015. "Industrial Policies and Implementation: Philippine Automotive Manufacturing as a Lens". Discussion Paper No. 2015-39, Philippine Institute for Development Studies. Makati City: Philippine Institute for Development Studies.

Lopez, Marie. 2019. "The Impact of Trade Liberalization on Labour in the Philippines: A Summary Report". Structural Adjustment Participatory Review International Network (SAPRIN). http://www.saprin.org/philippines/research/phi_trade_sum.pdf (accessed 10 May 2019.

Macaraeg, Pauline. 2020. " 'Sariling Diskarte': The Heavy Impact of Lockdown on Micro, Small Businesses". *Rappler*. https://www.rappler.com/newsbreak/in-depth/257179-heavy-impact-coronavirus-lockdown-micro-small-medium-enterprises (accessed 10 April 2020).

Magadia, Jose. 2003. *State-Society Dynamics: Policy Making in a Restored Democracy*. Quezon City: Ateneo de Manila University Press.

Manasan, Rosario. 2013. "Export Processing Zones, Special Economic Zones: Do We Really Need to Have More of Them?". Policy Notes No. 2013-05, Philippine Institute for Development Studies. Makati City: Philippine Institute for Development Studies.

McCoy, Alfred. 2009. *An Anarchy of Families: State and Family in the Philippines*. Madison: University of Wisconsin Press.

McKay, Steven. 2006. *Satanic Mills or Silicon Islands? The Politics of High-Tech Production in the Philippines*. Ithaca, New York: Cornell University Press.

Medalla, Erlinda. 1998. "Trade and Industrial Policy Beyond 2000: An Assessment of the Philippine Economy". Discussion Paper Series No. 1998-05, Philippine Institute for Development Studies. Makati City: Philippine Institute for Development Studies.

Mendoza, Ronald U. 2018. "Integrity, Good Governance and Development". Presentation to the Center for People Empowerment in Governance, 7 February 2018.

———, Edsel Beja, Victor Venida, and David Yap. 2012. "Inequality in Democracy: Insights from an Empirical Analysis of Political Dynasties in the 15th Philippine Congress". *Philippine Political Science Journal* 33, no. 2: 132–45.

———, Diyina Arbo, and Jerome Patrick Cruz. 2019. "In Search of Philippine Chaebols". ASOG Working Paper 19-009. Ateneo School of Government. Quezon City: ASOG.

Microfinance Council of the Philippines. 2016. "Realizing the Sustainable Development Goals Through Microfinance". https://microfinancecouncil.

org/wp-content/uploads/2016/05/2016-MCPI-Conference_Documentation-Report-Final.pdf (accessed 9 May 2019).

Mitra, Raja Mikael. 2013. "Leveraging Service Sector Growth in the Philippines". Economics Working Paper No. 366, Asian Development Bank. Mandaluyong City: ADB.

Monsod, Toby. 2008/9. "The Philippine Bureaucracy: Incentive Structures and Implications for Performance". Discussion Paper Series No. 4, Philippine Human Development Network.

Montes, Manuel, and Jerik Cruz. 2020. "The Political Economy of Foreign Investment and Industrial Development: The Philippines, Malaysia, and Thailand in Comparative Perspective". *Journal of Asia Pacific Economie*s 25, no. 1: 16–39.

Muyrong, Marjorie. 2020. "#StayAtHome #Bayanihan: Understanding the Profile of Displaced Workers due to ECQ". Department of Economics and Ateneo Center for Economic Research and Development Policy Brief 2020- 03, Ateneo de Manila University. http://ateneo.edu/sites/default/files/downloadable-files/Policy%20Brief%202020-03.pdf (accessed 10 April 2020).

National Economic and Development Authority. 2020. "Addressing the Social and Economic Impact of the COVID-19 Pandemic". Draft as of 19 March 2020. http://www.neda.gov.ph/wp-content/uploads/2020/03/NEDA_Addressing-the-Social-and-Economic-Impact-of-the-COVID-19-Pandemic.pdf (accessed 10 April 2020).

Nicholls, A.C. 2020. "Some Employers Still Awaiting DOLE Feedback on Cash Aid for Workers". CNN Philippines. https://cnnphilippines.com/news/2020/4/7/dole-cash-aid-covid-19.html (accessed 10 April 2020).

Ofreneo, Rene. 2013a. "Precarious Philippines: Expanding Informal Sector, 'Flexibilizing' Labour Market". *American Behavioral Scientist* 57, no. 4: 420–43.

———. 2013b. *Asia and the Pacific: Advancing Decent Work Amidst Deepening Inequalities*. Philippines: ITUC-AP.

Ogena, Nimfa. 2006. "The Low and Slow Ageing in the Philippines: Auspicious or Challenging?". University of the Philippines Population Institute. Quezon City: UPPI.

Paderon, Marissa Maricosa. 2017. "An Economic Evaluation of the ASEAN Free Trade Agreement (AFTA): The Case of the Philippines". Makati Business Club Research Report. Makati City: Makati Business Club.

Philippine Center for Investigative Journalism (PCIJ). 2007. "And the Clans Play On". https://pcij.org/stories/and-the-clans-play-on/ (accessed 9 May 2019).

Philippine Human Development Network. 2013. *Geography and Human Development in the Philippines: 2012/13 Philippine Human Development Report*. Quezon City, Philippines.

———. 2019. *Statistical Appendix*. Unpublished data.

Philippine Statistics Authority (PSA). 2013. *National Demographic and Health Survey, 2013 Round*. Quezon City: PSA.

———. 2015. *2015 Family Income and Expenditure Survey*. Quezon City: Philippine Statistics Authority.
———. 2016. *Women and Men in the Philippines*. Quezon City: PSA.
———. 2017. *National Demographic and Health Survey, 2017 Round*. Quezon City: PSA.
———. 2017. *Integrated Survey on Labour and Employment, 2017 Round*. Quezon City: PSA.
———. 2019a. *National Accounts of the Philippines*. Quezon City: PSA.
———. 2019b. *Labour Force Survey*. Quezon City: PSA.
———. 2019c. *Annual Per Capita Poverty Threshold, Poverty Incidence and Magnitude of Poor Families, by Region and Province—2006, 2009, 2012 and 2015*. Quezon City: PSA.
———. 2019d. *Regional Accounts of the Philippines*. Quezon City: PSA.
Porio, Emma. 2012. "Decentralization, Power and Networked Governance Practices in Metro Manila". *Space and Polity* 16, no. 1: 7–27.
Quimpo, Nathan. 2008. *Contested Democracy and the Left in the Philippines After Marcos*. Quezon City: Ateneo de Manila University Press.
Racelis, Rachel, Fe Vida Dy-Liaco, Lilibeth David, and Lucille Nievera. 2016. "Health Account Estimates for the Philippines for CY 2012 Based on the 2011 National Health Accounts". *Philippine Journal of Development* 41 & 42, no. 1–2: 185–210.
Raquiza, Antoinette. 2017. "The Philippine Growth Momentum, Services, and Contentious Politics". Australia National University and Philippine Institute for Development Studies Conference 2017, Marco Polo Hotel, Pasig City, 18–19 October 2017.
———. 2018. "The Changing Configuration of Capitalism". In *Routledge Handbook of Contemporary Philippines*, edited by M. Thompson and E.V. Batalla. London: Routledge, 2018.
Republic of the Philippines. 2017. "Republic Act 8371: An Act to Recognize, Protect and Promote the Rights of Indigenous Cultural Communities/Indigenous Peoples, Creating A National Commission on Indigenous Peoples, Establishing Implementing Mechanisms, Appropriating Funds Therefore, and For Other Purposes". Official Gazette of the Philippines, https://www.officialgazette.gov.ph/1997/10/29/republic-act-no-8371/ (accessed 1 September 2020).
Reyes, Celia, Audrey Tabuga, Ronina Asis, and Maria Blesida Datu. 2012. "Poverty and Agriculture in the Philippines: Trends in Income Poverty and Distribution". Discussion Paper No. 2012-09, Philippine Institute for Development Studies. Makati City: Philippine Institute for Development Studies.
Rodrik, Dani. 2015. "Premature Industrialization". *Journal of Economic Growth* 21, no. 1: 1–33.
———. 2017. "Populism and the Economics of Globalization". *Journal of International Business Policy* 1, no. 1: 12–33.
Rivera, Temario. 2016. "Rethinking Democratization in the Philippines: Elections, Political Families and Parties". In *Chasing the Wind: Assessing Philippine*

Democracy. Second Edition, edited by F. Miranda and T. Rivera . Quezon City: UNDP and Phil Commission on Human Rights.

Safir, Abla, Sharon Faye Piza, and Emmanuel Skoufias. 2013. *Disquiet on the Weather Front: The Welfare Impacts of Climatic Variability in the Rural Philippines.* Washington, DC: World Bank.

Salaverria, L. 2017. "Competition Commission to Start Probing Cartels". *Philippine Daily Inquirer,* 4 August 2017.

Serrano, Melissa. 2007. "Of Jobs Lost and Wages Depressed: The Impact of Trade Liberalization on Employment and Wage Levels in the Philippines, 1980–2000". Paper presented in the International Conference on "Labour and the Challenges of Development", 1–3 April 2007, University of Witwatersrand, Johannesburg, South Africa, convened by the Global Labour University, https://mronline.org/2008/08/26/of-jobs-lost-and-wages-depressed-the-impact-of-trade-liberalization-on-employment-and-wage-levels-in-the-philippines-1980-20001/ (accessed 19 May 2019).

Sharma, Ruchir. 2013. *Break-Out Nations: In Pursuit of the Next Economic Miracles.* New York: W.W. Norton.

Sidel, John. 2014. *Achieving Reforms in Oligarchical Democracies: The Role of Leadership and Coalitions in the Philippines.* Research papers No. 27, Developmental Leadership Program, Birmingham: DLP.

Tabunda, Ana Marie, and Jose Ramon Albert. 2002. "Philippine Poverty in the Wake of the Asian Financial Crisis and El Niño". In *Impact of the East Asian Financial Crisis Revisited,* edited by Shahid Khandkher. Makati City: The World Bank Institute and the Philippine Institute of Development Studies.

Tan, Edita, and Charles Irvin Siriban. 2016. "How Well Has Education Lifted Families from Poverty". Unpublished paper written for the Philippine Human Development Network, Quezon City, Philippines.

Tauli-Corpuz, Victoria. Ruth Sidchogan-Bati, and Jim Maza. 2006. "The Impact of Globalization and Liberalization on Agriculture and Small Farmers in Developing Countries: The Case of the Philippines". Third World Network, April 2006 http://www.twn.my/title2/par/vicky_ifad_paper.rev_21_april_2006.doc (accessed 8 May 2019).

Teehankee, Benito. 2017. "Conglomerates and Inclusive Growth". *Business World Online,* 6 April 2017. http://www.bworldonline.com/content.php?section=Opinion&title=conglomerates-and-inclusive-growth&id=143344 (accessed 10 May 2019).

Thompson, Mark. 2010. "After Populism: Winning the 'War' for Bourgeois Democracy in the Philippines". In *The Politics of Change in the Philippines,* edited by Y. Kasuya and N.G. Quimpo. Manila: Anvil Publishing.

———. 2016. "Bloodied Democracy: Duterte and the Death of Liberal Reformism in the Philippines". *Journal of Current Southeast Asian Affairs* 35, no. 3: 39–68.

Timberman, David. 1991. "The Philippines in 1990: On Shaky Ground". *Asian Survey* 31, no. 2: 153–63.

UNDP. 2008. *Creating Value for All: Strategies for Doing Business with the Poor.* New York: UNDP.

University of the Philippines Pandemic Response Team. 2020. "Estimating Local Healthcare Capacity to Deal with COVID-19 Case Surge: Analysis and Recommendations". Policy Note 3.

UP School of Economics – Health Policy Development Program. 2017. *The Challenge of Reaching the Poor with a Continuum of Care: A 25 Year Assessment of the Philippine Health Sector Performance.* Quezon City: UPSE-Health Policy Development Program (HPDP), University of the Philippines Diliman.

Usui, Norio. 2012. *Taking the Right Road to Inclusive Growth: Industrial Upgrading and Diversification in the Philippines.* Mandaluyong City, Philippines: Asian Development Bank.

World Bank. 2013. *Philippine Development Report: Creating More and Better Jobs.* Manila: World Bank.

———. 2016. *Philippine Economic Update: Outperforming the Region and Managing the Transition.* April 2016. Manila: World Bank.

———. 2018a. *Philippine Economic Update: Investing in the Future.* Macroeconomics, Trade and Investment Global Practice, East Asia and Pacific Region.

———. 2018b. *Making Growth Work for the Poor: A Poverty Assessment for the Philippines.* Manila: World Bank.

———. 2018b. *Riding the Wave: An East Asian Miracle for the 21st Century.* Washington, DC: World Bank.

———. 2018c. *Global Economic Prospects: East Asia and the Pacific.* Manila: World Bank.

———. 2018d. *Doing Business: Reforming to Create Jobs.* Washington, DC: World Bank.

———. 2019. *World Bank Open Data.* https://data.worldbank.org/ (accessed 9 May 2019).

———. 2019. *World Bank PovCal Net.* http://iresearch.worldbank.org/PovcalNet/povOnDemand.aspx. (accessed 9 May 2019).

———. 2020. *East Asia and the Pacific in the Time of COVID-19.* Washington DC: World Bank.

7

INEQUALITY AND THE SOCIAL COMPACT IN SINGAPORE
Macro Trends vs Lived Inequalities

Nathan Peng[1]

INTRODUCTION

Increasingly divisive levels of inequality are a global problem with profound consequences. With many countries in both developed and developing contexts seeing increasing disparities between the haves and have-nots alike, the potentially disastrous consequences for society and politics and their impact on businesses and productivity can no longer be ignored. Against this backdrop, Singapore's developmental context is shifting as the rate of economic structural transformation slows. The city-state finds itself at a turning point where hard choices must be made to safeguard the social stability previously upheld by breakneck growth speeds. With its policies historically being an object of study for China, Southeast Asia, and other developed and developing economies, the learnings from how Singapore tackles inequality will resonate beyond its shores.

Addressing parliament in February 2018, Singapore's Prime Minister Lee Hsien Loong bluntly observed that if widening income inequalities were allowed to create "a rigid and stratified social system", "Singapore's politics will turn vicious, its society will fracture, and the country will wither". Sounding the exact same warning in her inaugural speech three months later, President Halimah Yacob noted that inequality had broken the social compact in many countries and Singapore "must tackle inequality" before the problem became entrenched (Yacob 2018). The recasting of inequality as a serious societal problem in Singapore has become increasingly prominent in recent years, including during the 2020 General Elections.

Although few would question the seriousness of inequality, there is far less consensus on its extent and how to mitigate it. This paper contributes to this debate by juxtaposing empirical trends against the emerging realization that while the normative commitment to meritocracy in Singapore has never slackened, its increasing tension against the lived realities of unequal opportunities is posing a jarring contrast to the narrative of equal life chances, taking an increasing toll on Singaporeans' belief in the system's ability to arbitrate life chances based on talent and effort.

There are three takeaways. First, inequality for Singapore has become a matter of national survival, tied to the larger social compact of a functioning meritocracy in spite of constructive efforts by the government towards mitigating the ills of what I call "time two meritocracy". Next, the current approach, while innovative, has not sufficiently addressed the underlying inequality of opportunity and the kinds of "felt inequality" that threaten national cohesion, thus coming across as incrementalistic. Essentially, the problem is one of degree, not type. Current policies, while heading in the right direction and having had some success in recent years, do not go far enough in narrowing inequality in terms of outcomes. Finally, as seen from some of the empirical results (luxury cars, sense of alienation in the education system, etc.), I argue that it is not the overall state of inequality that matter, but the lived everyday experiences on issues for which no amount of normative justification via meritocracy can assuage, no matter how well entrenched the narrative.

My analysis makes two theoretical contributions to understandings of Singapore and the nature of meritocracy. It first speaks to the fact that purely emphasizing equality of opportunity without a healthy degree of equality of outcomes is insufficient for maintaining a functioning meritocracy across generations. Secondly, contrary to Ian Holliday's (2000) insight that social policy in Singapore is subservient to economic considerations, Singapore's strong economic growth has been predicated on a stable socio-political context, and both social and economic policies are subservient to considerations of national survival for which economic progress was just a means, not an end.

The first section provides an empirical overview from available data on inequality typically starting from 2000 up to 2018. Most measures reflect how inequality has been generally stable in the five years leading up to 2018, after an increase from the initial years to 2012. While inequality increased in absolute terms during this period, this fails to explain the sharp spike in public attention in 2018. To explain the timing of the backlash, I qualitatively review how Singapore's meritocracy evolved over time to create perceptions of an uncaring brand of elitism. I then review policy responses thus far and conclude that while the efforts are a step in the right direction, they do not sufficiently address the gap. For example, while growth in real income was faster for the lower deciles from 2014 to 2018, overall growth from 2000 to 2018 for higher income groups were far greater (see below). There has also been insufficient attention paid to "felt inequality", on issues that have an outsized impact on how Singaporeans experience inequality. All this poses the puzzle of why, if the government is so keenly aware of the critical importance of combating inequality, have policy shifts been so incremental. I suggest the answer is not found in previous hypothesis that the Singapore government prioritizes the economic over the social as a rule, but in perceived trade-offs. I conclude by arguing that, while the principle of not burdening individuals and companies to keep the economy vibrant as a way to foster mobility is not wrong, Singapore has reached the point when tackling the gap between the haves and have-nots more strongly and directly would improve Singapore's prospects for sustainable economic growth in the long run.

EMPIRICAL OVERVIEW

To paint a comprehensive picture of the state of Singapore's inequality, this section covers both macro quantitative indicators as well as relevant survey data from credible sources. The selection of categories is intended to reflect both the indicators that enable Singapore's case to be analysed comparatively (income, consumption, wealth) as well as those that reflect how inequality is perceived in the Singaporean context (intergenerational mobility, education, and sense of belonging). Table 7.1 provides a summary of the insights drawn.

TABLE 7.1
Singapore: Summary of Inequality Trends

Income Inequality—Gini Coefficient	Inequality, as portrayed by the Gini coefficient, was relatively stable between 2000 and 2018. The Gini coefficient increased starting 2000 before stabilizing at around 0.405 from 2014 to 2018. Reduction in the Gini, due to government taxes and transfers, increased from 6.3 per cent in 2000 to 11.8 per cent in 2018.
Income Inequality—top 10 per cent vs bottom 10 per cent real household income per member	There was an across-the-board increase in real income for all groups, but growth for better-off groups was greater even though the trend reversed slightly in years leading up to 2018. The ratio of top 10 per cent to bottom 10 per cent household income per member increased from 18.4 in 2000 to 23.8 in 2018. In terms of real change in household income per member from 2000 to 2018, that of the • Bottom 10 per cent increased by 29.4 per cent • Top 10 per cent increased by 85.8 per cent.
Consumption Inequality	Increases in expenditure was observed for all income quintiles. Ratio of expenditure for the top 20 per cent to bottom 20 per cent of households in terms of income increased from 3.53 in 2002/03 to 3.78 in 2007/8 before dropping again to 3.55 in 2012/13.
Wealth Inequality	After a sharp drop from 2010 to 2011, wealth inequality in Singapore has remained fairly stable. In absolute terms, the wealth Gini coefficient is consistently higher than the income Gini.
Intergenerational Inequality	Singapore fared better than selected economies like the US, UK, Denmark and Canada in terms of probability of those in the bottom quintile of income making it into the top quintile. Comparing the 1969–73 and 1978–82 cohorts, the association between parents' and children's income ranks is almost similar.
Educational Inequality	Tertiary completion rates by parents' education have converged over the years. However, according to PISA, socio-economic background plays a significant role in the determination of cognitive performance in Singapore.
Geographic Inequality	There was a clear concentration of households earning more than $20,000 per month versus those who earned less than $2,000 in certain areas, but the overall distribution was relatively even: • 7.1 per cent of regions had more than 10 times the higher income households • 25 per cent had between 2 to 5 times • 42.9 per cent had between 1 to 2 times • 25 per cent had less than 1 times (i.e., more lower income households). Similar patterns emerge breaking down residential property by types.
Inequality and Sense of Belonging	Those identifying with higher classes felt greater belonging to Singapore and felt prouder to be Singaporean. The gap in belonging between children from disadvantaged backgrounds versus those who are not has grown.

Income Inequality: Gini Coefficien

Singapore's Gini coefficient[2] has typically been high compared to other countries. A common caveat against using the Gini to measure Singapore's inequality in a comparative context is that it is unrealistic because of its predominantly urban economy. The argument is that urban inequality tends to be higher than rural inequality, and generally higher than country-level inequality (as measured by Gini), particularly in more developed contexts (OECD 2016a). Given Singapore's duality as both a city and a state, Singapore's Gini could thus be mechanistically higher compared to other countries.[3] Since city-states are extremely limited in number and those that exist developed in unique contexts (other modern city-states besides Singapore are Monaco and the Vatican), they make poor benchmarks.

Another strand of thought also derives from Singapore's geographical limitations but focuses on the absence of urban-rural divides and isolation of certain communities, as observed in other countries. Typically, Gini coefficients of urban areas exceed that of rural areas, but the national Gini is even higher. From this perspective, Singapore's inequality is expected to be lower than countries with a broader range of economic activities and wider disparity in income levels. Singapore's relatively high inequality becomes even more accentuated, considering the non-existence of a rural economy.

A further perspective holds that, regardless of what the "inherent" economic structure of a city-state is, what matters is the experiences of citizens, and whether redistributive efforts align with expectations within the Singapore context. Whatever its utility in a comparative context, changes in the Gini, particularly before and after taxes and transfers, still serve as useful benchmarks for reflecting shifts in overall income inequality and the degree of government intervention.

From Figure 7.1, we see that after 2000 income inequality rose steadily until 2007, before stabilizing and declining slightly after 2012. Overall, net inequality rose from 2000 to 2018 but progressive transfers and taxes stabilized it, leading to a relative drop after 2013. Specifically, the Gini coefficient before accounting for taxes and governmental transfers increased from 0.442 in 2000 to a peak of 0.482 in 2007 before declining and stabilizing at around 0.458 from 2016 to 2018. After accounting for taxes and transfers, the Gini increased from 0.414 in 2000 to a peak of 0.439 in

Inequality and the Social Compact in Singapore

FIGURE 7.1
Singapore: Gini Coefficient of Per Capita Household Income

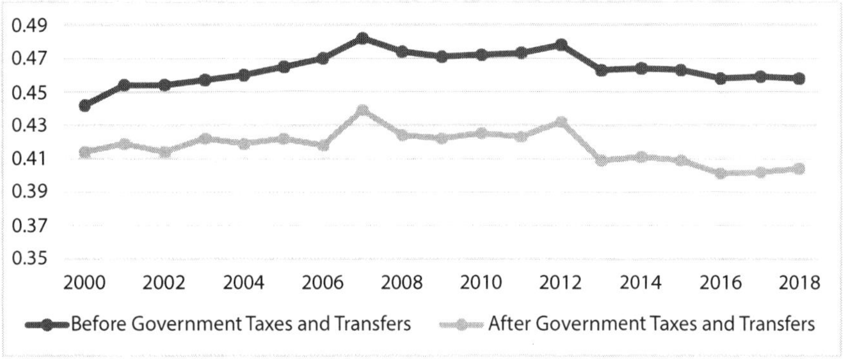

[Chart showing Gini coefficient from 2000 to 2018, with two lines: "Before Government Taxes and Transfers" (upper line, ranging from ~0.445 to ~0.48) and "After Government Taxes and Transfers" (lower line, ranging from ~0.39 to ~0.44)]

Source: Singapore Department of Statistics.

2007 before plateauing at about 0.402 over the last three years. In short, income inequality was relatively stable leading up to 2018.

Another insight we can draw from the Gini data is how far government intervention mediates this inequality. From Figure 7.2, we see the effect of government transfers and taxes has essentially doubled since 2000, reflecting increasingly progressive taxation and transfers from the government. In other words, the degree to which government efforts lowers inequality, as reflected by the Gini coefficient, has steadily and significantly increased since 2000. I discuss these measures in more detail in later sections.

Income Inequality: Top 10 Per Cent vs Bottom 10 Per Cent

For a more granular look at income differences, I examined household income from work (including businesses) per household member. I chose a per household member approach—as opposed to looking at the whole household—to account for potential differences in household size.[4] Trends from two indicators of household income inequality are of interest here: (i) changes in the nominal ratio of the income per household member of the top vs bottom 10 per cent; and (ii) the cumulative change of real income over the entire period.

We continue to see the trend of rising, then stabilizing, inequality, and a net increase over two decades. As shown in Figure 7.3, the income ratio of

FIGURE 7.2
Singapore: Percentage Reduction in Gini Due to Government Taxes and Transfers

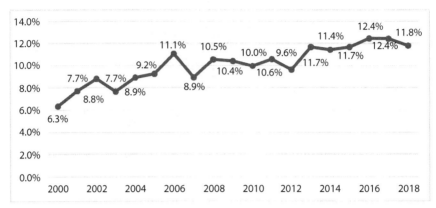

Source: Singapore Department of Statistics.

FIGURE 7.3
**Singapore: Average Monthly Household Per Capita Income
(Top 10 Per Cent vs Bottom 10 Per Cent)**

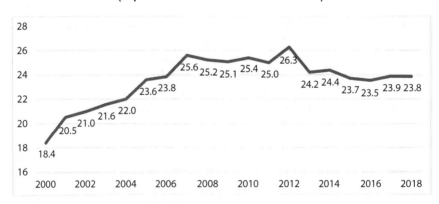

Source: Singapore Department of Statistics.

the top 10 per cent versus bottom 10 per cent increased significantly from 2000 to 2012, growing 42 per cent from 18.4 times in 2000 and reaching a peak of 26.3 times in 2012 before stabilizing at around 24 times from 2013 to 2018. In terms of real growth for each decile, we see from Figure 7.4 that cumulative change from 2000 to 2018 is biased heavily towards higher income groups. Each better-off decile's income grew faster than the poorer

Inequality and the Social Compact in Singapore

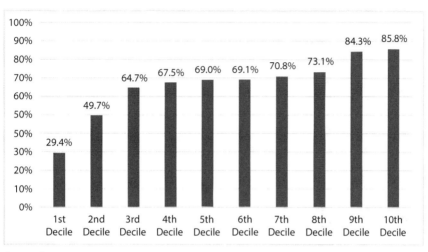

FIGURE 7.4
Singapore: Real Household Per Capita Income Change, by Decile, 2000–18

Source: Singapore Department of Statistics.

deciles', with the bottom 5 deciles seeing an average growth that was 20.6 per cent less than the top 5 deciles.

While it is true that for the latest five years of data (2014 to 2018) the cumulative real income growth for poorer five deciles outstripped the top five deciles, this was only by an average of 0.7 per cent (see Figure 7.5).[5] So, while the change in direction is applaudable, in substantive terms the real income per household member from 2000 to 2018 of the bottom 10 per cent of households only increased by 29.4 per cent while the real income growth for the top 10 per cent was almost triple that, at 85.6 per cent. A note is that while the disparity between the bottom and top deciles are large, the 3rd to 7th as well as the top and second deciles have seen comparatively similar growth in their incomes. This accounts for why there were no markedly higher shifts in the Gini coefficient presented earlier.

Consumption Inequality

Compared to income, consumption might be a better indicator of well-being since it reflects what Singaporeans actually receive in terms of goods and services. We use statistics from the Household Expenditure Survey (HES)

FIGURE 7.5
Singapore: Real Household Per Capita Income Change, by Decile, 2014–18

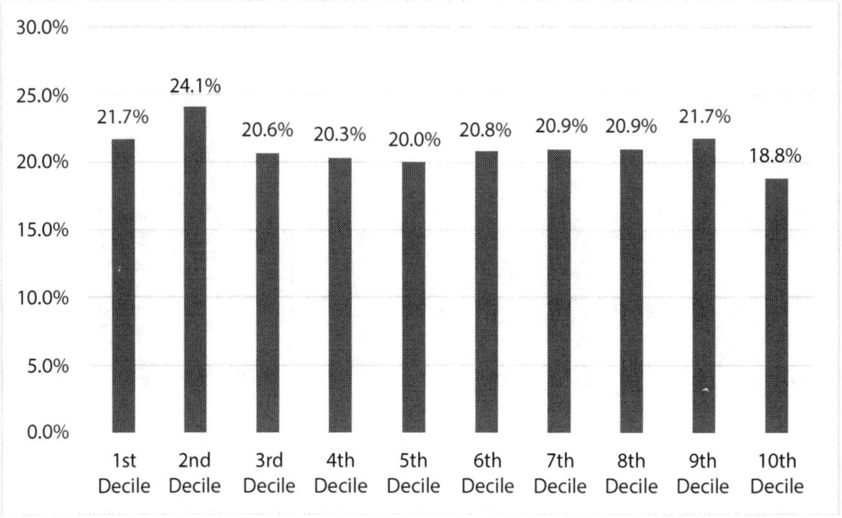

Decile	Change
1st Decile	21.7%
2nd Decile	24.1%
3rd Decile	20.6%
4th Decile	20.3%
5th Decile	20.0%
6th Decile	20.8%
7th Decile	20.9%
8th Decile	20.9%
9th Decile	21.7%
10th Decile	18.8%

Source: Singapore Department of Statistics.

reports from 2002/3 to 2017/18. Since the data is collected from surveys, there is less likelihood of underdeclaration as in the case of income or wealth data from taxation. And unlike usual surveys, it suffers less from non-response or recall errors since participation is mandatory and the journal method is used.[6]

From the latest 2017/18 HES results, we see the same patterns in how consumption inequality shifted; across-the-board increases in expenditure per member for households are observed across all income quintiles (Figure 7.6), with the difference between the top and bottom income quintiles increasing before reverting and then actually *decreasing*; the ratio of expenditure of the top 20 per cent versus bottom 20 per cent increased from the 2002/3 to 2007/8 HES, before successively declining from 2012/13 to 2017/18 and reaching levels lower than 2002/3 (Figure 7.7A). Comparing this to similar periods for income in Figure 7.7B, we see that consumption inequality is less severe, and that the *decrease* in consumption inequality from 2007 to 2017 (17.5 per cent) is more than double that of income inequality (8.6 per cent).

Inequality and the Social Compact in Singapore

FIGURE 7.6
Singapore: Average Monthly Expenditure Per Capita (S$), by Income Quintile

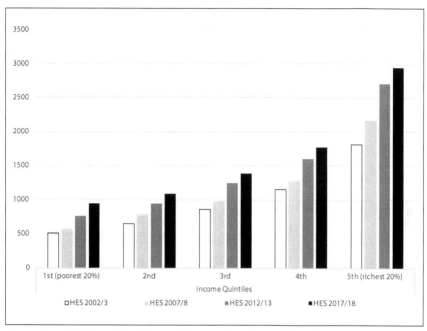

Source: Household Expenditure Surveys, Singapore Department of Statistics.

Wealth Inequality

Wealth inequality[7] in Singapore, according to Credit Suisse's Global Wealth Reports that started in 2010, has trended slightly differently. After a sharp dip in 2011, wealth inequality has been relatively stable albeit increasing slightly after 2015. Overall, wealth inequality in Singapore has been consistently lower than the global average (see Figure 7.8). Compared to the Asian Tiger economies, Singapore's level of wealth inequality between 2011 and 2019 had been less than Hong Kong's, and comparable with Taiwan and South Korea; although South Korea's u-shaped trend has seen increasingly lower levels of wealth inequality after 2016.

Another particularly salient manifestation of wealth inequality in Singapore comes in the form of luxury cars. In early 2019, it was reported that even as the general car market tightened with fewer Certificates of

FIGURE 7.7A
Singapore: Ratio of Average Monthly Expenditure Per Capita,
Top 20 Per Cent vs Bottom 20 Per Cent

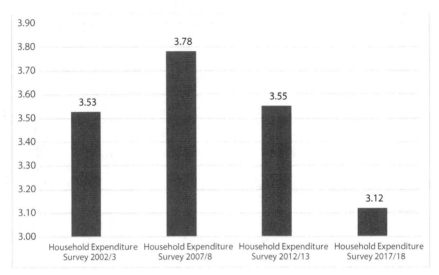

Source: Household Expenditure Survey, Singapore Department of Statistics.

FIGURE 7.7B
Singapore: Ratio of Average Monthly Income Per Capita,
Top 20 Per Cent vs Bottom 20 Per Cent

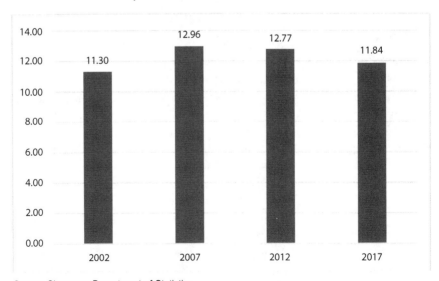

Source: Singapore Department of Statistics.

FIGURE 7.8
Singapore: Wealth Gini Coefficien

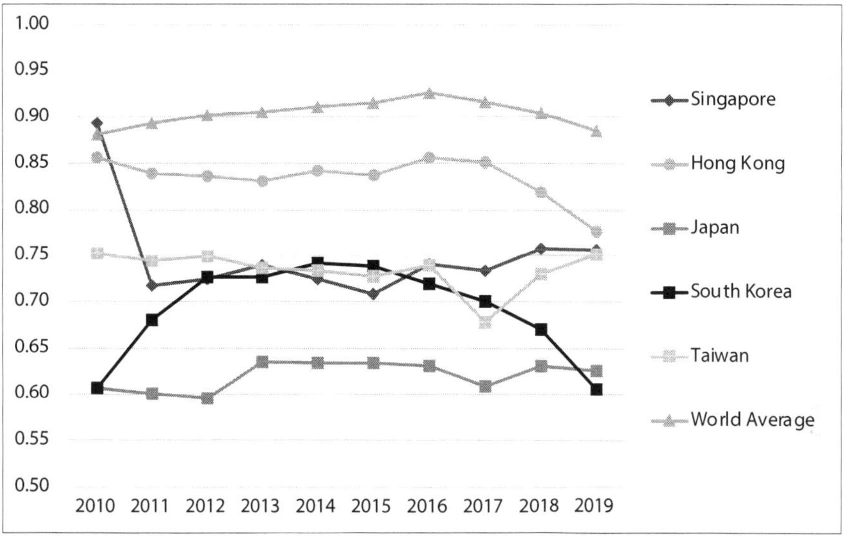

Source: Credit Suisse Global Wealth Database (2010–2019).

Entitlement (COE)[8] being issued, three of the six brands with models generally costing above S$750,000[9] posted significantly higher sales (Tan 2019). Figure 7.9 shows how the share of luxury cars has consistently and significantly grown from 0.094 per cent in 2005 to 0.384 per cent in 2018 translating to a more than fivefold increase in absolute numbers: from 414 to 2,376 vehicles. While such a form of conspicuous consumption is not a key driver of inequality, it might have a disproportionate impact on perceptions of its severity.

A third form of wealth important to the Singaporean context is residential property ownership. Home ownership in Singapore is known to be comparatively higher even among lower income groups. From Table 7.2, we see that overall home ownership[10] in the last twenty years is stable at above 90 per cent. That said, there has been a small decrease (1.6 per cent) in home ownership rates from 2000 to 2019. This was mainly caused by public housing ownership falling 1.2 per cent, with private apartment and landed property ownership (generally resided by higher income groups) in fact increasing by 2.3 per cent and 1.7 per cent, respectively. Breaking it down, however, we see a dramatic increase of 19.8 per cent for residents of 1- and 2-room public housing flats. This is likely due to the 2-room Flexi

FIGURE 7.9
Singapore: Share of Luxury Cars

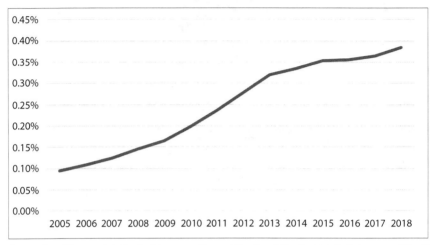

Source: Land Transport Authority, Singapore. "Annual Car Population by Make", Data.gov.sg. https://data.gov.sg/dataset/annual-car-population-by-make

TABLE 7.2
Singapore: Home Ownership Rate by Type of Dwelling

Variables	2000	2019	Percentage Change
Percentage of resident households who own their homes (per cent)	92	90.4	−1.6
Total HDB dwellings (per cent)	93.1	91.9	−1.2
HDB 1- and 2-room flats (per cent)	19.3	39.1	19.8
HDB 3-room flats (per cent)	96.1	94.5	−1.6
HDB 4-room flats (per cent)	98	97.2	−0.8
HDB 5-room and executive flats (per cent)	98.5	97.1	−1.4
Condominiums and other apartments (per cent)	80.8	83.1	2.3
Landed properties (per cent)	89.8	91.5	1.7
Other types of dwelling[a] (per cent)	56.1	31.6	−24.5

Note: a. These include non-HDB-owned shophouses, etc.
Source: Singapore Department of Statistics.

Scheme introduced in 2015 to allow seniors and other specific groups to own 2-room public housing units. The data corroborates this: from 2014 to 2015, the share of 1–2 room flats (public) jumped from 23.9 per cent to 33.9 per cent of total ownership,[11] before increasing further to 39.1 per cent in 2019.

While overall homeownership rates have been largely stable, public housing prices (resale) have grown faster than private residential property values: from 2000 (Q1) to 2019 (Q4), public housing prices increased by 64 per cent while that for private housing went up by only 55 per cent. That said, breaking down private property sales, a more nuanced picture emerges; landed private property prices rose 71 per cent during this period while non-landed ones increased by 52 per cent (see Table 7.3).

Taking the higher home ownership rates for smaller public housing apartments (where lower income households predominantly live) and the increase in property values for public housing flats together, this could suggest increasing wealth for Singapore's poorest. Whether this portends a decreasing gap in property wealth, however, would depend on this increase relative to changes in multiple-property ownership levels of larger HDB flats and private properties by higher income groups.

Overall, further investigation into trends and underlying mechanics of how homeownership rates and property values is required to understand what is driving these numbers, but it bears emphasizing that gaps in housing are potentially dangerous in the Singapore context. The government's narratives over the years has reframed home ownership from a purely economic issue to become a benchmark by which the current social compact and national identity is measured; owning a home in Singapore effectively represents having a stake in the country's

TABLE 7.3
Singapore: Nominal Changes in Property Prices, Q1 2000 to Q4 2019, by Residence Type

	HDB Resale Price Index	Private Residential Property Prices — Landed	Private Residential Property Prices — Non-landed	All Private Residential Property
2000 Q1 to 2019 Q4	64%	71%	52%	55%

Sources: Urban Redevelopment Authority and Housing and Development Board (from data.gov.sg).

national security and development. A widening gap in property values, compounded by increasingly unaffordable home ownership in the lower end of the distribution, portends debilitating social instability.

Intergenerational Inequality

Given that relative incomes can fluctuate, and households shift from being in one income decile to another within the same generation, information on intergenerational mobility is arguably the most informative indicator on Singapore's ability to provide equal opportunity for all regardless of background. In 2015, Singapore's Ministry of Finance (MOF) released an occasional paper releasing rare—and possibly unprecedented—analysis on the state of intergenerational inequality in Singapore.

The study estimated the proportion of children (in the 1978 to 1982 cohorts) born to the poorest quintile of parents who later reached the top quintile of income, and juxtaposed Singapore with comparable statistics in other develop nations like the United States, United Kingdom, Denmark and Canada. MOF found that Singapore's was the highest at 14.3 per cent. This was almost double that of the United States' at 7.5 per cent (see Figure 7.10). Checking the overall association of parents' and child's income between the two groups of cohorts for which data was available (1969–73 and 1978–82), they find that intergenerational mobility was relatively stable for these two groups a decade apart (Table 7.4). In other words, the degree to which both generations' income levels (relative to the rest of society) were determined by that of their parents were similar.

While achieving comparatively high levels of relative mobility is encouraging, the different contexts in which mobility is produced matter. The MOF report explicitly recognized this: "the relatively high mobility estimates for Singapore likely reflect the rapid economic transformation that occurred during the period when these cohorts grew up. During the 1980s and 1990s, Singapore's rapid transformation was accompanied by a significant expansion. Given this, they caveat that as "the pace of Singapore's development slows, it will be an increasing challenge to sustain such mobility in the future". Despite this, the report nonetheless emphasized that "it remains critical that society offers a level playing field for new cohorts of Singaporeans, especially early in life" (Ministry of Finance 2015, p. 19). The Singaporean government is thus clearly aware

Inequality and the Social Compact in Singapore 233

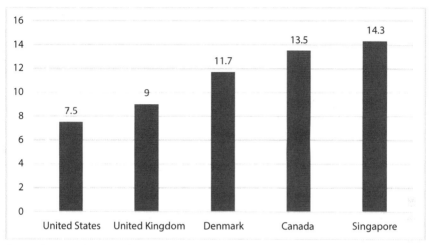

FIGURE 7.10
Singapore: Percentage of Children Born to Parents Earning the Lowest 20 Per Cent of Income Who Reached the Top 20 Per Cent of Income

Source: Ministry of Finance 2015.

TABLE 7.4
Singapore: Correlation of Parents' and Child's Income Rank

Correlation Coefficient of Parents' and Child's Income Rank	
1969–73 cohort	0.21
1978–82 cohort	0.22

Source: Ministry of Finance (2015).

of both the changing context and the importance of mitigating long term inequality in Singapore.

Educational Inequality

Next, education has played a quintessential role in Singapore's development strategy and continues to be a cornerstone in maintaining her social compact. As Ng (2013, p. 209) puts it: "The education system has been leveraged as an important tool for developing a productive workforce on the one hand, yet an equalizer of opportunities on the other." Others have argued that the combination of the Singapore government's hiring practices and the outsized influence it has on society has made educational credentials a key channel for progress in Singaporean society (Chua 2011). As such, how different groups experience the education system, whether equal opportunities actually exist, disproportionately influences how Singaporeans *feel* about the level of inequality and how meritocratic the system truly is in ensuring intergenerational mobility.

In terms of absolute educational outcomes, Singaporean students have consistently ranked top in mathematics and science performance in the Programme for International Student Assessment (PISA). However, there is a need to examine these results with respect to the social economic dimension to better understand the lived experience of Singaporean students with respect to socio-economic inequality. From PISA's index of economic, social, and cultural status (ESCS), parents may have some cause for concern; they found that Singapore students were the fourth most likely to perform worse due to disadvantage (bottom 25 per cent) relative to non-disadvantaged students (OECD 2016b). In terms of why this might be, the report noted that while the lack of disadvantage did not guarantee higher performance scores, it did provide a "floor" where students from better-off families do not fare too poorly; in the words of the report, Singapore's system is one where "socio-economic advantage acts more as a protection against low performance than as a springboard to high achievement" (OECD 2016b, p. 221). This contrasts sharply with the stable intergenerational mobility data shown earlier, but given its recency, is likely a better reflection of the contemporary state of intergenerational inequality.

One explanation for how this "shield" against poor performance operates as the result of socio-economic status is "tuition classes" (supplementary lessons offered by the private sector). It is a pervasive practice in Singapore for parents to send their children for such classes outside of school with the primary goal of improving examination scores. Here, how socio-economic disadvantage plays out as suggested by the PISA scores is consistent with the stratification in educational supplement spending as reported in the Household Expenditure Survey.

From Table 7.5,[12] we see that the ratio of this difference between the top to bottom quintiles decreased from 5.4 times in the 2002/2003 report to 3.7 in the 2017/2018 report. This shows that while households across

TABLE 7.5
Singapore: Average Household Monthly Expenditure on Private Tuition and Other Educational Courses (S$)

	Income Quintile					
	Bottom 20%	Lower middle 20%	Middle 20%	Upper middle 20%	Top 20%	Average
HES 2002/3	25.8	54.6	86.2	110.1	138.9	83.1
HES 2007/8	28.5	59.4	60.8	81.9	102.8	66.7
HES 2012/13	33.9	68.3	107.3	144.1	174.9	105.7
HES 2017/18	45.3	75.8	121.2	152.6	167	112.4
Percentage increase from 2002/3 to 2012/13	75.6%	38.8%	40.6%	38.6%	20.2%	27.2%

Source: Singapore Department of Statistics.

the board are spending more on tuition, the amount spent by the poorest quintile has increased the most during our period of interest, by 75.6 per cent. In absolute terms, however, the higher income quintile still consistently spends more on tuition and other educational courses.

In total, this means that the tuition industry almost doubled in size from 2002/3 to 2017/18 from around S$974 million a year to S$1.76 billion.[13] Beyond the absolute amount, we see from Figure 7.11 that the percentage households spend on educational supplements as a portion of their total expenditure has generally crept upwards for all income groups over the years.

In measuring educational inequality in Singapore, we should also look at the role of tertiary educational attainment in legitimizing meritocracy and strengthening the social compact. Over the past few decades, Singapore's rapid development and shift towards a higher value-added service economy, coupled with supporting educational policy, has increased the proportion of those with tertiary education.

A 2018 OECD report on educational equity estimated the probability of completing tertiary education based on parental education from survey data collected for the Programme for the International Assessment of Adult Competencies (PIAAC) (OECD 2018). In terms of absolute educational mobility, Singapore had the third highest (within the sample of thirty-

FIGURE 7.11
Singapore: Average Household Monthly Expenditure on Private Tuition & Other Educational Courses (Percentage)[a]

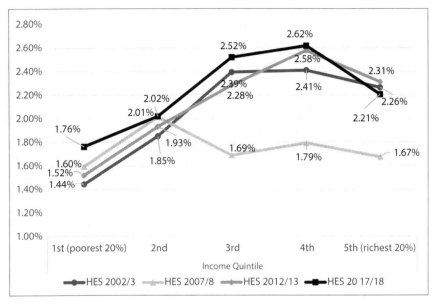

Note: a. The figure previously published in Peng (2019) misattributed household expenditure figures to the wrong HES reports. This has been corrected here and updated with the latest HES data.
Source: Singapore Department of Statistics.

three OECD countries and partners) proportion of adults aged 26 years or older who attained higher education levels than their parents, at 57.8 per cent, after only Cyprus and the Russian Federation. Comparing cohorts' likelihood of attaining tertiary education by their parents' education in Figure 7.12 in terms of "low" (neither parent attained upper secondary education), medium" (at least one parent attained upper secondary education) and "high" (at least one parent attained tertiary education),[14] we see a convergence across cohorts in the likelihood of attaining tertiary education between those with parents of different levels of education. Although Singaporeans with better-educated parents are still more likely to attain tertiary education, the gap between them and their peers with less educated parents have been closing. This leads the report to conclude that "Singapore is the only country where equity in the attainment of tertiary education improved markedly over time" (OECD 2018, p. 90).

Inequality and the Social Compact in Singapore   237

FIGURE 7.12
Singapore: Probability of Completing Tertiary Education Based on Parents' Education (Low/Medium/High)

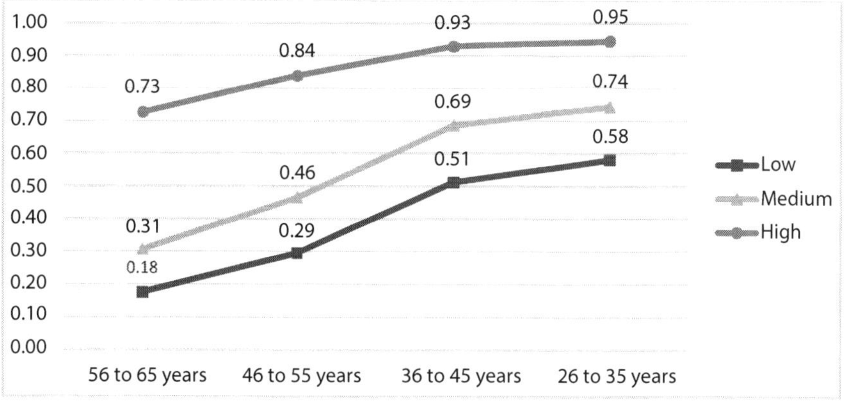

	56 to 65 years	46 to 55 years	36 to 45 years	26 to 35 years
Low	0.18	0.29	0.51	0.58
Medium	0.31	0.46	0.69	0.74
High	0.73	0.84	0.93	0.95

Source: OECD (2018), p. 89.

This result should not be read as opposing the OECD and PISA report results on how disadvantage affects educational outcomes. It represents longer term historical trends while the earlier segment provides a more contemporary reflection on educational inequality.

But there are fundamental problems with aggregating different kinds of tertiary programmes together. "Tertiary" generally covers a range of qualifications—in Singapore's context this includes universities, polytechnics, and the Institutes of Technical Education (ITEs). As tertiary education attainment becomes the norm rather than the exception, therefore, it becomes more expedient to examine the relative opportunities for advancement open to students who attain different qualifications. Also, to repeat the caveat from the previous section, even if the tertiary education gap has closed over the past few decades this could have been driven by shifts in economic structure and it remains to be seen if the gap would widen again as Singapore's economy matures.

Geographic Inequality

Another form of inequality is disparities across geographical regions. While this issue is structurally less stark for Singapore given its small geographical area, the government's housing policy has intervened very deliberately to make housing policy in Singapore driven by social considerations.

This is done on several fronts. First, as mentioned earlier, Singapore's home ownership policies providing public housing in the form of Housing and Development Board (HDB) flats has seen Singapore's home ownership reach heights of 90 per cent or more, with 80 per cent of all Singaporeans staying in these HDB flats. Next, the Ethnic Integration Policy and the Singapore Permanent Resident Quota, as their names suggest, aim to foster social integration by engendering a more equal distribution of racial and immigrant groups across different geographical regions. Finally, the planning of HDB locations fall within broader efforts at creating self-sufficient New Towns designed to ensure all the needs of lower income groups could be met within these locations, where employment, retail, education, sporting and other recreational infrastructure are planned alongside residential sites to ensure equal access to amenities (Yuen 2006).

While Singapore's limited land mass and integrative housing policy have certainly mitigated the felt impacts of lived inequalities, the problems are certainly not eliminated. Certain neighbourhoods are still widely recognized as being exclusively for higher income groups. This insight is corroborated by the findings of the latest data from 2015, where a breakdown of persons by income across town planning zones were provided for the first time. While the snapshot nature of this data cannot inform us of how geographical inequality has evolved over time, we can still glean basic insights of how persons from different socio-economic strata are spread across different regions in Singapore.

From Figure 7.13, we see that overall, differences in distribution of higher income and lower income Singaporeans are not too extreme. The majority of districts (around 43 per cent) had between one to two times the number of persons earning S$20,000 and above versus those earning S$2,000 and below, and the number of districts with more of the lower income group versus those where there were between two to five times the higher income group were equal at about a quarter each. However, there were two outliers, Bukit Timah and Tanglin, that had more than ten times the high earning group. So, while there is a fairly even distribution, there is still some concentration of the richest and poorest in certain regions. As the private sector redevelops the residential areas in these locales, it might bear watching if property ownership there become ostentatious status symbols, potentially exacerbating perceptions of class division.

Inequality and the Social Compact in Singapore 239

FIGURE 7.13
Singapore: Income Earners by Geographical Planning Zones

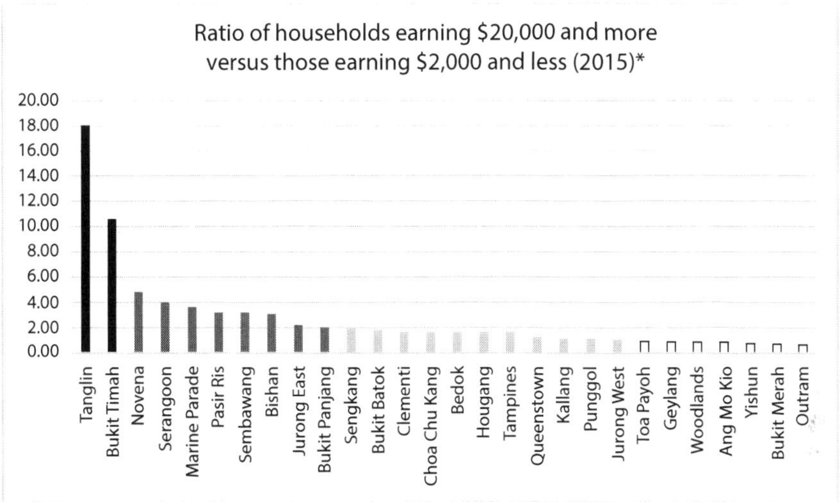

Ratio of households earning $20,000 and more versus those earning $2,000 and less (2015)*

[Bar chart showing ratios from highest to lowest: Tanglin (~18), Bukit Timah (~10), Novena, Serangoon, Marine Parade, Pasir Ris, Sembawang, Bishan, Jurong East, Bukit Panjang, Sengkang, Bukit Batok, Clementi, Choa Chu Kang, Bedok, Hougang, Tampines, Queenstown, Kallang, Punggol, Jurong West, Toa Payoh, Geylang, Woodlands, Ang Mo Kio, Yishun, Bukit Merah, Outram]

Note: * Numbers excludes persons with no income as these might include retirees who are not necessarily from lower income backgrounds. Planning zones are taken from Singapore's Urban Redevelopment Authority's Masterplan 2014 and excludes the "Others" category.
Source: Department of Statistics Singapore (From General Household Survey 2015).

The distribution of landed properties and condominiums to HDB 1–4 room flats provides a hint as to how this pattern emerged. From Figure 7.14, we see that Tanglin (not included in the chart because there are no HDB 1–4 room flats) and Bukit Timah have significantly more expensive residence types relative to other areas. While there are no restrictions as to the housing decisions of individuals, the state's design as to the number and type of public housing within each locale has had a heavy influence on the patterns of geographical inequality that emerge today.

The full intricacies of geographical disparities cannot be adequately explored here, but a good starting point for understanding the kinds of inequality dynamics at play between and within neighbourhoods can be found in Leong Chan-Hoong's commentary on the issue during the 2018 debates (Leong 2018). Finding similar patterns that certain neighbourhoods had significantly higher concentrations of higher income earners, he further observed the "distinct clustering of brand name schools" in some of these

FIGURE 7.14
Singapore: Ratio of Resident Households in Condominiums/ Apartments and Landed Properties vs HDB 1–3 Room Flats, by Geographical Planning Zones

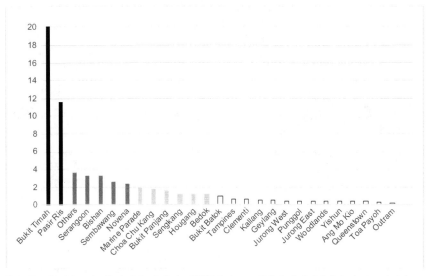

Note: Tanglin data not reflected due to lack of HDB 1–4 room flats (ratio is infinite); chart scaled down for ease of comparison with Figure 7.13 (Bukit Timah has ratio of 42.6, beyond the graph). Planning zones are taken from Singapore's Urban Redevelopment Authority's Masterplan 2014 and excludes the "Others" category.

neighbourhoods. Given that under Singapore's admissions system children residing in closer geographical proximity to these schools were more likely to be admitted, this potentially meant that "qualified and deserving students living in less well-off estates may have to travel a longer distance to these schools, and may therefore miss out on the opportunity to attend better institutions". Another interesting finding was that neighbourhoods with more mixing of lower and higher income groups were more prone to petty crime than those that were more equally poor or rich. In short, there are numerous deserving avenues of research on the interplay of policy, geography, and inequality in Singapore.

Inequality of Belonging

Finally, there is also a need to look beyond macro indicators of inequality to examine felt inequality and potential implications. A recent Channel

Inequality and the Social Compact in Singapore   241

NewsAsia survey found that class, not race or religion, was the most divisive factor in Singapore (Paulo and Low 2018). More worryingly, they found that those who identified themselves as upper class were more likely to feel a sense of belonging to Singapore and feel proud to be Singaporean. This suggests that as socio-economic inequality grows in severity, it corrodes national identity. This is corroborated by the 2000–4 and 2010–14 World Values Survey (WVS) reports, that a consistently smaller proportion of respondents in Singapore who identified themselves as lower class[15] felt "very proud" or "quite proud" of their nationality (Figure 7.15).

Interestingly, there was an across-the-board decrease in national pride felt by all classes except those identifying as lower class for the two WVS waves, with the self-identified upper class seeing the greatest drop leading to greater convergence across classes. One possible explanation is that the 2008 financial crisis had disproportionately affected the upper classes while the increasingly progressive government taxes and transfers during that period as discussed earlier might have pushed up positive perceptions of the lower class.

FIGURE 7.15
Singapore: World Values Survey – How Proud of Nationality

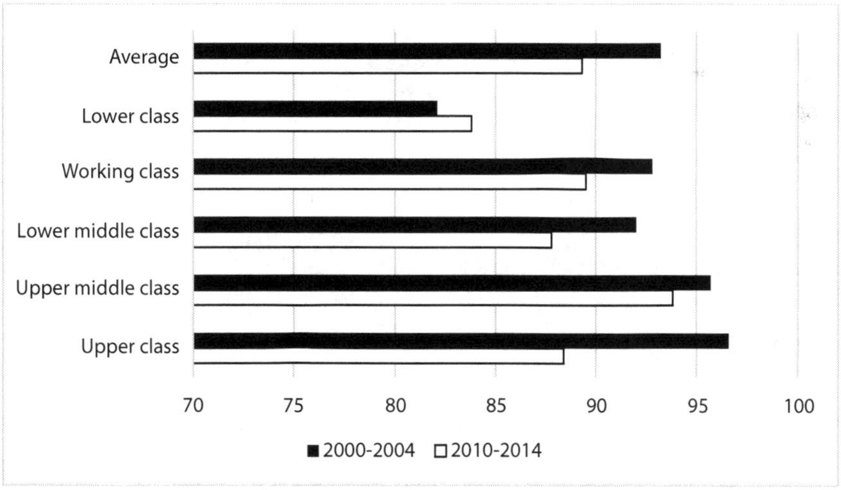

Source: World Values Survey.

This larger theme of socio-economic divisions increasingly affecting identity is further reinforced by OECD's examination of students' sense of belonging at school, which they found to be correlated with "feelings of security, identity and community ... (that) support academic, psychological and social development". Worryingly, while most OECD countries saw their gap between socio-economically advantaged and disadvantaged children to be stable or narrowing, Singapore was one of six countries[16] where disadvantaged children's sense of belonging in school had dropped relative to their better-off peers from the 2012 to 2015 PISA cycles, the largest decrease among all sampled countries (OECD 2018, pp. 69–71).

Feeling a healthy level of belonging is not just good-to-have in a normative sense; the report cites Baumeister and Leary (1995) and Ma (2003) on how it affects students' self-identity, their overall satisfaction with life, their motivation to learn and put effort into their own education. While the report only collected data over two time periods, there is value in studying the source of this disparity and closely monitoring it lest the divide grows further, causing students with academic potential to underperform.

The next section will explore some of these themes further and qualitatively by first highlighting the public discourse on inequality in 2018 and situate it in the evolution of Singapore's meritocracy.

SALIENT FEATURES, UNDERLYING FACTORS, AND POLICY RESPONSES

As illustrated in the previous section, inequality in Singapore can neither be characterized as a slow degradation of macroeconomic factors over the past two decades nor as sharply increasing in recent years. A salient question is then how Singaporeans experience inequality in the day-to-day, particularly with respect to their children's experiences within the education system, which disproportionately determines their chances at success. One issue has had an outsized influence on how Singaporeans experience inequality: the narrative and practice of meritocracy, and the normative winners and losers it entails. This section first highlights key milestones in the 2018 inequality debate and the pragmatic nature and origins of Singaporean meritocracy before discussing recent policy shifts towards more universalistic social protection policies in response.

2018 Inequality Debate

At the end of 2017, Singapore's Institute of Policy Studies (IPS) released the results of a study on social networks supported by the Ministry of Culture, Community, and Youth. The study found that people were more likely to be able to name an acquaintance of another age, gender, race or religion than another socio-economic class (Yong 2017). This prompted member of parliament Mr Gan Thiam Poh to file a Parliamentary Question in February 2018 about the current state of income inequality and if the state had plans to prevent income divisions to create fractures along class lines. In the same year, Teo You Yenn (2018) published her illuminating account of the poor in Singapore, propelling inequality to a prominent position in the Singaporean imagination, earning her widespread recognition and her position as a finalist for the accolade "Singaporean of the Year".

Subsequently, in response to parliamentary questions on the issue, Prime Minister Lee Hsien Loong said that "the issues of mitigating income inequality, ensuring social mobility and enhancing social integration are critical" but a specific committee was unnecessary as ministries were already working on these issues in "a concerted and coordinated effort". Two months later, Singapore's Minister for Law and Home Affairs (in charge of internal security) continued to echo the sentiment that inequality was one of the most serious issues facing Singapore today and "if the same few people keep winning eventually the rest will believe the system is flawed ... and we won't have a society", signalling that inequality in Singapore is no longer solely an economic, social, or even political problem (Tan and Chin 2018). It has become an issue of national security and long-term survival.

In the debate following President Halimah's address cited in the introduction above, Prime Minister Lee Hsien Loong defined what would be a good outcome by four indicators: (i) When every child has a good start in life, regardless of which family they are born in, (ii) when every talent is recognized and developed to the fullest, (iii) when every opportunity is open to anyone with the right attitude and ability, and (iv) when a capable person faces minimal social impediments to be accepted, to contribute and to lead in society. To understand why the issue of inequality took off when it did, we need to understand the role of meritocracy in Singaporean society, and how changing contexts have eroded its claim to legitimacy.

Singapore's Pragmatic Meritocracy

Meritocracy has been a core part of the social compact in Singapore since early in its history. Here, Singapore can be typified as a "pragmatic meritocracy", one that does not espouse meritocratic principles for its own sake but aims at maintaining equality of opportunity such that the most capable are identified and put into positions where they can benefit Singaporeans society the most. As I discuss shortly, this is one that recognized the impact of structural inequalities early on and sought to correct them. This by no means is likely to be unique to Singapore but given that the primary purpose here is not a comparative study of meritocracies, I leave the question of what other countries could be similarly classified to interested readers.

At independence in 1965, Singapore being a multiracial Chinese-majority state with a sizeable Malay-Muslim population in a Muslim-majority region had to carefully navigate racial sensitivities. Its closest neighbour, Malaysia, emphasized the primacy of Malays while Indonesia comprised predominantly of Muslims. Singapore had to take care not to create perceptions that the local Malay population was being unfairly treated to avoid the perils of providing political capital for interventions in the name of emancipation. At the same time, Singapore was a Chinese-majority parliamentary democracy so providing preferential treatment was not politically expedient. Given these circumstances and his firm belief that racial politics will cause society to be "finished" and "ripped apart" (Lee 2010), Singapore's then Prime Minister Lee Kuan Yew decided Singapore's system must not be seen to favour any racial group, particularly the Chinese.

Thus, the commitment to a meritocratic system was repeatedly emphasized in the early years of Singapore's founding: "Singapore would necessarily become an achievement-based meritocratic society, one in which reward, prestige, influence and advancement would go to those who were most able, most energetic, and most prepared to contribute actively and positively towards Singapore's national development and modernization" (Rajaratnam 1969). True to Singapore's famed pragmatism, however, this was a meritocracy with exceptions; Malays enjoyed preferential policy treatment like free education. This exceptionalism was explicitly enshrined in Singapore's Constitution (Article 152): to "recognize the special position of the Malays, who are the indigenous people of Singapore, and accordingly it shall be the responsibility of the Government to protect, safeguard, support, foster and promote their political, educational, religious, economic, social and cultural interests and the Malay language".

Beyond geopolitical expedience, this approach recognized the uneven starting point of Malays as a group, who had been historically disadvantaged in large part due to British colonial policy. Education of the local Malay population was limited towards the preservation of traditions, even as Chinese migrants streamed in for the conduct of commerce and a sizeable number of educated Indians were brought in to aid government administration (Betts 1980).[17] While such exceptions seemingly violated meritocratic principles, in actuality the legitimacy of Singapore's meritocracy was strengthened by ensuring different groups could compete on more even footing. Had the gap been allowed to widen, it would have been difficult to convince Singapore Malays of the authenticity of Singaporean's budding meritocracy.

A pragmatic meritocracy, one that recognizes the need to equalize outcomes and not just opportunities to correct for structural inequalities, was thus adopted. This philosophy, coupled with the demand for talent to drive Singapore's growth, pushed leaders to identify young, promising Singaporeans from all backgrounds and groom them for key positions in government and industry. Such candidates often hailed from families of modest means and few political connections. Notable examples are S.R. Nathan, whose father had committed suicide from poverty when he was eight years old but who rose through the ranks to become Singapore's sixth President (Nathan and Auger 2011); Lim Siong Guan, one of the most prolific Heads of Civil Service whose father was a taxi driver (Long 2014); and Philip Yeo, who spearheaded many of Singapore's major strategic projects like Jurong Island, was also born to a poor migrant family and later reflected in his memoirs how he had been too poor to afford even test tubes and chemicals for his own chemistry lessons during his schooling years (Peh and Han 2016).

After independence, Singapore's phenomenal transition to developed country status is well discussed in the memoirs of leaders such as Lee Kuan Yew and Goh Keng Swee, as well as writings of notable economists like Paul Krugman (Goh 2004; Krugman 1994; Lee 2000). As mentioned, social mobility during this period was relatively high (Ministry of Finance 2015). During this time, a strong belief in the determinism of inborn characteristics underlaid an approach of selecting the best students and investing in them.

A quote by Lee Kuan Yew on the issue, is telling: "The bell curve is a fact of life. The blacks on average score 85 per cent on IQ and it is accurate, nothing to do with culture. The whites score on average 100. Asians score more ... the bell curve authors put it at least 10 points higher. These are realities that, if you do not accept, will lead to frustration because you will be spending money on wrong assumptions and the results cannot follow." (Han, Fernandez and Tan 1998).

This philosophy coincided with a lower functional need for redistributive policies due to the large-scale economic changes at the time having a naturally redistributive effect. Effectively, this context mitigated the dynamic where students from families that were better off and could support their development are better able to display their potential earlier, snowballing their early advantage. Given the crucial function educational performance plays in determining one's socio-economic success, the nature over nurture stance taken by the state at the time and the meritocratic narrative espoused could be accepted only under those conditions of relatively equal starting points. However, once transition slowed and families became entrenched, the availability of emerging opportunities that were accessible to most and not immediately soaked up by entrenched interests dried up. This is the "Time Two" problem of meritocracy mentioned earlier, where unequal outcomes produced in an earlier instance—when competition might have been relatively fair—sets uneven starting points for the next generation.

The "old boys" problem thus began to emerge. Children of better-off families attended the same schools, shared and married within the same social circles, and generally went to the same prestigious professions (in Singapore, this was broadly law, medicine, and government) with minimal interaction with those of other socio-economic strata. While compulsory national service does provide some buffer to this by imposing some shared experiences on Singaporean males, the difference in academic calendars separate those from the more academically focused junior colleges (high schools) and polytechnics (technical institutions) into separate batches. Some vocations are known to consist predominantly of servicemen from certain educational groups.

Instances of ostentatious elitism during this time were then taken by some as evidence that the Singapore-styled meritocracy had gone too far. A widely debated incident in 2006 was when Wee Shu Min, a daughter of former member of parliament Wee Siew Kim, publicly dismissed concerns of job security and ageism in Singaporean society in an online post by former national debater Derek Wee, who asked him to "get out of (her) elite uncaring face". That she was both from a family that was part of the ruling class and attending an educational institution considered the pinnacle of achievement at the time made her outburst the perfect lightning rod for simmering sentiments against a system that was increasingly seen as skewed towards an entrenched elite.

With meritocracy taking on negative connotations and becoming associated with an uncaring brand of elitism that led to the unbridled go-for-growth and immigration policies in the early 2000s, the dominant political party, the People's Action Party (PAP), saw its lowest vote share since independence in the watershed 2011 General Elections. In response, the government changed its narrative on meritocracy, stepped up social support policies, organized a nationwide public consultation exercise to better understand citizens' concerns, and instituted more employment and immigration regulations to ensure lower skilled workers had better prospects and incomes. In the following years, redistributive policies in the areas of early childhood education subsidies, social support, and healthcare coverage were gradually ramped up. The next part of this section discusses some of these policy responses in greater detail.

POLICY RESPONSES TO INEQUALITY

This section discusses the policy responses to the emerging backlash against Singapore's pragmatic meritocracy against the backdrop of empirical trends depicted in earlier sections: that while both the income and wealth Gini coefficients has stabilized over the years, income growth for the better off has outstripped that of the worst off since 2000 despite improving in the last five years up to 2018. While consumption inequality and intergenerational inequality did not show significant changes, and estimates point towards high but stable wealth inequality. More salient is the lived reality that the gap in school performance and perceptions of belonging between the haves and have nots has persisted. Narrowing these gaps present new challenges as structural upheavals and growth in the economy slows.

Policy responses to inequality since 2000 can be viewed within four main thrusts: (i) expansion of social assistance policies with moves towards universalism; (ii) interventions to uplift the incomes of lower skilled Singaporeans; (iii) *relaxing pressures to compete and equalizing early childhood development outcomes*; and, more tangentially; (iv) making the taxation system more progressive. Ultimately, I argue that Singaporean meritocracy has not moved away from its pragmatic roots, having to deal with very real trade-offs, but policymakers are grappling with the uncertainty over where the balance should lie.

Expansion of Social Assistance Policies and Shift to Universalism

Redistribution in Singapore is characterized by some as minimalist. Programmes tend to follow the general principles of (i) self-reliance, where individuals and their families are expected to be first lines of support as seen from most social assistance schemes having household, not individual income, as the criteria; (ii) co-payment, where the state almost never fully subsidizes a service to lower potential abuse; and finally, (iii) conditioned on employment or efforts towards this—so many forms of help are dependent on a person's ability to work. While assistance schemes like the ComCare Long-Term Assistance (popularly known as Public Assistance) which provide lifelong assistance exist, they have strict criteria to first ensure that neither the individual nor their families can reasonably care for them. Also, their inability to work must either be medically certified or validated by being past the official retirement age. Overall, direct financial assistance is targeted at the neediest of families and provides only for basic needs. Singapore also does not have a minimum wage. Retirement security comes in the form of mandatory savings under the Central Provident Fund (CPF).

In this context, several shifts have occurred to tackle the problem of increasing inequality. First, the ComCare endowment fund was set up in 2005 to weatherproof social assistance funds from economic shocks. Next, its component schemes' benefit amounts—which includes the ComCare Long-Term Assistance—have been successively increased over the past ten years (including in the 2019 Budget). Thirdly, a key step towards universalist welfare schemes was taken with the introduction of the Silver Support scheme. This provides supplementary income for up to 30 per cent of all elderly in Singapore, one of the first large-scale, semi-universalistic schemes that were not contingent upon employment. Potential recipients automatically qualify if they meet criteria such as housing type, reported household income, and amount of savings in their individual CPF accounts.

The recent 2020 Budget saw its cash pay-outs raised by 20 per cent and its income eligibility criteria expanded.

Intervention in the Market to Uplift Low Incomes

For low income workers themselves, the absence of a minimum wage and the large-scale entry of low-skilled foreign workers has traditionally put downward pressures on their wages (even as other benefits might have been accrued). While the Singapore government does intervene in the market when it feels it is not delivering on objectives or not doing so quickly enough, economic policy is generally conducted within the ambit of letting market mechanisms operate (Peng and Phang 2018).

A similar approach is taken to closing the income gap. As economic growth slows and the structural upheavals that created room at the top during Singapore's rapid transformation become a thing of the past, the equality of opportunity that the first generations experienced began to disappear. Introduced in 2007, the first scheme promulgated in this regard was Workfare, comprising two components: Workfare Income Supplement (WIS) and Workfare Training Support (WTS). For WIS, pay-outs and eligibility criteria were revised upwards as part of the 2019 budget and will be implemented in 2020. There are two components, cash is 40 per cent and the other 60 per cent goes into workers' CPF accounts. This reflects the other intent of the scheme; to bolster lower income workers' funds for retirement and medical needs etc. In other words, this does not significantly close the income gap[18] and may also lead to perverse incentives where employers might decide to lower salaries or slow down increases. The other component, WTS, subsidizes training to upskill low income workers. Given its indirect impact on wages, its overall efficacy is less clear.

A second pillar of the government's strategy to close the income gap in the absence of a minimum wage is the Progressive Wage Model (PWM). Instead of instituting an across-the-board minimum wage that might lead to economic inefficiencies, Singapore targets specific sectors—namely, the cleaning, security (as in civilian security for facilities protection), and landscaping industries—where lower income Singaporeans are concentrated. It sets out different job tiers within each sector to help foster progression, and specifies the minimum income for these. The scheme is backed by a licensing regime that applies to all companies. These were implemented between 2015 and 2016 and so could have contributed to the increase in real income of the bottom deciles between 2014 and 2018 mentioned in earlier sections. In 2013, the Wage Credit Scheme was also introduced where the government co-funded wage increases for those earning up to S$4,000 per month. This income ceiling was later raised to S$5,000 together with the government's co-funding levels (from 15 per cent to 20 per cent), announced in the 2020 Budget Debates.

Relaxing Competitive Pressures in Education and Equalizing Early Childhood Development Outcomes

After 2011, the government adopted more compassionate narratives and emphasized multiple pathways to success. In 2013, amidst concerns about Singapore becoming too narrowly focused on examination results, then Minister for Education, Mr Heng Swee Keat, said "we should have a talent-centric meritocracy that recognizes talent in a wide range of areas" (*Straits Times*, 14 March 2013). Later, the subsequent Education Minister Mr Ong Ye Kung highlighted the philosophy of "lift the bottom, not cap the top". One effort that attempts to close the developmental and performance gap between children born to lower and higher income backgrounds was removing the number of examinations and rankings, to give students more time to adjust when transitioning to different stages of education and relax the competitive pressures students face (Chia 2018). An added benefit is the reduction of incentives for better resourced parents to provide advantages to their children beyond the classroom.

Next, recognizing the need to mitigate the impact of unequal family backgrounds on children's development, the Early Childhood Development Agency (ECDA) was set up in 2013 to oversee the early childhood education sector "to keep pre-school programmes affordable, especially for low and middle income families", among other objectives (Ministry of Social and Family Development 2013). Recognizing the importance of family in shaping home environments early to close the developmental gap, the Singapore government also introduced the KidStart pilot programme in 2016 to proactively identify and support children from vulnerable families (Early Childhood Development Agency 2016). In 2020, the government announced their intent to double annual early childhood spending from S$1 billion per year in 2018, along with enhancing other forms of support for lower income students at higher levels of education.

Making Singapore's Tax System More Progressive

Finally, the government has been reforming the tax system to be more progressive. In Singapore the overall tax burden is designed to be low to keep Singapore attractive to investments and talent. However, how much lower income households pay relative to the better off (how "progressive" the system is) impacts inequality and perceptions of fairness. So, even as demands for public services like healthcare continue to increase as Singapore's population ages, corresponding calls for the rich to bear a larger burden in financing public expenditure similarly arose.

A key issue was how to mitigate the regressive effects of the Goods and Services Tax (GST) introduced in 1994. Defining a tax system as efficient when "there cannot exist any reshuffling of its rate structure that improves social welfare", Leung, Low and Toh (1999) concluded that while the GST is relatively efficient, it exacerbated inequality. To counter this effect, the government absorbed the GST for public education and healthcare and implemented the Permanent GST Voucher (GSTV) scheme in 2013 to provide cash and utilities rebates for lower income Singaporeans, as well as top-ups to medical savings accounts (MediSave) for the elderly. An announcement to enhance GSTV's benefits was made during the 2018 budget and reiterated in the 2019 budget, together with the introduction of an offset package to facilitate adjustment to the new rates when they commence, for which lower- and middle-income households would receive greater support.

There have also been more efforts to make the income and properties' tax structure more progressive—personal income taxes for top income brackets increased in 2015, with a cap on tax reliefs introduced the following year. In 2019, the government also lapsed a scheme providing tax incentives for persons with regional or global responsibilities while increasing tax relief for working mothers with special needs children. A progressive property tax system was also introduced in 2010 and enhanced in 2013, with non-owner occupied and higher value properties seeing the greatest increase in taxes. In 2018, a higher top marginal rate was imposed on residential properties with values exceeding S$1 million.

A final strategy to ensure tax burdens remained competitive as demands for more government services and progressive distribution rose was by diversifying revenue sources. As Asher, Bali and Chang (2015) pointed out, while the GDP share of government revenue from 2003 to 2014 fluctuated between 20 and 25 per cent, tax revenue hovered at around 13 per cent, reflecting a significant reliance on non-tax revenues. One such is the Net Investment Returns Contribution (NIRC), generated from past accumulations of the government's consistent surpluses. In 2018, the Finance Minister pointed out that this had become the largest contributor to the Singapore government's revenues. While this does not change the progressiveness of the system, it keeps the overall tax burden stable.

While these efforts are commendable, the complexity of trade-offs involved makes it uncertain how the revenue collection system contributes to overall inequality relative to alternatives. For example, estimating the net effect on inequality of keeping income and corporate taxes low while increasing GST: while GST hits the poor harder, lower income and corporate taxes could attract more companies and individuals to Singapore. Measuring the implications of just these two effects is already no simple affair, much less the innumerable run-off effects each decision has and how they interact with one another. In short, the overall impact of Singapore's taxation and transfers system deserve more systematic analysis before any conclusions can be drawn. What deserves attention is that government efforts to balance against some of the more regressive features and keep the overall burden low have different levels of visibility, affecting "felt" inequality differently. For example, spending on goods and services occur every day with incremental burdens relatively small, potentially fading from salience after some time. In contrast, income and property tax payments occur in the form of one-off transaction, making any changes highly perceptible.

Overall, for the vast majority of Singaporeans the government's attempts in addressing the fundamental inequality of economic outcomes are generally indirect, focusing more on correcting longer-term equality of opportunity. For example, working through policies that foster more even educational performance and increasing wages of lower income groups indirectly through market mechanisms via training programmes increasing productivity (with the exceptions of certain industries). While there have certainly been positive innovations in the approaches taken in combating inequality, it remains ambiguous if their ultimate impact has been sufficient in closing the gap in equality of outcomes in a way that will improve or even maintain the perceived chasms in opportunities from one's background.

From the data presented here, the answer seems to be no. We see that despite good results in recent years on several macroeconomic measures such as the faster rise in poorer households' incomes and a generally stable wealth and income inequality (evidenced by the respective Gini coefficients), inequality remains a hot button issue. Lived inequalities seems to have fomented discontent sufficiently to have catapulted the issue to striking prominence in 2018 which led key political figures from the President to the Prime Minister and members of his cabinet to issue sombre statements that leave little doubt as to the cardinal role of relative equality in sustaining Singapore's stability and prosperity.

Other pieces of evidence regarding the worsening sense of belonging of poorer students in school and the persistent differences in how those identifying as specific classes differed in their reported levels of pride as Singaporeans signals the need for a greater understanding of what is driving some of these dynamics, and that current measures, however well-intentioned and designed, does not go far enough. Ultimately, the efficacy of these in mitigating such issues seems to have been incremental; a problem perhaps not of type, but of degree.

Given this, the next section discusses the bigger puzzle of why, if inequality is so fundamental to national well-being and clearly recognized as such, the government is not taking more drastic measures.

POLICY IMPLICATIONS

In the previous section, I proposed one understanding of the evolution of Singaporean meritocracy and detractors of its principles and outcomes, to put in perspective the policies the Singapore government has pushed out over the past decade or so. Despite general macro measures of inequality being relatively stable and governmental efforts towards maintaining this, lived inequalities does not seem to have been sufficiently mitigated.

Ian Holliday, building on Esping-Andersen's conceptualization of welfare states, offers one explanation: in Singapore social policy has always been subservient to economic considerations. I argue here that this is an inaccurate depiction of Singapore's policy approach; that both social and economic policy are subservient to larger goals of national survival.

Esping-Andersen in his landmark work *The Three Worlds of Welfare Capitalism* (1990) set out the logic that welfare states must be measured not in terms of aggregate spending, but by programme characteristics that follow different policy logics. Recognizing that his classification of contemporary, and largely Western, welfare state as liberal, conservative and social democratic did not adequately account for East Asian economies, Holliday (2000) proposed a fourth world of welfare capitalism he terms "productivist", where the policy logic is that social policy is subordinate to economic policies. He further classifies Singapore as "Developmental-Particularist", where social rights are minimal and help is linked to productive activity, the system reinforces the position of more productive elements of society, and the state basically directs the social welfare activities of families.

While Ian Holliday is correct that Singapore has seemingly put far more effort into economic growth over social welfare, this is not due to the lack of prioritization of social objectives but that economic progress was what the government perceived as the best way to achieve larger goals of national continuity. Singapore's survival is the penultimate goal. The means to achieve this could include, depending on the context, prioritizing either societal cohesion or economic competence at different points of time, the two not being mutually exclusive. The implication here is that where social objectives are more important than economic growth in achieving overall systematic stability and competitiveness, the Singaporeans government will prioritize social over economic objectives. We see this in the adoption of schemes such as Workfare, Silver Support, the Progressive Wage Model, and KidSTART; that when it was sufficiently clear a change in approach was necessary for sustaining Singapore's meritocracy in practice, the government has not been shy in moving away from previous approaches relying on the market to deliver desired outcomes, similar to its approach towards managing the economy.

Why the government did not adopt stronger measures then, is likely because of perceived trade-offs between pursuing direct redistribution and lowering Singapore's overall economic competitiveness, making it harder to pursue social objectives anyway. Emphasizing the importance of inequality, Deputy Prime Minister Tharman Shanmugaratnam's escalator analogy is a simplified representation of this conundrum. He says that like an escalator, everyone in society must continually progress, that "there is no point being better off than someone else if everyone is stuck in the same place". However, the analogy also aims to illustrate that the country must keep growing to sustain social mobility, that "an escalator that continues to carry everyone upwards also makes it much easier for a country to have social mobility" (Yahya 2018).

But as seen in some of the trends discussed earlier, Singapore could be at the point when relying on further economic growth to combat inequality is no longer feasible. At least not without more direct redistribution to mitigate the increasing entrenchment of the better off. Absent a more even playing field for the next generation, it is unlikely the kinds of long-term stability conducive to growth would exist. As Kenneth Paul Tan, a prominent observer of Singapore's political economy states, "in a densely populated city like Singapore inequality is palpably experienced at the day-to-day level of the person-in-the-street" and as "Singapore's income inequality increases further, which is not unlikely if the government continues merely to tweak their redistributive policies, there could be significant consequences for trust in the government." (Tan 2018, pp. 35 and 37).

In other words, while I recognize the potential trade-offs in economic competitiveness with more redistributive policies from higher taxation, and I agree that growth definitely benefits social mobility and well-being in general, my contention is that Singapore is at the stage where the marginal benefits of more redistribution has begun to outweigh the costs. While continued efforts towards ensuring equality of opportunities is commendable and necessary, these fall flat without a healthy degree of equality of outcomes. If we do not address such differences in outcomes head-on, the resulting inequality of opportunity, actual and perceived, would be a formula for future social unrest, creating a breeding ground for populism and other forms of toxic politics.

CONCLUSION

To summarize, while the overall empirical trends do not show a starkly increasing inequality over the past twenty years, felt inequality, especially on the issue of education and equal opportunities for children, has reached the stage where narratives of inequality strike a poignant chord.

What the Singapore case also illustrates is that the macroeconomic situation might not be a good proxy for how citizens perceive the severity of inequality. While not divorced from one another, the distinction of fact from perception, and their different drivers are important for policymakers and political actors to manage. Absolute improvements in economic equality might not translate to addressing the particular manifestations of inequality that people care and feel most about. In any case, addressing both is necessary to combat the kinds of entrenchment which most developed societies have experienced and that threatens Singapore today.

As a representation of the government's disposition, it is instructive to cite the Ministry of Finance's report: "While Singapore has been relatively successful in achieving broad-based prosperity so far, managing these issues of income growth, inequality and mobility will not get easier in any society. They require effective and sustainable economic and social policies" (Ministry of Finance 2015, p. 20). However, from the solutions adopted, the government's main attempt has been to correct for the ills of inequality without significant redistribution, which I argue is not enough to maintain the social compact required to provide a stable socio-political foundation for maintaining Singapore's competitiveness.

While the underlying principle of using economic prosperity for societal progress is sound, the balance has swung too far towards prioritizing the economic over the social. At this point, Singapore will benefit less from going for growth than from more progressive measures that generate greater equality of outcomes. The kind a functioning meritocracy, and society, requires.

Notes

1. This chapter updates an article previously published in the *Journal of Southeast Asian Economies* (Peng 2019). Main changes include a deeper look at property ownership and divergence in property price growth over the last twenty years, updated household expenditure numbers from the recently released Household Expenditure Survey 2017/18, and inclusion of relevant initiatives announced during the 2020 Budget Debates. The inclusion of these additional analysis does not change previous conclusions.
2. This measures to what extent (from 0 to 1) income needs to be redistributed for income to be completely equal, where 1 means 100 per cent needs to be reallocated (completely unequal) and 0 means none (completely equal).
3. Conversely, cities with rural hinterlands would have structurally higher levels of inequality, making them inaccurate comparisons as well.
4. For example, the average household size of those in the 1st and 2nd income deciles by average monthly household income from work (poorest two deciles) were 3.43 and 3.50 while that of the 9th and 10th deciles were 2.99 and 2.40, respectively.

5. This refers to the difference between the average real household per capita income change of the 1st to 5th deciles (poorer half) and the 6th to 10th deciles (better-off half) of households, for the period 2014–18.
6. While survey data is potentially prone to errors in recall, Singapore's Department of Statistics employ the journal method where selected households in Singapore are required to record their expenditure daily over two weeks.
7. Defined as the marketable value of financial assets plus non-financial assets (principally housing and land), minus debts.
8. To own a car in Singapore, a buyer must first obtain a COE through an open bid uniform price auction. These are limited in number and serve as a hard quota on the number of motor vehicles introduced to Singapore's roads each year.
9. These are Aston Martin, Bentley, Ferrari, Lamborghini, McLaren and Rolls Royce.
10. Home ownership rate here refers to the proportion of households where head or any other member owns the house, and is as reported by respondents (Singapore Department of Statistics).
11. From 2000 to 2014, this was relatively stable around 22.14 per cent.
12. If some of these numbers seem small, it should be noted that not all resident households have children and the Singapore's overall fertility rate stands at around 1.3 during the ten years (Singstat).
13. Given the surveys were conducted across two years, I used the average number of resident households across those years. For 2002/3 and 2017/18, this was 976,800 and 1,307,600 respectively.
14. Definitions from OECD report.
15. Results are taken from responses to surveys administered for the World Values Survey through their partner organizations in Singapore. Specific questions used in our analysis are "How proud are you to be Singaporean?" and "People sometimes describe themselves as belonging to the working class, the middle class, or the upper or lower class. Would you describe yourself as belonging to the …"
16. The other five were Australia, Brazil, New Zealand, the Slovak Republic and Sweden.
17. These racial categories should be understood as loosely representing the very diverse groups of people of all professions who resided in and came to Singapore over the years.
18. The range of possible pay-outs, depending on income and age, was increased from S$1,500 to S$3,600 to S$1,700 to S$4,000 annually. This means the cash component was increased from between S$50 to S$120, to S$56.67 to S$133.33 per month.

References

Asher, Mukul G., Azad Singh Bali, and Yee Kwan Chang. 2015. "Public Financial Management in Singapore: Key Characteristics and Prospects". *Singapore Economic Review* 60, no. 3: 1–18.

Baumeister, Roy F., and Mark R. Leary. 1995. "The Need to Belong: Desire for Interpersonal Attachments as a Fundamental Human Motivation". *Psychological Bulletin* 117, no. 3: 497–529.

Betts, Russell Henry. 1980. *Multiracialism, Meritocracy and the Malays of Singapore*. Singapore: University Microfilms.

Chia, Lianne. 2018. "Fewer Exams, Assessments in Schools to Reduce Emphasis on Academic Results: MOE". *Channel NewsAsia*, 28 September 2018. https://www.channelnewsasia.com/news/singapore/exams-assessments-scrap-mid-year-primary-secondary-schools-10767370 (accessed 4 June 2019).

Chua, Vincent. 2011. "Social Networks and Labour Market Outcomes in a Meritocracy". *Social Networks* 33, no. 1: 1–11.

Early Childhood Development Agency. 2016. "KIDSTART". https://www.ecda.gov.sg/Parents/Pages/KidSTART.aspx (accessed 3 February 2019).

Esping-Andersen, Gosta. 1990. *The Three Worlds of Welfare Capitalism*. Cambridge: Polity Press.

Goh, Keng Swee. 2004. *Wealth of East Asian Nations*. London: Marshall Cavendish Academic.

Han, Fook Kwang, Warren Fernandez, and Sumiko Tan. 1998. *Lee Kuan Yew, the Man and His Ideas*. Singapore: Singapore Press Holdings.

Holliday, Ian. 2000. "Productivist Welfare Capitalism: Social Policy in East Asia". *Political Studies* 48, no. 4: 706–23.

Krugman, Paul. 1994. "The Myth of Asia's Miracle". *Foreign Affairs* 73, no. 6: 62–78.

Lee, Kuan Yew. 2000. *From Third World to First: The Singapore Story, 1965–2000*. Singapore: Singapore Press Holdings.

———. 2010. "Transcript of Minister Mentor Lee Kuan Yew's interview with Seth Mydans of New York Times & IHT on 1 September 2010". Prime Minister's Office, Singapore. http://www.pmo.gov.sg/newsroom/transcript-minister-mentor-lee-kuan-yew%e2%80%99s-interview-seth-mydans-new-york-times-iht-1 (accessed 26 January 2019).

Leong, Chan-Hoong. 2018. "Commentary: Inequality Has a Geographic Dimension: Between and Within Neighbourhoods in Singapore". *Channel NewsAsia*, 27 May 2018. https://www.channelnewsasia.com/news/commentary/inequality-in-singapore-exists-across-within-neighbourhoods-10276898 (accessed 15 June 2020).

Leung, H.M., L. Low, and M.H. Toh. 1999. "Tax Reforms in Singapore". *Journal of Policy Modeling* 21, no. 5: 607–17.

Long, Susan. 2014. "Lim Siong Guan: Superman, Yoda, Change Crusader". *Straits Times*, 2 September 2014. https://www.straitstimes.com/singapore/lim-siong-guan-superman-yoda-change-crusader (accessed 7 April 2019).

Ma, Xin. 2003. "Sense of Belonging to School: Can Schools Make a Difference?". *Journal of Educational Research* 96, no. 6: 340–49.

Ministry of Finance. 2015. *Ministry of Finance Occasional Paper: Income Growth, Inequality and Mobility Trends in Singapore*. Singapore: Ministry of Finance.

Ministry of Social and Family Development, Singapore. 2013. "Launch of the Early Childhood Development Agency (ECDA)". Ministry of Social and Family Development, Singapore, 27 March 2013. https://www.msf.gov.sg/media-room/Pages/Launch-of-the-Early-Childhood-Development-Agency-(ECDA).aspx (accessed 3 February 2019).

Nathan, S.R., and Timothy Auger. 2011. *An Unexpected Journey: Path to the Presidency*. Singapore: Editions Didier Millet.

Ng, Irene Y.H. 2013. "The Political Economy of Intergenerational Income Mobility in Singapore". *International Journal of Social Welfare* 22, no. 2: 207–18.

OECD. 2016a. *Making Cities Work for All: Data and Actions for Inclusive Growth*. Paris: OECD. https://read.oecd-ilibrary.org/urban-rural-and-regional-development/making-cities-work-for-all_9789264263260-en (accessed 17 July 2020).

―――. 2016b. *PISA 2015 Results (Volume I): Excellence and Equity in Education*. Paris: OECD.

―――. 2018. *Equity in Education: Breaking Down Barriers to Social Mobility*. Paris: OECD.

Paulo, Derrick A., and Minmin Low. 2018. "Class—Not Race nor Religion—Is Potentially Singapore's Most Divisive Fault Line". *Channel Newsasia*, 1 October 2018. www.channelnewsasia.com/news/cnainsider/regardless-class-race-religion-survey-singapore-income-divide-10774682 (accessed 28 January 2019).

Peh, Shing Huei, and Han Fook Kwang. 2016. *Neither Civil Nor Servant: The Philip Yeo Story*. Singapore: Straits Times Press.

Peng, Nathan. 2019. "Inequality and the Social Compact in Singapore: Macro Trends versus Lived Realities". *Journal of Southeast Asian Economies* 36, no. 3: 355–79.

―――, and Sock-Yong Phang. 2018. "Singapore's Economic Development: Pro- or Anti-Washington Consensus?". *Economic and Political Studies* 6, no. 1: 30–52.

Rajaratnam, Sinnathamby. 1969. "Speech by the Minister for Foreign Affairs and Labour, Mr S. Rajaratnam, at the National Employers' Council Annual Dinner at the Chinese Chamber of Commerce Auditorium on Sunday, 6 July at 7.30 pm". 1969. Speech.

Straits Times. 2013. "Accepting Broader Definitions of Success". 14 March 2013. https://www.straitstimes.com/singapore/accepting-broader-definitions-of-success (accessed 20 March 2019).

Tan, Christopher. "Super High-End Car Sales Zoom Ahead, but Sink for General

Mass Market Brands". *Straits Times*, 30 January 2019. https://www.straitstimes.com/singapore/transport/sales-of-high-end-cars-soar-but-sink-for-general-market (accessed 30 May 2019).

Tan, Kenneth Paul. 2018. *Singapore: Identity, Brand, Power*. Singapore: Cambridge University Press.

Tan, Si Hui, and Nigel Chin. 2018. "Government to Tackle 'Serious Issue' of Inequality from Pre-School Years: Shanmugam". *Channel NewsAsia*, 20 April 2018. https://www.channelnewsasia.com/news/singapore/shanmugam-government-inequality-preschool-meritocracy-10157896 (accessed 4 April 2019).

Teo, You Yenn. 2018. *This Is What Inequality Looks Like*. Singapore: Ethos Books.

Yacob, Halimah. 2018. "Address by President Halimah Yacob for Second Session of the Thirteenth Parliament". 7 May 2018. Speech.

Yahya, Yasmine. 2018. "To Tackle Inequality, Ensure Everyone Is Progressing: Tharman". *Straits Times*, 26 October 2018. https://www.straitstimes.com/singapore/to-tackle-inequality-ensure-everyone-is-progressing-tharman (accessed 30 March 2019)

Yong, Charissa. 2017. "New Study Finds Clear Divide among Social Classes in Singapore". *Straits Times*, 28 December 2017. https://www.straitstimes.com/singapore/new-study-finds-class-divide-in-singapore (accessed 13 February 2019).

Yuen, Belinda. 2006. "Squatters No More: Singapore Public Housing". In *Land and Urban Policies for Poverty Reduction: Proceedings of the third International Urban Research Symposium*, edited by Mila Freire, Christine Kessides, Ricardo Lima, Jose Aroudo Mota, Dean Cira, Diana Motta, Bruce Ferguson, pp. 269–94. Washington, DC, and Brasilia: World Bank and IPEA.

8

INEQUALITY IN THAILAND
Income, Socio-economic and Wealth Dimensions

Vimut Vanitcharearnthum

INTRODUCTION

In late 2018, Credit Suisse's Global Wealth Report 2018 made headlines in Thai media after a well-known financier publicized the report's key findings on his Facebook page. The post subsequently became viral as his followers and the media shared it to wider audiences. The report placed Thailand among the most unequal countries in the world, thanks to a wealth concentration in a tiny fraction of wealthy families. This finding dealt a heavy blow to the junta-established government since it showed that inequality has worsened since the coup d'état of 2014. The report estimated that the top 1 per cent of population owns a staggering 66.9 per cent or two-thirds of total wealth in Thailand. This figure is up from the 2016 report which estimated that the richest 1 per cent held 58 per cent of the country's wealth. As a result, Thailand ranked in the top four of the world most unequal countries in terms of wealth distribution.

The report was quickly dismissed by the government, which argued that the wealth concentration indicators were estimated from inaccurate and outdated data. The government officials went further to claim that the current income distribution is much improved from the past. Meanwhile, the National Economic and Social Development Council (NESDC), a government think-tank, stepped forward to lend supporting evidence of reduced income and consumption inequality over the past years.

The debate between the government and its critics subsided as time passed but whether Thailand has become a more unequal nation remains a resonating question. Critics point to signs of wealth concentration, while the government rallies to its defence indicators of improved income and consumption distribution. Both sides need to be critically examined, but it is also possible that there is actually no conflict; opposing trends in wealth and income inequality can coexist. Underdeclaration of wealth-based income in household income and expenditure surveys, from which we derive income and consumption inequality, undercounts wealth ownership. Educational advancement and policy interventions such as minimum wage may foster reduced wage and income inequality, even while wealth concentration at the top increases.

This chapter unpacks the multiple facets of inequality, and engages with the debate. We begin by investigating recent trends in income and consumption inequality in Thailand, then expand the scope of inequality to wider dimensions, specifically, education achievement and access to healthcare, and account for disparities and imbalances, particularly along geographic lines.

The data generally document reductions in various aspects of inequality—income, consumption and proxies of well-being, especially education and health. These outcomes can be related to public policies that broadened socio-economic provisions over the past years, particularly universal access to education and the Universal Health Care (UHC) Scheme. The education reform in 1995 and the subsequent Education Act in 1999 helped provide free basic education to all Thai citizens. This initiative significantly promotes equality of opportunity and social inclusion in later generations, and contributes to increased earnings for low- to middle-income households. Similarly, the UHC, launched in 2001, provided adequate healthcare insurance to people who previously lacked access to medical services. Almost 100 per cent of the Thai population has some form of health insurance to keep them from falling into poverty due to health expenses.

While most dimensions of inequality have followed downward trends, some geographic disparities persist, hindering more even distribution of income and human development. The income gap between Bangkok and the rest of Thailand is evident and does not show any sign of convergence yet. In particular, Bangkok has gained an edge over other regions in various aspects, including financial, educational and medical resources. As a result, both income and wealth of the Bangkokians are well above those in other regions, which exacerbates regional inequalities and concentrates influence and power in the capital city. The latter sections of this chapter discuss the persistent advantage enjoyed by the rich, via their political connection and structural power. Despite changes in political regimes, it seems that the extreme rich can thrive well and accumulate more wealth.

WEALTH, INCOME AND CONSUMPTION INEQUALITY TRENDS

As of 2019, Thailand's total population equals 66.6 million while the working age population stood at 54.8 million (NSO 2020). The current public debate on inequality in Thailand was prompted by Credit Suisse's estimates of wealth ownership (Credit Suisse Research Institute 2018). The financial institution's Global Wealth Databook 2018 estimated that the total wealth in Thailand is US$525 billion, with the mean and median per adult wealth equal to US$9,969 and US$1,085, respectively. The staggering difference between the two—with the mean exceeding the median by more than 900 per cent—reflects the skewed distribution of wealth in Thailand. This indicates that there are small number of households at the right tail of the wealth distribution, whose exceeding riches inflate the mean value.

The Credit Suisse report also lends supporting evidence to the conjecture in the above paragraph. The report shows that there are about 40,000 adults with wealth valued at over US$1 million, while the majority of Thai adults (or 48.2 million) have wealth below US$10,000. This highly skewed wealth distribution is summed up by an astronomical Gini of 0.902 (Table 8.1).

The Gini index in the Global Wealth Databook 2018 is based on the estimated wealth holdings of Thai households which consists of both financial and non-financial assets. The report documented the methodology of estimation and acknowledged that the Thai data is only in a "satisfactory"

TABLE 8.1
Thailand: Wealth Distribution of Adult Population (Thousands Within Range)

	Wealth Range (US$)				Gini of Wealth Ownership
< 10,000	10,000–100,000	100,000–1 million	>1 million	All Ranges	
48,271	3,951	377	40	52,639	0.902

Source: Credit Suisse, The Global Wealth Databook 2018.

level since it requires interpolation of the past data in order to get the 2018 distribution.

The more accurate and up-to-date data to evaluate inequality in Thailand is the household income survey carried out by the National Statistical Office (NSO). The dataset, the so-called Socio-Economic Survey, is an annual household survey covering around 52,000 households nationwide. Researchers have used this series to calculate the Gini index of income distribution since the dataset was first available in 1962. The Gini index for Thailand in 1963 touched 0.413 which was on par with the average value observed in developing countries at that time. In the 1990s, at the height of a long phase of economic growth, the index rose to 0.536, the level considered to be among the highest in the world.

From a peak of 0.536 in 1992, the Gini coefficient showed a declining trend, in other words more equal income distribution, especially after the 1997 Asian Crisis. The turnaround in the inequality indicator coincides with the Kuznets hypothesis, i.e., as the economy begins an industrialization process, a distribution of income becomes worsen, but later in the phases of economic development, inequality subsides. The Gini index shown in Figure 8.1 captures the inflection in the index across time: rising in the late 1980s into the early 1990s, stabilizing in the 1990s, then declining. The longitudinal plotline, from the Gini of 0.413 estimated in the early 1960s will trace out an inverted-U shape often referred to as the Kuznets curve.

Similar patterns are also observed in the measurement of consumption inequality. The Gini coefficient of household consumption may not appear or be mentioned in the media as much as the income Gini, but economists regard it as a more informative indicator for an inequality in household "well-being". This is due to the fact that what households actually consume or spend reflects their standard of living more accurately than what they earn.

Inequality in Thailand 265

FIGURE 8.1
Thailand: Gini Coefficient of Household Income, 1988–2017

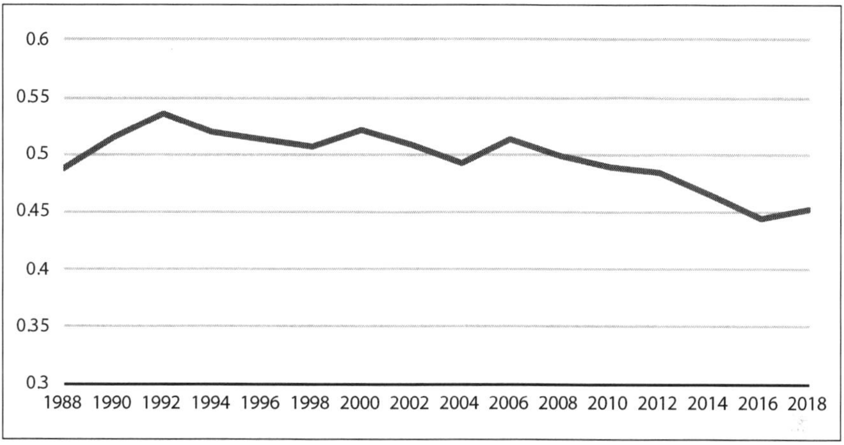

Source: National Economic and Social Development Council (2018).

Figure 8.2 exhibits a declining trend in the consumption Gini since 2002. It is noticeable that the Gini coefficients based on household income and consumption expenditure move in tandem and exhibit a downward trend in recent years. This empirical record supports the government's claims that both income and standard of living of Thai people have become more equal over the past years.

However, the national aggregate does not tell the full story. Thailand's economy is characterized by an exceedingly high concentration in greater Bangkok, to a greater extent than Manila, Jakarta and Kuala Lumpur, the capital cities and economic hubs of Southeast Asian neighbours (Rimmer and Dick 2009). Any investigation of inequality trends in Thailand should also look at inequalities within and between regions. We consider inequality within regions in this section, with reference to income and consumption (Figures 8.3 and 8.4). In particular, income distribution within each region has become more equal since 2000. The income Gini in all five regions, namely, Bangkok and its vicinities, the central, the north, the northeast and the south, in 2017 exhibit better income distribution than in 2000. It is noticeable that Bangkok had a worsening income distribution during 2000 to 2011, as the Gini indices kept rising over the period, while the indices for the other regions showed a continuous declining trend. However,

FIGURE 8.2
Thailand's Gini Coefficients Based on Household Income and Consumption Expenditure

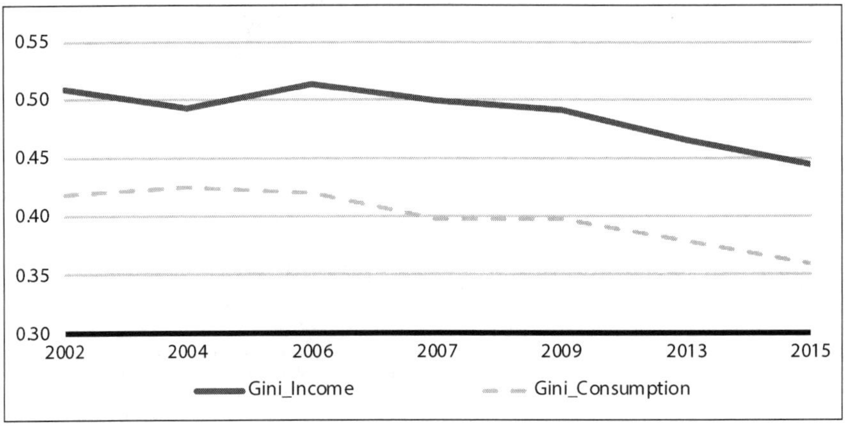

Source: National Economic and Social Development Council (2018).

things began to turn around after 2011 as the income Gini for Bangkok fell and continue on a downward path. In other words, Bangkok has turned itself from the most unequal to among the most equal regions within six years. Based on Figure 8.3 one may conclude that there is less disparity among households' income in each region than at the beginning of the new millennium.

Similar conclusion can be drawn from Figure 8.4 which shows trends in the Gini of consumption during 2007 to 2017. That is, there is tendency for more equal consumption among households in all regions. In addition, the inequality in consumption is less pronounced than the inequality in income, based on the magnitude of the Gini coefficient. This finding supports the government's claim that inequality, especially in standard of living, is less severe after the coup d'etat in 2014.

INEQUALITY IN LIVING STANDARDS

Sustained economic development in recent decades has fostered improvements in the material indicator of well-being, conventionally proxied by GDP per capita, and more broadly summarized by the Human Development Index, the UNDP's well-being indicator. The HDI attempts

Inequality in Thailand

FIGURE 8.3
Thailand: Income Inequality, by Region

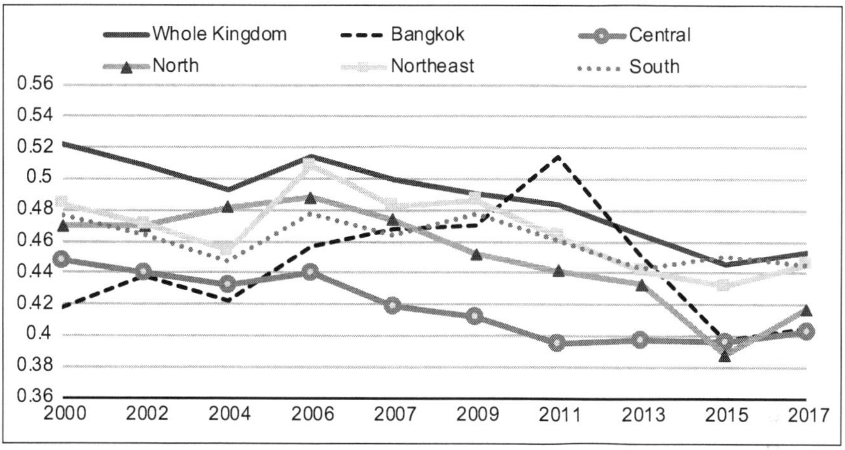

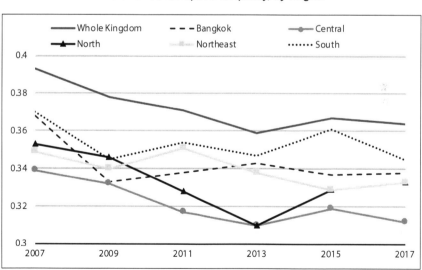

Source: NSO's Socio-economic survey various years.

FIGURE 8.4
Thailand: Consumption Inequality, by Region

Source: Author's calculation based on the NSO's Socio-economic survey.

to track progress in key human development dimensions, such as health, knowledge and decent standard of living. The higher HDI implies better achievement in these three areas.

Thailand has not only succeeded in raising average household income but at the same time also enhanced access to education and healthcare, two key aspects of human development which, together with income, are also components of the HDI (Figure 8.5). Thai citizens are now entitled to fifteen years of free schooling in public schools. In addition, every Thai has access to one of the three programmes of health insurance scheme, i.e., the Civil Servant Medical Benefit (CSMB) scheme, which is a welfare system for civil servants and their families, the Social Health Insurance scheme for private employees, and the UHC scheme for the rest of the population. As a result, 99.5 per cent of the Thai population enjoy healthcare protection.

Throughout the past decades, Thailand has narrowed education gaps between income classes. Figure 8.6 highlights educational attainment at secondary level classified by household income quartile from 1986 to 2010. It is evident that the rate of attainment has converged across income groups. In 1986, less than 10 per cent of the poorest households completed

FIGURE 8.5
Indicators of Thailand Improved Standard of Living: HDI and GDP per capita

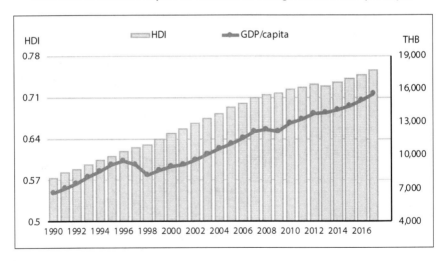

FIGURE 8.6
Thailand: Convergence in the Enrolment Rate in the Secondary School Level by Income Quartile

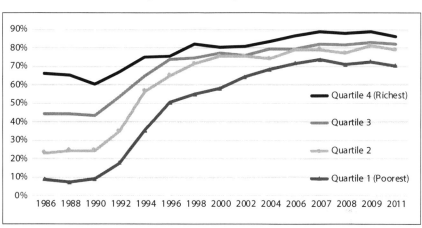

Source: World Bank (2015).

secondary school, compared to nearly 70 per cent of the top quartile. The completion rate has improved across income groups, notably the lowest quartile, and by 2010, 70 per cent of the lowest quartile accomplished the secondary school level.

These indicators show upward intergenerational mobility in education, thanks to the 1999 Education Reform Act. Under this Reform Act, the state will provide twelve years of free education to all Thai citizens. In 2010, the Ministry of Education extended free education to fifteen years so as to cover kindergarten level without making amendment to the constitution. The fifteen-year provision of educational expenses became a common practice in the subsequent government.

For further insight into how accomplishments in education have changed the landscape of educational attainment between generations, we looked at the data from the Global Database on Intergenerational Mobility (GDIM),[1] which collects information on education attainment and income across cohorts. From this dataset, several statistics are computed that reflect the educational mobility in Thailand and provide detailed comparison on education achievement between successive generations.

The lesser gap within generations is captured in the difference in the Gini of educational attainment (Table 8.2). The coefficient of the children's

TABLE 8.2
Thailand and International Comparison: Within-Generation Educational Inequality

	Thailand	GDIM Overall Average
Gini of parents' educational attainment	0.310	0.433
Gini of children's educational attainment	0.164	0.306

Source: GDIM (2018).

TABLE 8.3
Intergenerational Mobility in Education: Thailand vs Sample Average

	Thailand	Sample Average
Among children of parents not in the top quartile: the share of a child's generation that achieves a higher educational level than his/her parent	85.6%	51.3%
Among children of parents are in the bottom 50% by education attainment: the difference in the years of schooling between child and parents	6.58	4.07
The probability that a child of a parent in the lowest quartile will have education attainment in the highest quartile	0.155	0.153

Source: GDIM (2018).

cohort, at 0.164 is found to be smaller than that of the parents' cohort. That is, the indicator of inequality in education attainment is found to be 0.310 in the parent cohort, and 0.164 in the child cohort. Therefore, there are less disparity among individuals (and workers) in the later generations. This improvement in education attainment could lead to an upward mobility in the child cohort and the following descendants. In comparison to the sample average, Thailand is quite successful in reducing inequality over cohorts, regarding education attainment.

Three other statistics from the GDIM shed further light on upward mobility (Table 8.3). These statistics are chosen to highlight the education attainment of the child generation that surpasses their parents. First, for families in which parents' education is not in the top quartile, children tend to have higher education than their parents, overwhelmingly more so in Thailand than the GDIM average. 85.6 per cent of Thai families, compared to 51.3 per cent in the overall sample, fit this description. Globally, children of a parent with less education than average are likely to have more years of education than their parents. Of course, this varies across countries, with Thailand again showing up well against the average, with children of such families completing 6.58 years of schooling *more* than their parents, above the GDIM sample average of 4.07 years. Finally, GDIM also computes the probability that a child of parents in the lowest quartile of educational attainment will enter the highest quartile of educational attainment. Thailand does better than average, but only marginally; the country's estimated 0.155 probability on this score compares with 0.153 overall.

Universal access to basic education directly impacts on the labour supply in the ensuing years. From the Labour Force Survey, the average years of schooling of those in the labour force (aged 16–65) has increased from 5.3 in 1986 to 8.3 in 2010. Over this period, the proportion of the labour force with less than six years of primary education fell from 68 to 29 per cent, while the proportion of those with tertiary below bachelor degree level increased from 2.2 per cent to 5.3 per cent. Moreover, the proportion of the labour force with bachelor degree rose from 2.7 per cent in 1986 to 12.2 per cent in 2010. Evidently, Thailand has been successful in providing universal access to education and improve educational mobility across generations in a short period. Inequality in terms of education attainment has dramatically reduced.

Broad expansion in educational attainment, along with upward intergenerational education mobility, translates into improved economic mobility more generally. One approach to the dynamics of education and income, with earnings as an intermediating factor, is Corak's (2013) study of the United States, which finds a positive relationship between intergenerational earning immobility and income inequality. The key implication is that countries with high intergenerational earning immobility (i.e., the child generation is more likely to have the same earning as their parents) will also exhibit high income inequality—a relationship sometimes termed "the Great Gatsby curve". The robust improvement in educational access for Thailand's younger generation has presumably fostered their movement up the earnings ladder, and the documented decrease in income Gini index lends support to this postulate.

On health-related aspects of well-being, various indicators show Thailand on a converging path with developed countries. Life expectancy at birth has increased from 49.3 years in 1950 to 77.0 years in 2019, while infant mortality rate has declined from 138.2 per 1,000 live births in 1950 to 7.5 per 1,000 live births in 2019. Below-five mortality is basically nil. Better healthcare is one of the factors that contribute to the improving human development indicators. Thanks to the UHC which was introduced in 2001, all Thai population have some form of health insurance schemes to provide them accessible medical services.

In the 1970s, only 15 per cent of the population had access to the public health infrastructure, while 51 per cent of them was self-reliant or sought care from private or traditional healers. Government employees and their dependants enjoyed generous health insurance system, called CSMB, while the private sector employees had Social Security (SS) to partially cover their medical costs. The poor and underprivileged, lacking access to both healthcare financing options, constituted an estimated 34 per cent of the population.

Health provisions for the poor expanded. In 1975, the Medical Welfare (MW) scheme, a government-subsidized healthcare scheme was introduced, aiming to provide free care to the poor. The programme, also known as the low-income card scheme, was expanded to include the elderly and subsequently other vulnerable groups (e.g., children under the age of 12) in the early 1990s. In 1983, a subsidized Voluntary Health Card (VHC) was introduced to provide access to health services for workers in the informal sector and those who were not eligible for the other healthcare schemes. Under the VHC, each household could purchase one-year insurance coverage for THB500 (Thai baht), around US$16 at the current exchange rate. However, the MW and VHC ran into operational difficulties. Difficulty in verifying income marred the means testing process; many who gained access to MW were not necessarily the targeted low-income population. The VHC also encountered the adverse selection issues; a high proportion of those enrolling and utilizing the insurance had health problems, which entailed high pay-outs that financially stressed the insurance scheme.

The 1997 economic crisis accelerated the demise of the programme as the demand for the VHC surged, significantly due to massive lay-offs. Workers, especially from the financial sector, turned to the VHC as a replacement to the SS scheme, since their healthcare benefits from the SS automatically terminated once the workers became unemployed. Table 8.4 showed a rise in the proportion of population under the VHC from 1996

TABLE 8.4
Thailand: Percentage of Total Population with Healthcare Coverage

Scheme	1991	1996	1999
Insurance schemes:			
1. Medical Welfare (MW)	12.7	12.3	12.4
2. CSMB & State enterprise schemes	15.3	12.7	8.9
3. Social Security (SS)	0	5.5	7.1
4. Voluntary Health Card (VHC)	1.4	13.2	28.2
5. Private insurance	3.1	1.2	1.4
6. Others	0.9	1.1	1.7
Total insured	*33.5*	*46.0*	*59.8*
Total uninsured	*66.5*	*54.0*	*40.2*

Source: National Statistical Office 1991, 1996 and 1999.

to 1999. The surge also indicates that many previously uninsured persons took up the VHC.

The Universal Health Coverage, or the so-called the 30-baht Scheme, began in 2002 after the Thai Rak Thai (TRT) Party won the general election and became the core of the coalition government. This is due to the fact that the 30-baht Scheme was one of the party's grassroot-oriented election campaign. The TRT-led government quickly implemented this campaign promise. The UHC was launched in six provinces in April 2001, in an additional fifteen provinces by June 2001, and nationwide by April 2002.

The scheme is designed to provide equal access to quality healthcare according to beneficiaries' needs, regardless of their socio-economic status. Under this scheme, THB30 copayment (around US$0.9) is required for both outpatient and inpatient services except the vulnerable groups—the previous MWS beneficiaries including the poor, the elderly and children under the age of 12—who could obtain public health services for free. The UHC provides a comprehensive benefits package for curative as well as rehabilitation services. In 2006, the 30-baht copayment requirement was abolished, and services became free for the poor and vulnerable. The scheme is thus fully funded by the general tax revenue. Thanks to the UHC, those who are not eligible for the SS and CSMBS now have adequate health protection, and as a result, 99.8 per cent of Thai population has health protection coverage.

Prior to 2000, it is noticeable that the proportion of uninsured population remained relatively high. Tangcharoensatien et al. (2014) profiled the uninsured based on the Ministry of Public Health provincial health survey, finding that 31 per cent of the sampled households were uninsured. Unsurprisingly, the majority of the uninsured are households in the low-income bracket in which the head of household has attained, at most, primary schooling. The uninsured are required to pay all medical bills in full in both public and private hospitals. The study also found that a medical bill of THB6,000 or around US$200 is way above monthly income of many uninsured families. Such burdens can easily put these households in debt, potentially with informal lenders. The implementation of the UHC helped relieve the financial burden of the poor and prevent them from falling into impoverishment due to medical expenses.

Figure 8.7 depicts estimations of the numbers of households prevented from medical impoverishment thanks to the UHC. Without the UHC, up to 116,000 households might potentially fall into poverty due to medical expenses in 2009. However, the Socio-Economic Survey reveals that the

FIGURE 8.7
Thailand: Estimated Number of Households (Thousands) Falling into Poverty due to Medical Expenses (Protected from Health Impoverishment)

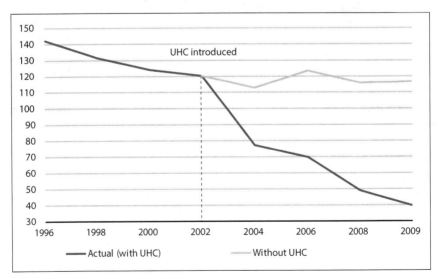

Source: Tangcharoensathien et al. (2014).

introduction of UHC in 2002 has saved the majority of those families, and there were only 39,700 households that belong to that category.

Persisting Capability Gaps

Despite various impressive indicators of more equal educational achievement across individuals, there are still issues of serious concern and needed to be addressed with urgency, particularly with regard to quality of education, tertiary-level qualifications and skills acquisition impacting on employment prospects and upward mobility. Beyond enrolment and certification, the acquisition of skills and knowledge increasingly matter. In this regard, the data from the World Bank Human Capital Project could help us evaluate the capacities of the soon-to-be labour force in Thailand. The Human Capital Project attempts to quantify the potential quality of the future labour force, based on health and education attributes of current children. The index has value between 0 and 1, indicating the worker's productivity relative to its full potential. For example, a score of 0.7 signals that a child at present will have future productivity of 70 per cent of its full potential. Put differently, this indicates that a typical worker will be 30 per cent below what could have been achieved with complete education and full health by the time he becomes a worker.[3]

The World Development Report 2019 showed that the Human Capital Index for Thailand is 0.6, implying the current children will develop into a worker who attains 60 per cent of its full potential (Table 8.5). The HCI for Thailand is higher than Indonesia, the Philippines and India, but lower than China and Vietnam. However, the index is slightly higher than the average of the whole sample and the upper middle-income group. Thus, there is room for improvement and all Thais as well as the policymakers should aim to achieve full potential.

Firstly, even though Thailand has improved education attainment at the primary and secondary levels, the attainment at the college level is still low, especially for households in lower income groups. The net enrolment rate in the college level is only 27 per cent in 2016, which seems to be minimal compared to the net enrolment rate of near 100 per cent in the primary level. The low net enrolment rate is due to the inability of children from poor families to further their study beyond the free twelve years basic education. Table 8.6 classifies household into ten equal groups, from lowest to highest based on the amount of household

TABLE 8.5
Human Capital Index: Thailand and International Averages

	Thailand	World Average	Upper Middle-Income Average	High Income Average
Human capital index	0.60	0.57	0.58	0.74

Source: World Development Report (2019).

TABLE 8.6
Thailand: Net Enrolment in the College Level by Expenditure Deciles (Percentage)

	2009	2012	2016
Decile 1 (Lowest)	1.4	4.0	4.2
Decile 2	5.4	6.4	11.1
Decile 3	6.3	8.6	13.6
Decile 4	12.4	14.2	16.4
Decile 5	15.1	15.1	18.4
Decile 6	21.0	21.9	22.1
Decile 7	26.2	30.9	29.9
Decile 8	29.6	44.4	37.0
Decile 9	43.8	53.1	51.3
Decile 10 (Highest)	59.3	66.0	65.8
Total	23.9	28.5	27.8

Source: NESDB.

expenditures, and calculates the enrolment rate in the college level of the family members. It is evident that the net enrolment ratio in the bottom half of expenditure deciles (i.e., decile 1–5) is below 20 per cent, while the top two expenditure brackets register above 50 per cent. The disparity between the richest and the poorest remains massive; in 2016, the net enrolment rate for the top decile was more than 15 times higher than the rate for the bottom decile.

Secondly, despite high education attainment in primary and secondary level, certain components in the HCI raise concern about the academic achievement of Thai students. One of the components in the HCI is international standardized test scores, which is a benchmark for comparing student competence across countries. Thai students achieved a score of

441 out of 625 in the OECD-administered Programme for International Student Assessment (PISA) of 2012. It is above the sample average, but still below 70 per cent. Moreover, in the most recent PISA 2012 reading assessment, only 1 per cent of 15-year-old students performed in the high level. About one-third of Thai students knew the alphabet and could read, but they could not locate information or identify the main messages in a text. This group of students is thus classified as functionally illiterate, which means that they lack critical skills for many jobs in an ever-evolving modern economy.

This test outcome became a major concern among academics and educators since Thai students performed poorer than counterparts in countries with lower income, like Vietnam. The average score of Vietnamese students are 66 points higher than their peers in Thailand, and more importantly, an average 15-year-old Vietnamese student is approximately 1.5 academic years ahead of the average Thai student. The average Thai student lags behind PISA-participating countries in the OECD and in East Asia and the Pacific, by 2.5 years and almost 3 years, respectively, in mathematics, reading and science. Another component in the HCI is learning-adjusted years of school, which indicates the academic achievement in terms of years-in-school. Under the 12 years education, Thai students have learning-adjustment years of 8.6, which means that even though Thai students spend 12 years in school, they learn only 8.6 years or about 72 per cent of the actual years.

What are the reasons behind the poor performances of an average Thai student? Disparities in the system—specifically, lagging achievements of rural and disadvantaged schools—are evidently contributing to the low national score. Low performing students are concentrated in remote villages. Table 8.7 shows the geographical distribution of 15-year-old student who took PISA in 2012. Students in villages accounted for 16 per cent of those participated in the test, and it is the group of students whose performances lag behind those in other groups. The average reading score of students in village areas in 2003 and 2012 are 394 and 410 respectively. The performances of the lowest 40 per cent of village-located students is even more worrying. This subgroup got only 337 and 344 in the 2003 and 2012 reading test. Students in large cities, at the other end, scored the highest—by wide margins. Correspondingly, functional illiteracy is more acute in villages; 47 per cent of students in villages were classified as functionally illiterate, compared to 16 per cent in large cities.

TABLE 8.7
Thailand: International Standardized Test Scores by Geographic Area

Area	% of 15-Year Student Population 2012	Pisa 2003 Reading Score	Pisa 2012 Reading Score	Functionally Illiterate in 2012 (% Within Area)	Point Gap with Large Cities 2003	Point Gap with Large Cities 2012
Village	16	394	410	47	68	73
Lowest-performing 40% in village		337	344		125	139
Highest-performing 60% in village		432	454		30	29
Small town, town, city	77	422	444	31	39	39
Large city	7	461	16	16	—	—
Thailand	100	420	441			

Source: World Bank (2015).

The World Bank's (2015) report on Thai education pointed out that lack of both material resources and staffs, along with inequality in allocating resources geographically, are responsible for the outcome. In particular, small village schools are severely under-resourced, in terms of teaching facilities and materials, and qualified teachers. A typical school in Bangkok has higher average ratio of teachers to classroom, and its teachers have more years of experience and higher graduate degrees. These evidences exemplify inequality in terms of education quality and expose the geographical disparities.

Bangkok vs the Rest

Political and economic power are persistently concentrated in Bangkok. The centrality of the metropolis continually contributes to national income and wealth inequality. In 2010, with almost 10 million residents within city limits, Bangkok accounted for nearly 15 per cent of Thailand's population. However, commerce operating or registered in Bangkok command around half of national GDP. As shown in Figure 8.8, the capital city's gross provincial product accounted for 54 per cent of GDP in 1995. The ratio

Inequality in Thailand 279

FIGURE 8.8
Bangkok's Gross Provincial Product (GPP) as Percentage of National GDP, 1995–2016

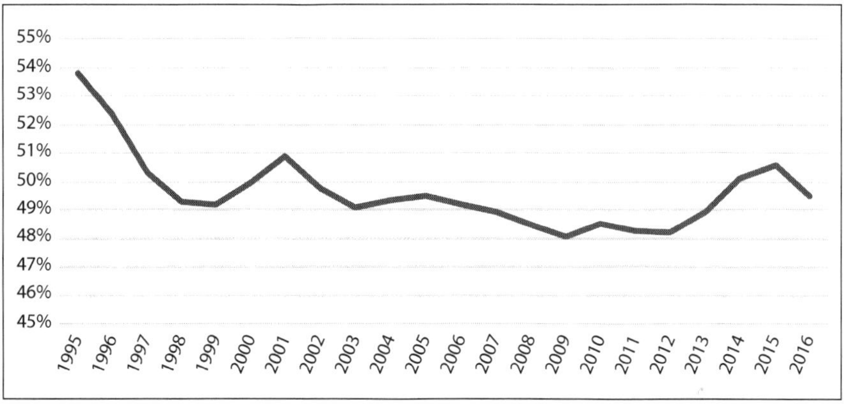

Source: Author's calculation based on the NESDC GPP data.

declined in the subsequent years, remaining under 50 per cent for a decade, but that trend seems to have reversed after 2012. The Bangkok share rose to above 50 per cent again in 2014 and 2015, and dipped again in 2016, but regardless of the fluctuations, the regional output distribution reveals disparities between Bangkok and the rest of the country.

The value of output produced has close connection with the income generated throughout the production process, sustaining an evident income gap between Bangkok and the rest of Thailand. Figure 8.9 shows the trend in average household income by regions over the period 2002–17. Though the average household monthly income in all regions steadily rose over the years, the gap between Bangkok and the rest of the country is relatively stable. The average monthly income of households outside Bangkok in 2017 are still below the level of average monthly income of Bangkokians observed in 2002—even in nominal terms. In other words, there is no convergence in average income across regions.

An income distributional profile based on the Socio-Economic Survey of 2017 finds variations in inequality within regions. Table 8.8 presents this finding in the form of cumulative distribution function of household monthly income in each region, and Thailand as a whole. Strikingly, 36 per cent of Bangkok households earn THB10,000/month or less, while around

FIGURE 8.9
Thailand: Average Household Monthly Income (in THB), by Region, 2002–17

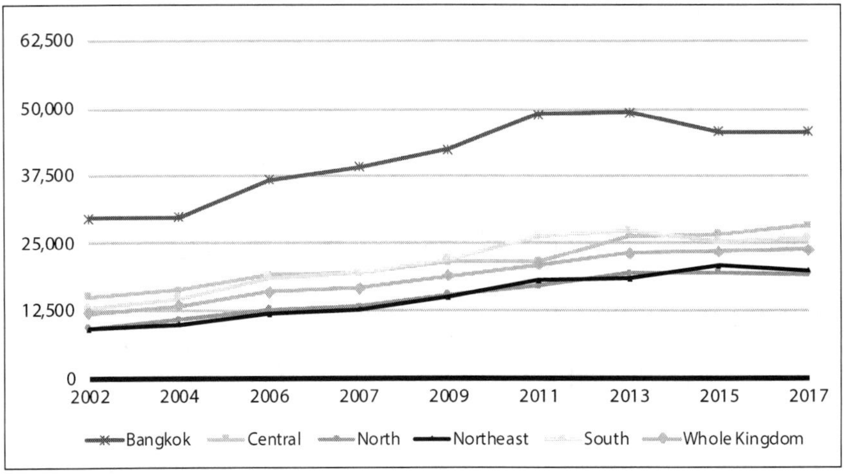

Source: National Statistical Office (2020).

TABLE 8.8
Thailand: Cumulative Distribution of Household Income by Regions, 2017

	Thailand	Bangkok	Central	North	Northeast	South
Below 500	0.4	0.2	0.5	0.4	0.3	0.5
500–1,500	1.4	0.3	1.2	1.6	1.9	2.2
1,501–3,000	10.2	0.8	6.6	12.9	18.4	11.3
3,001–5,000	30.3	4.5	23.6	42.0	48.4	32.2
5,001–10,000	65.1	35.8	62.7	80.1	80.9	66.1
10,001–15,000	81.8	65.1	81.1	90.8	90.2	81.6
15,001–30,000	95.5	90.9	96.2	98.0	97.2	94.8
30,001–50,000	98.6	97.0	99.0	99.4	99.0	98.6
50,001–100,000	99.8	99.5	99.9	100.0	99.9	99.7
> 100,000	100.0	100.0	100.0	100.0	100.0	100.0

Source: National Statistical Office (2020).

80–81 per cent of households in the north and northeast fall beneath the same income threshold. The ratio at the national level was 65.1 per cent which was in line with the fractions of households in the Central and the South, at 62.7 per cent and 66.1 per cent, respectively.

In terms of financial assets, households in Bangkok also have much larger holdings than other regions. Table 8.9 shows a similar pattern of cumulative distribution seen in Table 8.8. Only 35.9 per cent of households in Bangkok have financial asset valued at or under THB30,000, compared to 54.8 per cent of the households in the northeast, and nearly half of households in the central, north and south regions. Moving up to larger categories of asset holdings, we can notice that the fraction of households with asset values higher than THB1 million is 7.4 per cent in Bangkok, while this figure is only 1–2 per cent in other regions.

Bangkok is emphatically the financial centre of the country. The economic development over the years only reinforces its status as the core of Thailand's financial system. Figures 8.10 and 8.11 show shares of Bangkok and other parts of Thailand in terms of deposit and credit distribution in 1995 and 2019. Evidently, there is no significant change in the distribution of deposit and credit among regions in Thailand. Bangkok continues to command the lion's share of deposits (around 63 per cent) and of credit (71 per cent) in the financial system.

Apart from financial resources, Bangkok also has medical and educational resources in abundance relative to other regions. Table 8.10 compiles various indicators regarding medical resource adequacy, specifically, population per bed, population per physicist, population per dentist, population per pharmacist, population per professional nurse and population per technical nurse. Comparing the provinces in 2010 and

TABLE 8.9
Thailand: Distribution of Financial Assets across Regions, 2019

Value of Assets (THB)	Thailand	Bangkok	Central	North	Northeast	South
No saving assets	6.4	4.6	10.4	3.4	8.0	3.5
<= 10,000	26.3	15.4	29.5	26.8	32.7	25.1
10,001–30,000	47.7	35.9	49.4	48.9	54.8	48.6
30,001–50,000	59.0	47.2	59.1	62.0	65.8	60.4
50,001–100,000	74.3	64.1	73.0	78.3	79.9	76.3
100,001–500,000	93.7	87.1	94.7	94.8	96.6	95.7
500,001–1,000,000	97.0	92.6	97.9	97.7	98.7	98.5
1,000,001–5,000,000	99.6	98.7	99.8	99.8	100.0	99.9
5,000,001–10,000,000	99.9	99.5	100.0	99.9	100.0	100.0
>10 million	100.0	100.0	100.0	100.0	100.0	100.0

Source: National Statistical Office (2020).

FIGURE 8.10
Thailand: Deposit Distribution across Regions, 1995 and 2019

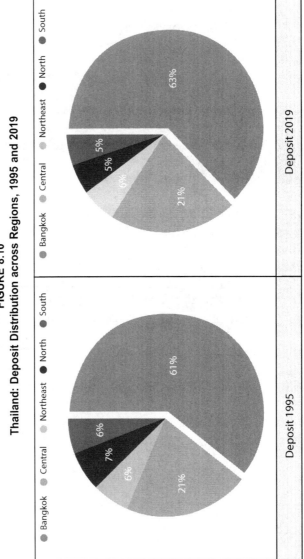

Source: Bank of Thailand (2019).

Inequality in Thailand

FIGURE 8.11
Thailand: Credit Distribution across Regions, 1995 and 2019

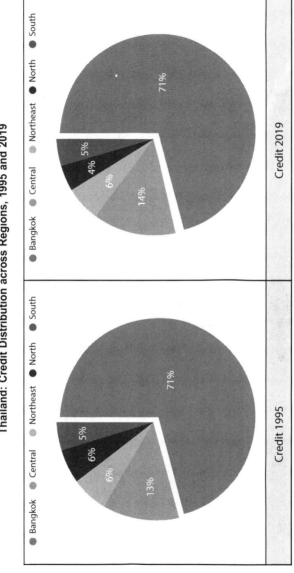

Source: Bank of Thailand (2019).

TABLE 8.10
Comparison of Medical Resource Adequacy Between Bangkok and Other Provinces

	Bangkok		Other Provinces	
	2010	2014	2010	2014
Total beds	21,451	28,085	112,654	122,265
Population/bed	266	203	515	504
Population/physicist	1,052	722	3,043	2,613
Population/dentist	7,865	5,957	14,209	10,542
Population/pharmacist	3,871	2,740	7,718	6,037
Population/professional nurse	282	203	581	474
Population/technical nurse	1,960	1,572	9,179	11,553

Source: National Statistical Office (2020).

TABLE 8.11
Thailand: Education Attainment by Regions, 2017

	Thailand	Bangkok	Central	North	Northeast	South
Never attended school	4.8	2.6	4.7	10.6	2.3	5.4
Kindergarten and pre-primary	40.2	21.1	38.1	48.2	54.1	35.6
Primary education	17.2	16.3	17.2	14.0	18.7	19.8
Lower secondary	10.8	15.4	12.5	8.2	7.6	10.9
Upper secondary	9.3	12.4	9.7	7.4	7.3	10.4
Vocational/technical education	3.2	6.3	3.3	1.8	1.9	2.8
Post-secondary education	3.7	5.7	4.7	2.3	1.7	4.4
University/bachelor	8.9	17.0	7.8	5.9	5.1	9.6
Postgraduate	1.6	3.3	0.9	1.3	1.3	0.9
Other education	0.3	0.1	1.1	0.2		0.1

Source: National Statistical Office (2020).

2014, it is obvious that Bangkok has better facilities and less congestion in medical services. Bangkok's advantages are further multiplied when we factor in education. Table 8.11 shows the highest educational attainment of populations within each region, in 2017. Bangkok has the highest proportion of individuals completing secondary education and above, in particular bachelor degree and higher, than other regions. As a result, households in Bangkok on average could earn higher income than their peers in other regions.

With abundance in resources that help promote human capital accumulation, spanning financial, medical and educational domains, Bangkok is able to draw the best talents in the country and enjoys an edge in productivity gain above the rest of the country, through human capital externalities. It is not surprising to see perennial differences in income and well-being between Bangkok and the rest of Thailand in the past decades. Predictably, the owners of financial capital, also concentrated in Bangkok, have exceedingly enjoyed gains from economic growth.

WEALTH INEQUALITY

Can the different scenarios of wealth inequality and income/consumption inequality be reconciled?

Arguably, the top tier of income distribution is critically underrepresented in the Socio-Economic Survey, which is the database for calculating income and consumption Gini.[4] The inability of household surveys to obtain responses from the ultra-rich, or tendencies for them to underdeclare income, is a global problem, but a major issue nonetheless for Thailand, in view of the massive wealth inequality documented through other empirical investigations. By missing the majority of the extreme rich, the higher end of the income distribution is truncated, consequently yielding lower value of the Gini index. In other words, the severity of income inequality is underestimated. The credential of the government's claims that income distribution has improved can certainly be contested. To overcome the problem of missing sample of the richest in the household surveys, researchers attempting to estimate the top income share have opted to use the income tax returns data in which the richest are more represented (Piketty 2003; Atkinson 2005; Alveredo 2011).

Two studies have combined household surveys with tax data. Vanitcharearnthum (2019) applied the methodology outlined in Alveredo (2011) in his study on income inequality and top income shares in Thailand, for the interval 2004–9. In particular, income tax tabulations were used to interpolate the top income earners in each year. The interpolations were then appended with the household survey income data so as to complete the missing right tail of the national income distribution. Then the Gini coefficients were recalculated based on the combined income data. The study found that the Gini indices from the combined data were higher than those based on the household survey. This implies that computations based on the Socio-Economic Survey alone under-report the magnitude of income inequality. Jenmana (2018) made important progress in this area of research in Thailand, for 2016, by combining data from tax returns and traditional household surveys with income information from national account that are not visible elsewhere, such as, imputed rents, investment income due to insurance policies and so on. The study reveals that the share of national income going to the top 10 per cent, 1 per cent and 0.1 per cent are, respectively, 52 per cent, 20 per cent and 8 per cent (Figure 8.12). These figures are higher than the calculation based on the Socio-Economic Survey in the corresponding years, in which the shares of the top 10 per cent, 1 per cent and 0.1 per cent are, respectively, 38 per cent, 11 per cent and 3 per cent.

Jenmana (2018) went further to recalculate the Gini coefficient, using a combination of data outlined above, and his findings are in line with Vanitcharearnthum (2019). That is, the corrected Gini coefficient remains in high level and does not fall rapidly as shown in the one computed from the survey data. Jenmana (2018) found that the inequality indicator fell slightly from 0.64 in 2001 to 0.60 in 2016, compared to the estimates from

FIGURE 8.12
Thailand: Top Income Brackets (Percentage of National Income), 2016

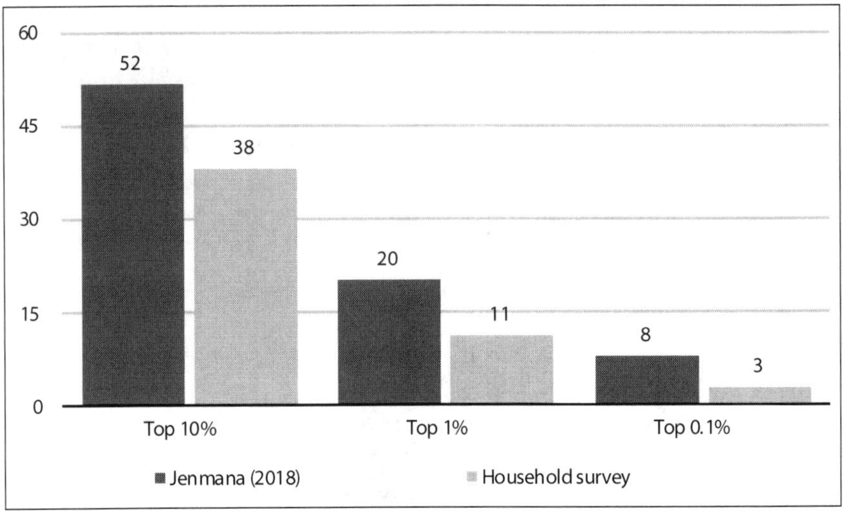

Source: Jenmana (2018).

the Socio-Economic Survey, which equals 0.508 in 2002 and 0.453 in 2017. Inequality in Thailand might actually be more severe and persistent than the official statistics suggest.

Crazy Rich Thais

Information about the richest are well exposed in various sources, such as stock ownerships, net worth or wealth ranking. The recent ranking of Stock Exchange of Thailand's richest shareholders reveals that the owners of big corporations witnessed substantial capital gain in their portfolio valuation. Table 8.12 provides the 2019 ranking along with portfolio value, as well as the percentage change from the previous year. These richest individuals draw their wealth from being owners of their business. For example, Sarath Ratanavadi is the CEO of Gulf Energy Development, and has 35.4 per cent stake in the company, while Prasert Prasarttong-Osoth owns various businesses ranging from medical services, airlines and digital TV.

It is noticeable that the majority of the major stockholders in Table 8.12 enjoyed astronomical rises in their wealth in 2019. The value of financial wealth among the top 8 has increased at a much faster rate, ranging from 15-495 per cent, compared to economic growth, which registered merely 1.9 per cent. This is in line with Thomas Piketty's argument, i.e., the wealth inequality that rose sharply in recent years is due to a rate of return on capital, whose ownership is highly concentrated among few individuals/

TABLE 8.12
Thailand's Richest Stockholders, 2019

Rank	Name	Value (THB billion)	Change from Previous Year (%)
1	Sarath Ratanavadi	121.0	109.8
2	Prasert Prasarttong-Osoth	66.1	−14.3
3	Niti Osathanugrah	48.6	52.1
4	Keeree Kanjanapas	43.1	51.8
5	Somphote Ahunai	42.1	−0.3
6	Vonnarat Tangkaravakoon	41.1	495.6
7	Daonapa Petampai	41.0	18.1
8	Chuchat Petampai	40.8	15.4

Source: Money and Banking magazine (2020).

families, greatly exceeding the rate of growth of the economy (Piketty 2003). Thus, the haves enjoy more prosperity than the have-nots.

Another source of information that exposes the wealth concentration and wealth inequality in Thailand is the Forbes' rich list. Forbes releases its ranking on an annual basis, thus providing more up-to-date estimates of individuals' and families' net worth. Table 8.13 provides the 2019 lists of the richest seven families and individuals along with their net worth and ranking in 2008.

It is noticeable that the names in the top four spots have not changed from eleven years ago. Four siblings in the Chearavanont family maintain the top spot in the rich list for four consecutive years. Their net worth ranked fourth in the Forbes list in 2008, with the values less than half of the 2008 top spot. Their business empire, Charoen Pokphand (CP) Group, encompasses agri-business, telecommunications and among others, wholesale and retail trade. Chalerm Yoovidhya, the Red Bull owner and the richest man in 2008 occupies the third spot in 2019. The Chirathivat family owns the country's biggest mall developer group, i.e., Central Group. They also own the upscale department store oversea as well. Charoen Sirivadhanabhakdi runs Thailand's largest brewer, ThaiBev, and recently became the country's largest property developer. He runs real estate development and owns hotels in Thailand, Asia, the United States, the United Kingdom and Australia.

The net worth of the Chearavanont family has grown more than ten times during the elevan years interval. The other top four's wealth has accumulated at a bit slower pace but still managed to accrue at least

TABLE 8.13
Thailand's Richest Persons/Families, 2008 and 2019

	2008		2019	
	US$ billion	Rank	US$ billion	Rank
Chearavanont family	2.0	4	29.5	1
Chirathivat family	2.8	3	21	2
Chalerm Yoovidhya	4.2	1	19.9	3
Charoen Sirivadhanabhakdi	3.9	2	16.2	4
Sarath Ratanavadi			5.2	5
Aiyawatt Srivaddhanaprabha	0.9	7	4.7	6
Prasert Prasattong-Osoth	0.3	22	3.4	7

Source: Forbes (2020).

US$1 billion per year. Such rates of increase among the wealthiest families have outpaced the growth rate of average income in Thailand, which averaged around 6.6 per cent during the past eleven years.

Political Ties and Big Business

Business-government ties have been recognized in Southeast Asia for long and the interdependence between them has implication on both political and economic development. In the build-up of the 2019 general election, Palang Pracharat Party (PPRP), a newly formed political party with close ties to the military junta, organized a fund-raising dinner which gathered THB622 million (around US$22 million) in donations. The PPRP won the election's popular vote and formed a coalition government that brought back the coup leader Prayut Chan-ocha as the prime minister. The main contributors in the fund-raising dinner includes the families listed in the Forbes's rich list 2019. That is, the Chearavanont family, the Chirathivat family, Charoen Sirivadhanabhakdi and the Srivaddhanaprabha family are among key donors for the PPRP.

The Srivaddhanaprabha family provide an outstanding example of the government-business nexus and monopoly capitalism. Aiyawatt Srivaddhanaprabha, ranked sixth in the 2019 Forbes' rich list, inherited the family business after his father, Vichai, died from a helicopter accident in England. The Srivaddhanaprabbha family business, the King Power International Group, built on its duty-free shops, and subsequently expanded to international sports and real estate developer. Since the opening of the Suvarnabhumi Airport in 2006, King Power was granted the exclusive right to operate as a sole provider of the duty-free shops at the Thailand international airport. When the duty-free concession in Suvarnabhumi Airport and another three regional ones open for concession bid last year, many expect a more open competition which might break down the King Power's monopoly. However, the King Power Group was awarded another ten-year extension so its monopoly in duty-free business at the Suvarnabhumi Airport will remain through March 2031. In addition, the Group won the bid for being sole operator in duty-free stores in other key regional airports as well. The Srivaddhanaprabha family now has a stronghold in this business for another decade.

The Srivaddhanaprabha family has close ties to various governments. From the Thaksin administration, which revived the construction of the

Suvarnabhumi airport and eventually put it into operation in 2006, to the current government, the family provides some forms of support to the running government for more than a decade. Since the inauguration of the new international airport, it is estimated that the wealth accrued to the family could top THB155 billion. Not surprisingly, the Group was also accused of wrongdoing, e.g., failing to pay the state the exact revenue specified under the concession, and corruption, which led to a lawsuit. On September 2018, the Central Criminal Court for Corruption and Misconduct Cases dismissed the lawsuit, ruling that the plaintiff was not affected party and cannot sue in this case.

The gain in income and wealth at the higher end of the income distribution due to monopoly power implies losses to the rest of the economy. Euromonitor, a leading global market research house, estimated that an average tourist spends only US$47 on duty-free items in Thailand, compared to an average spending of US$260 in South Korea. It is argued that the gap in the amount spent was due to lack of competition in Thailand duty-free retails. The South Korean government allotted twenty duty-free concessions at Incheon International Airport, which has a comparable retail area as the Suvarnabhumi Airport. It is obvious that more competition would lead to more equitable distribution of income and more revenue to the government. The opportunities lost in the duty-free business may remain for another ten years.

CONCLUSION

Inequalities in income and consumption, and dynamics of inclusion and exclusion, are structural consequences of capitalism. Those with skills and abilities, and privileged access to financial resources and educational opportunity, stand to reap the most returns and prosperity. Inequality in income reinforces inequalities in wealth and financial assets. Some degree of talent is innate, but children of a well-to-do family would have better chance to acquire and develop skills necessary to be successful in competitive markets—and to benefit from family networks and personal referrals. However, the less fortunate ones would find that their limited endowment and resources prevent them from acquiring better skills, maintaining health without adverse financial impact, and accessing networks—and may struggle to catch up with their peers and be hindered from moving up the income ladder. Across generations, many children born into disadvantage are stuck at the lower end of the income distribution. Therefore, it is the responsibility of the government to ensure that opportunities to prosper are available to all citizens, especially the less fortunate families. Public policies, such as free education for all and universal healthcare, are considered as a policy to reduce inequality of opportunities, and could help improve income distribution. Thailand has successfully launched these policies in the early 2000s and now began to see the evidence of more even income distribution. The Gini coefficients of household income distribution has declined from 0.536 in 1992 to 0.453 in 2018. This indicates that the distribution of household income become more equal. Thanks to the education reform that initiated in 1999 and the UHC Scheme in 2002, all walks of life in Thailand have more equal access to basic education and healthcare.

Despite the improving trend of inequality in general, different facets of inequality remain unchanged in Thailand. First, there is a huge gap between Bangkok and the rest of Thailand in terms of healthcare provision, education opportunity and income. While there are variations in per capita income across the north, south, central and northeast regions, the differences among these regions are not as substantial as their income gap relative to Bangkok level. Second, resources and financial assets are highly concentrated in Bangkok. Better schools, better hospitals, better financial services and better job opportunities all are clustered in Bangkok. As a result, Bangkok is in a good position to draw talents and capital relative to elsewhere and reinforce itself as a focal point of Thai economy. Finally, evidence has emerged, through combining insights from household surveys and tax return and national accounts data, that national income is more highly concentrated at the top than the official estimates—and this disparity has possibly remained steady in recent years. Augmented estimates of inequality show a lesser decline in income inequality over the past two decades, departing from the household survey-based estimates of more substantial decline.

Concentration of income in the uppermost extremities is confirmed by the net worth of Thailand's richest families. Based on Forbes' list of 2008 and 2019, we observe that the top four have not changed over this eleven-year period. In addition, their net worth has grown at much faster rate than the national income. This wealth inequality will surely persist in Thailand for a long while, considering how Thailand's plutocrats have secured their political ties to help them sustain their business advantages.

Such practices are not beneficial to Thailand's economic development in various ways. First and foremost, it prevents competition from domestic and foreign competitors who could have provide better and more efficient products and services to consumers. The wealth of few families in various ways comes at the expense of the majority of Thai nationals. Secondly, inability to compete fairly prevents innovation and creativity. Resources and efforts that could have been channelled to productive uses would be diverted to rent-seeking activities.

Despite the success in reducing inequality of opportunities in the past decades, the prospect of a more equal society may be jeopardized by the current uneven income and wealth distribution. While it is evident where the problems lie, it might be hard to remove the obstacles to better and more even income and wealth distribution.

Notes

1. GDIM collects data on educational attainment and income for ten-year cohorts covering individuals born between 1940 and 1989 from 148 countries. For Thailand, GDIM imputed inequality across generations using household information about parents' and children's educational attainment, based on the 2012 Socio-Economic Survey.
2. The Ministry of Public Health provincial health survey sampled 52,987 households countrywide.
3. The human capital index comprises of three components, i.e., survival, education and health. Based on the indicator in each component, such as under-five mortality rate, education expected to obtain by age 18, learning-adjusted years of schooling, and the rate of stunting of children under five, etc., the composite index is computed as a number in the range of 0 and 1.
4. The Socio-Economic Surveys of 2009 and 2013, which contain information about household's income from various sources, such as labour income, revenue (and cost) of business operations, and money received, as well as cost incurred, from agriculture, can be used to locate the highest income person in the survey sample. The richest person sampled in the 2009 survey had income of THB33 million or around US$1 million, resided in the central region, and engaged in an industry labelled "wholesale and retail, repairing motor vehicles, motorcycles and household goods". The richest person in 2013 has income of THB17 million or around US$0.5 million, lived in the south, and ran a business involving oleaginous fruits. These incomes clearly fall short of the billionaires who own multi billion-baht business in Thailand.

References

Alvaredo, Facundo. 2011. "A Note on the Relationship Between Top Income Shares and the Gini Coefficient". *Economic Letters* 110, no. 3: 274–77. https://doi.org/10.1016/J.ECONLET.2010.10.008

Atkinson, Anthony B. 2005. "Top Incomes in the UK over the 20th century". *Journal of the Royal Statistical Society: Series A (Statistics in Society)* 168, no. 2: 325–43. https://doi.org/10.1111/j.1467-985X.2005.00351.x

Bank of Thailand. 2019. *Commercial Banks' Deposits and Credits Classified by Provinces*. Bangkok: Bank of Thailand. https://www.bot.or.th/App/BTWS_STAT/statistics/BOTWEBSTAT.aspx?reportID=781&language=eng

Becker, Gary S., Scott D. Kominers, Keven M. Murphy, and Jorg L. Spenkuch. 2018. "A Theory of Intergenerational Mobility". *Journal of Political Economy* 126 (S1): 7–25. https://doi.org/10.1086/698759

Corak, Miles. 2013. "Inequality from Generation to Generation: The United States in Comparison". In *The Economics of Inequality, Poverty, and Discrimination in the 21st Century*, edited by Robert Rycroft. Santa Barbara, California: ABC-CLIO.

Credit Suisse Research Institute. 2018. *Global Wealth Databook 2018*. Zurich: Credit Suisse Research Institute.

Forbes. 2020. "Thailand's 50 Richest". *Forbes*. https://www.forbes.com/thailand-billionaires/list/#tab:overall (accessed 13 October 2020).

GDIM. 2018. *Global Database on Intergenerational Mobility*. Development Research Group, World Bank. Washington, DC: World Bank Group.

Jenmana, Thanasak. 2018. "Democratisation and the Emergence of Class Conflicts Income Inequality in Thailand 2001–2016". WID.world Working Paper No. 2018/15.

Money and Banking Thailand. 2020. "Thailand's 50 Stock Tycoons 2019". https://www.moneyandbanking.co.th/article/cover-story-mb452 (accessed 3 April 2020).

National Economic and Social Development Council. 2018 *Report on Poverty and Inequalities in Thailand 2017*. Bangkok: National Economic and Social Development Council.

National Statistical Office. 1991 *Health and Welfare Survey 1991*. Bangkok: Ministry of Digital Economy and Society.

———. 1996. *Health and Welfare Survey 1996*. Bangkok: Ministry of Digital Economy and Society.

———. 1999. *Health and Welfare Survey 1999*. Bangkok: Ministry of Digital Economy and Society

———. 2020. *Socio-Economic Survey 2019* . Bangkok: Ministry of Digital Economy and Society (in Thai).

Nikomborirak, Deunden. 2018. "Freeing up the Duty-Free Business". *Bangkok*

Post, 26 September 2018. https://www.bangkokpost.com/opinion/opinion/1546854/freeing-up-the-duty-free-business (accessed 26 September 2018).

Piketty, Thomas. 2003. "Income Inequality in France, 1901–1998". *Journal of Political Economy*, 111, no. 5 : 1000–42. https://doi.org/10.1086/376955

Rimmer, Peter, and Howard Dick. 2009. *The City in South East Asia: Patterns, Processes and Policy*. Singapore: NUS Press.

Tangcharoensathien, Viroj, Supon Limwattananon, Wilaiporn Patcharanarumol, and Jadej Thammatacharee. 2014. "Monitoring and Evaluating Progress towards Universal Health Coverage in Thailand". *PLoS Med*, 11 no. 9: e1001726. https://doi.org/10.1371/journal.pmed.1001726

Vanitcharearnthum, Vimut. 2019. "Top Income Shares and Inequality: Evidences from Thailand". *Kasetsart Journal of Social Sciences* 40, no. 1: 40–46. https://doi.org/10.1016/j.kjss.2017.07.010

World Bank. 2015. *Wanted: A Quality Education for All*. Washington, DC: World Bank.

9

TRENDS AND DRIVERS OF INEQUALITY IN VIETNAM

Trang Huyen Dang, Cuong Viet Nguyen and Tung Duc Phung[1]

INTRODUCTION

There is a broad consensus that inequality is harmful for sustainable development. Kuznets (1955) observed the historical record of growth and inequality in some industrialized countries. As incomes grew, inequality first increased and then decreased after a peak. However, recent studies show that inequality can reduce economic growth and increase poverty, and it is possible that an economy can grow without rising inequality, especially in the early stages (Alesina and Rodrik 1994; Persson and Tabellini 1994; Deininger and Squire 1998; Bourguignon 2003). Inequality can also increase the social conflict and violence (Cramer 2003; Østby 2013; Ferrer-i-Carbonell and Ramos 2014). Inequality is also found to be negatively correlated with happiness and life satisfaction (Dolan, Peasgood and White 2008; Schneider 2015; Tran, Nguyen and Van Vu 2018). Understanding the trends and drivers of inequality is, therefore, very important not only for researchers but also policymakers.

In this study, we examine changes in inequality in Vietnam over time and analyse potential drivers of inequality using decomposition and regression methods. Although Vietnam has achieved relatively broad-based economic growth, there is still a large gap in living standards between population subgroups. Thus, in this study we also investigate the gaps in living standards between the Kinh majority and ethnic minorities in Vietnam. Using the richly detailed Vietnam Household Living Standards Surveys (VHLSSs) of 2002 to 2016, we estimate inequality levels and patterns based on different living standards indicators.

Vietnam is an interesting case to look at. Since 1987, the economy of Vietnam has experienced rapid economic growth as well as structural transformation from a centrally planned economy to a market-based economy. As a result of economic growth, poverty has decreased dramatically with the poverty headcount ratio (using the international poverty line of US$1.25 a day (2005 PPP)) falling from 43.6 per cent in 1993 to 14.3 per cent in 2008 (World Bank 2013). In 2016, according to the international poverty line of US$3.20 a day (2011 PPP), the rate was around 8.6 per cent (World Bank 2018). Extreme poverty is almost eliminated, with only 2 per cent of the population living on less than 2011 PPP US$1.90 per day.

Economic growth is not associated with rising inequality in Vietnam. Estimates from VHLSSs show that inequality of expenditure has been very stable in Vietnam. The Gini coefficient of per capita expenditure is estimated at 0.357 in 1993, 0.358 in 2006 and 0.353 in 2016. However, there remains a large gap in living standards between groups, in particular between rural and urban people, poor and non-poor groups, men and women as well as the Kinh/Hoa group and ethnic minority groups. In 2016, per capita consumption of ethnic minorities was 45 per cent less than the Kinh and Hoa, and nearly 45 per cent of the ethnic minorities still live in poverty. Thus, ethnic minorities who make up only 15 per cent of the country's population, constituted 73 per cent of the poor in 2016 (World Bank 2018). There is still a gap in accessing public services between the ethnic minorities and majority. Even within the poorer areas where the ethnic minorities account for a large proportion of the population, the Kinh majority fares better than the ethnic minorities (Nguyen, Phung and Westbrook 2015). Together with economic growth, the number of super-rich people, who have US$30 million and more in assets, have been increasing in Vietnam (Kim 2017). Considering that the world today, including Vietnam, is facing an unprecedented inequality crisis, inequality has become a problem that needs to be thoroughly studied and seriously addressed (Oxfam 2017).

There is a considerable literature on inequality in Vietnam. A number of studies explore the income gap among different population subgroups such as between the Kinh and ethnic groups (Nguyen, Phung and Westbrook 2015; Bui, Nguyen and Pham 2017; Nguyen et al. 2017). All studies show a large gap in income, consumption and other welfare indicators between the Kinh and ethnic minorities. Few studies discuss the cost of inequality. Nguyen and Pham (2018) show that high inequality reduces the effect of economic growth on poverty reduction in Vietnam. Nguyen, Van der Weide and Truong (2010) and Lanjouw, Marra and Nguyen (2017) also find that districts with lower initial inequality have been more successful in poverty reduction.

Regarding the drivers of inequality, Nguyen, Tran and Van Vu (2007) conclude that welfare disparity between the urban and rural areas was mainly due to change in the returns or differentials based on household characteristics, i.e., the dramatic change in the returns to education, and income gaps associated with ethnicity and agricultural activities. Le and Booth (2013) also find that rural-urban expenditure inequality continued to increase over the years due to growth in covariates as well as returns to those covariates. Benjamin, Brandt and McCaig (2017) find that agricultural opportunities played an important role in dampening inequality-increasing pressures that may arise from rural underemployment, but more importantly, Vietnam's stable inequality levels are attributed to the steady development of wage-labour markets in both urban and rural areas. On the other hand, Nguyen, Doan and Tran (2020) show that wages and nonfarm business income are the two main determinants of income inequality. Over the 2004–14 period, wage income's contribution to total income inequality increased to 50 per cent, while the second largest source of inequality is nonfarm business income, accounting for 30 per cent.

Compared with previous studies, this study has different features. First, it uses VHLSSs from 2002 to the most recent one in 2016 to show the trend in inequality in Vietnam. Second, this study measures welfare by using multiple indicators, including per capita income, expenditure, electricity consumption and housing value. Most studies measure welfare by either expenditure or income. Measuring aggregate income and consumption is associated with measurement errors, since aggregate income and consumption consist of a large number of items. Data for electricity consumption, which draw on records of utility providers, are easier to collect compared to surveys, and less likely to be correlated with measurement errors. It is also more related to the asset level. We use the housing value to explore the inequality in assets in Vietnam. Third, this study uses several decomposition and regression methods to examine the drivers of inequality in Vietnam over time.

This chapter is structured into five sections as follows. The second section describes the data set used in this study. The third section presents the analysis method and the fourth section discusses the empirical findings. The fifth section concludes.

DATA AND METHOD

Data Set

The data used in this study comes from the VHLSS series. The VHLSSs have been conducted every two years since 2002 by the General Statistics Office of Vietnam (GSO), with technical support from the World Bank. The latest VHLSS was conducted in 2018, but this survey has not been released. Thus, our analysis covers the period 2002–16.

The VHLSSs are sampled from around 3,000 communes throughout the country. Officially, Vietnam is divided into three administrative tiers: provinces, districts and communes. In 2020, there are 63 provinces, 707 districts and 10,614 communes. The 1999 Population and Housing Census is used as the sampling frame for the VHLSSs from 2002 to 2008, while the sampling frame for the VHLSSs since 2010 references the 2009 Population and Housing Census. The 2002 VHLSS, with almost 30,000 households sampled, was designed to be representative at the provincial level, while the other VHLSSs, with about 9,200 to 9,400 households, are representative at the regional and urban/rural levels.[2]

The VHLSSs contain very detailed data on individuals, households and communes. Household data include durables, assets, production, income and expenditures, and participation in government programmes. Income and expenditure details are also collected through the questionnaire, as well as information on the demographics, education, employment, health and migration of individuals within the households.

Estimation Methods

Measuring Inequality

Income or expenditure inequality is often measured by the three most common indices: Gini, Theil L, and Theil T. The Gini coefficient, which is based on the Lorenz curve, is most widely used to measure inequality due to its straightforward calculation, flexibility across different population groups and independence from sample size and scale of the economy. The Gini coefficient is estimated by the difference between the distribution of income and the uniform distribution that represents equality (Deaton 1997):

$$G = \frac{n+1}{n-1} - \frac{2}{n(n-1)\bar{Y}} \sum_{i=1}^{n} \rho_i Y_i, \qquad (1)$$

where ρ_i is the rank of individual i by their income. ρ_i is equal to 1 for the richest and increase for individuals with lower income. The Gini coefficient lies in the range of 0 to 1, with a higher Gini coefficient representing greater income inequality.

The Theil L index of inequality is calculated as follows:

$$Theil_L = \frac{1}{n}\sum_{i=1}^{n} \ln\left(\frac{\bar{Y}}{Y_i}\right), \qquad (2)$$

The Theil L index ranges from 0 to infinity. A higher value of Theil L indicates more inequality.

The Theil T index of inequality is calculated as:

$$Theil_T = \frac{1}{n}\sum_{i=1}^{n} \frac{Y_i}{\bar{Y}} \ln\left(\frac{Y_i}{\bar{Y}}\right) \qquad (3)$$

The Theil T index ranges from 0 (lowest inequality) to ln(N) (highest inequality).

The overall inequality which is measured by the Theil indexes can be decomposed into inequality within groups (e.g., urban and rural areas, or Kinh and ethnic minorities) and inequality between groups. For example, the Theil T index can be decomposed as follows:

$$Theil_T = \sum_{i=1}^{m} s_i T_i + \sum_{i=1}^{m} s_i \ln\left(\frac{\bar{Y}_i}{\bar{Y}}\right) \text{ with } s_i = \frac{n_i}{n}\frac{\bar{Y}_i}{\bar{Y}}. \qquad (4)$$

T_i is the Theil index of within inequality of group i, n_i is the population size and $\bar{Y}_i$ is the mean income or expenditure of group i.

Regression Analysis

In order to understand the variables that affect inequality, we use the VHLSSs to estimate the provincial-level inequality indexes and other explanatory variables, and estimate the following standard model that explains the variation in inequality across provinces:

$$Inequality_{i,t} = \alpha + \beta Log(Y_{i,t-1}) + \gamma Poverty_{i,t-1} + X'_{i,t-1}\delta + \theta T_t + u_i + v_{i,t}, \quad (7)$$

where $Inequality_{i,t}$ is the inequality index of province i in year t. $Y_{i,t-1}$ is the lag of per capita income, $P_{i,t}$ is a poverty index, $X'_{i,t-1}$ is a vector of explanatory variables including high school completion rates, shares of the ethnic and the rural population, and different types of investments, T_t is a year dummy variable. The unobserved variables are decomposed into time-variant ($v_{i,t}$) and time-invariant components (u_i).

We estimate equation 7 using GMM estimators. OLS estimates can be biased. We address this selection bias as follows. First, we use lagged explanatory variables to avoid reserve causality. Second, we estimate the model of first-differenced variables, and the first difference transformation removes the time-invariant unobserved effect (u_i). The Arellano–Bond test for zero autocorrelation of the first order and second order in first-differenced errors shows no evidence of model misspecification. Third, we apply the GMM estimator which were developed by Holtz-Eakin, Newey and Rosen (1988) and Arellano and Bond (1991). The GMM-type instruments for the log of lagged per capita expenditure are higher order lags of the per capita expenditure variables. Although the exogeneity of these instruments may be questionable, we can perform the overidentification test to test the validation of the instruments. The Sargan test concludes that the null hypothesis that overidentifying restrictions are valid is not rejected.

EMPIRICAL RESULTS

Trends in Inequality

As mentioned above, we measure living standards by several indicators. The most popular indicators used to analyse inequality and poverty are income and expenditure. Table 9.1 reports estimates of per capita income and expenditure over time using the VHLSSs. We adjust all the variables to the price of January 2016 for comparison. Income per capita

TABLE 9.1
Vietnam Living Standards Indicators: Per Capita Income and Expenditure, and Housing Value, 2002–16

Years	Per Capita Income (VND thousand)	Per Capita Total Expenditure (VND thousand)	Per Capita Expenditure on Electricity (VND thousand)	Housing Value Per Capita (VND thousand)
2002	13,626	10,374	273	n.a.
2004	15,924	11,966	345	n.a.
2006	18,433	14,051	381	n.a.
2008	19,144	14,258	391	n.a.
2010	25,897	25,427	510	211,888
2012	28,890	26,568	577	203,939
2014	31,641	28,609	734	210,147
2016	35,943	32,538	865	219,997

Note: The variables are measured in January 2016 price. There are no data on house value before the 2010 VHLSS.
Source: Authors' estimation from VHLSSs.

and expenditure per capita both increased over time. During the 2014–16 period, per capita income and expenditure increased by nearly 7 per cent annually. In 2016, per capita income and expenditure was, in Vietnamese dong, VND35,943,000 and VND32,538,000, respectively.[3] The spending on electricity is around 2.7 per cent of the total expenditure.

The VHLSS has undergone some change in content over time, which affect the data series. It should be noted that there is a gap in expenditure between 2008 and 2010 because of changes in the sampling frame and questionnaires. The VHLSSs of 2002 to 2008 record food consumption for the whole year; from 2010 onwards, food consumption amounts are obtained for month prior to the sampling, then annualized. As a result, per capita expenditure was remarkably higher in 2010 than in 2008. Additionally, since the VHLSS 2010, there are data on the housing value of households. A real estate boom in 2009 raised housing prices in 2010. In 2016, the average per capita housing value was around VND220 million.

Gini coefficients of four living standard indicators over time show a general stability over 2002–10, and downward trends in the 2010–16 interval (Figure 9.1). Inequality in expenditure was lower than inequality in income. In 2016, the Gini coefficient of per capita expenditure was

FIGURE 9.1
Vietnam: Gini Coefficient of Income, Expenditure and Housing Value, 2002–16

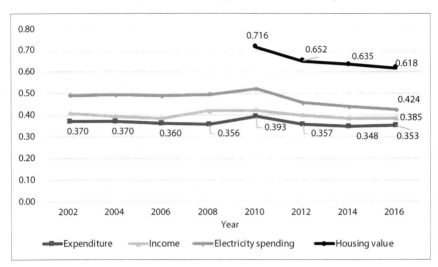

Source: Authors' estimation from VHLSSs.

0.353, while the Gini coefficient of per capita income was 0.385. Housing is even more unequally distributed, with the Gini coefficient at 0.618. As expected, inequality in this asset is much higher than inequality in income or consumption, particularly due to the capacity for high-end property prices to inflate markets are buoyant, coupled with zero property ownership of a segment of the population at the bottom end.

Figure 9.1 also shows a peak in inequality in 2010, especially in per capita expenditure and housing value. One reason is that there was a large increase in housing price in 2010 in big cities. The Gini coefficient in housing value was very high in 2010, hence the subsequent decline is quite expected. The per capita expenditure includes rent paid by tenants or imputed rent of owner-occupied houses, which in turn derives from the value of the property. Thus, disproportionate increases in housing value, between low expenditure and high expenditure households, can impact on overall inequality in expenditure as captured in the Gini.

Inequality in electricity consumption adds further insight. The Gini coefficient in electricity spending, at 0.424 in 2016, is higher than that of income and overall expenditure which were, respectively, 0.385 and 0.353.

These differentials in the level of inequality, together with the parallel downtrend of inequality in electricity consumption and housing value, concur with expectations that this particular item in household budgets moves in tandem with house size and lifestyle. Larger homes and more lavish lifestyles consume more electricity; middle class expansion may contribute to the decline in the electricity consumption Gini.

Income remains an important outcome, and the vital link between economic activity, consumption and living standards. The stability of income inequality in Vietnam is of importance and interest, and can be explained by several reasons. First, poor people can also benefit from economic growth. As mentioned in Benjamin, Brandt and McCaig (2017), the increase in agricultural production played an important role in dampening inequality-increasing pressures. The movement from agriculture to non-farm sectors can also help the poor to increase their income. Second, the government has implemented a large number of anti-poverty programmes, which can help to reduce inequality (Nguyen, Phung and Westbrook 2015). Third, VHLSSs cannot capture super-rich households. The number of super-rich people, who have US$30 million and more, have been increasing in Vietnam (Kim 2017). However, these people are not sampled in the VHLSSs. Thus, actual inequality might be higher than inequality observed from household surveys.

We also examine the sensitivity of the measurement of inequality to different inequality indices. Table 9.2 reports the inequality indices of per capita expenditure. The inequality indexes of other indicators of living standards (income, electricity consumption and housing value) are presented in Appendix Tables A9.1 to A9.3. The results show that inequality measured by the Theil indexes and the ratio of 90th to 10th percentiles were stable over time—and all also recorded a peak in 2010. However, the ratio of 95th to 5th percentiles has increased slightly, from below 8.0 in 2006–8 to 8.1–8.3 in 2014–16.

For a snapshot of the inequality level to income relationship, we compare the GDP per capita and Gini coefficient of countries with both these variables in 2012, using World Bank's World Development Indicators, and also observe Vietnam's location on this plot. Overall, the correlation is weak—reflecting the complexity of the income-inequality relationship—but the fitted line points to an inverted-U shaped, mainly negative correlation between inequality and GDP per capita. Countries with higher income per capita tend to have lower inequality, while the

TABLE 9.2
Vietnam: Inequality Measures of Per Capita Expenditure

Year	Gini	Theil's L	Theil's T	Ratio 90th/10th	Ratio 95th/5th
2002	0.37	0.22	0.25	4.9	7.9
2004	0.37	0.22	0.24	5.1	8.4
2006	0.36	0.21	0.23	4.9	7.8
2008	0.36	0.21	0.23	4.8	7.6
2010	0.39	0.26	0.29	5.5	9.4
2012	0.36	0.21	0.23	4.9	8.0
2014	0.35	0.21	0.22	4.8	8.1
2016	0.35	0.21	0.22	4.9	8.3

Source: Estimation from VHLSSs.

FIGURE 9.2
Gini Coefficient and GDP, Vietnam and the Countries Worldwide, 2012

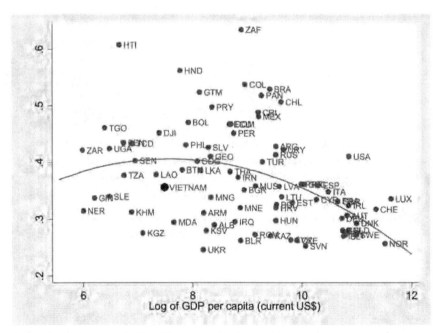

Source: Preparation using the World Development Indicators data.

highest inequality tends to be found in middle- and upper middle-income countries. Vietnam's Gini coefficient is lower compared with countries at similar economic levels. In other words, Vietnam's position below the curve indicates that its inequality is below that expected based on its income level and the income to inequality relationship observed around the world. Two reasons are worth mentioning here. First, Vietnam has achieved broad-based economic growth. Both poor and non-poor have experienced growth of income and expenditure (Nguyen and Pham 2018). Second, Vietnam has implemented a large number of poverty reduction programmes, which could help the poor to increase their income, consequently reducing inequality.

Inequality between the Kinh and Ethnic Minorities

Vietnam has fifty-four ethnic groups, of which the Kinh majority accounts for 85 per cent of the total population. Ethnic minorities live in mountains and highlands, while the Kinh tend to live in delta and coastal areas. Vietnam has achieved remarkable success in economic growth and poverty reduction during the past decades. However, there is still a large gap in living standards between the Kinh and ethnic minority groups (Bui, Nguyen and Pham 2017). Figure 9.3 shows that the absolute gap in per capita expenditure between the Kinh and ethnic minorities has been widening over time. Figure 9.3 also shows a gap in living standards between urban and rural areas. However, this gap is smaller than the gap between the Kinh and ethnic minorities. Thus, in this study, we focus on the gap between the Kinh and ethnic minorities.

As mentioned above, the sampling frame and questionnaires of VHLSSs before 2010 and those since 2010 are different. This can explain why there is a large difference in per capita expenditure between 2008 and 2010.

Vietnam has achieved a great success in poverty reduction. Figure 9.4 shows the expenditure poverty rates of the Kinh and ethnic minorities over time. We used the expenditure poverty lines, which are estimated by the World Bank (WB) and GSO of Vietnam. It should be noted that the real poverty line increased in 2010. As a result, the poverty rates increased between 2008 and 2010.[4]

Although both the Kinh and ethnic minorities have experienced poverty reduction, the poverty rates were much higher for ethnic minorities than the Kinh group. The poverty rate of the whole country in 2016 was 9.8 per

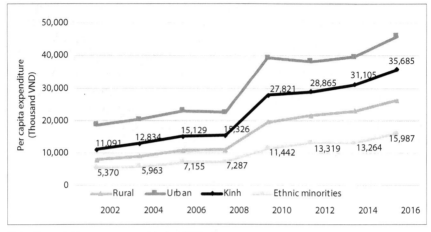

FIGURE 9.3
Vietnam: Per Capita Expenditure of Kinh and Ethnic Minorities

Note: The variables are measured in Jan 2016 price.
Source: Estimation from VHLSSs.

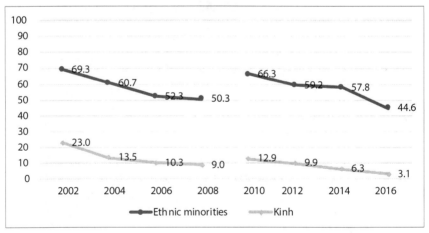

FIGURE 9.4
Vietnam: Expenditure Poverty Rates of Kinh and Ethnic Minorities

Source: Authors' estimation from VHLSSs.

cent. The poverty rate of the Kinh was 3.1 per cent, while nearly 45 per cent of ethnic minorities still live in poverty (Figure 9.4). Thus, ethnic minorities who make up only 15 per cent of the country's population, constituted 73 per cent of the poor in 2016.

Using the poverty estimate in 2009, Lanjouw, Marra and Nguyen (2017) find that even within the poorer areas where ethnic minorities account for a large proportion of the population, the Kinh majority fares better than the ethnic minorities. In this study, we estimate the poverty rate of districts for rural areas in 2016. We employ the small area estimation method from Elbers, Lanjouw and Lanjouw (2002, 2003) and combine data from the 2016 Fishery, Agricultural and Rural Census and data from the 2016 VHLSS to estimate the poverty rate of all fifty-four ethnic minorities and the poverty rate of districts in rural areas for 2016.

Since we predict the poverty rate using the small area estimation, we also compute relative standard errors associated with the estimates, from which we can report 90 per cent confidence intervals (Figure 9.5). We find that all groups are poorer than the Kinh, and poverty among the Hoa (Chinese) is also low. However, poverty rates vary widely between the groups, and some differences are statistically insignificant. Additionally, small ethnic groups with population less than one million tend to have higher poverty rates than large ethnic groups. Ethic groups such as La Hu, Mang and Lo Lo have very high poverty rates at around 80 per cent. The Mong constitute a special case, as a large ethnic group that also has a very high poverty rate.

Along with higher poverty rates, Vietnam's ethnic groups also attain lower levels—compared with the Kinh and Hoa—in the basic human development categories of education and health (Le et al. 2014; Bui, Nguyen and Pham 2017; Nguyen, Phung and Westbrook 2015; Nguyen et al. 2017). Although Vietnam has achieved universal primary education, there is great variation in the quality of primary education. MDRI (2016) found that the scores of literature and math test of students at grades 3 and 5 were significantly lower in areas with high concentration of ethnic minorities than other areas. Inequalities in education quality between schools and within schools are also noteworthy. In a report by Dang and Glewwe (2018), there was evidence that the variation within schools contributed 60 per cent of the overall variation in students' test scores, while the variation across schools and provinces accounted for the other

FIGURE 9.5
Vietnam: Poverty Rate of Ethnic Groups, with 90 per cent Confidence Interval, 2016

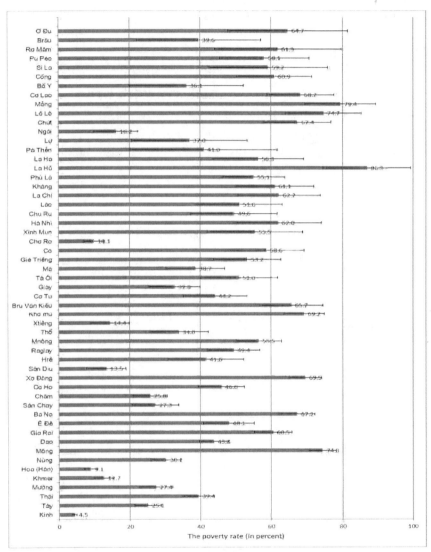

Source: Authors' estimation using small area estimation of the 2016 VHLSS and the 2016 Fishery, Agricultural and Rural Census of Vietnam.

40 per cent, which implied the effect of "special" classes on disparities in education quality within schools.

There is also a large gap in higher education between the Kinh and ethnic minorities. Figure 9.6 shows the proportion of tertiary education of the Kinh aged 18 to 23 is more than three times higher than that of ethnic minorities. Nguyen et al. (2017) conclude that difficulty in the Vietnamese language is one of the obstacles for ethnic minorities to have higher education and better employment opportunities.

Decomposition of Inequality by Population Categories

To understand the drivers or sources of inequality, we conduct decomposition analyses of inequality to estimate how much of the total inequality can be attributed to inequality within categories, and how much is due to inequality between categories (using the formula in equation 4). This exercise assigns all categories the same mean household expenditure

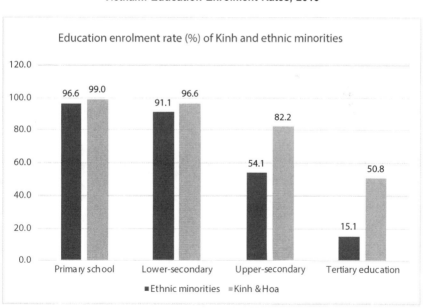

FIGURE 9.6
Vietnam: Education Enrolment Rates, 2016

Source: Authors' estimation from VHLSSs.

while computing inequality within the categories separately—a different Theil index for each category. This is the basis for the "within-category" contribution. We then assign equal levels of inequality across the board—the same Theil index to each category—while varying the mean household expenditure between categories, thus obtaining the "between-category" contribution.

A first round of decompositions uses spatial categories: urban/rural areas and provinces (Figure 9.7). We report the decomposition of the Theil's L index. The results from the decomposition of the Theil's T index are very similar and therefore not presented. Panel A of Figure 9.7 shows that the main contribution to total inequality is the inequality within urban or rural areas instead of the inequality between urban and rural areas. The within-category inequality accounted for 70.6 per cent of the total inequality in 2006, and its contribution increased to 83 per cent in 2016. There is a large variation in the per capita expenditure within urban areas as well as within rural areas. Panel B of Figure 9.7 also shows a large contribution of inequality within provinces towards total inequality.

We repeat this decomposition exercise with reference to ethnic groups (Figure 9.8). We first divide the population into two groups—Kinh and all other ethnic minorities. Panel A shows that the inequality within the Kinh and within ethnic minorities accounted for 86.9 per cent of the total inequality in 2016. Inequality between Kinh and ethnic minorities accounted for only 13.1 per cent. However, this share increased over the 2006–16 periods, which implies that the gap between Kinh and ethnic minorities tended to increase over this period. Panel B presents estimates of the same decomposition using all fifty-four ethnic groups. The Kinh remain as one group, but instead of the minorities being combined into one group as in Panel A, we incorporate every minority as a group on their own. The inequality within each group is still the main contribution to the total inequality. However, the inequality between ethnic groups tended to contribute more to total inequality between 2006 and 2016. So, the gap between the ethnic groups increased over time.

We then decompose total inequality in 2016, with households are categorized by head of household characteristics (Figure 9.9). Inequality between households with heads of different age and gender contributes little to the total inequality (Panel A). It means that age and gender of household heads have minimal impact on household expenditure. Almost all of total inequality derives from inequality within the categories, which

Trends and Drivers of Inequality in Vietnam 311

FIGURE 9.7
Vietnam: Decomposition of Expenditure Inequality by Urban/Rural Areas and Provinces, 2006 and 2016 (Theil-L Index)

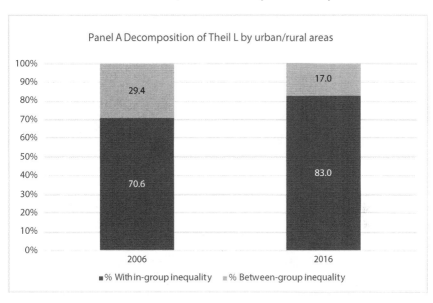

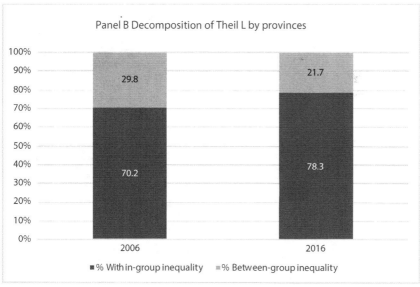

Source: Authors' estimation from VHLSSs.

FIGURE 9.8
Vietnam: Decomposition of Expenditure Inequality by Ethnic Groups, 2006 and 2016 (Theil-L Index)

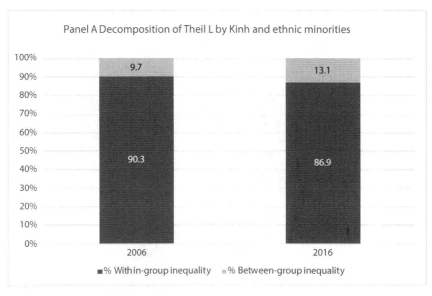

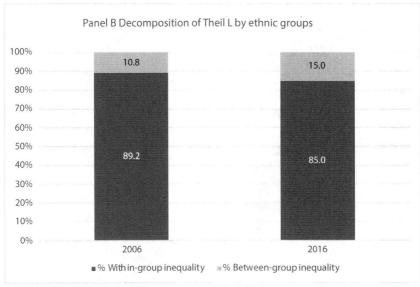

Source: Authors' estimation from VHLSSs.

Trends and Drivers of Inequality in Vietnam

FIGURE 9.9
Vietnam: Decomposition of Expenditure Inequality by Head of Household Characteristics, 2016 (Theil-L Index)

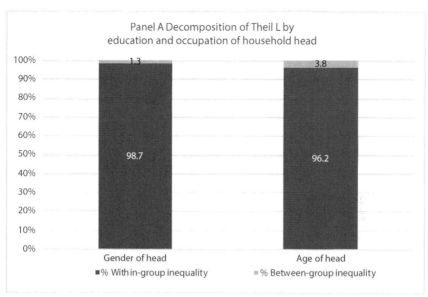

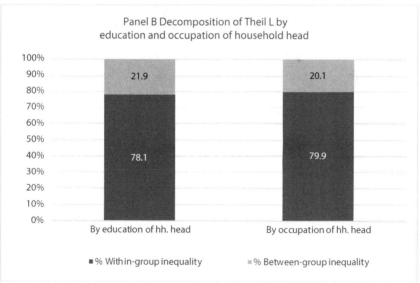

Source: Authors' estimation from VHLSSs.

is in turn due to other factors besides gender and age. Education and occupation are more important in determining household expenditure. The inequality components due to the differences in occupation and education contribute larger to total inequality (Panel B of Figure 9.9). Specifically, the between-education level inequality and the between-occupation inequality contribute 21.9 per cent and 20.1 per cent to the total inequality, respectively. It should be noted that these decompositions are based on household expenditure; if income is used instead of expenditure, these head of household characteristics will most likely show up as more important determinants accounting for a larger share of between-category inequality to total inequality.

Regression Analysis of Provincial Income Level: Income Inequality

We now apply the province as the unit of analysis, and examine relationships between income level and income inequality. Figure 9.10 presents the correlation between the Gini coefficient of income and log of per capita income of provinces, based on provincial-level inequality and per capita income that we compute from the VHLSSs.[5] It does not suggest any distinct relationship between income level and income inequality, although a fitted line traces out an inverted-U shaped relationship. As the income level rises, inequality also rises, and after achieving a peak inequality tends to decrease while income increases further.

Finally, we use regressions to examine the association between inequality and several socio-economic variables. The observations are provinces over the period 2002–16. The dependent variables are inequality indices of per capita income. We use two models: a small model with lagged log of per capita income, lagged poverty rate, year and province dummies, and a large model with additional explanatory variables. In the GMM models, the endogenous variables are lagged log of per capita income, lagged poverty rate, while the instruments are lagged variables of these endogenous variables. We use lags of explanatory variables to avoid reverse causality, i.e., the effect of inequality on the explanatory variables.

Table 9.3 shows that provinces with high initial income level and poverty rate tend to subsequently have higher inequality.[6] It is plausible that, in provinces with high initial income level, higher income households

FIGURE 9.10
Vietnam: Income Inequality and Per Capita Income, by Province, 2002–16

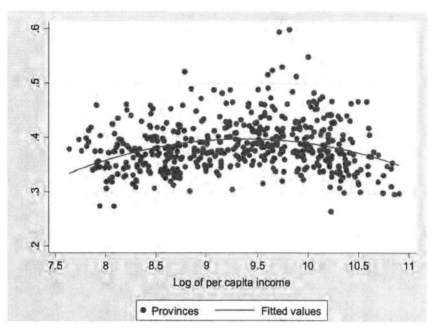

Source: Authors' estimation from VHLSSs.

may enjoy higher income growth. As a result, inequality within provinces increase as provinces grow richer. At the same time, provinces with a high poverty rate have a higher share of poor people, which is associated with higher inequality levels. On the whole, these two possible dynamics move inequality in different directions: as incomes grow and poverty declines, inequality also declines; income growth may also disproportionately boost higher income households and raise inequality. The net effect derives from the balance of these counteracting trends—among other factors, of course, due to the complexity of inequality determinants. In the context of this growth-poverty-inequality relationship, though, Vietnam's record of declining inequality indicates that robust income growth among lower income households is a greater driving force than income growth of rich households.

According to the large model of Gini coefficient, higher investments tend to increase inequality. Provinces with a higher share of urban

TABLE 9.3
Vietnam: GMM Regressions of Income Inequality Indexes

Explanatory Variables	Gini Small Model	Gini Large Model	Theil's L Small Model	Theil's L Large Model	Theil's T Small Model	Theil's T Large Model
Lagged log of per capita income	0.0572*** (0.013)	0.0334** (0.017)	0.0549** (0.023)	0.0606** (0.030)	0.1387** (0.060)	0.1113 (0.082)
Lagged poverty rate	0.2269*** (0.024)	0.1529*** (0.030)	0.2611*** (0.043)	0.1674*** (0.054)	0.4109*** (0.115)	0.3197** (0.145)
Lagged log of other State spending		0.0003 (0.001)		0.0002 (0.002)		−0.0018 (0.005)
Lagged log of investment spending		0.0055* (0.003)		0.0082 (0.005)		0.0094 (0.014)
Lagged log of population density		0.0006 (0.003)		−0.0077 (0.005)		0.0030 (0.014)
Lagged share of urban population		0.0004** (0.000)		0.0001 (0.000)		0.0005 (0.001)
Lagged share of population with high school diploma		−0.0002 (0.000)		−0.0003 (0.000)		−0.0007 (0.001)
Lagged share of ethnic minority population		0.0005*** (0.000)		0.0008*** (0.000)		0.0010* (0.001)
Lagged share of wage income		−0.0663** (0.030)		−0.0803 (0.053)		−0.1950 (0.143)
Lagged share of non-farm income		0.0689* (0.041)		0.1796** (0.074)		0.3867* (0.198)
Lagged share of other non-farm income		0.0059 (0.050)		0.0158 (0.090)		−0.0599 (0.243)
Year fixed effects	Yes	Yes	Yes	Yes	Yes	Yes
Province fixed effects	Yes	Yes	Yes	Yes	Yes	Yes
Constant	−0.1637 (0.117)	−0.0044 (0.158)	−0.2715 (0.209)	−0.4091 (0.285)	−1.0166* (0.558)	−0.7500 (0.769)
Observations	441	441	441	441	441	441
Number of provinces	63	63	63	63	63	63

Notes: Robust standard errors in parentheses.
*** $p < 0.01$, ** $p < 0.05$, * $p < 0.1$

population as well as a higher share of ethnic minority population are more likely to have higher inequality than others. Interestingly, provinces with a higher share of wages have lower inequality, while provinces with a high share of non-farm income have higher inequality.

CONCLUSION

Vietnam has been very successful in economic growth and poverty reduction, and maintaining steady income distribution. This study examines inequality in Vietnam over the 2002–16 period using data from the VHLSSs. Consistent with previous studies on inequality in Vietnam, which also use data from the VHLSSs, we find that inequality in income and expenditure have remained stable, with a downward trend in some aspects. Compared with other countries at similar economic level, Vietnam has lower inequality.

Vietnam has achieved pro-poor economic growth (Nguyen and Pham 2018). Income and expenditure have been increasing for all population subgroups. In addition, the government has carried out a large number of programmes providing the poor, ethnic minorities and other disadvantaged groups with support on infrastructure, education, health and production activities. However, large gaps in living standards between ethnic groups remain. The Kinh and Hoa have the lowest poverty, while small ethnic groups have very high poverty. Poverty varies across ethnic groups as well as geographical areas. At the same time, inequality within groups and provinces are substantial. Inequality between provinces accounts for 22 per cent of total inequality, while inequality between ethnic groups accounts for 15 per cent of total inequality. Our regression analysis shows that inequality tends to be higher in provinces with higher income level and higher poverty.

There are concerns about high and possibly rising inequality, particularly in terms of wealth. The number of super-rich people have been increasing (Kim 2017). Inequality in assets, measured by housing value, is significantly higher than inequality in income or expenditure. The VHLSSs capture the effects of a housing bubble around 2010; inequality in housing value has declined since. However, due to the inherent volatility of property markets, there remains the possibility of housing inequality increasing again.

To reduce poverty and foster equitable distribution, Vietnam must expand and enhance its inclusive growth policies. The poor as well as ethnic minorities often work in the agricultural sector and informal sector with low wages. The government should have policies to promote agricultural productivity, while facilitating a vibrant private sector and FDI, which can attract labour from rural and ethnic minority areas. Inequality can only be reduced if the poor achieve an economic growth proportionally more than the rich. In addition, income-redistribution policies can reduce poverty and promote income growth in the lower- and middle-income segments, thereby decreasing inequality.

APPENDIX

TABLE A9.1
Vietnam: Income Inequality Measures

Year	Gini	Theil's L	Theil's T	Ratio 90th/10th	Ratio 95th/5th
2002	0.409	0.279	0.340	5.6	9.6
2004	0.396	0.262	0.290	5.7	9.9
2006	0.386	0.248	0.281	5.5	8.8
2008	0.421	0.299	0.365	6.0	10.8
2010	0.424	0.312	0.388	6.6	11.0
2012	0.401	0.279	0.313	6.6	11.0
2014	0.385	0.262	0.266	6.5	11.2
2016	0.385	0.264	0.267	6.4	11.1

Source: Authors' estimation from VHLSSs.

TABLE A9.2
Vietnam: Electricity Consumption Inequality Measures

Year	Gini	Theil's L	Theil's T	Ratio 90th/10th	Ratio 95th/5th
2002	0.49	0.42	0.47	8.8	17.1
2004	0.49	0.43	0.47	10.0	19.7
2006	0.49	0.42	0.46	9.0	17.6
2008	0.50	0.43	0.48	9.2	19.1
2010	0.52	0.49	0.50	11.7	22.5
2012	0.46	0.38	0.37	9.6	18.8
2014	0.44	0.36	0.33	9.1	18.2
2016	0.42	0.34	0.31	9.0	19.6

Source: Authors' estimation from VHLSSs.

TABLE A9.3
Vietnam: Housing-Value Inequality Measures

Year	Gini	Theil's L	Theil's T	Ratio 90th/10th	Ratio 95th/5th
2010	0.716	1.117	1.117	46.7	120.0
2012	0.652	0.881	0.841	31.9	80.0
2014	0.635	0.823	0.823	29.2	74.3
2016	0.618	0.769	0.781	25.0	60.0

Source: Authors' estimation from VHLSSs.

Notes

1. We would like to thank Lee Hwok Aun, Christopher Choong Weng Wai, and other participants in the workshop on Inequality and Exclusion in Southeast Asia, 29 March 2019, ISEAS – Yusof Ishak Institute for their very useful comments on this study.
2. The sample sizes of each VHLSS 2002 are as follows: 29,530 households with 132,376 household members (2002); 9,188 households with 40,437 household members (2004); 9,189 households with 39,071 household members (2006); 9,189 households with 38,253 household members (2008); 9,399 households with 36,999 household members (2010); 9,399 households with 36,655 household members (2012); 9,399 households with 36,077 household members (2014); 9,399 households with 35,788 household members (2016).
3. In January 2016, US$1 was equivalent to VND22,300.
4. The poverty line for the 2002–8 period is equivalent to the expenditure level that allows for food consumption securing 2,100 calories per day per person and some essential non-food consumption. From 2010 onward, minimum calories used to construct the poverty line was increased to 2,230 per day per person. The consumption basket is also updated since the 2010 VHLSS.
5. The sample of households with income data in VHLSS is representative at the provincial level, while the sample of households with expenditure data in representative at the regional level. Thus, we estimate the income inequality but not expenditure inequality at the provincial level.
6. It should be noted that we tried to include the squared log of per capita income to examine whether there is a quadratic relation between inequality and income. However, the squared log is not statistically significant, and we do not include this variable in the final model.

References

Alesina, A., and D. Rodrik. 1994. "Distributive Politics and Economic Growth". *Quarterly Journal of Economics* 108, no. 2: 465–90.

Arellano, M., and S. Bond. 1991. "Some Tests of Specification for Panel Data: Monte Carlo Evidence and an Application to Employment Equations". *Review of Economic Studies* 58, no. 2: 277–97.

Benjamin, D., L. Brandt, and B. McCaig. 2017. "Growth with Equity: Income Inequality in Vietnam, 2002–14". *Journal of Economic Inequality* 15, no. 1: 25–46.

Bourguignon, F. 2003. "The Growth Elasticity of Poverty Reduction: Explaining Heterogeneity Across Countries and Time Periods". In *Inequality and Growth. Theory and Policy Implications*, edited by T.S. Eicher and S.J. Turnovsky. Cambridge: MIT Press.

Bui, A.T., C.V. Nguyen, and T.P. Pham. 2017. "Poverty Among Ethnic Minorities: The Transition Process, Inequality and Economic Growth". *Applied Economics* 49, no. 31: 3114–28.

Cramer, C. 2003. "Does Inequality Cause Conflict?". *Journal of International Development: Journal of the Development Studies Association* 15, no. 4: 397–412.

Dang, H.A., and P. Glewwe. 2018. "Well Begun, But Aiming Higher: A Review of Vietnam's Education Trends in the Past 20 Years and Emerging Challenges". *Journal of Development Studies* 54, no. 7: 1171–95.

Deaton, Angus S., ed. 1997. *The Analysis of Household Surveys: A Microeconometric Approach to Development Policy*. Washington, DC: World Bank.

Deininger, K., and L. Squire. 1998. "New Ways of Looking at Old Issues: Inequality and Growth". *Journal of Development Economics* 57, no. 2: 259–87.

Dolan, P., T. Peasgood, and M. White. 2008. "Do We Really Know What Makes Us Happy? A Review of the Economic Literature on the Factors Associated with Subjective Well-Being". *Journal of Economic Psychology* 29, no. 1: 94–122.

Elbers, C., J. Lanjouw, and P. Lanjouw. 2002. "Micro-level Estimation of Welfare". Policy Research Working Paper No. WPS 2911. World Bank.

Elbers, C., J. Lanjouw, and P. Lanjouw. 2003. "Micro-level Estimation of Poverty and Inequality". *Econometrica* 71, no. 1: 355–64.

Ferrer-i-Carbonell, A., and P. Frijters. 2004. "How Important Is Methodology for the Estimates of the Determinants of Happiness?". *Economic Journal* 114, no. 497: 641–59.

Ferrer-i-Carbonell and Ramos 2014 [Authors to supply bibliographic information]

Holtz-Eakin, D., W. Newey, and H. Rosen. 1988. "Estimating Vector Autoregressions with Panel Data". *Econometrica* 56, no. 6: 1371–95.

Kim, C. 2017. "How Many Super-Rich Are There in Vietnam?". VietNamNet, 6 July 2017. https://english.vietnamnet.vn/fms/business/181234/how-many-super-rich-are-there-in-vietnam-.html (accessed 2 March 2019).

Kuznets, S. 1955. "Economic Growth and Income Inequality". *American Economic Review* 45, no. 1: 1–28.

Lanjouw, P., M. Marra, and C. Nguyen. 2017. "Vietnam's Evolving Poverty Index Map: Patterns and Implications for Policy". *Social Indicators Research* 133, no. 1: 93–118.

Le, C., C. Nguyen, T. Phung, and T. Phung, T. 2014. "Poverty Assessment of Ethnic Minorities in Vietnam". MPRA Paper 70090. Germany: University Library of Munich.

Le, H., and A. Booth. 2013. "Inequality in Vietnamese Urban-Rural Living Standards, 1993–2006". *Review of Income and Wealth* 60, no. 4: 862–86.

MDRI. 2016. Report of the Vietnam: Global Partnership for Education—Vietnam Escuela Nueva (GPE-VNEN) Project, Mekong Development Research Institute, Hanoi, Vietnam.

Nguyen, H., T. Doan, and T.Q. Tran. 2020. "The Effect of Various Income Sources on Income Inequality: A Comparison Across Ethnic Groups in Vietnam". *Environment, Development and Sustainability* 22: 813–34.

Nguyen, H.-T.-M., T. Kompas, T. Breusch, and M.B. Ward. 2017. "Language, Mixed Communes, and Infrastructure: Sources of Inequality and Ethnic Minorities in Vietnam". *World Development* 96, no. C: 145–62.

Nguyen, C.V., and N.M. Pham. 2018. "Economic Growth, Inequality, and Poverty in Vietnam". *Asian-Pacific Economic Literature* 32, no. 1: 45–58.

Nguyen, V.C., D.T. Phung, and D. Westbrook. 2015. "Do the Poorest Ethnic Minorities Benefit from a Large-Scale Poverty Reduction Program? Evidence from Vietnam". *Quarterly Review of Economics and Finance* 56, no. C3-14.

Nguyen, C.V., T.Q. Tran, and H. Van Vu. 2017. "Ethnic Minorities in Northern Mountains of Vietnam: Employment, Poverty and Income". *Social Indicators Research* 134, no. 1: 93–115.

Nguyen, C., R. Van der Weide, and T.N. Truong. 2010. "Poverty and Inequality Maps in Rural Vietnam: An Application of Small Area Estimation". *Asian Economic Journal* 24, no. 4: 355–90.

Østby, G. 2013. "Inequality and Political Violence: A Review of the Literature". *International Area Studies Review* 16, no. 2: 206–31.

Oxfam. 2017. "Even It Up: How to Tackle Inequality in Vietnam". Oxfam Briefing Paper, 12 January 2017. Hanoi: Oxfam in Vietnam.

Persson, T., and G. Tabellini. 1994. "Is Inequality Harmful for Growth?". *American Economic Review* 84, no. 3: 600–21.

Schneider, S.M. 2015. "Income Inequality and Subjective Wellbeing: Trends, Challenges, and Research Directions". *Journal of Happiness Studies* 17, no. 4: 1719–39.

Tran, T.Q., C.V. Nguyen, and H. Van Vu. 2018. "Does Economic Inequality Affect the Quality of Life of Older People in Rural Vietnam?". *Journal of Happiness Studies* 19, no. 3: 781–99.

World Bank. 2010. *Vietnam Development Report 2010: Modern Institutions*. Washington, DC: World Bank.

———. 2018. *World Development Indicators*. Washington, DC: World Bank.

10

CONCLUSION
Old Frontiers, New Fractures

Lee Hwok Aun and Christopher Choong

Inequality and exclusion prevail across Southeast Asia, in various forms and to different degrees from country to country. Patterns of distribution are shaped by structural factors, some of which are durable and some in flux, as well as policy measures, which also witness continuity and change over time. The forms and dimensions of inequality covered in the preceding chapters underscore the breadth of problems—and the value of interdisciplinary study on this subject. The contributions of this volume have also examined both the enduring and emerging features of inequality. As noted in the introduction, inequality is highly specific to each country. This premise has been underscored by the unique experiences of each Southeast Asian country unpacked in the chapters. Readers will make connections of their own between the countries. Nonetheless, some common themes that stand out to us merit a brief discussion. We conclude this book by unpacking some commonalities and differences that emerge in the preceding chapters.

FORMS OF INEQUALITY AND EXCLUSION: INCOME, CONSUMPTION, WEALTH, HUMAN DEVELOPMENT

Inequalities manifest in various forms, from income, the most widely referenced, to consumption, wealth and human development. The breadth and granularity of information depend on data disclosures, and hence differ across countries—but we also observe that more data have become available in recent years, as countries increasingly conduct household surveys. Happily, we have been able to meet this project's goal of updating the empirical record into the 2010s.

Household income and expenditure surveys constitute the foremost resources for gauging the magnitude of inequality and exclusion and tracing patterns across time. Our chapters underscore the general trend, as captured in the Gini coefficient and overviewed in the Introduction, of stable or declining expenditure and income inequality from the mid-2000s to the mid- or late 2010s. However, the preceding trend of the early 2000s varies across the region, with Indonesia and Singapore registering rising inequality, while in Thailand, Malaysia and the Philippines, the downward trend was already in motion. Vietnam's inequality stays quite even throughout. Notwithstanding this progress, inequality levels remain high, with Gini of income exceeding 0.40 in Malaysia, the Philippines, Singapore and Thailand, and Gini of expenditure close to 0.40 in Indonesia. Additionally, concerns over the household surveys' under-representation of high-income households continually raise questions about the reliability of these figures, specifically regarding income concentration at the top.

The countries with lower inequality levels are also at an earlier stage of development, with economic conditions that pose a different set of challenges. Cambodia and Myanmar stand out in this regard. Income disparity is less acute; greater priority is placed on poverty alleviation and basic needs provisions for large swathes of the population. Vietnam, similarly, registers relatively low inequality, but as economic diversification and urban agglomeration proceed, so will the pressures of rising disparities. Wealth inequality is already proving testy in Vietnam.

Indeed, wealth inequality reverberates as a zeitgeist issue in Southeast Asia and the world over. Public resentment at dominant and aloof elites pervades the region. Wealth is inherently more difficult to measure at any one moment, let alone across time, but some efforts at estimating asset

Conclusion: Old Fractures and New Frontiers

holdings or observing proxies such as ownership of housing and luxury cars, find high—and potentially rising—levels of disparity. Our Malaysia, Singapore, Thailand and Vietnam chapters venture into this space. The capacity for wealth to accumulate, to be transmitted across generations, and to be leveraged for influence and power, reinforce the importance of the subject.

Wealth, of course, can be further removed from the lived experiences, and the welfare and development conditions, of the masses. Income and consumption, as noted earlier, reflect well-being more directly. Inequality can also be approached from other angles, and associated with data that correspond with living conditions and household consumption, such as electrification (Myanmar) and electricity usage (Vietnam). Inequalities in human development—reflected in education, health, and living inequalities—provide further granularity, as we can see in the Cambodia, Philippines and Thailand chapters.

Education is a public good in itself, but also instrumental to knowledge and skills acquisition which subsequently impact on wage bargaining power and income generating capacity. Reduced inequalities in education directly reflect improvements in the distribution of well-being, but should also translate into equity in income distribution. One angle on the change across time is captured by the dispersion of educational attainment across generations. Evidence from Thailand indicates that inequality of educational attainment within younger generations is lower compared to their parents' generation. These patterns are consistent with the observed downtrend in income inequality.

Expansion of education is a hallmark of Southeast Asia and a contributing factor to equitable development in various countries. However, certain inequalities persist. Our Thailand and Myanmar chapters include discussion on disparities in educational access and attainment, especially at the tertiary level and between provinces or states, or urban versus rural location.

Test scores and socio-economic data from the PISA international standardized test allow for examination of relationships between these variables. In Singapore and Thailand, disparities in PISA scores correlate with socio-economic class, mirroring the limits of meritocracy for levelling the playing field in the former and the entrenched advantages due to status and geography in the latter. Gender divides in education, on the other hand, have been significantly bridged, and it has become quite common in Southeast Asia for girls to outperform boys in school and to constitute the majority of higher education students.

Health, like education, is another vast issue that warrants a book shelf of its own, and is both a policy outcome of interest, as well as a determinant of broader inequality. Nonetheless, we have uncovered some issues surrounding health inequality, as well as psychological ramifications of exclusion. Our Philippines chapter, indeed, argues that health inequalities are even more pronounced than education inequalities, and disparities in nutrition, food security and prevalence of stunting illustrate the harsh realities for considerable swathes of the populace. A less researched issue, but an important one nevertheless, concerns the impacts of inequality on peoples' psychological well-being. Class inequality in Singapore is found to affect citizens' sense of belonging, with those from the lower-income backgrounds feeling less affinity to the country, and perhaps consider their experiences and struggles are excluded in the national narrative, with its emphasis on achievement based on standardized yardsticks.

DIMENSIONS AND DETERMINANTS OF INEQUALITY AND EXCLUSION

Structure, Political Economy, Geography

Beyond mapping out magnitudes and trends of the problem at hand, this book explored various dimensions of inequality and exclusion, to delve deeper into the issues and provide some explanation for the patterns observed. We synthesize the myriad findings of this book in three parts. The first revolves around Southeast Asian economies' broad range of developmental, structural and geographic features. The composition of economic activity—the shares of agriculture, industry and services, and dynamics at the sub-sector level—along with urbanization, and differences across provinces and islands, impact on the distribution of income, well-being and wealth. As societies progress, notions of social justice and expectations of remedial action against inequality and exclusion may also come to bear on public policy.

While we must be circumspect in generalizing based on an eight-country sample, linkages between income level and inequality cannot go unnoticed. Lower-income countries Cambodia and Myanmar record lower inequality, and are more engrossed in addressing poverty reduction, labour-intensive industrialization and wage growth. These challenges correspond with a large share of low-wage jobs in overall employment, and consequently, relatively lower inequality on aggregate. Pressures of rising inequality may commence, however, depending on development trajectories. Southeast Asia's lower income and newly industrializing countries also experience outmigration to the region, which generates returns in the form of remittances, but clearly has limits as a development strategy in the long run.

Among middle and upper-middle income countries, inequalities have unfolded in the context of industrialization and, in recent years, deindustrialization and transitions to service-based economies. These turning points, arguably arriving prematurely before economies have attained high skilled and high productivity levels, pose challenges for generating employment, positive spillovers, and export potential of manufacturing activities. The shift into services has also been characterized by low-quality and more precarious jobs, which is a regionwide phenomenon but saliently noted in the Philippines case. Another outcome, even more pronounced in the Philippines, is the work migration that substantially supports households and the economy more broadly through remittances, but ultimately domestic economies must sustainably provide quality jobs.

Other structural aspects of inequality, from political economy angles, comprise class-based contestations over economic resources, bargaining over the distribution of income between wages and profits, and economic integration with global capitalism. As shown in the Indonesian case, disjunctures between productivity growth and wage growth, and parallel movements of increasing resource-based windfalls and increasing inequality, featured in the first decade and a half of the post-Soeharto era. Generating productivity growth, and fostering wage growth in tandem, are key to a sustainable and equitable economic trajectory in Southeast Asia's largest economy, and all others as well to a substantial degree.

The region's economies are generally open, with international trade and foreign investment comprising a large share of national income, and thus impacted by global capitalism. The book has not addressed the international political economic dimensions in depth, but our Philippines chapter insightfully points out the ramifications of structural adjustment agendas from the 1980s, which have limited the capacity for redistributive policy. Indonesia's small tax base persistently constrains the state's redistributive scope. In countries with relatively more established and effective governmental capacity, social programmes and inequality-reducing interventions can be executed more effectively, but it seems fair to say, even among Southeast Asia lead countries in these areas—Singapore and Malaysia—the progressiveness of taxation can be bolstered, which to some extent will entail confronting fears and presumptions about loss of international "competitiveness".

Turning briefly to spatial dimensions, urban-rural disparities remain important all around, and require particular attention in countries with majority rural populations. The chapter on Cambodia, where three quarters of the population are classified as rural residents, highlights how rural economies need to be managed with sustainability and resource management as guiding principles, given the considerable dependence on land for income and livelihood. Likewise, rural populations in Myanmar are more vulnerable to natural disasters and even face greater food insecurity than urban denizens. The indirect health effects of environmental degradation and climate change on all, including urban populations, will have immediate relevance to all countries, whether predominantly rural or urban. The archipelagic geography sets apart Southeast Asia from other regions worldwide, but also presents hurdles in terms of income, wealth and development disparities between islands, particularly in Indonesia and the Philippines.

Population Groups

Inequalities between population groups—predominantly defined by race, ethnicity and nationality, but also gender, religion, disability, and other categories—remain salient in Southeast Asia. These problems arise from a complex of factors, including social exclusion or stigma, unequal opportunity and unfair discrimination, which may perpetuate disparities between groups. Moral imperatives of equal opportunity and non-discrimination, coupled with socio-political pressures to redress stratification and promote equitable representation, have engendered specific group-targeted policies that go beyond general pro-poor, means-tested, class-based redistribution.

The impetus for group-based inequality responses necessarily vary by country, particularly when it comes to race and ethnicity that are demographically unique and historically contingent. Malaysia is an outstanding case of extensive, majority-favouring ethnic affirmative action, not just regionally but also globally. The long-term trend of declining inter-ethnic household income inequality marks major policy achievements, but much work remains to be done to overcome deficits in economic participation and capability among the bumiputras, beneficiaries of Malaysia's affirmative action. Vietnam's targeted assistance for minority groups, whose socio-economic development substantially lags that of the majority Kinh population, has fostered some catch-up—but the gulfs remain very wide.

Ethnicity is invariably a complicated issue, exemplified not just in the challenges of overcoming legacies of inequality and exclusion, but also in the hesitancy of some countries in revealing ethnicity-based data, as noted in our Indonesia and Cambodia chapters.

Gender-based inequalities have received more widespread, albeit perhaps less robust, attention. All countries certainly declare policy commitments towards promoting gender parity, and redressing multiple injustices women face, from a cumulation of lesser educational provision and labour participation, to workplace discrimination and constrained self-employment opportunity. Gender issues are interwoven to some extent through all chapters of this book, with some highlighting the compounded disadvantages of women, especially when engaged in informal employment and located in rural areas. In the educational sphere, advancements are quite apparent—indeed, to the point that women comprise a substantial majority of higher education students, such in Malaysia. Simultaneously, the country has also articulated more gender conscious policy making, and set gender quotas and targets in labour force participation and decision-making positions. At the same time, these gender targets must also be evaluated for their qualitative aspects, namely job security and decent wages, as noted in the chapter on Cambodia. However, gender parity across myriad socio-economic dimensions remains a long way off, and will entail an ensemble of changes in legislation, public budgeting, social mindsets and national leadership.

It is also pertinent to broaden the analytical frame of gender-based inequalities beyond the productive sphere to the social reproductive sphere. While not a dominant focus across all the chapters in this book, some findings have already pointed in this direction, suggesting not only critical gender-based disparities and biases in non-market institutions such as families and schools, or societies more generally, but also their eventual impact on a variety of labour market outcomes. Unequal distribution of the care burden at home, with persistent feminization of social reproductive responsibilities, influences patterns of gender wage gaps in Malaysia. Internalized and imposed gender stereotypes, when cultivated into social norms, may shape gender sorting in universities and occupational choices, as highlighted in the chapters on Malaysia and Myanmar. All these suggest important and fertile research areas to expand on, as Southeast Asia grapples with the question of social reproduction in pursuing its diverse but inter-related growth trajectories.

Dynasty, Oligarchy, Society

Inequality and exclusion invariably overlap with power. Oligopolistic or monopolistic market power are widely acknowledged sources of suboptimal distribution; closer to the experience of ordinary people, wage disparity also essentially derives from imbalances of bargaining power. These power dynamics play out in the backdrop of this book. A few chapters have placed in the foreground the business-political nexus of power that entrenches wealth concentration at the top, procures policy influence and can pre-empt inequality-reducing reforms. These can operate in a range of modes, from making partisan donations and securing monopolies, as described in Thailand and Indonesia, to reproducing dynastic politics in the Philippines, all of which preserve plutocratic profits and interests. The prominence of the issues in our chapters underscores the momentum of critiques against economic systems that favour the rich and marginalize the poor.

Focus on the elite-skewed structures of Southeast Asian states, however, should not be overstated. Problems in policy execution and service delivery arise from weak institutional capacity, and should not be simplistically attributed to vested interests of plutocrats. We should not negate attention to and acknowledgment of efforts to foster equitable distribution and alleviate exclusion, and of limitations in policy execution that are more rooted in operational deficiency than political expediency.

Society is emphatically not deprived of agency in the process. The story of social protection—in political regimes uniquely located somewhere within the authoritarian to democratic spectrum—is one of expansion, with minimum wage raised or introduced in recent years and social protection enhanced. Civil society and trade union advocacy, and signals from electorates, have produced some fruit. As drawn out in the Cambodia chapter, these positive trends have also included efforts to extend unemployment insurance or workplace injury insurance for the self-employed, or seasonal and irregular work, and those in the informal economy. Undoubtedly, there is immense room for growth and improvement, but there has also been positive momentum to build on.

OLD FRACTURES, NEW FRONTIERS

The book's overarching theme seeks to encapsulate how structures and trends, which have endured from the past and that emerge in the present, confront Southeast Asia moving forward. As noted in the Introduction, this book does not delve deeply into policies mitigating inequality, although all the chapters have covered policy matters to some extent, and the subject matter warrants a few remarks here. Policy specifics will continually be unique to each country, and our goal has decidedly not been to derive formulas, but we conclude this book with a few policy principles drawn out of this project.

We begin at the inception stage and most general level of policy making: how inequality features in the formulation of national objectives. Rich-poor gaps and disparities between classes and groups, while perpetually present from each country's emergence as a nation-state, have grown in prominence on policy agendas, and have been expressly addressed at the aggregate level in Malaysia and Indonesia. Both countries have in recent years targeted reductions in the national Gini coefficient. Our chapters have also drawn out how inter-regional disparities loom large in policy declarations, whether based on provinces (Vietnam, Myanmar), capital conurbation and the rest (Thailand), urban-rural areas (Cambodia), or islands (Indonesia, the Philippines). These are just the starting points, but such articulations importantly place inequality as a high priority.

Empirically, the primary focus on income and consumption will likely remain, and for good measure, given the determinative role of income in welfare, but also the continuing power of household income and expenditure surveys as the empirical basis. Some points on data should be registered here. A crucial requirement in policy design, implementation and monitoring is quality and availability of data. Household income and expenditure surveys remain the paramount empirical source; in this light, improvements in coverage, frequency and validity will certainly benefit policy making and progress tracking. In writing this book's chapters, authors repeatedly encountered difficulty obtaining access to microdata for independent inquiries, with many relying on official disclosures of processed statistics. Of our eight chapters, only Vietnam secured raw data to perform original calculations and analyses. All of Southeast Asia must continue, or begin, to cement inequality reduction as a high priority, and to undergird the process with rigorous empirical work. And while income and consumption remain the baselines, the multiple forms of inequality whose importance is increasingly recognized, demand policies and analyses that address all dimensions.

A second policy principle extends from the recurrent theme in this book: the multiple dimensions and multiple determinants of inequality. Economically, structural changes, human development trends and labour market developments impact on relative wages and incomes. Socially, virtuous cycles of inclusion and privilege can deliver benefits to some, while vicious cycles of exclusion and disadvantage continually marginalize others. Politically, concentration of power and wealth at the top can effect policies that further entrench such a system. Multidimensional approaches to poverty estimation and policy targeting are gaining traction—all chapters demonstrate to some extent. In practical terms, countries should avoid over-relying on macro data and household income surveys and to recognize the tangible well-being on the ground which may be at odds with the official account of income growth or distributional trends.

A further issue pertains to the public's relationship with inequality, and disconnects between official macro evidence and personal experience. The power of perception of inequality—especially of wealth as shown in the Malaysia case, in which popular discourses insist that inequality has risen, contradicting the official record of declining household income inequality—underscores the importance of empirical veracity and clarity. Mainstreaming wealth might enhance efforts to measure and mitigate inequalities in this domain. The Singapore case, showing that lived inequality ultimately matters to ordinary citizens, also highlights how research and policy formulation must also go to the ground.

A third principle emerging from our deliberations addresses the political economic structure within which distribution plays out. Southeast Asian countries need to sustain their efforts in combating systemic, persistent inequalities, and enhance responsiveness to emerging inequalities and exclusion. Some of the most entrenched and concentrated inequalities, which are both outcomes and causes of broader inequality, are at once necessary and difficult to confront, especially oligarchic or dynastic holds on power that can perpetuate wealth inequalities and skew economic systems in favour of elite interests. This challenge stands out in Indonesia, the Philippines and Thailand. Other systemically embedded elements, sometimes in the form of norms and ideas, may also be ripe for change, including the current modes of Singapore's meritocracy and some of its proclivities for reproducing privilege, and Malaysia's ethnic preferential policies that may need to intensively focus on developing capability and participation. For the industrializing economies of Cambodia, Myanmar and Vietnam, the overarching challenge will be to chart equitable growth strategies that meet the needs of rural populations that constitute the substantial majority, and of urbanizing masses, while mitigating pressures of rising inequality and wealth concentration.

The chapters of this book reflect a broad disposition across Southeast Asia that is conducive to reducing inequality and mitigating exclusion, whether driven by ideological adherence or pragmatic response to socio-political demands and policy trends. Although at the time of writing the world is still in the throes of the COVID-19 pandemic, and its long-term consequences are yet to unfold, the flux and fallout of 2020 has already driven home the importance of institutions to provide stability, protection and resilience, while also maintaining agility and room for discretionary actions. Southeast Asia is, therefore, poised to handle challenges of inequality and exclusion, old and new.

INDEX

A
Aburizal Bakri, 78
"affirmative action" laws, 178
ageing population, 43–44
ageism, 247
Agenda for Sustainable Development, 65
Ahok (Basuki Tjahaja Purnama), 78
Aiyawatt Srivaddhanaprabha, 289
Anis Baswedan, 78
anti-Chinese riots, 73
Aquino administration, 201
ASEAN (Association of Southeast Asian Nations), 139, 141, 154, 172–73, 194, 202
 tariff levels, 207
ASEAN Centre for Energy, 150
ASEAN Economic Community, 134
Asian Development Bank (ADB), 3, 9–10
Asian financial crisis, 52–55, 206, 264, 272
Asian Tiger economies, 227
Aung San Suu Kyi, 133, 137

B
"Back to Work" programme, 111
Bangkok, and disparity with rest of country, 278–85, 291

Bantuan Rakyat 1Malaysia (BR1M), social assistance, 95
Basuki Tjahaja Purnama (Ahok), 78
"Bottom-Up Budgeting" process, 201
BPS (Statistics Indonesia), 55
"break-out nation", 175
Brexit, 52
bumiputra, 96, 98, 101, 103, 113
business-government ties, 289–90

C
Cambodia
 birth rate, 28
 demography, 25–26
 development goals, 23–24
 development policies, 44
 gender inequality, 33–34
 government grants, 47
 income inequality, 29–33
 Land Law, 27
 Ministry of Labour and Vocational Training, 32
 outmigration, from rural areas, 39
 policy interventions, 39–43
 political regime, 27
 poverty rate, 26, 28–29
 public services, access to, 38–39
 socio-economic development, 26–27

unemployment rate, 26
urban-rural disparity, 34–39
Cambodia Socio-Economic Survey 2017, 34
Cambodian Sustainable Development Goals, 33, 45
Cambodian Labour Union Federation, 32
Cambodian Law on Investment, 27
capital flight, 62
capitalism, 253–54, 289–90, 327
cash-based economy, 27
cash transfer programme, 201
Census of Agriculture, 181
Central Criminal Court for Corruption and Misconduct Cases, 290
Central Group, 288
Central Provident Fund (CPF), 248
Central Statistical Agency, see BPS
Certificates of Entitlement (COE), 227, 229, 257
Chalerm Yoovidhya, 288
Channel NewsAsia, 240–41
Charoen Pokphand (CP) Group, 288
Charoen Sirivadhanabhakdi, 288–89
Chearavanont family, 288–89
"child penalty", 119
Chirathivat family, 288–89
city-state, 218, 222
Civil Servant Medical Benefit (CSMB) scheme, 268
class inequality, and sense of belonging, 240–42, 326
Cold War, 53
ComCare Long-Term Assistance, 248
Commonwealth of Independent States (CIS), 3
Comprehensive Education Sector Review (CESR), 157

Comprehensive National Industrial Strategy, 194
"conglopolistic" competition, 197
constitutional monarchy, 27
consumption inequality, 225–27
Convention on the Elimination of all Forms of Discrimination against Women (CEDAW), 33
corruption, 27, 37, 77–79, 171, 198, 290
Corruption Eradication Commission (KPK), 79
Corruption Perceptions Index, 27
coup d'état, 261, 266
COVID-19 pandemic, 2, 43, 46, 169–70, 175, 177, 201, 203, 205–6, 333
Credit Suisse, 5, 54, 227, 261, 263
cronyism, 171, 199

D
deforestation, 36–37, 46, 150
deindustrialization, 11, 17, 57, 79, 172, 200, 204, 327
Duterte administration, 201
dynastic power, 7, 18, 171–72, 197–99, 203, 206, 208, 330, 333

E
Early Childhood Development Agency (ECDA), 250
East Asian miracle, 54
Economic Land Concessions, 36
educational inequality, 233–37
electrification, and inequality, 150–51
"elite democracy", 171
elitism, 220, 246–47
Employees Provident Fund (EPF), 105–9
ethnic inequality, 73, 96–102, 296–97, 305–10, 312, 317
Ethnic Integration Policy, 238

Index

Euromonitor, 290
European Union, 32

F
"felt inequality", 219–20
Fisheries Code, 178
food poverty, 28, 147, 149
Forbes' rich list, 288–89, 291
forest destruction, *see* deforestation

G
Gan Thiam Poh, 243
Garment Manufacturers Association of Cambodia, 32
Gender Development Index (GDI), 141
gender division of labour, 156–60
gender inequality, 33–34, 89, 102, 111–22, 134, 136, 141–43, 155–63, 187–90
"gender sorting", 117
General Statistics Office of Vietnam (GSO), 298, 305
geographic inequality, 237–40
gig economy, 121
Global Database on Intergenerational Mobility (GDIM), 269–71, 292
global financial crisis (GFC), 2, 51–52
Global Forest Watch, 36
Global Gender Gap Index, 162
Global Wealth Report, 5, 54, 227, 261, 263
globalization, 51
Goh Keng Swee, 245
Goldman Sachs, 169
Golkar, 78
Goods and Services Tax (GST), 251–52
grants, from government, 47
"Great Gatsby curve", 271
GSTV (Permanent GST Voucher), 251
Gulf Energy Development, 287

H
Halimah Yacob, 219, 243
Hary Tanoesoedibjo, 78
Health Equity Fund, policy, 33
Heng Swee Keat, 250
Hindu nationalists, 52
Holliday, Ian, 219, 253–54
household income inequality, 2, 88–89, 95, 104, 223, 329, 332
Housing and Development Board (HDB), 238
human capital, 23, 45, 152, 184, 195, 202, 275–76, 285
Human Capital Index (HCI), 275–77, 292
Human Capital Project, 275
Human Development Index (HDI), 24, 28–29, 138–41, 194, 266, 268
Human Development Statistical Update Report, 139

I
Incheon International Airport, 290
income, and employment inequality, 178–81, 190–92
income inequality, 2, 29–33, 88–89, 95, 104, 134, 222–25, 314–17, 319, 329, 332
indigenous peoples, 207–08
Indonesia
  anti-Chinese riots, 73
  decentralization, 63
  education qualification, 68
  ethnic inequality, 73
  "furthest-behind" group, 70
  inequality in, 53–62
  infrastructure development, 76
  Java, and economic dichotomy, 57, 59, 63, 76
  Kalimantan, economy, 59, 61, 81
  land reform, 77

military, dual functions of, 78
mining industry, 61, 81
natural resource boom, 61
oligarchy, 18, 61–62, 77–80, 330–31
people with disabilities, 70, 73
poverty rate, 53–54, 62
presidential election, 78
richest families, 54–55
Sakernas (*Survei Angkatan Kerja Nasional*), 55, 65, 68–70, 73
sectoral inequality, 65
social assistance programme, 76, 81
urban-rural divide, 68
village funds, 76–77
wage divergence, 65–75
wealth inequality, in, 54, 62
Indonesian Democratic Party of Struggle (PDI-P), 78
industrialization, 5, 11, 17, 37, 61, 90, 135, 199, 205, 264, 327
inequality, consequences of, 75
Inequality Human Development Index, 140–41
Inequality Predicament, The, report, 51
Institute of Policy Studies (IPS), 243
intergenerational inequality, 232–33
Integrated Household Living Conditions (IHLCA) survey, 147
International Funds for Agricultural Development, 77
International Labour Organization (ILO), 27, 136
International Monetary Fund (IMF), 8, 51–52, 57, 75
"in-work poverty", 176
Islamist transnationalist, 52

J
Java, and economic dichotomy, 57, 59, 63, 76
Joko Widodo, 75–76, 78

journal method, data, 226, 257
Journal of Southeast Asian Economies, 15
Jusuf Kalla, 78

K
Kalimantan, economy, 59, 61, 81
KidSTART programme, 250, 254
King Power International Group, 289–90
Kinh, and inequality with other ethnic groups, 296–97, 305–10, 312, 317
KPK (Corruption Eradication Commission), 79
Krugman, Paul, 245
Kuznets Curve, 145, 264
Kuznets, Simon, 5

L
labour force participation rate (LFPR), 154
land and wealth inequality, 181–84
Land Law, 27
Least Developed Countries (LDC), 145
Lee Hsien Loong, 218, 243
Lee Kuan Yew, 244–46
Leong Chan-Hoong, 239
Lim Siong Guan, 245
Local Government Code, 170, 206
local government units (LGUs), 171, 178, 206
London School of Economics and Political Science, 5

M
Malaysia
"Back to Work" programme, 111
"Bottom 40" (B40), 87–90, 93, 98–101, 103–4, 123
bumiputra, 96, 98, 101, 103, 113

Index 339

civil service, employment in, 115
Employees Provident Fund (EPF), 105–9
ethnic disparity, 96–102
gender inequality, 89, 102, 111–22
household income survey (HIS), 89, 91–95, 104–5, 111, 124–27
Labour Force Survey, 113, 115
labour market policy, 105, 110
"Middle 40" (M40), 93, 98–101
Ministry of Education, 117
National Advisory Council on the Integration of Women in Development, 111
National Employment Returns (NER), 113–15
National Policy for Women, 111
Orang Asli, 102–3
public policy, inequality in, 96–110
Salaries and Wages Survey Report, 101, 105, 121
"Top 20" (T20), 93, 98–100
Malays in Singapore, preferential policy of, 244–45
Malaysia Plan, 89, 103, 111
Malaysia Standard Classification of Occupations, 113, 127
Malaysian Indian Blueprint, 103
Marcos, Ferdinand, 170–72, 184, 199, 202–3
"marriage penalty", 119
"matriarchal" society, 33
Medical Welfare (MW) scheme, 272–73
MediSave (medical savings account), 251
"Medium Human Development" category, 139
Mekong River, 25, 35
meritocracy, 219–20, 234–35, 242–47, 250, 253–56, 325, 333

middle class, 190–91, 193, 202–5, 208
Millennium Development Goals (MDGs), 1, 23–24, 28, 43
minimum wage, 8–9, 30–32, 34, 43, 95, 101, 103, 110, 181, 248–49, 262, 330
mining industry, 61, 81
monopoly capitalism, 289
Myanmar
  economic growth, 135–37
  food and nutrition, in, 147–50
  gender inequality, 134, 136, 141–43, 155–63
  higher education, 152–53
  income inequality, 134
  labour, gender division of, 156–60
  labour market structure, 153–55
  life expectancy, 139–40
  National League for Democracy (NLD), 137
  poverty rate, 139, 142, 144–46
  public infrastructure, 150–51
  Rakhine State, 137
  school enrolment, 155–56
  textiles, clothing and footwear (TCF) sector, 136
  wage inequality, 160–63
Myanmar Demographic and Health Survey, 149
Myanmar Sustainable Development Plan, 133, 148

N
Nargis, cyclone, 135
Nathan, S.R., 245
National Advisory Council on the Integration of Women in Development, 111
National Ageing Population, 43
National Anti-Poverty Commission, 200

National Commission for Indigenous
    Peoples, 178
National Development Strategic Plan,
    44
National Economic and Social
    Development Council (NESDC),
    262
National Employment Returns (NER),
    113–15
National Health Insurance Program,
    204
National Household Targeting
    System Poverty Reduction, 205
National Housing Authority, 200
national identity, 231, 241
National Labour Force Survey,
    see Sakernas
National League for Democracy
    (NLD), 137
National Policy for Women, 111
National Population Policy, 43
National Social Protection Policy, 43
National Social Security Fund (NSSF),
    32–33
National Socioeconomic Survey,
    see Susenas
neoliberal globalization, 51
Net Investment Returns Contribution
    (NIRC), 252
New Economic Model (NEM), 93
New Order, 53–54, 61–62, 79
"new rich", 90
"Next-Eleven", 169

O
"oligarchic economy", 177
"oligarchical democracy", 171
oligarchy, 18, 61–62, 77–79, 330–31
Ong Ye Kung, 250
Orang Asli, 102–3
outmigration, 39, 44–45

Overseas Development Assistance
    (ODA), 30, 33
Oxfam, 5, 55

P
Palang Pracharat Party (PPRP), 289
Palma index, 53, 80
pandemic, see COVID-19 pandemic
"party-list" system, 171
PDI-P (Indonesian Democratic Party
    of Struggle), 78
People Power Revolution, 170
People's Action Party (PAP), 247
Permanent GST Voucher (GSTV), 251
Philippine Economic Zone Authority,
    200
Philippine Central Bank, 181–82, 196
Philippine Competition Commission,
    198
Philippine Human Development
    Network, 194, 208
Philippines
    "affirmative action" laws, 178
    Agriculture and Fisheries
        Modernization Act, 194
    Aquino administration, 201
    cash transfer programme, 201
    Department of Agrarian Reform,
        200
    dividend ownership, in, 207
    Duterte administration, 201
    economic structure, 193–94
    education and health inequality, in,
        184–87, 203–4
    employment structure, 174–76, 205
    gender inequality, 187–90
    geography, infrastructure and
        connectivity, 194–95, 204
    human capital, 195
    income, and employment
        inequality, 178–81, 190–92

Index 341

indigenous peoples, 207–8
Local Government Code, 170, 206
local government units (LGUs), 171, 178, 206
middle class, 190–91, 193, 202–5, 208
National Anti-Poverty Commission, 200
National Health Insurance Program, 204
National Household Targeting System Poverty Reduction, 205
National Housing Authority, 200
Net Primary Income from Abroad account, 173
policy regime, 199–202
political dynasty, 197–99, 203, 206, 208
political economy, 170–78, 196–203
poverty rate, 177
remittances, from overseas, 173
small and medium enterprises (SMEs), in, 196
social protection programme, 205
Universal Access to Quality Tertiary Education Act, 203
UPEcon Health Policy Development Program, 204
wealth and land inequality, 181–84
Philippine Stock Exchange, 176
"PINEs" (Philippines, Indonesia, Nigeria, and Ethiopia), 169
place-based people-centred (PBPC) model, 44–46
population groups, inequalities between, 328–30
populism, 52–53, 73, 75, 78, 255
Prabowo Subianto, 78
Prasert Prasarttong-Osoth, 287
Prayut Chan-ocha, 289

Presidential Commission for the Urban Poor, 178
productivity, and wage, 5, 23, 52, 55, 57–58, 68, 79, 81, 327
Programme for International Student Assessment (PISA), 234, 237, 242, 277, 325
Programme for the International Assessment of Adult Competencies (PIAAC), 235
progressive taxation, 8, 251–53, 328
Progressive Wage Model (PWM), 249, 254
Public-Private-People-Partnership, 46

R
racial politics, 244
Rakhine State, 137
Red Bull, 288
reindustrialization, 57
remittances, from overseas, 173
"rising tiger", 175
RPJMN (*Rencana Pembangunan Jangka Menengah Nasional*), 75–76

S
Sakernas (*Survei Angkatan Kerja Nasional*), 55, 65, 68–70, 73
Salaries and Wages Survey Report, 101, 105, 121
Sarath Ratanavadi, 287
sectoral inequality, 65
Sen, Amartya, 5, 146
Shanmugaratnam, Tharman, 254
"sick man of Asia", 169
Silver Support scheme, 248, 254
Singapore
    Certificates of Entitlement (COE), 227, 229, 257
    class inequality, and sense of belonging, 240–42, 326

ComCare Long-Term Assistance, 248
consumption inequality, 225–27
educational inequality, 233–37
Ethnic Integration Policy, 238
General Election, in, 219, 247
geographic inequality, 237–40
government intervention, 223–24, 249–50
home ownership, in, 229–32, 238, 257
Household Expenditure Survey (HES), 225–26, 234–36
household income, 223–26
Housing and Development Board (HDB), 238
income inequality, 222–25
inequality trends, 221
intergenerational inequality, 232–33
Malays, preferential policy of, 244–45
meritocracy, 219–20, 234–35, 242–47, 250, 253–56, 325, 333
Ministry of Culture, Community, and Youth, 243
Ministry of Finance, 232, 256
national service, 246
progressive tax system 251–53
social assistance policies, 248–49
"tuition classes", 234–35
wealth inequality, 227–32, 247
Singapore Permanent Resident Quota, 238
"Singaporean of the Year", 243
Social Health Insurance scheme, 268
Socio-Economic Survey, 274, 279, 285–87, 292
Soeharto, 53, 61, 77–78, 327
Southeast Asia, economic profile, 12–14, 16
"state capture", 7

Statistics Indonesia (BPS), 55
Stock Exchange of Thailand, 287
stunting, prevalence of, 148–49
Sukarno, 61
Susenas (*Survei Sosial Ekonomi Nasional*), 55, 75
Susilo Bambang Yudhoyono (SBY), 76
Sustainable Development Goals (SDG) 2030, 1, 9, 23, 65, 139, 150
Suvarnabhumi Airport, 289–90

T
Tan, Kenneth Paul, 255
tariff levels, among ASEAN countries, 207
tax evasion, 62
Teo You Yenn, 243
textiles, clothing and footwear (TCF) sector, 136
Thailand
    Bangkok, and disparity with rest of country, 278–85, 291
    business-government ties, 289–90
    Civil Servant Medical Benefit (CSMB) scheme, 268
    coup d'état, 261, 266
    Education Act, 262, 269
    education attainment, 275–78
    household income, 264–66, 291
    Labour Force Survey, 271
    life expectancy, 271–72
    living standards, inequality in, 266–85
    Medical Welfare (MW) scheme, 272–73
    population, 263
    richest families, 287, 288–89, 292
    Social Health Insurance scheme, 268
    Socio-Economic Survey, 274, 279, 285–87, 292

Universal Health Care (UHC)
    Scheme, 262, 268, 272–75
Voluntary Health Card (VHC),
    272–73
wealth inequality, 285–90
Thai Rak Thai (TRT) Party, 273
ThaiBev, 288
Thaksin administration, 289
"Third Wave", 170
Three Worlds of Welfare Capitalism, The,
    253
Time magazine, 169
"time two meritocracy", 219, 246
"TIMPs" (Turkey, Indonesia,
    Malaysia, Philippines), 169
Tonle Sap Great Lake, 25, 35
tourism industry, 37, 43, 45, 47, 158,
    161, 173–75
Trade and Development Report:
    Inclusive and Balanced Growth,
    2012, 2
Transparency International, 27
"trickle-up" economics, 3
Trump presidency, 52
"tuition classes", 234–35
Turner Investment Partners, 169

U

U Thein Sein, 133
UN Convention on the Rights of
    People with Disabilities, 70
UNCTAD, 2
UNDP, 142, 266
UNESCAP, 9–10
UNESCO Institute of Statistics, 157
United Nations, 75
United Nations Convention on
    Sustainable Development, 23
United Nations Food and Agriculture
    Organization, 138
United Nations Sustainable
    Development Goals,
    see Sustainable Development
    Goals 2030
United Nations Universal Declaration
    of Human Rights, 22
Universal Access to Quality Tertiary
    Education Act, 203
Universal Health Care (UHC)
    Scheme, 262, 268, 272–75
University of London, 5
University of the Philippines, 201
UPEcon Health Policy Development
    Program, 204
Urban Development and Housing
    Act, 178
urban-rural disparity, 34–39, 68

V

Vietnam
    income inequality, 314–17, 319
    inequality, measuring of, 299
    inequality trends, 300–05
    Kinh, and inequality with other
        ethnic groups, 296–97, 305–10,
        312, 317
    poverty rate, 305–8, 314–15, 320
Vietnam Household Living Standards
    Surveys (VHLSSs), 296–98,
    300–09, 314, 317, 320
village funds, 76–77
Voluntary Health Card (VHC),
    272–73

W

wage, and productivity, 5, 23, 52, 55,
    57–58, 68, 79, 81, 327
Wage Credit Scheme, 250
wage inequality, 160–63
"war on drugs", 201

wealth inequality, 6, 54, 62, 80, 104, 181–84, 227–32, 247, 285–90, 324–25
Wee, Derek, 247
Wee Shu Min, 246
Wee Siew Kim, 246
welfare capitalism, 254
Workfare Income Supplement (WIS), 249, 254
Workfare Training Support (WTS), 249
World Bank, 9, 51, 75, 136, 144, 172, 176, 181, 196, 205, 208, 298, 303, 305
World Bank Human Capital Project, 275
World Development Report, 275
World Economic Forum, 162
World Economic Outlook, 52
World Health Organization, 186
world's richest people, 33
World Values Survey (WVS), 2, 241, 257

Y
Yeo, Philip, 245